# PSYCHIC EMPIRE

MODERNIST LATITUDES

## MODERNIST LATITUDES

Jessica Berman and Paul Saint-Amour, Editors

Modernist Latitudes aims to capture the energy and ferment of modernist studies by continuing to open up the range of forms, locations, temporalities, and theoretical approaches encompassed by the field. The series celebrates the growing latitude ("scope for freedom of action or thought") that this broadening affords scholars of modernism, whether they are investigating little-known works or revisiting canonical ones. Modernist Latitudes will pay particular attention to the texts and contexts of those latitudes (Africa, Latin America, Australia, Asia, Southern Europe, and even the rural United States) that have long been misrecognized as ancillary to the canonical modernisms of the global North.

Barry McCrea, *In the Company of Strangers: Family and Narrative in Dickens, Conan Doyle, Joyce, and Proust*, 2011
Jessica Berman, *Modernist Commitments: Ethics, Politics, and Transnational Modernism*, 2011
Jennifer Scappettone, *Killing the Moonlight: Modernism in Venice*, 2014
Nico Israel, *Spirals: The Whirled Image in Twentieth-Century Literature and Art*, 2015
Carrie Noland, *Voices of Negritude in Modernist Print: Aesthetic Subjectivity, Diaspora, and the Lyric Regime*, 2015
Susan Stanford Friedman, *Planetary Modernisms: Provocations on Modernity Across Time*, 2015
Steven S. Lee, *The Ethnic Avant-Garde: Minority Cultures and World Revolution*, 2015
Thomas S. Davis, *The Extinct Scene: Late Modernism and Everyday Life*, 2016
Carrie J. Preston, *Learning to Kneel: Noh, Modernism, and Journeys in Teaching*, 2016
Gayle Rogers, *Incomparable Empires: Modernism and the Translation of Spanish and American Literature*, 2016
Donal Harris, *On Company Time: American Modernism in the Big Magazines*, 2016
Celia Marshik, *At the Mercy of Their Clothes: Modernism, the Middlebrow, and British Garment Culture*, 2016
Christopher Reed, *Bachelor Japanists: Japanese Aesthetics and Western Masculinities*, 2016
Eric Hayot and Rebecca L. Walkowitz, eds., *A New Vocabulary for Global Modernism*, 2016
Eric Bulson, *Little Magazine, World Form*, 2016
Aarthi Vadde, *Chimeras of Form: Modernist Internationalism Beyond Europe, 1914–2014*, 2016
Ben Conisbee Baer, *Indigenous Vanguards: Education, National Liberation, and the Limits of Modernism*, 2019
Claire Seiler, *Midcentury Suspension: Literature and Feeling in the Wake of World War II*, 2020
Jill Richards, *The Fury Archives: Female Citizenship, Human Rights, and the International Avant-Gardes*, 2020
Daniel Ryan Morse, *Radio Empire: The BBC's Eastern Service and the Emergence of the Global Anglophone Novel*
Hannah Freed-Thall, *Modernism at the Beach: Queer Ecologies and the Coastal Commons*
Adam McKible, *Creating Jim Crow America: George Horace Lorimer, the Saturday Evening Post, and the War Against Black Modernity*

# PSYCHIC EMPIRE

*Literary Modernism and the Clinical State*

CATE I. REILLY

Columbia University Press
*New York*

Columbia University Press
*Publishers Since 1893*
New York Chichester, West Sussex
cup.columbia.edu



Library of Congress Cataloging-in-Publication Data
Names: Reilly, Cate I., author.
Title: Psychic empire : literary modernism and the clinical state / Cate I. Reilly.
Description: New York : Columbia University Press, [2024] | Series: Modernist latitudes | Includes bibliographical references and index.
Identifiers: LCCN 2023049515 (print) | LCCN 2023049516 (ebook) | ISBN 9780231214643 (hardback) | ISBN 9780231214650 (trade paperback) | ISBN 9780231560399 (ebook)
Subjects: LCSH: Psychiatry in literature. | Modernism (Literature)
Classification: LCC PN56.P914 R45 2024 (print) | LCC PN56.P914 (ebook) | DDC 809.93353—dc23/eng/2021226
LC record available at https://lccn.loc.gov/2023049515
LC ebook record available at https://lccn.loc.gov/2023049516

Cover design: Julia Kushnirsky
Cover image: Meret Oppenheim, *X-ray of My Skull*, 1964–1981, gelatin silver print; 9 3/4 x 8 in. (24.9 x 20.3 cm), San Francisco Museum of Modern Art. Gift of Elaine McKeon. © Artists Rights Society (ARS), New York / ProLitteris, Zürich. Photograph: Don Ross

*For Tim, with love*
*and for all those to whom I am related*
*if not by blood*

*Schizophrenia*

*Diagnostic Criteria* 295.90 (F20.9)

*A. Two (or more) of the following, each present for a significant portion of time during a 1-month period (or less if successfully treated). At least one of these must be (1), (2), or (3):*

1. *Delusions.*
2. *Hallucinations.*
3. *Disorganized speech (e.g., frequent derailments or incoherence).*
4. *Grossly disorganized or catatonic behavior.*
5. *Negative symptoms (i.e., diminished emotional expression or avolition) . . .*

—*Diagnostic and Statistical Manual of Mental Disorders*, 5th edition

*For the Enlightenment, anything which cannot be resolved into numbers, and ultimately into one, is illusion; modern positivism consigns it to poetry.*

—Max Horkheimer and Theodor W. Adorno

*Ought we not to remind ourselves—we who believe ourselves bound to a finitude which belongs only to us and which opens the truth of the world by means of our cognition—ought we not to remind ourselves that we are bound to the back of a tiger?*

—Michel Foucault

*When dealing with determined relationships between classes of phenomena, the ordering principles that form the basis of these classes must be made explicit. Classification, however, is not a self-serving aim for the literary scholar. Its use is instrumental: only when classification helps achieve greater insight into the phenomena constituting the classes is it meaningful in describing the text.*

—Mieke Bal

# CONTENTS

# ACKNOWLEDGMENTS

This is a book about naming. It is perhaps only appropriate that there should be many names to thank for its existence. I am grateful to all the people who have supported its creation through their feedback, insights, and conversations. There is no acknowledgment I could write that would be adequate to your contribution. The book's greatest debt is to the Duke Program in Literature. This is not any one person but an extraordinary collection of ideas, thinkers, and ongoing discussions, minimally articulable in the following names, here alphabetically: Nima Bassiri, Rey Chow, Roberto M. Dainotto, Anne Garéta, Markos Hadjioannou, Mark B. N. Hansen, Michael Hardt, Fredric Jameson, Ranjana Khanna, Walter D. Mignolo, Toril Moi, Negar Mottahedeh, Luciana Parisi, Antonio Viego, Robyn Wiegman. Thank you as well to Caryl Emerson, Peter Brooks, Devin Fore, Nancy Armstrong, Leonard Tennenhouse, Deborah Jenson, Leonard White, Marco Iacoboni, Charlotte Sussman, Stefanos Geroulanos, Veronika Fuechtner, Camille Robcis, Anna Parkinson, Jehanne Gheith, Carol Apollonio, Stefani Engelstein, Kata Gellen, Saskia Ziolkowski, Henry Pickford, Helen Solterer, Corina Stan, Sarah Milne Pourciau, Anne-Gaëlle Saliot, Jocelyn Olcott, Richard Langston, Robert Mitchell, Katherine Brading, Harris Scott Solomon, Nicole Rizzuto, Martin Miller, Karen Bell, and Sylvia Miller. I am grateful to my students, teaching assistants, and research assistants who have contributed to this project in invaluable ways: Julien Fischer, Melissa Karp, Carson Welch, Mandana Naviafar, Britt Edelen, Francesca Magario, Aaron Dowdy, Mike Sokol, Jessica Ginocchio, Amanda Bennett, Veronica Davis,

Evan Pebesma, Alexa Coucopulos, and Jessica Gokhberg. The book would not have been possible without the friendship and love of Timothy and Jen Reilly, Carolyn Irene Hejna, Andrew Arthur Reilly, Elizabeth Villari, Jill Jarvis, Alexa Garvoille, Alexis Priestly, Mert Bahadir Reisoglu, and Alisa Ballard. Most of all, it would not have been possible without you, Ben. Why write I still all one?

*Psychic Empire* was generously supported by a grant from the John Hope Franklin Humanities Institute at Duke University and has also benefited from a Humanities Unbounded grant funded by the Andrew W. Mellon Foundation. The final stages of its development are thanks to conversations with the EcoBrain research group, a collaborative endeavor between Duke University and Exeter University in the United Kingdom. I am grateful to the editors of the Modernist Latitudes series at Columbia University Press, Jessica Berman and Paul Saint-Amour, who both brought this book within the circle of their world and gave it latitude.

A special thanks to my editor at Columbia University Press, Philip Leventhal, who saw this manuscript through a global pandemic that reconfigured academic publishing, along with everything else.

# INTRODUCTION

## After Analysis
## Literary Modernism and Diagnostic Reading

In 1964, the Swiss surrealist artist Meret Oppenheim took an X-ray of her skull. Mostly what the viewer sees in the image, however, are her large earrings. The slither of a necklace enfolds her cervical vertebrae, and two chunky rings adorn the phalanges of the ring and pinkie fingers on her raised right hand. In the background of the contact silver print she made from the X-ray plate (figure 0.1), it is just possible to make out the faint outline of her nose and lips, which, like her jewelry, spectrally trouble this portrait of interiority. *Go ahead, try to get inside*, the image seems to say. *When you have captured my bones and beheld what lies in my head, when you have entered me in the most intimate of ways, when you have run your eyes through my marrow, what will you have? Only this strange residue, a mess of shades bedecked in jewels, only this Röntgen-wattage echo of a life, only still the skin of Meret.* In the quiet idiom of the *nature morte*, the photograph asks the viewer to tarry with the question of how one sees into another being. Turning medical imaging into artistic practice, it asks what a scientific picture of the head shows. This book does the same.

*Psychic Empire* offers a new chapter in the debates on language, the mind, and modernist literature that have defined conversations in structuralist and poststructuralist scholarship, as well as in psychoanalytically informed literary studies. The book considers the ways in which an immense project of psychiatric disease classification that began in the late nineteenth century now configures both the subject and narrative accounts of psychical health and suffering. It has culminated in the twenty-first century's vast, standardized

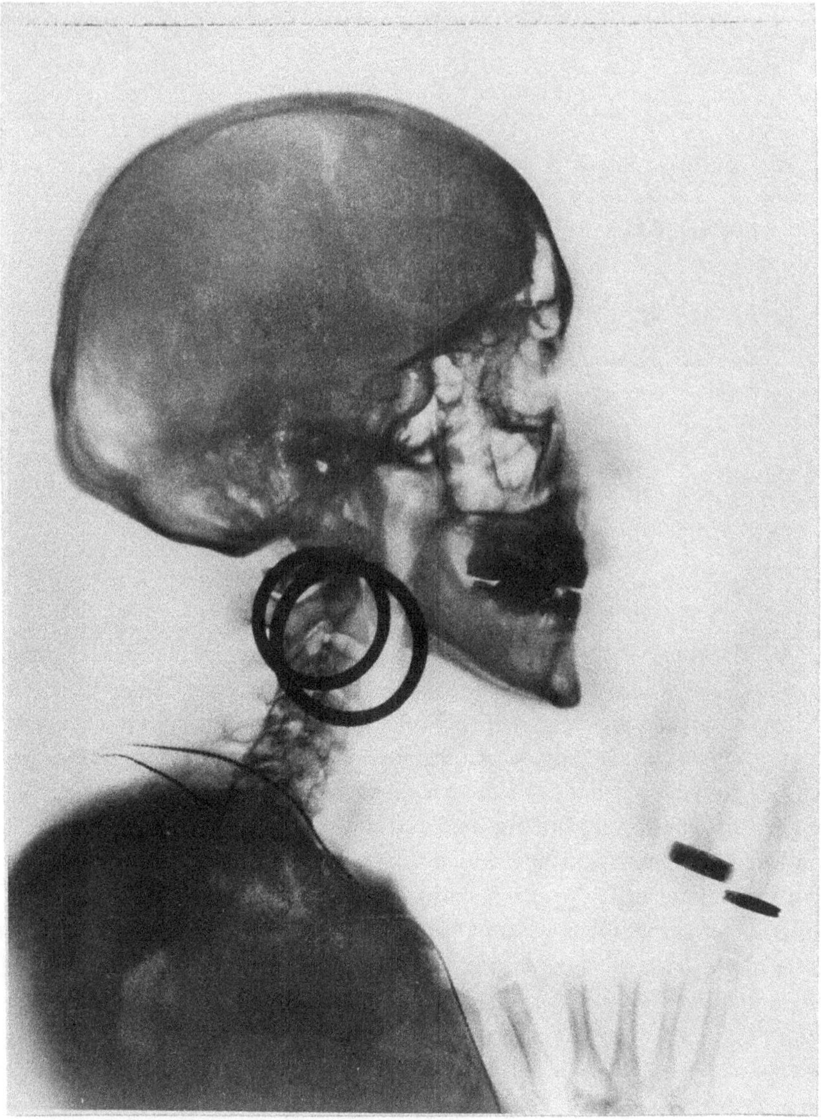

**0.1** Meret Oppenheim, *Röntgenaufnahme des Schädels M.O. / X-Ray of M. O.'s Skull* (1964). Contact silver print from the original X-ray plate, 15 7/8 × 12 inches (40.3 × 30.5 cm).

*Source*: Photography by Nicholas Knight. Courtesy Peter Freeman, Inc., New York.

clinical lexicon of mental disorders. This book turns to the critical and epistemological dimensions of the nineteenth-century precursor, developed by the German psychiatrist Emil Kraepelin (1856–1926), that informs the present system to offer an archaeology of psychopathological naming. Rather than beginning from a question of whether the unconscious is structured like a language

(Sigmund Freud, Jacques Lacan) or the mind organized by a plastic neural biology that allows the brain to speak (Antonio Damasio, Catherine Malabou, Oliver Sacks) or indeed whether consciousness is organized by categorical laws determining the perception of reality (Georg Wilhelm Friedrich Hegel, Immanuel Kant), I consider how the rise of a semantic regime of rigorously codified mental illnesses, developed in diagnostic manuals like the American *Diagnostic and Statistical Manual of Mental Disorders* (DSM, published by the American Psychiatric Association) and the *International Statistical Classification of Diseases* (ICD, published by the World Health Organization), now shapes globalized accounts of telling and selfhood in modernity.

Psychoanalysis, the philosophy of mind, and neuroscientific research provide three differing accounts of mental life. The conflict between them has long been perceived in terms of models vying to provide the most accurate explanation of psychical reality. *Psychic Empire* sets that question aside. This frees the book to consider the literary, epistemological, and philosophical consequences of representing mental life in the lexicon of standardized psychopathological terminology (e.g., anorexia, obsessive-compulsive disorder, post-traumatic stress disorder) rather than make claims about what mental life is "really" like.

These clinical terms are now the dominant mode of describing mental illness and are increasingly tied to the assertions of cognitive neuroscience. Given their prominence in affect theory, trauma studies, disability studies, and new interdisciplinary frameworks such as neuropsychoanalysis and the neurohumanities, not to mention branches of media studies concerned with artificial intelligence, it is of the utmost import that humanists take account of these terms.[1] Insofar as they were created as an alternative to psychoanalysis but are regularly treated as synonymous with its vocabulary, a distinction is overdue. The problem, then, is that these two systems—the psychoanalytic and the clinical psychiatric—are at work everywhere, without there being sufficient critical attention to their differences. Persistent focus on psychoanalysis and Freud within critical scholarship in the humanities reiterates a longstanding academic preoccupation with critiquing the psychoanalytic paradigm while leaving the far more globalized, economically impactful, and clinically dominant understanding of the mind untouched. The latter is nevertheless even more in need of the resources of the interpretive humanities. What does it mean to declare oneself "schizoid" (DSM-5 295.90 [F20.9]) or "autistic" (DSM-5 299.00 [F84.0]) in literature or in life?[2] Or to be declared as such? This is different from a question about the experience of *being* schizoid or autistic. Whereas the latter is concerned with *Dasein*, the former remains on the level of the *nomos*. *Psychic Empire* is less concerned with accounting for the contents of mental life in any of its myriad lived forms or evaluating modernist literary works' ability to do so. It is focused instead on the semiotic issues posed by the clinical language for psychical experience, as that language emerged historically and as used at present.

Modernist literature from the late nineteenth and early twentieth century offers a key perspective on this little-explored iteration of the "mad" person's speech. It provides a rich vantage point from which to address the question of what it means for literary characters, aesthetic objects, critical practices, and indeed individuals to define themselves (or be defined) in terms of psychopathological categories. The body of literary texts written in industrializing Central and Eastern Europe around the turn of the nineteenth century were conceived at the same time and in the same region that the modern account of psychopathological classification was born. Modernist literary and dramatic works have long been read as representing or as being influenced by the findings of (then) newly emergent disciplines like empirical psychology, clinical psychiatry, psychoanalysis, and neuroscience. They have also regularly been treated as narratological reflections of these field's accounts of mental functioning (stream of consciousness, interior monologue, double-voiced discourse). *Psychic Empire* proposes that modernist aesthetic works could equally well be considered as fraught negotiations of a newly scientized understanding of the psyche.[3]

For that reason, the book shifts from a focus on Anglophone modernism and figures like Virginia Woolf, Henry James, Gertrude Stein, and James Joyce to writers who worked in the same geographic and geopolitical region that gave rise to empirical psychology and standardized psychiatric classification. Focusing on authors such as Georg Büchner, Nikolay Evreinov, Vsevolod Ivanov, Santiago Ramón y Cajal, Daniel Paul Schreber, and Ernst Toller, all of whom who were in direct dialogue with the development of the modern mind sciences (and in some cases patients or researchers within it), provides a fresh perspective on psychopathological categories in the Anglophone canon and beyond. Although *Psychic Empire* is in conversation with the key advances of French psychiatry in the late eighteenth and early nineteenth centuries (associated with Jean-Martin Charcot, Jean-Étienne Esquirol, Philippe Pinel, among others), its focus on nineteenth- and twentieth-century Central and Eastern Europe tracks French psychiatry's role as a precursor to the renaissance in German-language psychiatry and clinical practice that unfolded beginning in the 1850s.

I am concerned specifically with the regional crucible in which the modern mind sciences took shape: Germany, Austro-Hungary, the Baltic States, and Russia. This is where Sigmund Freud (1856–1939) developed psychoanalysis, Gustav Theodor Fechner (1801–1887) created psychophysics, and Wilhelm Wundt (1832–1920) crafted empirical psychology. It is where neuroanatomy came of age, in the work of figures like Theodor Meynert (1833–1892) and Carl Wernicke (1848–1905). It is where Emil Kraepelin (1856–1926) changed the face of clinical psychiatry by proposing the existence of distinct natural categories of mental diseases, beginning with dementia praecox. It is also the same geographic arena that gave rise to transcendental philosophy two centuries earlier. As the alternately German and Russian possession of Königsberg/Kaliningrad—Immanuel Kant's home—makes evident, it was enormously geopolitically contested terrain that underwent a major structural reorganization in the nineteenth century.

German Unification in 1871 transformed the loose alliance of the nearly forty different member states in the German Confederation (1815–1866) into a more cohesive federal entity, now equipped with a constitution, a unitary legal code, and universal male suffrage. It substantially redefined and solidified German boundaries within Europe, while shoring up the connections between Germany's now smaller set of constituent states. The Austrian Empire (1804–1867), previously part of the German Confederation, separated after the Austro-Prussian War of 1866 dissolved the confederation as a whole. With the Austro-Hungarian Compromise of 1867, the Austrian Empire united with the Kingdom of Hungary in a diplomatic alliance subsequently known as the Austro-Hungarian Empire, which persisted until the Allied victory over the Central Powers in World War I.

Like other emerging European nation-states, imperial Germany, Austro-Hungary, and the Russian Empire embarked on national assimilation campaigns in the 1880s and 1890s, designed to stamp out or minimize regional heterogeneity and foster a monoculture. Working-class struggles like those of 1848 and the Paris Commune, alongside the rise of anarchist and communist movements lent a particular sense of urgency to the project of imagining a cohesive socius. Nationalization involved, among other things, new policies emphasizing the import of a single (standardized) language, religion, and set of national cultural values. In Alexander III's Russia, it also included renaming towns and revoking autonomy in regions like the Baltic States (modern-day Latvia, Lithuania, and Estonia) that had been under the autonomous control of a German-speaking local elite for more than a century.

Germany, Austro-Hungary, and Russia also expanded their territorial holdings during this time. During the so-called scramble for Africa that swept Western Europe, imperial Germany colonized portions of sub-Saharan Africa and the western Pacific, retaining them until its defeat (and dissolution) after World War I. Meanwhile, Austro-Hungary took control over the Kingdom of Croatia-Slavonia and annexed Bosnia-Herzegovina in 1908. Alexander III continued to expand into Eurasia until his death in 1894, extending the borders of the Russian Empire into the area on the southeastern edge of the Caspian Sea (present-day Turkmenistan) and into the Pamir Mountains (present-day Tajikistan), then bordering British Afghanistan. The acquisition of colonial holdings put an even finer point on the quest for standardization and uniformity while simultaneously making possible racialized comparisons between imperial hubs and so-called outposts.

The linguistic standardization, ethnic homogenization, and bureaucratic centralization that went along with efforts to forge a single national culture had a direct impact on medicine. It conditioned everything from the type of patient records collected by the state to the official language of doctor-patient interactions. So too did it bring changes in how medical care was funded (introducing health insurance for the first time in some areas) and amplify the ongoing shift of medical clinics from isolated rural regions to more urban ones. The Belgian astronomer and sociologist Adolphe Quetelet pioneered the use of statistics to study social phenomena beginning in the 1830s, which paved the way for the emergence of demography (rather than political arithmetic) as a tool in nationalization movements and medicine alike.[4] One only need look to the titles of the *Diagnostic and Statistical Manual of Mental Disorders* and the *International Statistical Classification of Diseases* to see the link between Quetelet's nineteenth-century creation of statistics and systematized classification systems for mental illnesses. As the advent of statistical science illuminates, these changes marked a more general turn to the management of health (and mental health) on the level of the population, not individuals.

Works by Büchner, Evreinov, Ivanov, Schreber, and Toller navigate the dilemma of psychopathological naming as it was created and applied to populations in this region and at this time. Such naming both holds out the possibility for liberating the subject (by legitimating mental experience and guaranteeing associated rights) and carries the risk of pathologizing, racializing, and gendering the subject (thereby retracting rights) in the name of objectivity. The book tracks the complexities arising from the contemporaneous consolidation of modern nation-states and standardized psychodiagnostic disease categories in the late nineteenth century. In this environment, efforts to provide large-scale mental health care overlapped with attempts to figure the popular mass as a rights-bearing *people*. Western political philosophy has long understood the idea of a people as synonymous with being compos mentis—sufficiently capable of *Mündigkeit* (maturity), in Kant's terms. For this reason, the notion of popular sovereignty and popular sanity go hand in hand.[5] *Psychic Empire* adopts the position that the operation of standardizing definitions of mental health and illness was interwoven with the project of imagining and representing (on the level of *Darstellung* and *Vertretung*) the people as the bearers of sovereignty in the wake of the French Revolution.

The problem of just how to portray popular sovereignty is one that multiple scholars have already identified as formative for modernist aesthetics. T. J. Clark and Eric Santner argue that sovereignty's politico-theological dilemmas appear as representational crises across modernist media. Modernist aesthetic objects reflect the difficulties produced by Louis XVI's execution, which symbolically divided the king's two bodies of medieval political theology (Kantorowicz) by dislodging the sublime body politic associated with the office of the king from its housing in the monarch's body natural. This second immaterial body then had to be reconstituted in the plural *bodies* of the people. Modernism, Clark and Santner suggest, captures the troubled migration of these "royal remains" (Santner) from monarch to multitude, symptomatically marking the field of figuration in the process. Clark and Santner frame the problem in terms of bodies and flesh. My own contention is that the issue of representing popular sovereignty was also entangled with a nineteenth-century scientific shift in the representation of the mind.[6] This period witnessed a transition from Cartesian mind-body dualism to the advent of new empirical sciences premised on a presupposition that psychical experience had measurable external manifestations and biological correlates. The need to represent the multitude as a single self (Jean-Jacques Rousseau's "moi" of the 1762 *Social Contract*) meant that the figuration of popular sovereignty was also tied to the changing scientific perspectives on the first person that emerged in the years following 1793. Standardized categories for mental illness developed in the nineteenth century participated in the aesthetic and political problem of popular representation by shifting the focus from individuals to the mental health of national populations.

Establishing a link between the emergence of standardized psychiatric diagnostics and representations of the body politic is important for modernism and modernist scholarship. It adjusts the limiting but persistent *idée reçue* that modernist depictions of non-normative mental states are restricted to reflecting and responding to the descriptions of powerful unconscious forces of unreason at work in the human mind from Freud, Friedrich Nietzsche, and others. The supposition that modernist experimentation is synonymous with an individually liberatory and socially progressive madness—whether because modernist works were created by deviant "mad" authors (Antonin Artaud, Vincent van Gogh), featured "mad" countercultural characters (Septimus Smith, Madame Bovary, Malte Laurids Brigge, the Underground Man, Chris Baldry), or responded to psychoanalytic theories about primitive libidinal forces—neglects that this era also gave rise to the quantitative, empirical, Enlightenment-driven accounts of the mind that form the basis for the contemporary mind sciences and so too an unprecedented mass rationalization of collective life.

Emphasis on modernism's mad qualities and, more specifically, on modernism's debt to the psychoanalytic unconscious can thus function as a kind of screen memory.[7] It leaves out the possibility that modernism perhaps also marked the psychical subject's more trenchant (re)inscription into reason's expanding scope. The ethically inspired move to recover depictions of contemporary diseases like obsessive-compulsive disorder, attention-deficit/hyperactivity disorder, and post-traumatic stress disorder in prior eras' literature (and so draw stigmatized groups and experiences back into the social circle) unintentionally subsumes the equally ethical possibility of reading literature for its commentary on psychiatric classification systems' marginalizing and normative dimensions within a tradition of instrumental reason. This normative dimension is as much a product of the mind sciences' conflicted formation in tandem with modern nation-states as it is a debt to what scholars in the philosophy of science term psychiatric reification. This is the premise, originating in Emil Kraepelin's work, that mental illnesses are *natürliche Krankheitseinheiten* ("natural disease entities"). Reification presents mental illnesses as given *things* (*Einheiten*, units, entities) in the natural world. Both the contemporary DSM and ICD psychiatric classifications are built on Kraepelin's ontological stance that, as Paul Hoff writes, "psychiatric disease entities, being natural kinds, are to be detected, not constructed, by research" (an observation different from suggesting that psychical suffering is not real or that it cannot be scientifically studied). The history of the subject must thus be thought as encompassing not merely the history of the "interpretive concepts and categories" that overtly structure a political and economic Imaginary but also the historical genesis of a scientific account of subjective consciousness, whether understood in its Hegelian, Leninist, Wundtian, Freudian, or Kraepelinian terms.[8] *Psychic Empire* argues it is inadequate to frame attention to consciousness per se as a defining feature of modernist aesthetics and instead engages with the historical advent of new scientific *accounts* of consciousness.[9]

Karl Marx's well-known comment on consciousness in the preface to *A Contribution to the Critique of Political Economy* (1859), written at the same time that the German founder of empirical psychology, Wilhelm Wundt, was trying to measure the speed of thought, speaks to the need to consider modernist works as dialogically conversant with scientific accounts of consciousness.[10] Marx writes, "The mode of production of material life conditions the general process of social, political, and intellectual life [*geistigen Lebensprozeß*]. It is not that consciousness [*Bewußtsein*] of men determines their existence, but their social existence [*gesellschaftliches Sein*] determines their consciousness [*Bewußtsein*]."[11] Following Marx, it makes sense to consider that the "mode of production of material life" also determines accounts of consciousness.[12] Modernist works do not just recount the experience of consciousness as such but reflect the coming into being of particular explanations of and for consciousness.[13]

Emphasis on accounts of consciousness and madness within modernist texts is important for another reason. Modernist works sketch the theoretical contours of a new technology of knowledge-power and new mode of subjectivation that began in the nineteenth century but has dramatically grown in scope and force since its inception. Psychopower, as I term it in this book, entails the mass management of popular mental health through measurement as a new expression of sovereignty in modernity. Michel Foucault's account of biopower has long held sway in critical commentary in the academy. Because the prevailing interpretations of Foucauldian biopower often concentrate on the body, however, they have drawn attention away from the possibility that the mind experienced a parallel transformation in the period Foucault describes, a possibility that is both interwoven into and incompatible with his ideas. This is an observation that literary theorists of biopolitics have yet to address and that remains unacknowledged by the concepts of immunitas (Roberto Esposito), precarity (Judith Butler), and bare life (Giorgio Agamben).[14] I elaborate the unifying concept of psychopower as it pertains to my own argument in the book's first chapter.

The texts I consider in this book are selected to illuminate psychopower's features and reveal ways in which psychopower conditions first-person statements about mental health and illness. On the one hand, modernist works disclose psychopower's basic components: a commitment to the quantification of mental experience, a population-level conceptualization of psychical life, and a partnership between the systematized classification of mental pathology and a normative definition of mental health. Georg Büchner's *Woyzeck* (written in 1836, published 1875), Daniel Paul Schreber's *Denkwürdigkeiten eines Nervenkranken* (*Memoirs of My Nervous Illness*, 1903), and Ernst Toller's *Masse-Mensch* (1919–1921) illuminate the mind's representational transformation into a measurable entity during this time. This transformation is similarly evident in the work of the Spanish neuroscientist Santiago Ramón y Cajal, whose neural drawings in the 1890s helped put in place the neuron doctrine (the concept that the nervous system is made of discrete cells called neurons). Alongside texts such as Nikolay Evreinov's play *V kulisakh dushi* (*In the Stage Wings of the Soul*, 1912) and Vsevolod Ivanov's novel *Y* (written 1929–1933), they disclose the formalization of a scientifically based concept of the popular mind, equipped with interpellative force and often working in partnership with capitalism and the law.

On the other hand, recognizing psychopower as it is sketched by these literary works provides a different account of the politics of mental life than that offered by the Frankfurt School, its inheritors, or contemporary philosophical accounts of affect and the brain as the basis for progressive social transformation. In my argument, neither DSM/ICD categories nor an affectively charged brain biology supply neutral terms for self-description or the formation of political community. Both must be contextualized as the conflicted products of a generalizable model of mental life developed a century earlier and different in nature from Freud's psychoanthropology. The *fin de siècle* German, Russian, and Soviet texts I examine show subjects and groups in the process of navigating this model's interpellative dimensions through Foucauldian games of strategy (directed against psychopolitical mechanisms), deterritorializations (configuring psychopower's terms for new ends), and the postcolonial dilemma of being able to speak at all. The story of psychopower is hence not a resistance narrative of the modern subject's heroism in the face of structurally violent obstacles to minoritarian self-expression. Neither is it an affirmation of ego-psychological selfhood given in the grammar of the clinic: "Speaking as an (insert psychiatric diagnosis here) . . ." Rather, it is a question of how to relate to the history of being hailed into consciousness.

Why tell this history through literature and art? My methodological premise is that it cannot be fully recognized from elsewhere. Because aesthetic objects are located outside rationalism's calculable logic, they are not amenable to either measurable performance or fixed meaning (save in the crudest possible instances). This allows such objects to remain in productive tension with the findings of scientific fields that, out of necessity, must base their claims on measurement and reproducible experimental results. The epistemological gap that separates aesthetic works (and the fields studying them) from the scientific method provides the quantum of critical distance necessary to identify crises not legible from within the scientific systems producing such crises. Properly speaking, the methodological approach that respects the generative conflict between aesthetic and scientific epistemologies is not interdisciplinary but counterdisciplinary, a distinction I elaborate below. Regarded from the perspective of the DSM and ICD, standardized psychiatric nomenclature provides an evidentially based and hence (in theory) universally generalizable typology of human psychical experience with supralinguistic explanatory power. Regarded from the (counterdisciplinary) perspective of aesthetic objects written as the foundations of these diagnostic systems took shape, such classificatory nomenclature remains entangled in the very complexities of representation, universality, and language it outwardly shuns.

Aspects of this entanglement are of course legible in studies of the history of individual psychiatric diseases (as in work by Georges Didi-Huberman, Ian Hacking, David Healy, Allan Horwitz, Ruth Leys, Edward Shorter, and Max Fink) that do not engage with aesthetic objects. Consideration of the history of individual diseases or attention to psychiatric reification alone, however, cannot easily situate mass mental diagnostics in the representational double-binds of Enlightenment ordering as they collided with the standardizing processes of modern nation-states. The book shows, then, how modernist literature articulates a fundamental historical transformation occurring midway through the nineteenth century that figuratively converted a generically labeled philosophical concept of *thought* (*das Denken*) into scientifically measurable terms like *cognition*, *response*, *impression*, *behavior*, *affect*, and *disorder*.

Scholarship in the history of science is already familiar with aspects of the shift. Anson Rabinbach has tracked its expression as industrial modernity's trope of energetics in *The Human Motor: Energy, Fatigue, and the Origins of*

*Modernity.* Katja Guenther has followed its developments in her work on psychoanalysis and brain localization and in her history of self-recognition in the human sciences. It is a feature of Laura Otis's writing on nineteenth-century neurobiology's metaphors of invasion and Nikolas Rose's studies on globalized psychiatry and neuroscience.[15] Its consequences appear in Kurt Danziger's discussion of psychology's language, Fernando Vidal's description of "brainhood," Ian Hacking's writing on multiple personality disorder and transient mental illnesses, and across Stefanos Geroulanos's work.[16] Accounts of the transformation that made the mind into an object of scientific study also appear in the many capacious volumes addressing the nineteenth-century disciplinary history of psychoanalysis, psychology, and psychiatry.[17] I build on that rich body of scholarship. My contention, however, is that the unique problems of semiosis and nominalization posed by psychiatric classification as it emerged out of the split between continental philosophy and the human sciences in the nineteenth century are most capaciously addressed by scholarship on literature and aesthetics, which deals with issues of narrative, language, meaning, and representation. To return briefly to the German psychologist Wilhelm Wundt's early work on the speed of thought, it is of course possible to see his scientific experiment and its associated device, the thought meter (*der Gedankenmesser*, lit. thought gauge, though *Messer* may also mean knife), as the foundation of modern experimental psychology. The thought meter (figure 0.2) operated by measuring the time it took the test subject to shift attention from the sound of its bell to the swinging pendulum that struck it. Wundt's device, however, is remarkably like another time measurement technology of its era: the metronome, patented in 1815. From the Greek *μέτρο-* (relating to measurement or regulation) and *νόμος* (law, rule), Johann Maelzel's ticking metronome that keeps musical time is the physical instantiation of the law of measure its etymology names. One way, then, to see Wundt's innovation is as a scientific breakthrough that inaugurated modern empirical psychology. Another is as opening a scientifically destabilizing question that troubles modern empirical psychology from within: What is or should be the "law of measure" for thought?

Because not premised on a commitment to calculability, literature (broadly defined) offers a site at which such "metronymy" can finally be considered. The rhetorical term "metonymy" refers to a figure of speech in which a part is made to stand for a whole. Metonymic constructions therefore first assume a definition of part and whole and so also a system of measurement. The related idea of metronymy involves questioning the law(s) that would guide such measurement.[18] How should one establish what is part and what is whole in the psyche? Who should be responsible for doing so? According to what metrics? In interrogating nineteenth-century scientific accounts of consciousness, modernist literary texts written by Büchner, Evreinov, Ivanov, Schreber, Toller,

**0.2** Wilhelm Wundt. Diagram of the thought meter in *Die Geschwindigkeit des Gedankens* (The speed of thought, 1862).

*Source*: Anonymous.

and the other authors I explore in this book metronymically take up the rules that formalized measures of thought and put in place their accompanying names.

These aesthetic works (and this book) are thus also a source for troubling one of the most outwardly unassailable components of evidence, knowledge, and truth: measurement. If literary-style analysis resituates findings such as Wundt's by drawing them out of the timeless universality of pure fact, it is also the source of a larger critical practice that resists the tendency to regard measurement as a natural end to interpretation, as if measurement were devoid of context. It is impossible to see that Wundt's thought meter is the foundation of modern psychological science *and* its own dialectical negation without a rhetorical detour through etymology (*μέτρο-νόμος*), use of an unprogrammed and incalculable associative linkage (between the metronome and the thought meter), knowledge of ancient and modern non-English languages (Greek, German), attention to the complexities of translation, and above all a training that cultivates a desire to read in this way.

Such reading shows that problems of naming, language, and representation remain at the core of the nonpsychoanalytic mind sciences, which nevertheless base their scientific legitimacy on a commitment to objective hard evidence and not fungible, subjective linguistic mediation. In this way, neuroscience, empirical psychology, and modern clinical psychiatry return to rather than escape from Hegelian and Enlightenment paradoxes of universality that even the most interdisciplinary practitioners among them nevertheless often write off as the irrelevant concerns of metaphysics, too seemingly dated and speculative for modern science to take seriously.[19] The metaphysics-critical stance makes good historical sense given that modern-day psychiatry, psychology, and neuroscience established themselves as sciences in the nineteenth century by rejecting speculative philosophy's claims to the study of the mind. The problem, however, is that this historical breach has since also come to neutralize the possibility of inquiring how scientific fields dealing with the mind remain inflected by subjective considerations without losing their objective scientific validity. It prevents consideration of how clinical psychiatry, empirical psychology, and neuroscience might interface with capitalism and globalization, generate a picture of the socius, and repeat racialized and gendered presuppositions. These questions have long been the subject of discussions focused on the social contract's and popular sovereignty's exclusions. They deserve to be extended into scientific domains, which are no less conversant with issues of rights or the body politic for having different objects. Physicists' recent consideration of the racialized metaphorics of "dark matter," humanists' ongoing exploration of algorithmic bias, and Black feminist scholarship on the representational dimensions of economic value all provide recent models suggesting that the human sciences could critically engage the Enlightenment's paradoxes without defaulting to a crude antiscientism or jeopardizing their own legitimacy.[20] The humanities' preoccupation with debating Freud's relative scientificity unfortunately amplifies the problem of neutralization by distracting attention from the rise of a far more medically dominant nonpsychoanalytic clinical psychiatry. While psychoanalysis seems to be the proper domain for humanistic inquiry, mainstream psychiatry, psychology, and neuroscience continue to do all the work without significant attention from humanists. Humanists too often miss that these fields' joint configuration by language and storytelling means that their objective findings—while in no way invalidated—also fall within the purview of humanities' analysis.

What one sees taking place in modernism, however, is the problem of who or what speaks (and in what terms) in the case of emergent nineteenth-century accounts of mental health and illness focused on the use of evidence, observation, and measurement. Modernist literature from Central and Eastern Europe shows the subject's struggle in the context of a new, jointly clinical and juridical code defining madness and sanity. This code's formalization during the nineteenth and early twentieth century affected the subjectivation of individuals as much as it did definitions of the group. As such, naturalized psychopathological categories developed in Germany and Russia that seemed only to scientifically describe the features of interior life also interfaced with a changing legal and bureaucratic system responding to the rise of workers' movements, communism, and the conflicts produced by imperial expansion.

The book's chapters investigate who or what speaks in such cases by reading the nonpsychoanalytic dimensions of modernist literature's mad persons. This allows *Psychic Empire* to revisit some of modernism's most iconic associated genres and tropes. Chapter 1, for example, questions schizoid speech as a pervasive account of modernism's fragmentary language and semiotic collapse, while chapter 2 comparatively considers diagnostic language in Freudian psychoanalysis versus non-Freudian clinical psychiatry. Chapter 3 explores self-diagnosis in psychiatric patients' clinical memoirs, and chapter 4 revisits expressionist accounts of pathological subjectivity. Chapter 5 reflects on the modernist novel's relationship to metaphors of psychic economy. Chapters 6 and 7 respectively discuss the genre of monodrama and modernist visual media's representations of the brain.

The book's organization maps the growth of psychopower from within a German and Russian context convulsed by the French Revolution and Napoleonic Wars, to the mid-twentieth century emergence of the Soviet Union and beginnings of decolonization. The first chapter introduces and explains my theory of psychopower through a reading of Georg Büchner's play *Woyzeck* (written 1836, published 1875). While *Woyzeck* is often treated in secondary criticism as a canonical example of schizophrenia and stylistically schizoid language, the chapter instead engages the play as commentary on the post-revolutionary scientific and legal transformations that gave rise to standardized psychodiagnostic disease categories, including schizophrenia. Through its source material (a historical trial involving the insanity defense) and Büchner's own medical training, *Woyzeck* is in conversation with the 1830s scientific shift from a transcendental philosophical account of the mind to one emphasizing its biological underpinnings and relationship to the nervous system. *Woyzeck* reworks this source material to dramatize how the "artificial soul" of sovereignty, described by Thomas Hobbes as animating the body politic, was itself transformed by changing scientific accounts of mental life. These cast the immaterial artificial soul, or psyche politic, of medieval sovereignty in new anatomical terms. The position is not one that can be accommodated by Michel Foucault's concept of biopower. Neither is it reducible to the various theories of psychical politics advanced by contemporary philosophers such as Bernard Stiegler and Byung-Chul Han and historians of science like Kurt Danziger, sociologists such as Nikolas Rose, and medical anthropologists like Fernando Vidal. By treating Büchner as a literary theorist of psychopower, chapter 1 provides the conceptual armature structuring the book's subsequent consideration of psychopower's role in the modernist canon and beyond.

Chapter 2 focuses on how psychopower configured the meaning of diagnostic language in a psychoanalytic versus nonpsychoanalytic context. The chapter argues for the existence of a basic epistemological divergence—created by the use of quantification and physics—between Freudian psychoanalysis and the German clinical psychiatry practiced by Freud's contemporary Emil Kraepelin. Kraepelin's research is an essential precursor to today's DSM and ICD. Examination of the distinction between Freud's and Kraepelin's diagnostic approaches offers insight into a division that continues to separate psychoanalytic nosology from outwardly similar DSM and ICD categories. I focus here on a single patient whom both men treated: the Wolf-Man (Sergey Pankeyev, 1886–1979). Pankeyev's case history and autobiography raise questions about the use of a generalizable psychiatric system, indebted to the mid-century claim that mental life obeyed Newtonian laws, as an ethical alternative to the psychoanalytic focus on reading individual cases. It simultaneously complicates Friedrich Kittler's influential account of the relationship between the mind sciences and modernist literature, showing that Kittler's neglect of the key distinction between Freud's and Kraepelin's systems imperils his overall claim about technology in modernist aesthetics.

Chapter 3 explores how the rise of psychopower helped formalize a picture of popular sanity, instead of just illness, within imperial Germany's new 1871 civil code. This chapter centers on the clinical memoirs of the German judge Daniel Paul Schreber (1842–1911), who was institutionalized against his will and placed under legal guardianship in 1893. Written while interred in a psychiatric institution, *Memoirs of My Nervous Illness* offers a first-person account of Schreber's allegedly delusional system. It made him a key psychoanalytic case for Sigmund Freud and Jacques Lacan. Both Freud and Lacan read Schreber's apocalyptic experiences of celestial voices, divine insemination, and metamorphosis into a woman as a psychotic crisis of paternity, investiture, and symbolic authority. Schreber also had close ties to the psychiatric court case that inspired Georg Büchner's *Woyzeck* (chapter 1) and Emil Kraepelin's psychiatric research, which he cites at length in his *Memoirs* (chapter 2). His ability to deploy the findings of German clinical psychiatry and make use of it standardized nomenclature in successful defense of his sanity nuances the reading of Schreber as having foreclosed the Name-of-the-Father and dropped from the order of representation. This chapter resituates the *Memoirs* at a gendered boundary between an Enlightenment project of standardization committed to semiosis, sanity, and the law and Schreber's fall out of language and into the Real.

The antisemitism and Bismarckian nationalism that appear in Schreber's *Memoirs* provide the basis for chapter 4's discussion of psychopower's racializing role in imperial German criminal law. I look at how Kraepelinian psychiatry informed interwar antisemitism through a reading of the expressionist play *Masse-Mensch* (written 1919, published 1921), by the German-Jewish playwright Ernst Toller (1893–1939). Toller had been treated by Kraepelin for alleged psychopathy in 1918, a diagnosis that returned to haunt him during his trial for treason in 1919. At first glance, *Masse-Mensch* seems little more than a politically ambivalent commentary on Toller's time as a revolutionary leader of the short-lived Bavarian Socialist Republic. Reconsideration of the play, however, discloses the drama as an analysis of Kraepelinian classification's racialized descriptions of the popular mass in the Weimar Republic. In *Masse-Mensch*, Toller's reworking of his revolutionary experience addresses the impasses of representing the psyche politic that were generated by Kraepelin's concept of "natural disease entities." Toller shows how the notion of natural disease entities helped carve the social body into a hierarchy of groups.

Chapter 5 considers psychopower's economic implications by investigating the fate of Kraepelinian psychiatry in the Soviet Union. The chapter focuses on the question of non-Freudian psychic economies. I engage with the socialist writer Vsevolod Ivanov's untranslated novel *У* (U, pronounced "oo"), composed during 1929–1933 and posthumously published in 1987. Written as the Soviet Union was in the process of banning psychoanalysis and shifting its scientific focus to neurology and behaviorism, Ivanov's novel takes a surprisingly critical stance on the economic implications of Kraepelin's psychiatry. Against the growing Soviet critique of psychoanalysis as bourgeois and individualistic, *У* frames Kraepelinian clinical psychiatry as more capitalist than Freud's work. The novel subtly suggests that Kraepelin's classification generated a psychical version of the value form that replaced the Freudian economy of desire with a mental model structurally mirroring capitalist economic exchange. Confined to a drawer in the 1930s, *У* nevertheless speaks to a Lukácsian commodification of consciousness in which psychiatric and economic reification worked in tandem. In Ivanov's novel, the same scientific model offering a biologized picture of mental illness that should have provided an alternative to the ideologically dubious investments of Freudian libidinal exchange instead created a portrait of mental life with similar problems.

Chapter 6 follows the complexities of a naturalized model of the mind further into the Soviet context by turning to psychopower's key role in representing the Soviet people *as* a people in the tumultuous years following the Russian Revolution. I show that the Russian playwright Nikolay Evreinov's monodrama *In the Stage Wings of the Soul* (1912), which engaged with theories from psychophysics and empirical psychology, was the basis for a Soviet mass spectacle that consolidated a picture of the Soviet popular will pivotal to the Bolsheviks' narrative about the Russian Revolution. Strikingly, Evreinov's bourgeois, slapstick monodrama about the psychical dilemmas of a married man in love with a cabaret singer nevertheless became the foundation for a giant public spectacle aimed at fostering a sense of collective psychical solidarity and public unity at a moment of factional strife. Evreinov's prerevolutionary play, built on his theory of theatrical "co-experiencing," helped generate a sense of collective consciousness and the imagination of a "we" that proved strategically useful to the postrevolutionary Bolshevik cause.

Chapter 7 expands on the prior chapter's attention to a biological model of mental life by turning to psychopower's place in the contemporary neurosciences and neuroimaging. This chapter traces neurobiology's entanglements with colonial history beginning with the neuroscientist Santiago Ramón y Cajal's famous neural drawings of the 1880s. These important drawings established the neuron doctrine, the concept that the nervous system is made up of discrete cells, for which Cajal won the Nobel Prize in 1906. Cajal's images, however, also track his anxieties about the Spanish Empire's loss of its colonies in the Spanish-American War of 1898. His exquisite representation of the neural landscape is entwined with a contemporaneous nationalist celebration of the Spanish countryside in the Spanish literary and visual arts seeking to compensate for the territorial losses of 1898. Because twentieth- and twenty-first-century functional neuroimaging practices are indebted to Cajal's nineteenth-century drawings, this perspective offers a new way of understanding the visual genealogy of brain-based mental functioning. Cognitive literary criticism and cognitive film studies have stressed that aesthetic objects are expressions of brain-based processes. A counterdisciplinary perspective shows that aesthetic objects also offer a vantage point from which to read the neuroscientific visualizations depicting brain-based processes. Both Cajal's images and modern films like Lucrecia Martel's *La mujer sin cabeza* (2008), on the traumatic legacy of the Argentine Dirty War, situate aesthetic objects as sites through which to engage the social and cultural dimensions of neuroimaging.

The afterword reflects on *Psychic Empire*'s counterdisciplinary juxtaposition of aesthetic objects with scientific claims. It considers the role of the interpretive humanities and the fate of what Friedrich Schiller called an "aesthetic education" in the wake of the neurocognitive turn. The afterword proposes that extant paradigms for integrating subjectivity into the mind sciences, such as neuropsychoanalysis, tend to force subjectivity into the established scientific model for objectivity. While stressing the importance of storytelling and art in a clinical context, current neurocognitive models for integrating subjectivity into a scientific framework incorporate creative objects and practices only to the extent as these objects and practices can be made commensurate with instrumental ends. Working against the reduction of the humanities to an information delivery model that delegitimates irreducibility and doubt, the afterword proposes that the brain does not explain away creative works but requires the interpretive practices their analysis cultivates.

The remainder of this introduction outlines the key gap in current humanities scholarship to which this book responds. To do so, it surveys extant critical approaches to psychodiagnostic categories within literary theoretical research. The introduction then explains the methodological concept of counterdisciplinarity and shows why it is needed to address this gap. In the final section, I discuss the book's title.

## Reading Diagnostically: Three Paradigms and the Case for Counterdisciplinarity

Imagine Jacqueline Rose, Catherine Malabou, and Gayatri Chakravorty Spivak in conversation. They are discussing the Freudian diagnostic category of narcissism in relationship to trauma, psychical violence, and modernist literature. In a sense, their dialogue is already ongoing, although carried out in sufficiently separate spheres as to seem nonexistent. Gathering their voices together here makes it possible to survey existing humanities models for interpreting diagnostic language. Far from being a new practice, diagnostic reading has already made such deep but unrecognized inroads into literary study, modernism, and accounts of the subject as to seem as if it were not there at all. This "as if" is an extraordinary supposition, with important implications for and beyond literary study.

By "reading diagnostically" I have in mind the diagnostic interpretation of literary texts (for example, diagnosing a literary scenario as "narcissistic") and the humanities' attention to specific diagnostic terms (for example, etymologically analyzing the term "narcissism"). As I see it, there are currently three basic paradigms for reading diagnostically, which I here designate the "literary critical," the "clinico-critical," and the "postcolonial psychoanalytic."

In broad strokes, the first of these paradigms, the "literary critical," advocates reading literary texts and aesthetic objects on their own terms first rather than through the lens of a clinical lexicon. It nevertheless acknowledges this lexicon as a potentially helpful interpretive tool, while rejecting the crude application of psychoanalysis to characters or authors. Here, individual psychodiagnostic terms—mostly from a psychoanalytic context—deserve the same careful consideration as aesthetic objects. Writers in this paradigm, like the British psychoanalytic literary critic Jacqueline Rose, tend to emphasize that these clinical terms must not be taken at face value let alone applied to aesthetic works or their writers to explain them. These terms are still productive, however, as a frame for describing psychical patterns literature may respond to, mediate, narratologically reproduce, or symptomatically illustrate.

The second paradigm, "clinical criticism," takes the opposite approach. In this scenario literary texts and aesthetic objects illustrate the evidence-backed diagnostic categories used in clinical psychiatry, empirical psychology, and neuroscience. Here, psychodiagnostic terms do not require interpretive analysis, as their meaning has already been defined in a (nonpsychoanalytic) clinical context. The seemingly cold accounts of mental life these scientific fields produce must nevertheless be supplemented by more affective, narrative ones (written by patients or their doctors) that ethically humanize these field's empirical findings by connecting them to real patients' daily lives and struggles. I examine the clinico-critical paradigm through the work of the French philosopher Catherine Malabou, in dialogue with the neuroscientist Oliver Sacks.

In the third paradigm, "postcolonial psychoanalysis," literary texts and aesthetic objects illuminate psychoanalysis. They show psychoanalysis's debt to a narrow cultural, historical, and linguistic context that is in tension with its more universal account of the psyche. Here, recognition of the limited purview of Freud's nineteenth-century oeuvre nonetheless encourages a reinterpretation of his concepts that opens them in new, more capacious ways. In this paradigm, psychoanalysis's emphasis on interpretation supplies an escape hatch allowing readers to acknowledge and subvert the racism, classism, and misogyny in Freud's work without being forced to abandon psychoanalytic insights. I consider the postcolonial psychoanalytic paradigm through the work of Gayatri Chakravorty Spivak.

The literary-critical, clinico-critical, and postcolonial psychoanalytic paradigms nevertheless leave out the possibility that nonpsychoanalytic research on the mind might still require interpretive analysis of its diagnostic language. They neglect, that is, a missing fourth paradigm, one I call counterdisciplinarity and suggest is contained in Meret Oppenheim's modernist photograph *X-ray of M.O.'s Skull.*

## The Literary-Critical Paradigm: Reading Sylvia Plath with Jacqueline Rose

The British psychoanalytic scholar Jacqueline Rose remarks at the beginning of *On Violence and On Violence Against Women* (2021) that while "it is a truism to say that everyone knows violence when they see it," what has become "clear over the past decade [is that] the most prevalent, insidious forms of violence are those that cannot be seen."[21] Pair this claim with the assertion by the French philosopher Catherine Malabou in *The New Wounded: From Freud to Neurosciences, Thinking Contemporary Trauma* (2007) that psychoanalysis "ignores the suffering of the brain, and along with it, the emotive and emotional dimension of the brain," and a curious paradox arises.[22] Is psychical violence and suffering a matter of visibility, self-evidentiality, and indeed biological physicality, or isn't it? Does psychical violence and suffering require interpretation?[23] One approach to this question would be to follow the paroxysms of mind-body dualism into their twenty-first-century iterations. Another would insist that the disjuncture between the invisible (and hence only ambiguously "real") violence Rose psychoanalytically describes and the one Malabou presents as demonstrably real by virtue of the brain's materiality points to a more fundamental rift. It tracks the gap between the dematerialized psychoanalytic representation of mental life and an embodied neurophysiological portrait of cognitive functioning, each possessing different perspectives on how to figure the psyche and correspondingly different epistemological standpoints on how to describe its operations.[24]

Rose writes of the "deadly mix" in male violence toward women established by a "link between the ability to inflict untold damage and a willed distortion—whether conscious or unconscious—in the field of vision."[25] It is this link that permits the seeming ease, she argues, among White House staff photographed watching Donald Trump sign the 2017 "global gag rule" into effect, which barred foreign NGOs receiving U.S. global health assistance from providing legal abortion or counseling for abortion. The men's complacency in the photograph visually belies the enormous increase in "deaths by illegal abortion for thousands of women throughout the developing world" by the gag rule, which anticipated the overturning of *Roe v. Wade* by the Roberts court in 2022.[26] The problem, then, is that this violence is not one that bloodily or bodily declares itself in media-ready snapshots or statements but—absent interpretive scrutiny—will always proceed invisibly. This violence is the impalpable expression of a psychoanalytically configured narcissism. In Rose's argument, such violence takes the form of a childlike royal right to aggression (a lèse-majesté) like that possessed by "His Majesty the Baby" in Freud's essay "On Narcissism" (1914). The infant's belief in its status as the center of creation, coupled with its faith in immortality and immunity to all realities that would restrict the free expression of its will, leads it to interpret injuries as violations of its god-given sovereign rule, deserving a proportionately aggressive response. For Rose, the infant's narcissistic entitlement persists in contemporary expressions of violence like the global gag rule. Perpetuators of this violence nevertheless publicly frame themselves as defending innocent lives and do so with the conviction of the screaming infant defending its (nominally) sovereign right to enforce its will. "Violence in our time thrives on a form of mental blindness," she writes, contending that such violence is perpetuated and sustained by its outward invisibility (as in the photograph, for example) *and* by its psychical nonappearance, its status as a "willed distortion—whether conscious or unconscious—in the field of vision."[27]

Rose's argument develops a point from her earlier writing on literature. Midway through *On Violence*, she returns to her 1992 book *The Haunting of Sylvia Plath*. As she recounts, in the early 1990s the Plath estate vigorously resisted publication of *Haunting* on the grounds that it deformed the established narrative of Plath's life story, of which Olwyn and Ted Hughes saw themselves as the sole proprietors. Reflecting on this frustrating experience twenty years later, Rose remarks that the central premise of her present book is inspired by that earlier work's conviction "that feminism has nothing to gain by seeing women solely or predominantly as the victims of their histories." In order to step outside the willed distortion described in *On Violence*'s opening, feminism must "confront violence as a part of the psyche," Rose writes, and avoid unwittingly supporting "psychic processes that lead to the enactment of violence."[28] This means, in particular, avoiding diagnostic thinking that frames the female subject first and primarily in terms of her medical history. Plath's suicide seemed to justify knee-jerk retroactive interpretations of her life and her work, as if everything had inexorably led to that fatal point. Her every word and action were thereby all too easily mustered as evidence for a preestablished suicide master narrative:

> Anything negative or violent in her writing is then read as a stage in a myth of self-emergence . . . an allegory of selfhood which settles the unconscious and ideally leaves its troubles behind. . . . In fact, despite appearances, those diagnoses of Plath remove the problem of the unconscious even more than the criticism that has come in reply. There is nothing like the concept of a purely individual pathology for allowing us, with immense comfort, to conjure it all away. . . . For me, one of the central challenges presented in Plath's writing has been to find a way of looking at the most unsettling and irreducible dimensions of psychic processes which she figures in her writing without turning them against her—without, therefore, turning her into a case. . . . I do not believe we can take writing as unproblematic evidence for the psychological condition or attributes of the one who writes. . . . Even from inside the space of her writing, Plath offers no singular form or vision on which such a diagnosis could safely alight.[29]

In this passage, Rose identifies multiple reasons for avoiding facile diagnostic labeling in literature and life. First, the use of psychoanalysis as a diagnostically explanatory key to either is a profound abuse of psychoanalysis: "Those diagnoses of Plath remove the problem of the unconscious even more than the criticism that has come in reply." This is because such diagnostic labeling is a way of dispensing with interpretation and so of avoiding truly difficult problems. In place of a frightening insolubility, applied psychoanalytic diagnosis in the literary sphere offers the comfort of an explanation. "There is nothing like the concept of a purely individual pathology for allowing us, with immense comfort, to conjure it all away." To write about Plath, Rose notes, her task as a scholar was to steer clear of this trap. She had to engage with all that was "unsettled and irreducible" in Plath's writing by treating it as unsettled and irreducible, by not, that is, "turning her into a case." This is in line with Plath's own practice as a writer. "Even from inside the space of her writing, Plath offers no singular form of vision on which such a diagnosis could safely alight," Rose remarks. The link between *On Violence* and *The Haunting of Sylvia Plath*, then, is Rose's unstated thesis that facile psychodiagnostic interpretation constitutes a form of narcissistic mental blindness, which unwittingly distorts the psychoanalytic method and perpetuates violence by ignoring the "unsettling and irreducible" dimensions of psychic processes that literary works figure.

Her thesis about literature's unsettling and irreducible qualities forms the basis of Rose's argument about modernism in *On Violence*.[30] Scholarship on modernism seems to be caught between accounts stressing the disintegration of consciousness and those framing modernism as the resurgence of a violent Enlightenment dream (apropos Max Horkheimer and Theodor Adorno's *Dialectic of Enlightenment*). For Rose, this is a false binary. The real question, she states, is how a history or histories of violence fit the mind's loss of authority over itself. Turning to Virginia Woolf, Toni Morrison, and Eimear McBride's novels, Rose advances the position that modernist literature's hallmark use of fragmentary language translates the entanglement of violent historical crisis and "the collapse of the belief in the integrity of the self."[31]

*On Violence* and *The Haunting of Sylvia Plath* help show that the literary-critical paradigm for diagnostic reading begins from the careful interpretation of literary works and brings in diagnostic concepts from psychoanalysis only secondarily, when these concepts can serve that task rather than condition, inhibit, or distort it. Ethical reading involves stepping away from pathologizing disease narratives that characterize the subject exclusively in terms of their disease history. Resistance to both diagnostic nomenclature and framing people as "cases" is thus essential. Both strategies merely serve to conjure away the challenges of interpretation. Literary works remain on the level of the unsettling and irreducible and accordingly cannot provide evidence for a psychological state. Modernism captures the struggle for language in response to a historical violence effacing the self. The Freudian concept of narcissism names the failure of reading that sustains physical violence by (consciously or unconsciously) occasioning the subject's turn to victimization narratives as means of protecting the ego's right to mastery and thereby avoiding uncertainty.

## The Critico-Clinical Paradigm: Reading Marcel Proust with Catherine Malabou

For Catherine Malabou, by contrast, literary modernism is a diagnostic tool par excellence. Her Proustian experience of her grandmother's suffering and death from Alzheimer's disease leads her to question whether "psychoanalysis hasn't said everything on the subject of psychic suffering."[32] The grief Marcel Proust's fictional protagonist experiences at his grandmother's death (from stroke) in *À la recherche du temps perdu* (*In Search of Lost Time*, 1913–1927) moves Malabou to consider in *The New Wounded* whether the brain is capable of suffering, not just the mind. What if the anguished brain in cases of cerebral pathology (like Alzheimer's and stroke) represents an instance of wounding that the Freudian account of traumatic neurosis (rooted in Freud's concept of narcissism), has massively neglected? She retraces the psychoanalytic relationship to war via Freud's experiences with soldiers in World War I and the Austrian psychoanalyst Bruno Bettelheim's (1903–1990) account of autistic children's similarities to the "'musulmans' in the concentration camps." Malabou then contends that accounts of psychic disturbances are consistently historically contemporaneous with "a certain state or a certain age of war."[33] Trauma is consequently at the core of psychopathology in general. This can no longer be Freudian trauma, however, but one that, in the present, has quite literally exceeded psychoanalytic terms:

> Taking into consideration changes in weaponry and the very form of military conflict [*l'état changeant des conflits*] in the course of the twentieth century, the contemporary psychiatry of war has been compelled, on its own, to assimilate the evolution that led from what was called traumatic neurosis during Freud's time to what has more recently been called PTSD, or posttraumatic stress disorder [*état de stress post-traumatique*]. War psychiatrists have a more convincing explanation for the inability of psychoanalysis to think this evolution, I believe, than *Le livre noire de la psychanalyse*. This explanation can be reduced to a single word: trauma. It might be—as all the conflicts of the twentieth century and the dawning twenty-first century have shown—that, for a long time now, psychoanalysis has had little of relevance to say on this subject.[34]

War, in other words, drives psychiatric research (just as it did in the nineteenth century), but military psychiatry now offers a more convincing description of war-induced pathologies in the form of PTSD, a diagnostic category that Malabou correctly observes was created to characterize the experiences of Vietnam veterans in the United States.

Although she does not discuss the backstory in *The New Wounded*, it is deeply pertinent to her claims and this book's argument.[35] In the late 1960s, psychiatrists aligned with the U.S. political advocacy group Vietnam Veterans Against War (VVAW) made the case—against the reigning antipsychiatry movement's rejection of clinical language and view that psychiatry was a form of coercive social control—that psychiatric labels actually benefited their recipients by drawing needed public and medical attention to their problems.

Vietnam veterans with experiences of untreated war trauma had failed at the time to carry political weight because the dominant contemporaneous medical perspective on Vietnam by the U.S. military was that it had little negative psychical impact.[36] Against the initial protestations of researchers on the clinical task force developing the contemporary DSM at Washington University in St. Louis, psychiatric representatives for VVAW convinced the task force leader, Robert Spitzer, to include a new diagnostic category in the DSM that would reflect Vietnam veterans' struggles and publicly legitimate them.[37] Political pressure driven by 1960s antiwar sentiment meant no clinical trials were performed for this new category, which was integrated into the DSM on the basis of veterans' statements alone.

Spitzer's DSM-III of 1980 was a particularly good choice for VVAW's objectives because Spitzer's goal in creating it was to generate a psychiatric manual that would replace psychoanalysis with a research-oriented clinical psychiatry based on measurable evidence, not the vagaries of analytic storytelling.[38] Earlier editions of the DSM (I and II) had been psychoanalytic and promoted largely data-free methodologies conducted outside the parameters of the established scientific method. Spitzer, however, wanted psychiatric diagnoses to become consonant with the disease specificity theory of illness operative in the rest of medicine. This meant psychiatric diagnoses had to be understood as "existing outside the unique manifestations of illness in particular [individuals]" and should conform to increasingly "tightly specific, agreed-upon, disease categories" that did not vary from place to place or patient story to patient story. The categories had to be identified *without* reference to the "lived experience of those who suffered from them," as linking diagnoses to personal experience would defeat the purpose by tying the general categories to individuals.[39] This made the DSM-III an ideal vehicle for the VVAW's aims. Obtaining a special category in Spitzer's DSM-III for the veterans' experiences ensured not only that their concerns were valid but also that they were universally so.

Malabou links the DSM's recognition of PTSD with Bettelheim's 1960s proposal that autistic patients' behavior resembled that of concentration camp survivors.[40] Extreme violence and oppression caused the individuals who lived through Vietnam or the Holocaust to completely emotionally withdraw in a manner resembling autistic patients' emotional coolness and the disaffection of brain-damage victims. This leads her to the book's central claim: that patients with brain lesions (like her grandmother and Proust's Marcel's) behave as if suffering from war trauma (like the Vietnam veterans), and patients with war trauma have responses "comparable in every respect" to those with brain lesions. These "new wounded" (*nouveaux blessés*), can now be related to one another in a "general theory of trauma" under an expanded concept of PTSD. Their pathologies are not the consequence of psychosexual development, as Freud argued, but organized by a cerebral eventfulness that is foreign to psychoanalysis. "From sex to the brain," she writes. Given that the DSM has already defined PTSD, there is no need to interpret the term.[41]

For Malabou, shifting to a generalized theory of trauma stops the undue victimization of patients with cerebral pathology. She argues that Freud's account of traumatic neuroses makes patients responsible for their pain. In her view, the psychoanalytic focus on ingrained psychosexual triggers forces everyone from individuals with war-related brain injuries to the dehumanized survivors of Nazi concentration camps to become answerable for their own suffering.[42] Freudian traumatic neuroses originate in a narcissistic withdrawal of the libido that causes the ego to take itself as an erotic object of desire, resulting in a personality change. Malabou contends that Freud's attribution of personality change to narcissism instead of brain injury absurdly sexualizes the origins of trauma at the price of acknowledging its physical basis. "Sexuality thus intervenes itself in every case in order to activate or efface the psychic effects of organic damage, especially brain damage." By contrast, the work of contemporary neuroscientists like Antonio Damasio, Oliver Sacks, Jaak Panksepp, and Mark Solms shows that affect is indeed constituted in the brain. This means that subjective experience is cerebrally determined. Patients with cerebral pathology resemble those traumatized by war, who resemble individuals with mental disorders, because all are experiencing physical changes (wounds) to the brain, the very wounds Freud disregards: "The concept of PTSD should thus *extend to any and all cases of trauma* . . . today's victims of sociopolitical trauma present the same profile as victims of natural catastrophes (tsunamis, earthquakes, floods) or grave accidents (serious domestic accidents, explosions, fires). We have entered a new age of political violence in which politics is defined by the renunciation of any hope of endowing violence with a political sense."[43] PTSD is hence an ideal choice for a "complete theoretical reinvention of psychopathology" because it stresses the unanticipatable nature of these catastrophes, to which blameless victims can only respond afterward.[44] Whereas Freudian narcissism denies the brain its voice, PTSD grants rights, recognition, and speech to mentally wounded cerebral sufferers in a global field. "*The new wounded, people with brain lesions, have replaced the possessed or the madmen of ancient medicine and the neurotics of psychoanalysis.* The specter of such phenomena hints at the scope of a posttraumatic condition that reigns everywhere today [*partout regnant*] and demands to be thought."[45]

Channeling the language of the *Communist Manifesto* (a specter, reigning everywhere, that demands to be thought), Malabou foregrounds the Hegelian universality of her position on PTSD in *The New Wounded*, linking it back to her earlier work on the brain and plasticity. "It would even be necessary . . . to enlarge the scope of posttraumatic stress disorder . . . in order to designate a multiple and differentiated—one might even say universal—state of stress," she writes. Neurology shows "psychic pain in the age of globalization [*à l'heure de la mondialisation*]" that generates the "worldwide uniformity [*l'uniformasion globale*] of neuropsychological reactions." It is high time to replace the Freudian unconscious with the concept of cerebral autoaffection, discard neurosis, abandon psychic energy, set aside primary narcissism and start talking about nervous energy alone. Considering a "globalized [*mondialisée*] psychic pathology that is identical in all cases and all contexts," it is time to embrace destructive plasticity as an alternative to the (sexually determined) death drive.[46] The random, mentally destructive external shocks of the contemporary world are not explained by individuals' psychobiographies. War and globalization subjugate victims everywhere to an unpredictable reign of trauma that changes the constitution of their brains.[47]

Despite *The New Wounded*'s bid for a liberatory, antiglobalist approach to trauma, the Marxist Lacanian philosopher Slavoj Žižek responded critically to Malabou's claims.[48] Žižek took issue with Malabou's rejection of psychoanalytic hermeneutics and her related assertion that mental suffering was meaningless when caused by senseless violence.[49] A universalized post-traumatic subject, Žižek argued, was none other than the Lacanian split subject by another name. "Malabou seems to pay the price for her all too naïve reading of Freud, taking Freud too (not literally, but) 'hermeneutically,' not distinguishing the true core of Freud's discovery and all the different ways in which he himself misunderstood the scope of his own discovery," he remarked.[50] "How, then, would it be necessary to read Freud?" Malabou queried in reply.[51] To this one could also add the question: How would it be necessary to read Proust?

Malabou's opening reference to Proust demonstrates that modernist literature's role in the clinico-critical paradigm is illustrative: it proves the findings of neuroscientific and clinical psychiatric research. Proust's description of Marcel's grandmother's suffering anticipates Malabou's grandmother's own experiences with Alzheimer's. Likewise, the expostulations on the powers of the X-ray by the French protosurrealist poet Guillaume Apollinaire in his essay *The New Spirit and the Poets* (*L'esprit nouveau et les poètes*, 1917) are made to corroborate twenty-first-century neuroscientific imaging's ability to offer insight into the cerebral self. A few of Apollinaire's lines form *The New Wounded*'s epigraph: "How could it be! An X-ray was made of my head. I, a living being, have seen my cranium—is that not something new? Come on!" The lines are presented as if ventriloquizing contemporary neuroscientists' frustration with their psychoanalytic counterparts. "Come on!" the poet seemingly pleads from 1917 to modern-day psychoanalytic holdouts still committed to the sexual etiology of trauma.[52]

The focus on literature and art's ability to illustrate scientific findings is a feature of Malabou's work as well as that of the British neurologist Oliver

Sacks, whom Malabou cites at length. In Sacks's *The Man Who Mistook His Wife for a Hat* (1985), *An Anthropologist on Mars: Seven Paradoxical Tales* (1995), and subsequent works, modernist figures like Samuel Beckett, Fyodor Dostoevsky, James Joyce, Marcel Proust, and Vincent van Gogh all make regular appearances. For Sacks, their role is to showcase the causal relationship between art and mental illness. Dostoevsky's fiction, for example, was a product of his Interictal Personality Syndrome and epilepsy.[53] Tourette's syndrome helped Samuel Johnson and Mozart. Autism enabled Bartok and Einstein. Manic-depressive illness inspired Baudelaire.[54] Modernist literary works also describe real illnesses, as in the case of Henry James's *The Turn of the Screw* (1898), which Sacks reads as an expression of Hughlings Jackson's 1880s description of psychical seizures.[55] To Sacks, modernist art offers case studies of real diseases that inspire his own affectively humanizing neurological stories. Building on the premise that literary works are diagnostically illustrative, Sacks sets himself the task of writing what he terms empathetic "neurological novels" about his patients that return to the descriptive heights of Freud and Alexander Luria's case histories but take modern neurological patients as their subject matter.

Influenced by Sacks (as well as the writings of Gilles Deleuze and Félix Guattari), Malabou's 2007 book describes the need to similarly narrate the experiences of the new wounded. "Indeed, for Sacks, it is necessary to weave the patient's coolness and indifference . . . into a narrative intrigue that must not be disaffected itself . . . stylistic indifference is not an adequate response to subjective indifference. *Narrative work is a clinical gesture.*" This means, she remarks, that the task is to "make people with brain damage into cases in the strong sense" by transforming them into "paradigms, into mirrors in which we learn to look at ourselves."[56] Quoting Sacks's *Anthropologist*, she notes that compelling narratives about the new wounded allow readers to " 'travel to unimaginable lands—lands of which otherwise we should have no conception or idea.' "[57] The brain may be a fundamentally a nonrepresentational space, devoid of Freud's symbolic elaboration of internal excitations, but the new wounded's foreign terrain nevertheless deserves to be explored in rich narrative detail.

In Catherine Malabou and Oliver Sacks's clinico-critical work, modernist literary texts and aesthetic objects thematically describe objective neuroscientific findings about cerebral existence in affectively compelling terms. Exegesis of these literary and aesthetic works can stop, however, once the appropriate psychopathological diagnosis, correlated to a cerebral change, is identified in them. Reading in this way has an ethical component because modernist literature (Proust, Apollinaire, Joyce) offers a model for composing modern-day patient case histories that give suffering brains a voice. It is socially progressive because enabling the brain to speak illuminates a universal psychical suffering—identifiable under the heading PTSD—generated by late capitalism's globalized violence. PTSD can and should replace a dated, victim-blaming Freudian narcissism and its related account of the traumatic neuroses.

## The Postcolonial Psychoanalytic Paradigm: Reading Sigmund Freud with Gayatri Spivak

Gayatri Chakravorty Spivak approaches narcissism from a different angle, seeking to discern whether Freud's definition is all that psychoanalysis can say on the matter. In an essay from 1993, later published as a chapter of *An Aesthetic Education in the Era of Globalization* (2012), Spivak points to the irony that narcissism is commonly a trait assigned to women, when the mythical figure of Narcissus was male.[58] Female narcissism is a major feature of Freud's 1914 piece. It characterizes women as paradigmatic narcissists and diagnoses non-European cultures as developmentally backward because purportedly never able to rise to the Oedipus complex given their alleged narcissistic arrest in psychosexual infancy. Psychoanalysis cannot, Spivak argues, be deployed as a generalized cultural critique. It can only be responsibly used in a clinical context where transference is possible. Readers and analysts set aside the geopolitical and historical factors determining group behavior at their peril. For this reason, a postcolonial and feminist account of Freudian narcissism may yet be possible after all.[59]

Observing that neither Freud nor Lacan took the time to carefully engage Ovid's account of Narcissus, Spivak then rereads the *Metamorphoses*.[60] Like Malabou and Sacks, she explains the move to literature as an ethical one, if for different reasons. Drawing on the insights of the philosopher Bimal Krishna Matilal, she points out that the Indic tradition of rational critique turns to the interpretation of literary texts in place of recourse to formalized European moral philosophy. Reading literary works replaces systematized philosophizing.[61] Demeaned as "popular" by Western European high culture, the practice of relying on literature as a source for navigating ethical dilemmas is nevertheless a global phenomenon, she argues. Literature read in this "popular" way becomes the site for an incalculable truthfulness that is irreducible to either illustration or symptom. Literary works are not dependent upon the speaker's intention because no longer conceived as direct expressions of authoritative first-person perspectives that the reader is obliged to recover.

Assuming the ethical validity of deintentionalized "popular" readings makes it possible for Spivak to refuse fixed interpretations of even well-known texts. This justifies Spivak's decision to focus on the minor figure of Echo in Ovid's myth of Narcissus. In Ovid's tale, Echo, a nymph sentenced by Juno to repeat the words of others, falls in love with Narcissus but can neither call to him nor answer his call because of her divine punishment. As such, he rejects her. When Narcissus instead becomes enamored with his own reflection in a pool of water and dies of starvation there, Echo returns in time to repeat his dying farewell to himself. Echo then dies, leaving only her bones (which turn to stone) and her resounding voice.

Spivak's reading stresses the ambivalent status of Echo's speech in the myth. She aligns Echo's absence of egological plenitude—and her echoing words' inability to express intentionality—with the subaltern difficulty of speaking directly Spivak examined in her earlier work on Bhubaneswari Bhaduri.[62] In her reading of the myth, Ovid's story of Echo's seeming punishment becomes one of reward. Deprived by Juno of the ability to speak for herself, Echo, Spivak argues, is also invested with an identity beyond the boundaries of the self that Narcissus is denied. Whereas the tale of Narcissus is the "story of the construction of the self as an object of knowledge," Echo marks the "withheld possibility of a truth outside intention." Situated beyond the braggadocio of the first-person, Echo is a "self that cannot accede to an 'I.' "[63] The limpid mirrorlike clarity of the reflecting pool, which endlessly gives back Narcissus his own image, is none other than the prohibitive clarity of self-knowledge, so lucid that it proscribes relation, quite literally knowing no other. This circle of self-affirmation leaves no alternative but for Narcissus to die, as he can no longer experience the world. Echo, however, continues to be open to the other because of her suspended intentionality. An "(un)intending subject," the bones she leaves behind upon her death are a tribute to the risk of response that foils Narcissus's willful choice of himself as the object of his own desire.

Reading Ovid and Freud in this "popular" way, Spivak argues, shows that the psychoanalytic diagnosis of narcissism exceeds Freud statements about it in his 1914 piece. The temptation to simply condemn Freudian narcissism as racist and misogynist must be met with a recognition that psychoanalytic narcissism is also the name for the Echo-Narcissus pair, in which determinate self-knowledge is supplemented by a responsiveness not dependent upon the intentionality of the first-person. This is important for interpretations of modernist literary texts in Spivak's argument. James Joyce's novel *Finnegan's Wake* (1939) and Wallace Stevens's poem "Peter Quince at the Clavier" (1915) call for a truth not dependent on self-knowledge that resembles Echo's own call in Ovid's myth.

Spivak's approach to narcissism is different from the clinico-critical paradigm in which literary works offer case studies of real clinical diseases told in the first person by cerebrally wounded patients/characters or by doctors speaking on their behalf. In the postcolonial psychoanalytic paradigm, diagnostic terms are themselves a site of deintentionalized storytelling. Freud's narcissism contains the story of Ovid's Narcissus, which must be read and carefully analyzed to disclose a dimension of narcissism of which psychoanalysis was not consciously aware. The ethical move is in the reading, not the telling. Exegesis of Ovid's myth removes the burden of narcissism from women and non-European cultures. It simultaneously questions the project of making one's voice heard, by undercutting a gendered, first-world supposition (in a gesture to Bhubaneswari Bhaduri) that it is possible for everyone to speak truth to power in every context. To Malabou's call for a new wounded, Spivak offers narcissism and Echo as "the impossible experience of identity as wound."[64]

## The Problem: Only Psychoanalysis

Rose, Malabou, and Spivak reveal that the problems of nominalization and semiosis raised by psychodiagnostic categories are crucial to modernist literary studies and contemporary critical theory. At the same time, their work also illuminates the absence of attention by humanists to the nonpsychoanalytic diagnoses used in the DSM and ICD classificatory systems. In focusing on narcissism and other psychoanalytic concepts, the literary-critical paradigm neglects the rise of non-Freudian accounts of the mind with the power to ascribe meaning to modernist literary works by framing them as disease histories. This paradigm is also relatively unconcerned with exploring the universalizing aspects of psychoanalysis. Rose's shift in *On Violence* from Freudian narcissism, created in nineteenth-century Central Europe, to a global contemporary context of trauma (South Africa is a key site for her) passes without remark. Absence of attention to the cultural and linguistic specificity of psychoanalysis returns to the potential for fundamentalist uses of Freud's work alongside more progressive ones.[65]

Malabou, Sacks, and the critico-clinical paradigm resolve the issue of Freudian universality by turning to the biological brain. They nevertheless fail to note that the DSM produces its own problems of linguistic and cultural relativism. Why should the English-language diagnostic category of PTSD designed for Vietnam War veterans at the behest of a political activist movement in the 1970s apply everywhere? The DSM's struggle to deal with what one edition called "Culture-Bound Syndromes" makes this point nicely.[66] Malabou's push to establish a generalized theory of trauma and a unified notion of psychopathology is, however, consonant with the objectives of the DSM-III's creators in 1980. It repeats the clinical task force's goals. Like the DSM-III, *The New Wounded* seeks standardized, universalized disease categories to supplant the idiosyncrasies of patient storytelling. The principle "wager of [her] book" is that "*cerebral eventuality will replace sexual eventuality within the psychopathology to come.*"[67] Pointing to the "evolution from what was called traumatic neurosis during Freud's time to what has more recently been called PTSD" risks tautology. The argument follows the same logic that created PTSD as a diagnostic category. Malabou's interest in a "complete theoretical reinvention of psychopathology" retraces the Kraepelinian classificatory evolution from personal, experience-based narratives to generalized diagnostics that drove the DSM-III and its subsequent editions.[68] Because of its refusal of hermeneutics, however, *The New Wounded* is unable to critically read its own gesture. Neither can it assess the DSM diagnostic terms it deploys or the literary works it frames as evidence of those diagnoses.

Given that the DSM was designed as an alternative to psychoanalysis, moreover, it is inevitable that the DSM's account of PTSD would not fit a Freudian model. This makes it difficult to sustain the claim that PTSD's more modern account of trauma is modern because the result of scientific discoveries facilitated by new technology.[69] That the DSM's validity is now under tremendous scientific scrutiny both in terms of its basic viability as a psychiatric model and its relationship to the brain also creates significant problems.[70] Even first-person speech that makes use of diagnostic categories is not as straightforward as it appears in Malabou and Sacks. As Ian Hacking has indicated in his work on the DSM, the compilation of diagnostic categories in a medically verified encyclopedia encourages a "looping" effect, in which the individuals supposedly only described by the DSM's psychopathological disease names interact with those names in ways that change them and make the names scientific "moving targets."[71]

Spivak's attention to the cultural specificity of psychoanalysis overlooks that psychoanalysis is no longer the clinical paradigm with the largest worldwide scope or the one with the most fraught ties to questions of race and gender. It neglects that nonpsychoanalytic clinical psychiatry is equally in need of the resources of postcolonial and decolonial theory. In *Anthropologist*, for example, the British Oliver Sacks stylistically compares his neurological narratives to the entertaining tales of the *Arabian Nights*. He identifies those Arabic-language stories in their English translation (heavily configured by British colonial reception) as a literary model for his own work. Sacks's writing is likewise intended to be anthropological and entertaining. He frames his task as presenting exotic stories about distant (psychical) lands to intrigue audiences at home. A postcolonial reading, by contrast, might stress how reliance on the trope of anthropological exploration tacitly endorses a psychological Orientalism. Spivak's brilliant analysis of the Narcissus myth, focused on the psychoanalytic literary sphere, allows this narcissistic quality of the non-Freudian mind sciences to pass without mention. Like Ovid's Narcissus, however, the non-Freudian mind sciences could potentially be framed as both gazing into the reflecting pool of a self-iterative truthfulness determined by intentionality *and* as opening, if one knows how to listen, to the echo of the other.

Turning to Deleuze and Guattari, as Malabou implicitly does in her work, to address the problem posed by psychopathological semiosis and naming does not significantly help. Deleuze and Guattari do focus on psychodiagnostic terms at length across their oeuvre. In *Coldness and Cruelty* (1967), for example, Deleuze analyzes the German sexologist Richard von Krafft-Ebing's coinage of the term "sadomasochism" based on a combination of the proper names of Austrian writer Leopold von Sacher-Masoch (*Venus in Furs*, 1870) and the French revolutionary writer the Marquis de Sade. Finding fault with Krafft-Ebing's clinical definition of this psychopathology, Deleuze advocates for a "literary approach" to sadomasochism. "We need to go back to the beginning and read Sade and Masoch . . . we must take an entirely different approach, the literary approach, since it is from literature that stem the original definitions of sadism and masochism."[72] Deleuze then proceeds to unpack the word "sadomasochism's" debt to literature and show why the combination of Masoch's and Sade's proper names in a single diagnosis creates a false binary between their creative enterprises that undermines the clinical term. This becomes the basis for affect theory's argument to read literary works as diagnostic. In Deleuze and Guattari's subsequent writing, their symptomatological view treats literature (and modernist writing especially) as interchangeable with case histories. Creative writers articulate the possibility of new forms of existence by bringing together groups of signs and symptoms in their work. Deleuze and Guattari's influential methodological concept of "schizoanalysis" draws on this unique feature of creative works, showing that aesthetic objects formulate noncapitalist modes of being that disrupt industrialized modernity's fragmentation of the social body and enable more viable forms of political community.

Affect studies' approach nevertheless remains limited to the few diagnostic terms that carry literary authors' names (sadomasochism), leaving out all those clinical terms—the "schizophrenia" of schizoanalysis included—that do not carry anyone's proper name but instead have come to acquire the status of proper names and identity categories. Deleuze and Guattari's 1970s-era focus on literature as a symptomatology naturally cannot account for the 1980s-era rise of nonpsychoanalytic psychiatric nomenclature. Neither is it well suited to assess the place of nonpsychoanalytic terms within literary modernist texts. The project of *critique et clinique* compellingly frames literature as a source of diagnostics but is for that same reason ill-equipped to question what happens when an ontologized and biologized psychodiagnostics becomes the basis for interpreting literature.

At the same time, affect theory clearly identifies the importance of disease names in the semiotic field. "When a doctor gives his name to an illness this is a major linguistic and semiological step, in as much as a proper name is linked to a given group of signs, that is, *a proper name is made to connote signs*," Deleuze writes in *Coldness and Cruelty*. Recognition of the semiological status of psychopathological terms counters the notion that there is no hermeneutic dimension to contemporary cerebral psychopathology. "The principles behind this labeling process deserve closer analysis."[73] With that said, little attention had been paid to what the differences between psychoanalytic and nonpsychoanlaytic diagnostics might be, beyond arguments that the more contemporary is the more accurate.[74] This leaves the problem of how these systems configure stories and lives unexamined. It also restricts assessments of cultural specificity, coloniality, gendering, and violence to psychoanalysis, as if psychoanalysis alone intersected with those issues.

Of these two models of imagining psychopathology, only one is seen as having ethnocentric presuppositions. Only one is framed as requiring historicization. Only one possesses a questionable relationship to subjectivity and the scientific method. Only one is embedded in language. Only one hails the subject into a symbolic social order. Only one connects with the ills of late capitalism. Only one imperils women and minorities. Only one is plagued with issues of power and authority. Only one has a problem with substance abuse. Only one must be closely supervised. Only one can be questioned. Only psychoanalysis.

## Counterdisciplinarity: Reading *M.O.'s Echo Bones*

I suggest the need for another paradigm of diagnostic reading: counterdisciplinarity. Inspired by Rose, Malabou, Spivak, and Deleuze and Guattari on diagnosis, this style of reading is nevertheless not reducible to any one of their positions. In the counterdisciplinary paradigm, close readings of irreducible aesthetic objects (Rose, Deleuze and Guattari) form an ethical basis for illuminating the unseen epistemological presuppositions of empirical research about the mind and brain (Malabou) and thereby the diagnostic terms such research creates and deploys to characterize both literary works and people (Spivak). Counterdisciplinarity suggests that the fields studying aesthetic objects are in productive tension with those fields committed to measurable evidence and interpretive fixity. It situates the humanities methodologies as important *because* of their divergence from the testable and quantitative commitments of the scientific method, not despite it. Whereas interdisciplinarity takes the combinatory nature of different disciplines for granted, counterdisciplinarity is premised on the idea that conflict between disciplines is generative, ethical, and indeed unavoidable.[75] It develops Kant's notion of *Streit* in *The Conflict of the Faculties*, dialectical criticism's emphasis on negation, the Derridean concept of *différance*, and Bruno Latour's notion of scientific irreductionism in Actor Network Theory. It is nevertheless distinct. Counterdisciplinarity emphasizes aesthetic objects' ability to bidirectionally engage, in their own idiom, the truth claims of nonhumanities fields rather than unidirectionally narrate or support those claims.

Meret Oppenheim's *X-Ray of M.O.'s Skull* provides an example of the counterdisciplinary work that "popular" readings of modernist texts are well suited to perform. The photograph is outwardly a portrait of victim-blaming, sexualized female narcissism. It appears to show the self-decorating and ego-infatuated woman whose jewelry appears even in her X-ray, as if so crucial to her identity as to show up in her bone structure. It outwardly celebrates modern science and technology. Advances in modern medical imaging (the X-ray) make it possible to visualize the self in radically new ways. Like Guillaume Apollinaire in his essay *The New Spirit and the Poets*, Oppenheim's image outwardly declares: "How could it be! An X-ray was made of my head. I, a living being, have seen my cranium—is that not something new? Come on!"

Apollinaire's comment is also deeply ironic. As much a send-up of the modernist (and especially futurist) invocation to "make it new!" as it is a serious celebration of the X-ray, Apollinaire pushes back on a (clichéd) modernist embrace of technoscientific progress by mocking grandiose pretensions to a utopia just over the next motorway and radiology clinic. *The New Spirit* critically relativizes newness. Its "Come on!" offers a critique of the "new"-found ability to see inside one's own head. Is the old Cartesian *esprit* truly made new by medical imaging's ability to delve under the human skin and show what's inside?

Oppenheim's image channels the ambivalence in Apollinaire's lines. The image outwardly seems to be a techno-scientific exposé of bone-deep female narcissism. While permitting this reading, however, the image also contests it. To begin with, the figure is demonstratively nongendered (a feature of Meret Oppenheim's work more generally). Its lack of gender identity is configured both in terms of what the image shows, a skeleton wearing jewelry, and on the level of the photograph's title: *X-ray of M.O.'s Skull*. "M.O.," not "Meret Oppenheim." There is nothing in the image that necessitates the figure be either biologically female or even female-identifying. Instead, Oppenheim's image comments on the viewer's assumption that would make it so.

This nominal X-ray is also exceptionally obtuse for a medical image. The figure's chest cavity is illegible to the point of obscurity and the skull opaque. The bones of the hand—the (would-be) artist's hand, no less—almost disappear into the background and are further diminished by the prominent bars of rings that have the effect of bisecting, not adorning, the fingers. The image's blurriness and opacity visually comment on the limits of X-ray imaging. That the X-ray includes jewelry and depicts the outline of the figure's lips and neck alongside a skeletal structure further troubles the matter of medically picturing interiority. In place of a clear bone structure, the viewer is confronted with a confusing simultaneity of inside and outside. Even the label "X-ray" in its title is a misnomer. This is a gelatin silver contact print of an X-ray, not an X-ray proper. The fact is evident from the color inversion: black bones on a white background. The change subtly emphasizes the image's status as a mediated representation, visually disputing readings that would frame it solely as an indexical transcript of biological reality.

The "not-X-ray" of "not-Meret-Oppenheim's skull" produces a crisis of self-representation in place of a self-portrait. The title's seeming first-person claim to authorship is negated by the image's refusal to be an X-ray or female or its creator's self-image. In place of sustaining a claim to female narcissism, the image places the egocentricity of medicalized self-portraiture under erasure. The viewer, exiled from the diagnostic role of radiologist and cast adrift, finds only a set of echo bones, in Spivak's sense. They repeat the words of another: another being (the self of the proper name), another image (the original X-ray), another technological medium (radiation beams passing through a body), an other-gender. Because an X-ray is a negative, the possibility of making an endless series of photographic prints from it destabilizes the auratic singularity of selfhood in any resulting "portraits" and so too disrupts that self's presumed unity. It would be possible to print an entire series of "M.O.s" from one X-ray, as Meret Oppenheim in fact did. *X-Ray of M.O.'s Skull* counterdisciplinarily deconstructs the monolith of selfhood, refusing, like Echo, to gaze only at its own reflection.

## Mapping Global Modernist Madness

Counterdisciplinarity offers a fresh standpoint on modernism's "possible geographies."[76] Discussions within modernism studies and, indeed, new modernism(s) have tended to focus on the geospatiality of modernist works, modernist political alliances, and modernist writers' travels across the face of the globe. Work on global modernism might also attend to psychospatiality and psychogeography: the imagined communities (Benedict Anderson) produced by the worlding processes of the nonpsychoanalytic mind sciences.[77]

What I am describing, however, is not quite the same as Anderson's imagined communities. Anderson tracks the imaginative projections of community cast on the earth's surface by everything from brightly colored geopolitical maps to print media like national censuses. *Psychic Empire* engages with global modernism by suggesting—following both Jacques Derrida and postcolonial writing on psychoanalysis—that nonpsychoanalytic studies of the mind also have a worlding function, in Martin Heidegger's sense of "*weltend*."[78] Alongside Derridean "geopsychoanalysis" (the worlding of the earth by psychoanalytic institutions), one might also think of a "geopsychiatry," "geopsychology," and "geoneuroscience," which point to the nonpsychoanalytic mind sciences' role in producing a picture of the world, as much through their institutional configurations as their premises.

One need not look exclusively to deconstruction or postcolonial critique, however. In *Our Psychiatric Future* (2018), Nikolas Rose describes the inherently political nature of psychiatry, made evident in recent efforts like the Movement for Global Mental Health. That there is a correlation between so-called internal mental disorders and external geopolitical space is also evident in the work of scholars such as Danziger, Vidal, and Hacking. It is further on display in the many books, both academic and popular, fictional and nonfictional, that suggest this link. The titles of these works speak for themselves: *Prozac Nation* (1995), *An Anthropologist on Mars: Seven Paradoxical Tales* (1996), *Crazy Like Us: The Globalization of the American Psyche* (2011), *One Nation Under Stress: The Trouble with Stress as an Idea* (2013), *Nervous States: Democracy and the Decline of Reason* (2019), *Mind Ecologies: Body, Brain, and World* (2020), *Dopamine Nation: Finding Balance in the Age of Indulgence* (2021).[79] Whether one looks to these relatively contemporary texts or earlier ones—Wilhelm Wundt's ten-volume *Völkerpsychologie* (1900–1920) or Georges Dumas's *Traité de psychologie* (1923)—a widespread scholastic recognition exists outside of global modernism and critical theory of an overlap between descriptions of interior life and external geopolitics.[80] Camille Robcis has traced its pathways through the postwar impact of institutional sociotherapy in Western Europe.[81] Others have identified the conjunction of interior and exterior worlds as a missing crossover between sociology and psychiatry in the study of the city and the brain, a topic that harks back to the German sociologist Georg Simmel's reflections on "The Metropolis and Mental Life" in 1903.[82] Laura Salisbury and Andrew Shail do the same by telling the cultural history of nervous systems.[83] David Freis recounts it in his history of how interwar German, Austrian, and Swiss psychiatrists attempted to diagnose society at large.[84] The collapse of this interior/exterior boundary is further evident in the "wander lines" made by the French educator and psychiatric renegade Fernand Deligny during the 1960s and 1970s. Ten years earlier, the psychoanalyst William G. Niederland had proposed the concept of "psychogeographies," or the "study of how issues, experiences, and processes that result from growing up in a male or female body become symbolized and played out in the wider social and natural worlds, which serve as 'screens' for these inner dramas."[85] Add to this the vast contemporary collection of research on psychoanalysis in translation, and the need for a global modernist account addressing *mondialisation* (Derrida) in the fields of psychiatry, psychoanalysis, and neurosciences becomes clear.

In certain ways, this is already Malabou's observation in *The New Wounded* about the "worldwide uniformity [*l'uniformisation globale*] of neuropsychological reactions" and "psychic pain in an age of globalization [*mondialisation*] and globalized [*mondialisée*] pathology identical in all cases and all contexts." It is indeed a question of the Enlightenment's role in the expanding scope of the human. Sylvia Wynter observes that the "struggle of the new millennium" will be centered on a conflict produced by, on the one hand, the overrepresentation of Man "as if it were the human itself" (a position that asserts Man's unbounded global purview) and efforts to secure, on the other hand, the "cognitive/behavioral autonomy of the human species itself."[86] Denise Ferreira da Silva points out that a technique of "engulfment" present in Hegel's work helps institute the Western European human condition as a normative basis for accounts of human beings everywhere, who become mere "variations" of it.[87]

The topic of psychic interiority and geopolitical exteriority nevertheless has yet to find its way into discussions of global modernism. The capacious *Oxford Handbook of Global Modernisms* does not attend to it, nor do modernist anthologies like *The Cambridge Companion to Modernism* or *The New Modernist Studies*. There is nothing on the topic of the mind that appears in *A New Vocabulary for Global Modernism*.[88] Considering how clinical psychiatry, psychology, and neuroscience world the earth would not only build on the rich extant humanities research addressing colonial psychiatry but also carry the study of modernism and madness in new directions. It would allow modernists to think about how aesthetic objects engage the development and spread of non-Freudian investigations of the mind and brain by looking specifically at how those fields shaped and imagined national and international communities. This would further develop research on cosmopolitanism (Berman, Walkowitz), planetary modernism (Susan Stanford Friedman), transnational modernism (Berman), and modernist internationalism (Balthaser, Clark, Djagalov, Lee, Rizzuto, Vadde).[89] It would augment works like Lisa Siraganian's *Modernism and the Meaning of Corporate Persons* and Natasha Wheatley's *The Life and Death of States*, which focus on sovereignty and the fate of the body in modernity but do not do so for the mind.[90] It is in dialogue with scholarship in Slavic studies that has already stressed the impact of psychophysics and a Soviet sensory revolution on everything from Russian futurism to Soviet film (Olenina, Widdis).[91] In German, it is in conversation with work on classification and standardization, like Stefani Engelstein's *Sibling Action: The Genealogical Structure of Modernity* (2017) and Jakob Norberg's *The Brothers Grimm and the Making of German Nationalism* (2022), that have highlighted how the use of highly organized knowledge structures interfaced with the making of modern nation-states.[92]

Attending to how pathopathological terminology produces an imagination of community rather than focusing on the alleged uniformity of individuals collected under the "same" disease heading would help offset persistent confusion about the meaning of diagnostic terms.[93] It would encourage reading for the contextual nuance and historical specificity of diagnostic categories, instead of assuming various versions' basic equivalence. Fredric Jameson's concept of cognitive mapping emphasizes the need for the subject in late capitalism to step outside its disorienting colonization of Nature and the Unconscious.[94] To Jameson's concept one could add the idea of mapping cognition: the practice of tracking how human sciences like clinical psychiatry, empirical psychology, and the neurosciences have historically configured global space through their accounts of sanity, consciousness, and cognition. The study of global modernist madness, rather than representation of madness in global modernism, would explore literary works as they track the creation of communities through the dissemination of representations of the mind.

* * *

This book's title, *Psychic Empire: Literary Modernism and the Clinical State*, is inspired by the idea of broadening global modernism's conceptual scope to incorporate the Enlightenment dilemmas produced by psychiatric classification. "Psychic empire" names the book in the form of an open-ended critical problem. Read as the parataxis "psychic/empire," the title calls on the reader to consider the relationship between its two component parts. Begin with "psychic," and the title interrogates the psyche's sovereign self-possession. Begin with "empire," and it asks about the geopolitical and juridical concerns with which the emerging mind sciences were entangled as they first took shape in imperial nineteenth-century Central and Eastern Europe.

I do not restrict the term "empire" to the political regimes that dominated Central Europe and Eurasia during the late nineteenth and early twentieth century. This is as much to remain attentive to this period's links to the present as to avoid producing an undesirable equivalency. This move can, by tending to make the Russian, German, and Austro-Hungarian empires seem interchangeable with those of contemporaneous imperial powers like Britain and France—the common denominator being "imperiality"—have the effect of closing off questions about the specificity of their respective contexts, instead of opening them. It betokens, or can betoken, a spurious comparativism. The differences, however, are significant.

While the German Reich did acquire a set of overseas colonial holdings in sub-Saharan Africa and the Western Pacific during the 1880s, these colonial possessions were neither as extensive nor enduring as those of Britain, France, or even Spain up until 1898. Neither did imperial Germany have the same relationship to economic extractivism, slavery, or colonial revolt as the British, French, and Spanish empires (which is hardly to say the *Kaiserreich* did not support their practice or have profoundly racist policies). There is a similar difficulty in the case of the Russian Empire. Imperial Russia was a land empire, with the exception of a brief foray into Africa the late 1880s and early 1890s. My approach to the relationship between postcolonial theory and both Russia and the Soviet Union is hence also one that stresses the nonequivalence of imperial structures. It turns instead to think what critical resources the established study of the British, French, and Spanish empires offers to a German, Russian, and Soviet context.

My use of empire is thus closer to Michael Hardt and Antonio Negri's in *Empire* (2000) and in their trilogy. Hardt and Negri redefine empire as a new juridical constitution of the world order in the twenty-first century built around an all-encompassing reign of biopower that fundamentally compromises the social body.[95] For them, this biopolitical understanding of imperial dominion replaces the older concept of empire restricted to specific imperial regimes. Relatedly, I am concerned with the way in which a globalized twenty-first-century psychopower at once guarantees the social body (through making possible an imagination of the social mind) and imperils the very psyche politic whose representation it seems to secure.

The main title's parataxis informs my use of term "clinical state" in the book's subtitle. I draw here on the polysemy of the French word *état*, which may mean mental state, national state, sovereign authority, the estates of the Ancien Régime (*États généraux*), and hesitations or qualms. To speak of literary modernism and the "clinical state" in this sense involves situating modernist works as engaged with the nonpsychoanalytic mind sciences' role in determining individuals' mental states (for which they provide the technical terms), interfacing with the history of modern nation-states, defending their own scientific authority, responding to revolutionary movements, and simultaneously wrestling with the Enlightenment as a dialectical legacy of both axiomatic certainty and doubt. This clinical state is also implied by Catherine Malabou's references to an *état de stress post-traumatique* (state of posttraumatic stress) and an *l'état posttraumatique* (posttraumatic state) and evoked (if unexplored) in Giorgio Agamben's notion of the "state of exception."[96] Malabou is entirely right when she remarks on a "posttraumatic condition that reigns everywhere today [*partout regnant*] and that demands to be thought."

## After Analysis

In Jacques Lacan's seminar on *The Sinthome*, which draws extensively on James Joyce's literary work, Lacan argues there is a residue left after analysis, an unanalyzable leftover that refuses to disappear. Constituting the subject's jouissance, the sinthome makes it possible for the subject to bind together the psychical orders (Imaginary, Symbolic, Real) in a "*synth-homme*" (synthetic person) whose artificial existence nevertheless supports the experience of lived reality. The sinthome emerges at the crossroads of hope for a solution to desire's self-reproducing excesses and the despair born of acknowledging the impossibility of any solution that is not psychosis.[97]

Moving from clinical to critical, one could perhaps also say there is a left-over that remains after the heyday of psychoanalytic literary criticism and psychoanalytic medical practice. Neither passed with perfect finitude. The debates that now plague the DSM-5, the difficulty correlating between DSM and ICD psychopathological classifications, the issue of psychiatric reification that besets both, the rise of neuropsychoanalysis, and the question of knowing who speaks in self-diagnostic statements all attest to psychoanalysis's sinthomic remainder. On the one hand, it stimulates consideration of the role of representation, semiosis, and naming in modern psychology, psychiatry, and neuroscience. On the other, it provokes a return to modernist literary texts, like Lacan's return to Joyce, as sources of counterdisciplinary tension and enjoyment. Such a postanalytic position, one that is "after analysis" (pursuing psychoanalysis, following on psychoanalysis), sustains interpretation—and perhaps so too the experience of lived reality—through acknowledging the hope for a psychical unity that would constitute the positive object of scientific research as that hope encounters the mind sciences' own fragmentation of mental life in their attempt to define it once and for *all.*

## CHAPTER 1

# BÜCHNER'S BRAIN

## On Psychopower

*Perhaps we can say that every poem is marked by its own "20th of January"?*

—Paul Celan, "The Meridian"

*Immer zu . . . immer zu* . . . on and . . . on and . . . on August 27, 1824, the convicted murderer Johann Christian Woyzeck was beheaded in the Leipzig market square on account of his sanity. An eyewitness to the scene, part of the large crowd that gathered on that sunny Friday morning to watch the execution, describes the imposing line of mounted cuirassiers stationed around the scaffold suddenly parting to permit the condemned man through just before noon.[1] Woyzeck exited the town hall accompanied by his lawyers. He ascended the steps of the execution platform alone. The eyewitness, a local schoolteacher, states that the condemned kneeled and prayed loudly. He then tied on the blindfold himself and settled on the prepared chair. The executioner so swiftly and skillfully lopped off his head that it allegedly remained balanced on the drawn sword and only fell at the turn of the blade. A trapdoor opened on the scaffold, and Woyzeck's body was thrown down into it, before being placed in a coffin and carried, under guard, to the morgue. Silence. *Exeunt.*

It had taken several years to reach this fatal scene. Woyzeck's sanity in 1821 at the time he murdered his lover, the widow Johanna Christiane Woost, had already long been questioned. It was only after multiple medical examinations and a failed clemency plea to the king of Saxony, Friedrich August I, that his eligibility for the death penalty could finally be established.[2] The case hinged on the expert testimony of Dr. Johann Christian August Clarus (1774–1854), the state medical examiner and a prominent professor of anatomy and surgery at Leipzig University, with ties to the Saxon court.[3] Despite the accused's long record of hearing voices and seeing visions, Clarus's multiple medical reports found Woyzeck in full possession of his mental faculties and hence "*zurechnungsfähig*" (legally compos mentis, lit. able to be held accountable).[4] There were "no grounds whatsoever for the assumption that he was of unsound mind [*im Zustande einer Seelenstörung*] at any time in his life, and in particular directly before, during and after the homicidal act perpetrated by him."[5] So it was that Johann Christian Woyzeck was executed for being sane.

Thus concludes the first drama. Enter the second. The case and its source materials are the basis for the German writer Georg Büchner's play *Woyzeck*, often framed as a forerunner to modernism. Written in 1836, the play was left unfinished at the time of Büchner's abrupt death in 1837. Büchner, a child at the time the events took place, likely found the case history in his father's library. The protracted trial and public execution—the first beheading in Leipzig in decades—had caused a flurry of legal and medical controversy at the time, in which Büchner's father took part.[6] It would have been familiar in their Darmstadt household. In this early, unsuccessful, iteration of the insanity defense, it was the demonstration of Woyzeck's sanity and full possession of free will that enabled him to be beheaded. A medical report that he had been insane (in the grips of a *Seelenstörung*, or a disruption of his mental faculties) when he murdered Woost would, paradoxically, have saved his life.

Perhaps that is the nature of Büchner's play: to be the medical report diagnosing Johann Christian Woyzeck as *non compos mentis* that would have preserved his head. Perhaps. One cannot help but wonder, however, about a play where all the action has already taken place (and been so fatally resolved as to see both the audience disperse and the theater taken down) without any of the characters having set foot on the boards.

The curtain had already long fallen on the drama of the trial when Büchner put pen to paper to write about it. "*A posteriori*—that is how everything begins," Büchner remarked in his play *Leonce and Lena* (composed in 1836). The comment seems to apply here as well. If Büchner's play is supposed to save the confessed murderer Johann Christian Woyzeck, it is already manifestly too late. If the play is supposed to dramatize his trial, that too is redundant. The scaffold-stage on which the historical figure lost his head was disassembled following the execution and the attendant Leipzigers all sent about their

Friday business on that bright summer day in 1824. Here Woyzeck is again, nevertheless, in 1836, head still firmly affixed to his shoulders, ready to play his part. He is even speaking the same lines. And here lies the dilemma. How many times does Woyzeck die? Or live? How many times Woost? How many dramas are there? How many Woyzecks? How to count?

The tension between the countable and the uncountable that twists the play's relationship to its intertext also warps its characters' statements. Büchner's fictional protagonist gives his biography, reading it aloud out from a scrap of paper. "Friedrich Johann Franz Woyzeck, enlisted infantryman in the second regiment, second battalion, fourth company, born . . . Today on the feast of the annunciation, the 20th of July, I am thirty years, seven months and twelve days old."[7] What 20th of July? An infantryman in the second regiment, second battalion, fourth company of what army? The seeming precision in the personal history—with its many numbers but little meaning—gives way at the slightest touch. So too in the case of the "original" drama of the trial and Büchner's secondary "adaptation" of it. It is unclear if the first drama (J. C. Woyzeck's legal struggle and public execution) is indeed the first, of which Büchner's *Woyzeck* is merely the lightly fictionalized recapitulation, or whether there are two Woyzecks (Johann Christian Woyzeck of 1821 and Friedrich Johann Franz Woyzeck of 1836) whose lives and stories bear only a tenuous relationship to each other.

The poet Paul Celan commented on this drama of numbers in his postwar reflections on Georg Büchner's oeuvre and the relationship between art and sovereignty. Written on the occasion of Celan's receipt of the Georg Büchner prize in 1960, "The Meridian" observes that Büchner's novella *Lenz* begins on an ambiguous "20th of January." Celan pauses to ask whether this little phrase said something about the "newness" of contemporary art related to its being "written most plainly to be mindful [*eingedenk*] of this kind of date." His use of the word "mindful" is an odd choice. *Lenz*, for example, begins with its protagonist's exasperation at his own inability to walk on his head. *Woyzeck* centers on a question about the protagonist's capacity for reasonable thought (*das Denken* of Celan's *eingedenk*), indeed about his ability to be mindful at all—let alone in particular ways.

Celan can be read as suggesting that art's mindfulness of punctuality, calculability, and exactitude (embodied in phrases like "the 20th of January") should also occasion a reflection on how rationalized, techno-scientific modernity's focus on precision affected the definition of the mind, changing what it would mean for art to be mindful in turn. This small observation alters the framework for engaging with Büchner's 1836 drama. A long tradition of secondary criticism presents Büchner's *Woyzeck*, like *Lenz*, as a literary case study of schizophrenia and stylistically schizoid language because dealing with insanity and the insanity defense. Celan's comment, by contrast, intimates that Büchner's *Woyzeck* is sensitive to the genesis of new standards of exactitude in the nineteenth century (including diagnostic terminology like schizophrenia) designed to govern what counted as thought.

*Woyzeck*'s flirtations with precision are then the cipher of a historical shift in Büchner's era that jointly obliged art to keep calculable precision "in mind" and changed the conception of the mind art portrayed by making it more calculable. In the 1830s, this shift involved a scientific turn away from the account of mental life offered by René Descartes on the *res cogitans* (thinking substance) and Immanuel Kant on a transcendental *Vernunft* (reason) and toward a quantifiable, biological understanding of mental life. Büchner's play, Celan intimates, is in conversation with this key transition as it produced a mutation in the field of sovereignty, understood both as the capacity for self-governance and the exercise of force. *Woyzeck* reflects on the paradox that sanity was, on the one hand, a precondition for legal personhood (linked to sanity's implied role in the classical politico-theological definition of sovereignty), and on the other, a new site of juridical regulation and violence in the 1830s. While an execution connected to a somatic account of mental life might appear to be a paradigmatically biopolitical phenomenon, Büchner's play exposes that the shift from a transcendental account of mental life to an empirical one generated circumstances that exceed Michel Foucault's concept of biopower. In Büchner's literary treatment, the historical execution of Johann Christian Woyzeck becomes a *psycho*political supplement to Foucault's account of Damiens the regicide, described at the opening of *Discipline and Punish*. If Damiens's execution showed the "soul as the prison of the body," Johann Christian Woyzeck's reveals the strange persistence of the body as the prison of the soul, made possible by the rise of German somatic psychiatry. By attending to the Cartesian soul's transformation at this time, *Woyzeck* aesthetically illuminates the advent of what I term psychopower, or the genesis of the mass management of popular mental health based on measurement. The play shows the initial phase of its development, on which psychopower's expansion and consolidation within the mind sciences built during the latter half of the twentieth century (the subject of the next chapter). *Woyzeck*'s use of broken speech and its focus on non-normative mental experience map psychopower's redefinition of the human as it took shape in the 1830s. The play engages with this reconfiguration of the "name of man" in the legal sphere to comment on how a new scientific conception of the psyche interfaced with questions about representation, popular sovereignty, and the body politic recently raised by the French Revolution.

Because it is concerned with populations, not individuals, the concept of psychopower nevertheless has implications well beyond the nineteenth century and scholarship on biopower. It intersects with recent discussions in contemporary philosophy, sociology, the history of science, and medical anthropology about the reprogramming of modern mental life. Büchner's account of psychopower expands the idea of psychical politics advanced by contemporary philosophers such as Bernard Stiegler and Byung-Chul Han. It shows the partnership they describe between information technology and late capitalism, which they argue forces collective thought out of *Mündigkeit*, has earlier roots and is not limited to technology. Psychopower similarly works in tandem with propositions advanced by Nikolas Rose (on the brain as an antidote to anthropocentrism), Fernando Vidal (on "brainhood"), and Kurt Danziger (on psychology's language), while highlighting the limits of interpretive strategies that present aesthetic objects as peripheral to the investigation of the mind sciences' cultural investments.

The first part of the chapter carefully reads the case and the play. The second explains the philosophical and medical backdrop against which both unfolded. The third discusses psychopower.

Almost everything about Büchner's *Woyzeck* is fragmentary: its manuscript, plot, characters, language, above all its protagonist's mental state. To speak of Büchner's *Woyzeck* as a play in any traditional sense of the term is to radically misstate the case. Büchner died before completing the work, and its posthumous legacy has involved heterogeneous efforts to "reconstruct" the drama from its fragments, spread across four manuscript drafts, each of which lacks crucial sections possessed by the others.[8] There is no standard version. After Büchner's death, moreover, the work remained unpublished for decades until 1875.[9] Yet more time had to pass before it appeared on stage: *Woyzeck* was not performed until 1913. The play did not receive the recognition that has since stimulated everything from multiple Woyzeck-themed operas, films, and novels, however, until Max Reinhardt's 1921 expressionist staging at the Deutsche Theater in Weimar Berlin.

Having languished for years without acknowledgment, *Woyzeck* was put on the map as a modernist icon by Reinhardt's production. Its exploration of the human psyche, depiction of the theater's first "proletarian" protagonist, violence, bawdy humor, forays into collective consciousness, and use of a broken, fragmented dialect that seemed to emulate expressionism's telegraphic speech all helped ensure its prominent status within a postwar German artistic landscape already celebrating the physicalization of the playing space and emphasis on troubled psychical interiority. Integrated into the expressionist tradition through Reinhardt's staging, the play has also been read as a precursor to existentialism, an illustration of György Lukács's "transcendental homelessness," and an early form of Soviet socialist realism. Its stammering, haunting, crisis, sense of apocalypse, and jittery lack of causality led the poet Rainer Maria Rilke to speak of it in 1915 as an "incomparable play." The "misused" protagonist, Rilke remarked, "cannot prevent, now here, now there, before, behind, beside his dull soul, horizons from being torn open onto violence, immensity, the infinite."[10] For similar reasons, *Woyzeck* is a key text in Paul Celan's speech "The Meridian," his poetological account of art in the wake of the Holocaust. Remarkably, then, if one includes the lifespan of J. C. Woyzeck (1780–1824), the play covers historical ground spanning from the French Revolution to the establishment and fall of Nazi Germany and literary movements ranging from Romanticism to high modernism, while nevertheless lacking any fixed order of exposition or even a definitive conclusion. *Immer zu.* On and on.

The play appears to tell the story of a fictional soldier named Woyzeck stationed in an unnamed German province. Woyzeck struggles to earn money for himself, his lover (Marie), and their child, born out of wedlock. This leads him to take on a series of odd jobs including tasks for his army captain and participation in a bizarre medical experiment for a local physician that requires he eat nothing but peas. While on this diet, Woyzeck begins to hear voices and see visions. His doctor is delighted and offers to increase his payment for what he diagnoses in one draft as an "*aberratio mentalis partialis*" and another as an "*alienatio mentis*." Meanwhile, Marie is growing increasingly enamored with a drum major in the army. Consumed by jealousy and suspicion and in an ever more tenuous state of mind, Woyzeck stabs Marie to death. In many editorial arrangements of the drama's fragments, the play closes with Woyzeck's disposal of the murder weapon in a nearby pond. Multiple commentators have also assumed that he drowns there, though others suggest (based on a scrap in the first manuscript) that Büchner had a trial scene in mind.[11]

Even this plot is tenuous, however, as the numerous drafts and variety of subsequent editorial arrangements leave a wide margin for interpretation. *Woyzeck* could conceivably unfold in any order. This flexibility contributes to the ambiguity surrounding the relationship between the source materials and the play. The difficulty of establishing how *Woyzeck* concludes reflects the larger problem of fixing legible coordinates in it and for it. It is unclear whether the fictional drama's outcome is a forgone conclusion (determined by the historical trial) or an imaginative reworking of its historical precursor's tragic end. If the pond scene is indeed the protagonist's death, is it Johann Christian Woyzeck's second death or merely the fictional character's first? Are the play's allusions to bloody knives ill omens or the return of a repressed historical past? And the voice the protagonist hears demanding he "stab the Woyzeck widow"? Is this the record of Woost's murder creeping in or the motive that drives the play?

Like the body of the text, the human beings that populate the drama also seem to be made from an assemblage of broken parts roughly hewn together or mixed with the bodies of animals. Characters in *Woyzeck* regularly compare one another to everything from horses, canaries, monkeys, dogs, and hedgehogs to oxen, lions, and beetles. A scene set at a fairground explicitly raises the issue of the human being's relationship to the animal by having a carnival barker suggest that a simple change of dress can make a monkey into a human. "Gentlemen! Gentlemen! [Points to a monkey.] Look at this creature, as God made it: he's nothing, nothing at all [*nix, gar nix*]. Now see the effect of art [*Kunst*]: he walks upright wears coat and pants [*geht aufrecht hat Rock und Hosen*], carries a sword! Ho! Take a bow [*Mach Kompliment!* ] Good boy [*So bist brav*]."[12] These comparisons draw additional force from the play's liberal references to bodily fluids. Both humans and animals regularly urinate or defecate in scenes that deliberately mock the nature/culture distinction. "Look how the sun's coming out of the clouds, like a bedpan being emptied out," the barber states at one point.[13] In *Woyzeck*, sunlight is an incandescent fecal sludge poured from a human solar toilet.

The carnival barker and barber help show the disjointed linguistic register in which the play is conceived. Its bizarre verbal distortions and agrammatical constructions seemingly anticipate the linguistic fragmentation of modernist psychoses.[14] Written in dialect ("*nix*" versus "*Nichts*"), the play also portrays characters whose speech is altered by their economic status, a stylistic feature that has contributed to its reception as a proletarian drama composed before Marx's account of class struggle. Pronouns vanish ("*So bist brav*" versus "*Du bist brav*"), and sentences are boiled down to their most abbreviated possible form, stripping away nuance to replace it with raw force ("*Mach Kompliment*," lit. "Pay a compliment!"). Woyzeck pushes this literary agrammatism even further. His lines in the play often entail only the semisensical paratactic repetition of set words and short phrases. The little phrase "*Immer! zu!—Immer zu!*" (On! and on!) is one of the most common such instances. Woyzeck's use of language foils the nominally educated technical jargon of the play's doctor, who pompously overuses Latin medical terminology with little greater rhetorical effect or meaning. This diminishment of speech as the exchange of meaningful signs lends the play a cacophonous quality. Combined with the incorporation of rhyming folk songs as a running chorus, it enhances the sense of the work as a carnivalesque drama of voices from nowhere.

The play's sonorous recursion to something between glossolalia, verbal sputtering, and an existential howl appears to predict the modernist communicative failures on display in everything from Freudian aphasia and Russian futurist transrational language to Hugo von Hoffmansthal's *The Lord Chandos Letter* and Samuel Beckett's oeuvre. Because lapses in syntax and hearing voices are so closely tied to the clinical psychiatric definition of schizophrenia created decades after Büchner's death, *Woyzeck* has split its literary diagnosticians into opposing camps. Critical responses are caught between evaluating the play and its protagonist as an example of the historically contemporaneous Romantic melancholia—on display in Johann Wolfgang von Goethe's *The*

*Sorrows of Young Werther*, from the 1770s—and a more modern (and modernist) dementia praecox, schizophrenia, or psychoanalytic psychosis, all of which only appeared as diagnostic categories beginning in the late nineteenth century. Proponents of melancholia support their position by citing Büchner's familiarity with the English writer Robert Burton's 1621 *Anatomy of Melancholy*, his own medical training, and research by the French alienist Philippe Pinel. Woyzeck is afflicted with a pathological variant of melancholy that connects him to the prominent topos of *Melancholie* among Romantic contemporaries like Goethe, Heinrich von Kleist, E. T. A. Hoffmann, and Clemens Brentano.[15] The opposing perspective, which includes Gilles Deleuze and Félix Guattari's psychoanalytically inflected remarks on *Woyzeck* in *Anti-Oedipus* (1972), frames Woyzeck as psychotic or as speaking in a psychotic language conditioned by his socioeconomic deprivation, while nevertheless recognizing that the clinical categories of dementia praecox, schizophrenia, and psychoanalytic psychosis all postdate Büchner's era. Many of these readings draw energy from the abundance of complementary interpretations that conclude Büchner's Lenz is schizoid.[16] Some go further. Building on the schizophrenia diagnosis, multiple commentators frame Woyzeck's "paranoid" ideas and auditory hallucinations as biopolitical in nature. In these assessments, Foucauldian "discipline, hygiene, diet and economy" are all at work on Woyzeck's body, where they combine to generate a specific form of subjectivation.[17] Biopower allegedly reduces Woyzeck to Agambenian bare life and the distorted speech accompanying it.[18] Woyzeck's statements form the biopolitical expression of a modern-day *Homo sacer*, whose reduction to the mere fact of being alive and status within the state of exception they orally transcribe. "Doctor, have you ever seen anything of double nature? When the sun's high at noon and the world seems to be going up in flames, I've heard a terrible voice talking to me!" Woyzeck states.[19]

Secondary criticism stressing the protagonist's affliction with Romantic melancholia, clinical schizophrenia, psychoanalytic psychosis, or the effects of biopower distorts a fundamental ambiguity in the play. All conflate Büchner's departure from Clarus's finding about Johann Christian Woyzeck's sanity with an assumption about the fictional Woyzeck's necessary insanity, overlooking that Büchner's text is inconclusive about the nature of its protagonist's experiences. The very plurality of positions in secondary criticism on this point reinforces Woyzeck's mental state as site of key equivocation in the play. The drama departs from Clarus's medical conclusion *without* taking the opposite position: that J. C. Woyzeck or his fictional counterpart were, in some way, diagnosably insane. Refusing to provide a clear account of Woyzeck's condition allows the play to instead aesthetically focalize the trial's scientific drama between an older eighteenth-century account of the psyche, associated with Cartesian dualism, and a newer early-nineteenth-century one framing consciousness as physical and biological in nature.[20] Turning to the details surrounding the historical trial helps make the conflict between transcendental philosophical dualism and psychiatric somaticism clear.

## Revolutionary Science: The Medical Case of Johann Christian Woyzeck

In the summer of 1821, the former mercenary Johann Christian Woyzeck (1780–1824), orphaned son of a Leipzig barber and veteran of the Napoleonic wars, was arrested for the murder of his lover, the Leipzig widow Johanna Christiane Woost (1775–1821). The legal documents associated with the case state that Woyzeck and Woost had been lovers for several years. During this time, Woyzeck's jealousy at Woost's liaisons with other soldiers purportedly became increasingly severe. His poverty drove him to theft and, combined with an assault on Woost in early 1821, led to a first arrest. Unable to find work after spending time in prison, Woyzeck's economic situation substantially worsened. He found himself homeless and was forced to resort to begging. Twentieth-century commentators on the case observe that the unhappy combination of hunger, unemployment, social degradation, infidelity, and possible affliction with mental illness proved a toxic mix. Johann Christian Woyzeck stabbed Johanna Christiane Woost to death in June 1821 in an entryway in Leipzig.[21]

He was arrested shortly thereafter, asking at the time only to learn whether his victim was indeed dead, as she had "deserved it."[22] His imprisonment, however, prompted one of his former landlords—a physician—to publish a newspaper article calling for the defendant's medical examination, on the grounds that Woyzeck had long exhibited signs of hallucinations (*Wahnvorstellungen*).[23] The case was assigned to the Leipzig minister of public health, Clarus, who produced an official medical report for the Leipzig court in September 1821 after personally examining the defendant. Contrary to the landlord's reports and Woyzeck's statements, Clarus's first report found Woyzeck in full possession of "*freie Selbstbestimmung*" (free self-determination) and hence ineligible for a legally mitigating designation of a disturbed psychic state (*Seelenzustand*). He could be sentenced to the maximum penalty under the law. As Clarus was a senior professor of medicine at Leipzig University, head of the university hospital there, and a medical advisor to the Saxon court in the Kingdom of Saxony (then part of the German Confederation), his opinion carried special weight.[24] The expert testimony he provided significantly influenced the decision to sentence Woyzeck to *Strafe durchs Schwert* (death by beheading) in October 1821.

Use of the death penalty nevertheless had to be authorized by the Saxon king. The defense thus made a clemency plea to Friedrich August I in 1822, who turned it down even against the recommendation of his nephew, crown prince Duke Friedrich August of Saxony. The defense, having found further witnesses to testify to Woyzeck's insanity, requested that the trial be reopened and that Clarus conduct a second medical examination. Woyzeck, the defense claimed, had been hearing voices and seeing apparitions (*Geistererscheinung*) for years before the murder. Clarus wrote the second report in February 1823. It nevertheless confirmed the findings of the first, if at greater length.[25] In line with Clarus's second report, Johann Christian Woyzeck was beheaded a little over a year later.

In Clarus's assessments, Woyzeck's so-called *Wahnvorstellungen* (hallucinations) were in fact nothing of the sort. As Clarus concluded in 1823, the voices and visions Woyzeck supposedly experienced were, in fact, *Sinnestäuschungen* (sensory misperceptions) produced by a "disorder of blood circulation" (*Unordnung des Blutlaufes*), which meant he was still in a state of perfect psychical health.[26] The patient's characterologically superstitious nature had unfortunately caused him to mistake a basic biological phenomenon—a circulatory disorder—within his own body for "objective and supernatural causes" originating from outside of his person.[27] As such, a healthy Woyzeck had acted of his own free will in killing Woost, a crime that could in no way be considered the expression of a "blind instinctual impulse" exempting him from legal responsibility.[28] Saxon criminal law at the time acknowledged only full responsibility or full incapacitation in cases of madness. It did not recognize *diminished* legal responsibility, meaning that Woyzeck's sensory misperceptions carried no legal weight.[29]

Clarus's position was controversial. His publication of his case history after Woyzeck's death spurred a flurry of legal and medical debate about the appropriate relationship between mental illness and criminal responsibility. It highlighted an emerging scientific conflict in Europe between an older, medical trend known as dualist psychiatry (derived from the dualism of the Cartesian tradition) and a newer one that advocated for a materialist or "somaticist" psychiatry and saw mental illness as the product of physical disease.[30]

Psychiatry in the modern medical and scientific sense did not yet exist. Instead, patients deemed mad were largely placed in the care of asylum directors or general physicians who developed their own accounts and diagnostic terminology to explain their patients' illnesses. German psychiatry (alienism), in its early stages at this point, still adhered to the British model of "moral treatment." Following the work of figures such as John Conolly (1794–1866) and William Tuke (1732–1822), practitioners in Germany advocated nonrestraint and basic humane regard for asylum patients. They nevertheless lacked established, standardized guidelines for these patients' diagnosis or treatment, a situation did not change until the middle of the nineteenth century. At that point, transformations in French clinical practice, led by figures such

Jean-Martin Charcot, inspired a scientifically based approach to mental life in Germany and beyond, which became the basis for modern psychiatric science.[31] Both the trial of J. C. Woyzeck and Büchner's play unfolded in this transitional phase between the philosophical alienism of the seventeenth and eighteenth centuries and the scientific psychiatry of the nineteenth century and thereafter.

## The Measure of Mind: Burton, Descartes, Kant, Hegel

J. C. Woyzeck's legal trial is as a much the drama of the defendant as it is a public exposé of conflicting currents within German medical practice, Saxon jurisprudence, and Enlightenment-era continental philosophy about the divisibility of the mind. At stake in the secondary literature's diagnostic opposition between schizophrenia and melancholia is a deeper problem connected to the separate stances that early-nineteenth-century Romantic alienism and late-nineteenth-century clinical psychiatry took on treating the psyche as if it were a material thing.

Dualists writing in the tradition of transcendental philosophy during Büchner's time—like the German physicians Adolphe Henke (1775–1843), Johann Christian August Heinroth (1773–1843), and Christian Heinrich Ernst Bischoff (1781–1861)—were committed to the mind-body separation advocated by René Descartes and also promoted in the philosophical works of Immanuel Kant and Georg Wilhelm Friedrich Hegel. Dating back to the 1640s, dualism assumed a basic distinction between the type of partitioning possible in physical bodies and that possible in the immaterial mind. This position is already evident in the English writer Burton's *Anatomy of Melancholy* (1621), citations from which appear in Büchner's *Leonce und Lena*, and that informed the German Romantic understanding of melancholy. In the *Anatomy*, Burton openly mocked the endeavor of dividing the "corpus" of melancholy, of an-atomizing it (from the Greek "*ana*" and "*temnein*," to cut up) as if it were a physical thing. The gridded frontispiece (figure 1.1) prefacing Burton's *Anatomy* of 1628 displays species of melancholy (*zelotipia*, *solitudo*, *inamorato*, *hypochondriacus*, *superstitiosus*, *maniacus*) in neat boxes, alongside a portrait of the pre-Socratic philosopher Democritus, responsible for the theory of atomism. Counterintuitively, however, both the reference to Democritus and these divisions satirize the idea of slicing melancholy into its component parts as if it were material substance. In the same manner, the voluminous *Anatomy*'s division into "three Partitions with their severall Sections, members & subsections" (named prominently on the frontispiece) ironically foils the *Anatomy*'s labyrinthine disorder and tendency to defy classification by meandering in innumerable different directions. Instead of providing an argument about melancholy, the

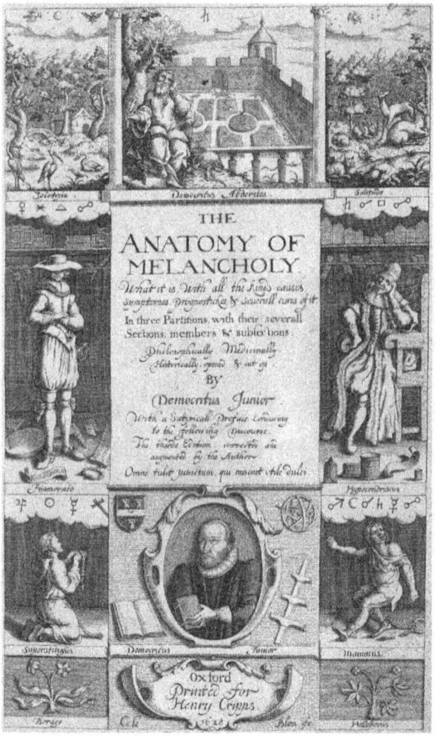


**1.1** Frontispiece to Robert Burton, *The Anatomy of Melancholy*, 3rd ed. (1628). Etching by Christian Le Blon.

*Source*: The British Museum.

book offers Democritus Junior's compilation of a huge array of disconnected citations on every possible topic, heaped together in a jumble. The body of Burton's text proves as resistant to anatomization as the hypothesized "body" of melancholy.

Burton's prefatory poem, "The Argument of the Frontispiece," further foregrounds the absurdity of dividing melancholy's corpus in the early seventeenth century. The poem's numbered stanzas initially seem to explicate the engraved frontispiece's respective divisions. Yet rather than supplying justification for the latter, the poem reveals their arbitrary nature. "Now last of all to fill a place / Presented is the Author's face," the closing stanza announces, highlighting that the author's (i.e. Democritus Junior's) portrait at the engraving's center is only there to prevent that section from remaining blank. The lines cast doubt on the motive for filling the other quadrants of the image and, by proxy, the pages of the book. Are *solitudo* and *hypochondriacus* fundamental parts of melancholy or simply expedient means of taking up space on the page? The poem's assertion that "Ten distinct squares here seen apart / Are joined in one by cutter's art" uses a pun—the "cutter's art" is both anatomical incision and the incision of engraving—to foreshadow issues of part and whole that plague the *Anatomy* overall. That "the cutter's art" paradoxically *joins* these distinct squares in the poem, rather than dividing them, succinctly captures the sense in which the *Anatomy*'s stated intention to provide a clarifying rhetorical division of melancholy instead yields a macabre textological monster stitched together from heterogeneous elements. Promising a treatise on melancholy's component organs, Burton instead offers a comically meticulous demonstration of the challenges, if not impossibility, of treating melancholy as if it were just like the physical body. The Renaissance anatomist Andreas Vesalius may have been able to clean up the anatomical body's messy viscera in his meticulous drawings, but the same is not the case here. Melancholy's uncontainable "innards" spew across the pages of Burton's *Anatomy* less as a reflection on the characteristic properties of the illness than as a satirical commentary on melancholy as the spiritual malaise of existence itself.[32]

Burton's position on melancholy aligns well with that of his French contemporary René Descartes, who adopted a similar stance on the soul's indivisibility in the *Meditations* (1641–1647). In the sixth and final meditation, Descartes makes his case for mind-body dualism on the grounds that the body is divisible but the mind is not. "There is a vast difference between mind [*mentem/l'esprit*] and body [*corpus/le corps*], in respect that body, from its nature, is always divisible, and that mind is entirely indivisible," Descartes writes in VI, §19. Proof for this can be seen, he observes, in that he is unable to distinguish discrete parts of the mind when he considers himself in his own capacity as a "thinking thing" (*res cogitans/une chose qui pense*). Moreover, removal of a physical limb from the body nevertheless leaves the mind intact. In addition, one and the same mind "in its entirety" (*una et edeam mens/ la même esprit s'emploie tout entier*) appears to be at work in faculties like willing, perceiving, and conceiving. This makes it inaccurate to say such faculties constitute the mind's "parts" (*partes/parties*). "This would be sufficient to teach me that the mind or soul of man [*mentem/l'esprit ou l'âme*] is entirely different from the body, if I had not already been apprised of it on other grounds," he concludes in §19, referring to his argument about the *cogito* in the more famous first meditation.

Read in light of the sixth meditation, Descartes's subsequent text, *The Passions of the Soul* (*Les passions de l'âme*, 1649), seems just as resistant to psychic corporealization as Burton's *Anatomy*. Indeed, Descartes reaffirms his earlier claim about the soul's indivisibility in the later work:

> It is necessary to know that the soul is truly joined to the whole body, and that one cannot properly say that it is any one of its parts to the exclusion of

> others . . . because [the soul] is of a nature which has no relation to extension, or to the dimensions or other properties of the stuff the body is composed of, but only to the whole collection of [the body's] organs—as becomes apparent from the fact that one cannot in any way conceive of a half or a third of a soul, or of what extension it occupies, and from the fact that [the soul] does not become small from some part of the body being cut off, but separates from it entirely when the collection of its organs is dissolved.[33]

Descartes repeats that the soul lacks spatial extension, a quality he restricts exclusively to "the stuff the body is composed of." As such, there can be no question of "half a soul" in the way one might speak of "half the intestinal tract." The soul cannot be materially spatialized.[34]

Philosophers following Descartes reiterated his claim about the soul's fundamental indivisibility. Nicolas Malebranche's *The Search After Truth* (*De inquirienda veritate*, 1674–1675) noted: "One need not imagine, as most philosophers do, that the mind becomes material when united with the body, and that the body becomes mind when it unites with the mind."[35] For Malebranche, as for Descartes, "each substance remains what it is," and the soul continues to be "incapable of extension and movement" even when its thoughts are "allied" with the "brain traces" and its emotions "with the movements of the animal spirits."[36]

One hundred years after Descartes, the soul's indivisibility also remained the case for Immanuel Kant. His *Metaphysical Foundations of Natural Science* (*Metaphysische Anfangsgründe der Naturwissenschaft*, 1786), published just before the second ("B") edition of the *Critique of Pure Reason* was released in 1787, reasserts the soul's inseparability. Based on this claim, Kant states that psychology cannot be grouped among the sciences at all.[37]

> Yet the empirical doctrine of the soul [*empirische Seelenlehre*] must forever remain even further from the rank of a properly so-called natural science [*so zu nennenden Naturwissenschaft*] than chemistry. In the first place, because mathematics is not applicable to the phenomena of inner sense [*des inneren Sinnes*] and their laws [. . . In the second place,] however, the empirical doctrine of the soul can also never approach chemistry even as a systematic art of analysis [*als systematische Zergliederungskunst*] or experimental doctrine [*Experimentallehre*], for in it the manifold of inner observation [*das Mannigfaltige der inneren Beobachtung*] can be separated only by mere division in thought [*Gedankentheilung*], and cannot then be held separate and recombined at will. . . . Therefore, the empirical doctrine of the soul can never become . . . a science of the soul [*Seelenwissenschaft*], nor even, indeed, an experimental psychological doctrine [*psychologische Experimentallehre*].[38]

Kant identifies that the phenomena of inner sense and by proxy the soul (*Seele*) are immune to division except on the level of thoughts (which he characterizes elsewhere in the passage as sufficiently arbitrary units not to merit real consideration). The impossibility of mathematizing these phenomena and their laws leads Kant to differentiate between a feasible "natural description of the soul" (*Naturbeschreibung der Seele*) and an impossible "science of the soul" (*Seelenwissenschaft*) or "experimental psychological doctrine" (*psychologisches Experimentallehre*). A *Naturbeschreibung* establishes classification systems for natural things based on their similarity. It forms part of the "historical doctrine of nature" (*historische Naturlehre*), or the systematic ordering of facts about the natural world.[39] This is separate from "natural science" (*Naturwissenschaft*) proper, linked to mathematics. "In any special doctrine of nature there can be only as much proper science as there is mathematics therein."[40] Since mathematics is not applicable to inner sense, Kant rules out the possibility of *Seelenwissenschaft*, or a science of the soul.[41] He instead assigns the fields that would come to be disciplinarily designated as "psychology" and "psychiatry" in the nineteenth century to the realm of pragmatic anthropology, which deals with human conduct. This is, indeed, exactly the position Kant takes in the *Anthropology*. There he describes "mental deficiencies" (*Gemütsschwachen*) and mental illnesses (*Gemütskrankheiten*) as "defects in the cognitive faculty [*Erkenntnisvermögens*]," which disrupt the understanding (*Verstand*) and so deprive the individual of Enlightened maturity (*Mündigkeit*).[42]

Like Kant, Georg Wilhelm Friedrich Hegel (1770–1831) also prohibits the localization of the mind directly in the brain on the grounds that it is specious to analogize between *Geist* (spirit, mind) and the physical world. In §309–346 of the *Phenomenology of Spirit* (1807), he refutes the validity of both physiognomy, developed by Johann Kasper Lavater (1741–1801), and phrenology, created by Franz Joseph Gall (1758–1828). Each thinker, Hegel argues, makes the mistake of treating external physical matter (facial features in the case of Lavater, the skull for Gall) as an equivalent to *Geist*. The brain is only a "middle term [*eine Mitte*] between the Spirit's pure essence [*Sein*] and its corporeal articulation [*körperlichen Gliederung*]."[43] If this were not the case, Hegel suggests, matter—whether in the form of the brain as the "living head" or the skull as the "*caput mortuum*" (dead head)—would need to be capable of *Geist*'s intricate operations.[44]

The transcendental prohibition on mathematizing the soul as if it were analogous to the body did not prevent eighteenth-century physicians from either treating patients considered to have a psychical affliction or from endeavoring to classify their illnesses. Their work, however, remained focused on extrapolating from individual cases and did not make the leap to a naturalized taxonomy of mental disease entities. The English physician William

Battie, for example, published *A Treatise on Madness* in 1758 designed to initiate a conversation about the care of such patients within the hospital system. In Florence, the Italian physician Vincenzo Chiarugi undertook a series of reforms at the Bonifacio Hospital and wrote *On Insanity and Its Classification* (*Della pazzia. In genere e in specie*, 1793–1794). Perhaps most famously, the French physician Philippe Pinel improved conditions for mental patients at the Bicêtre Hospital and Hospice de la Salpêtrière in Paris, giving rise to the apocryphal story of his having heroically "liberated" the insane from their chains during the French Revolution. His *Treatise on Insanity: In Which Are Contained the Principles of a New and More Practical Nosology of Maniacal Disorders Than Has Yet Been Offered to the Public* (*Traité médico-philosophique sur l'aliénation mentale ou la manie*, 1800) was one of the first to establish mental illness as a disease rather than as a form of demonic possession or symptom of moral depravity. No separate academic discipline or medical approach to studying mental illnesses yet existed. Throughout the seventeenth and eighteenth centuries, the study of the mind remained split between therapeutic treatments for madness that various practitioners of medicine like Battie, Chiarugi, and Pinel might choose to provide and speculative philosophy's related reflections on the *cogito*, informing an all-or-none position in European jurisprudence. If the mind was not divisible, only a distinction between sanity and madness made sense.

The creation of biology as a discipline distinct from both natural history and medicine in the early nineteenth century changed the picture, as did the research conducted between 1800 and the 1830s that put in place cell theory. During this time, physicians in Germany like Friedrich Gross (1768–1852), working in Heidelberg; Carl Wigand Maximilian Jacobi (1775–1858), in Siegburg; and Christian Freidrich Nasse (1778–1851), in Bonn, took a new materialist position that viewed free will as a product of somatic organization. They saw it as physical in nature.[45] These "somaticists" hence viewed both mental and physical ailments as grounds for mitigated legal responsibility in a criminal context. Their position had the unintended effect of suggesting that the soul, against Burton's and Hegel's claims, was indeed anatomizable and therefore amenable to mathematical measurement, in contrast to Kant's arguments. The German philosopher Johann Friedrich Herbart (1776–1841), who held Kant's former chair in Königsberg for a time, developed the idea that the soul obeyed the mathematical laws of physics in *Psychologie als Wissenschaft. Neu gegründet auf Erfahrung, Metaphysik und Mathematik* (Psychology as a science: newly founded on experience, metaphysics, and mathematics, 1824, 1825). Herbart pioneered the notion that all mental phenomena were dependent on "psychological laws linked by necessity."[46] In order for psychology to be a proper science, Herbart claimed, one would need to "research the soul in the same way that we research nature inasmuch as this implies presupposing a ubiquitous, completely regular relationship of phenomena, and investigating this by surveying facts, making careful deductions, by using novel, tested and corrected hypotheses, and finally, whenever possible, by contemplating values and calculation." To avoid the transcendental objection, his *Psychologie* argued that the indivisible *Geist* (mind) contained within it a *Gemüt* (or disposition) that was subject to varying degrees of increase or decrease in feeling in response to different stimuli, making a physics of affective states possible after all.

Herbart's law-governed scientific psychology and somaticists' stance on the physical divisibility of the mind overlapped with a related position that alienists from the transcendental tradition were beginning to advance: the idea of mental diseases that only affected a portion of the individual's mental faculties (*Seelenvermögen*) and not those faculties in their entirety. If so, would such diseases be grounds for mitigated legal responsibility because limiting individuals' capacity for free will? The French alienist Philippe Pinel, for example, had already argued for the existence of psychopathological categories such as "manie sans délire" in his *Treatise* of 1800, a disease Pinel characterized as exclusively limited to patient's affect and therefore devoid of the hallucinations typically used to evaluate the presence of a *Seelenstörung* preventing the exercise of free will. Patients who did not experience delusions could nevertheless then still be considered legally insane. The Leipzig physician Ernst Platner (1744–1807) similarly described *amentia occulta* (or "hidden madness"), in which the patient appeared outwardly sane but could be suddenly and unpredictably overcome by an irrational urge to commit an otherwise unmotivated crime. The Kantian philosopher Johann Christian Hoffbauer (1766–1827) remarked in his psychiatric textbook in 1808 about the concept of partial manias, in which individuals would behave perfectly normally until presented with a particular trigger (an object), in the presence of which they would lose the capacity for reason.[47]

Claims like Pinel's and Platner's about the existence of partial mental disorders pushed criminal defense lawyers in the German Confederation in the opening years of the nineteenth century to try their hand at reducing their clients' sentences by arguing that these disorders did indeed impair their clients' will. In cases such as that of Daniel Schmolling, for example, an assistant tobacconist who murdered his lover in 1817, the defense (unsuccessfully) argued that Schmolling was not guilty because he had "manie sans délire" at the time of the murder. The judge, none other than the writer E. T. A. Hoffmann, threw out the diagnosis and condemned Schmolling to death in a blow against the legal viability of partial psychiatric disorders. It was also in terms of a partial psychiatric disorder (Hoffbauer's monomania) that crown prince Duke Friedrich August of Saxony argued equally unsuccessfully against use of the death penalty to his uncle, the Saxon sovereign.

Clarus's conclusion about Woyzeck did not take a position on psychiatric dualism or somaticism. By simply writing off Woyzeck's hallucinations as sensory misperceptions, Clarus avoided either having to affirm the mind was biological or to deny its relationship to the body outright. In his view, the uneducated, superstitious Woyzeck had simply mistaken the internal noises of his own body for something supernatural. Clarus nevertheless did argue clearly against Woyzeck's possession of a legally mitigating partial psychiatric disorder. His 1823 report criticized the view that Woyzeck was a case of Platner's *amentia occulta*. Clarus's insistence that Woyzeck was suffering from a "disorder of blood circulation" reflected a rejection of partial psychiatric disorders as legally viable.

From his conservative standpoint, somatictist and alienist ideas about psychical divisibility represented a threat to the law because they seemed to provide new ways of allowing criminals to escape punishment. The somaticist stance diminished perpetrators' legal responsibility in cases of physical ailment. Pinel, Hoffbauer, and Platner's partial mental disorders had the same effect because they appeared to mitigate sentencing even in instances where the perpetrator did not show demonstrable signs of mental disturbance. Whether by somaticization, mathematicization, or the creation of partial mental disorders, the early-nineteenth-century division of the Cartesian mind into physicalized parts did less to protect accused individuals from being unjustly assigned legal responsibility than it did to expose their sanity to juridical force, making mental health a site of normative regulation while also rationally typologizing its (supposed) antithesis, madness. As Clarus's medical examination of Woyzeck demonstrates, sanity was suddenly more of a threat to life than insanity. The alleged danger posed by partial mental disorders in the legal sphere pushed Clarus to focus on proving Woyzeck's status as fully compos mentis as a way of guaranteeing his punishment.

This left the historical Johann Christian Woyzeck in an impossible position. To be found sane was not only to be sentenced to death but also to be legally and medically identified as a homicidal social pariah. If he had acted of his own free will, Woyzeck was a confirmed threat to society (not a victim of its violence). To be found insane was to live on, but in the form of a legal and philosophical nonperson, the mental equivalent (at least within Saxon jurisprudence) of children, sleepwalkers, drunkards, and maniacs.

## *Woyzeck's* Antidiagnosis

Had Büchner's play identified Woyzeck as insane, it would merely have perpetuated this game of nominalization that entrapped the historical figure by reducing the difference between sanity and madness to a distinction between a lethally regulatable reason and a dehumanizing expulsion from Enlightenment. The play's originality lies in its ability to identify and aesthetically transcribe this double bind as the central issue of Johann Christian Woyzeck's historical case while also strategically moving within it. The play's outwardly modernist "fragmentariness" is a historically specific response to the possibilities and perils of diagnostic thinking in the early nineteenth century. The play's refusal to quantitatively divide the mind is sensitive to the transformation that a jointly transcendental and empirical understanding of the human being produced in the 1830s. Rather than showing a case of modernist schizophrenia or aesthetically schizoid speech, Büchner's *Woyzeck* discloses the semiotic determinism within the clinical name "schizophrenia" and disturbs modernism's use of that term to characterize psychical disintegration resulting in a loss of the capacity for symbolization.

Büchner's play thus not only avoids a clear explanation for Woyzeck's experiences but also allows the various psychodiagnostic perspectives of the era to negate one another. Each would-be diagnosis becomes the antithesis of the others. The drama first suggests a physical basis for the phenomena the protagonist sees and hears, in line with the materialist stance. These visions and voices are the result of Woyzeck's diet of peas.[48] At the same time, the doctor overseeing the experiment repeatedly insists to Woyzeck that he is a human being possessed of free will, not an animal, and needs to start acting like it. Woyzeck urinates on the wall outside the doctor's office, instead of conserving his urine for the doctor to analyze and is sharply taken to task for it. "I saw it, Woyzeck—you pissed on the street, you pissed on the wall like a dog. . . . The call of nature, the call of nature! Nature! Haven't I proved that the *musculus constrictor vesicae* [urinary bladder muscle] is subject to the will? Nature! Woyzeck, man is free; in man alone is individuality exalted as freedom [*in dem Menschen verklärt sich die Individualität der Freiheit*]."[49] This returns to the dualist hypothesis about the immaterial and indivisible nature of the soul, affirming the will as sovereign within the human being and positioning it as the basis for the human/animal distinction. The doctor nevertheless also formally diagnoses his test subject with an "*aberratio mentalis partialis*" (i.e., a partial mental disorder) during the same consultation scene. This suggests a preexisting psychical malady with an (at best) unclear relationship to either the dualist or materialist arguments about the mind, like the diseases described by Platner, Pinel, and Hoffbauer.[50] "Woyzeck, you've got a marvelous *aberratio mentalis partialis*, second species, beautifully developed," the doctor states.[51] The overall degree of Woyzeck's economic and social abasement tend to frame his experiences of visions and voices as socially determined, the product of years of poverty and want. This sociogenic and (retrospectively) biopolitical position contradicts the previous three.

With the best intentions, discussions in secondary literature focused on the play's representation of a mental illness sustain the epistemic and juridical violence Büchner's play seeks to subvert, while missing that the clinical paradigm Büchner *Woyzeck* indirectly describes (involving the somatic and Herbartian shift from a transcendental philosophical to a scientific model of mental life) provided the basic epistemological conditions that enabled German clinical psychiatry in the 1890s to name and classify ailments like schizophrenia. Eschewing diagnosis, by contrast, Büchner's *Woyzeck* shows that the act of clinically ascribing a mental illness to a patient was entangled with the possibility of exercising sovereign force over the sane and insane alike. In dialogue with the French Revolution's political legacy in the reactionary years following the Treaty of Versailles, the play also recognizes, however, the necessity of a definition of popular sanity, showing the psyche politic as a key component in the representation of popular sovereignty.

## Revolutionary Science and Enlightenment

"A scientific revolution is taking place! A revolution!" the doctor declares in one version of the play's consultation scene. The conclusion could not be more appropriately put.[52] *Woyzeck*, like Büchner's 1835 drama *Danton's Death*, was conceived in response to the French Revolution and the 1830 Paris uprising (the July Revolution) that marked a shift from constitutional monarchy, under the Bourbons, toward popular sovereignty under Louis Philippe I. Written in 1836, *Woyzeck* also followed closely on the heels of the Paris Uprising of 1832 (the inspiration for Victor Hugo's *Les misérables*), in which dissatisfied republicans in Paris rose against Louis Philippe I for two days of fighting that culminated in their defeat. Closer to Büchner's home in the Grand Duchy of Hesse-Darmstadt, Napoleonic occupation had long acclimated the local population to the liberties of the French revolution.[53] Spurred on by the July Revolution and the June Uprisings in France, the heavily taxed peasant population of Upper Hesse revolted in 1830, destroying government offices and local shops, before being brutally suppressed by the military.[54]

Radicalized while at the University of Strasbourg (1831–1833), Büchner cowrote a revolutionary treatise entitled *The Hessian Messenger* in 1834. The piece opened with a call for "Friede den Hütten! Krieg den Palästen!" (Peace to the huts! War on the palaces!), a translation of the French revolutionary slogan "Guerre aux châteaux! Paix aux chaumières!"[55] Sometimes regarded as a forerunner to Karl Marx and Friedrich Engels's *Communist Manifesto* of 1848, *The Hessian Messenger* accused the German princes of abandoning the principles of the French Revolution and deliberately impoverishing those with the least economic stability: the Hessian peasantry. Büchner's creation of a secret

Society for Human Rights (*Gesellschaft der Menschenrechte*) and the publication and distribution of *The Hessian Messenger* nearly cost Büchner his life when the society was infiltrated by the police the same year.

As the literary scholar Peter J. Schwartz points out, however, the French revolutionary reference to the "huts and palaces" in the *Hessian Messenger* was already present in Clarus's 1823 medical report, in a much different form. There Clarus made the French revolutionary slogan into the basis for an Enlightenment morality lesson in which he equated respect for established order with humankind's progressive betterment. Clarus twisted the republican call to protect the huts from the palaces into an assertion that the safety of both huts and palaces was exclusively ensured by respect for the law. The law, in turn, had to rely on a "strict scale" of measure (that Clarus associated with a narrow definition of Enlightenment), which set aside feelings in the pursuit of truth.

> If things are not to end simply in sickly sentimentalism or even in farce [*Grimasse*], the thought must arise of *the inviolable sanctity of the law*, which, to be sure, is capable, like mankind itself, of a progressive mitigation [*Milderung*] and improvement [*Verbesserung*], but which, so long as it exists, must, in defense of the throne and the cottages, weight on a strict scale where it shall spare and where it shall punish, and which demands from those who serve it and from whom . . . it seeks enlightenment [*Aufklärung*], *truth* [*Wahrheit*]—and not feelings [*Gefühle*]. Such enlightenment was requested of me, as a physician of this city, when in Woyzeck's criminal trial it had become questionable whether he was *in his right mind*, and thus *accountable* for his actions [*ob er seines Verstandes mächtig, und mithin zurechnungsfähig sey*].[56]

Clarus's 1823 report presents the question of Woyzeck's sanity in terms of a concern about mass enlightenment. He turns a Kantian defense of civic duty into something closer to a normative mass injunction to intellectual guardianship:

> May the generation of youth now coming of age [*heranwachsend Jugend*], gazing upon the bleeding criminal or thinking of him, take good note of the truth [*Wahrheit*] that the reluctance to work, gambling, drunkenness, unlawful satisfaction of sexual lust, and bad company can lead, gradually and unexpectedly, to crimes and to the gallows [*zum Blutgerüste*].—Finally, may all return from this dreadful event with the firm resolution: To *be* better, so that things may *become* better [Besser zu *seyn*, damit es besser *werde*].[57]

"To be better, so that things may become better." In Clarus's hands, the Woyzeck case becomes an injunction to a generalized psychical health: "*being* better." This better being to which the report compels the youth of the future is defined by willingness to work, sexual propriety, sobriety, and the ongoing exclusion of perceived social outsiders. Condemning Woyzeck to lose his preeminently sound head, Clarus also managed to eke out a defense of public mental health that made a mockery of the same free will it nominally defended. If Woyzeck was sane but deviant, he could be held up as a case study showcasing the importance of collective mental hygiene and defining its constituent features.

As Clarus's reliance on the phrase "Guerre aux châteaux! Paix aux chaumières!" demonstrates, however, there was also a genuinely republican dimension to the idea of popular sanity. Even the Rousseauian concept of the general will (*volonté générale*) exposes the import of popular will (*volonté*) to the republican formulation of popular sovereignty. The people's mind could no more be mad than that of the sovereign's in medieval political theology. Imbecility might afflict the king's material person but could never disturb the sublime body politic.

As such, Büchner's play cannot exclusively be understood as an evisceration of Clarus via his reactionary rewriting of the Enlightenment's progressive, republican legacy. Instead, the play unfolds in the space of a conflict between the necessity of a popular free will or psyche politic (now also a site for capital punishment) and a "liberating" condemnation to madness that still causes individuals to lose their heads (by barring the subject from legal personhood). In this respect, the play offers a rejoinder to the apocryphal story of Philippe Pinel heroically unchaining the insane during the French Revolution. This fantasy assured the happy liberation of "mad/people" from their chains. *Woyzeck*, by contrast, questions what the Enlightenment tradition—caught between positivist rationalization and a progressive defense of citizen's rights—meant for the freedom of both mental patients and for a postrevolutionary public as bearers of the psyche politic.

*Immer zu. Immer zu.* In his reading of *Woyzeck* and *The Hessian Messenger*, Jacques Rancière suggests that Büchner discovers a twofold scandal at the heart of both scientific truth claims and revolutionary dogma. These texts foreground the "double scandal of science and utopia: the knowledge of their identity, the knowledge that revolutions are just as reasonable as mad, just as aleatory as ineluctable."[58] In Rancière's reading, *Woyzeck* brings to the fore a collision between scientific truth claims based on measurement, which reduce the mind and revolutionary strategy to quantifiable variables (the *Hessian Messenger* is full of statistics), and an incalculably aleatory dimension that sustains both.

The clinico-critical focus on sanity nevertheless helps keep *Woyzeck* confined to an "aesthetic sandbox."[59] Focus on *Woyzeck* the work as an illustration of scientific facts about the mind involves "purifying [these other disciplines'] various theories and inquiries from all those questions about culture and ideology and consciousness that are so messy . . . and that threaten to reintroduce the non-quantifiables of human freedom back into a carefully delimited and positivizing, testable, falsifiable, area of tests and questionnaires, of statistics."[60] Büchner, however, hollows out numerical precision across his play without allowing it to disappear entirely. Büchner's gesture sustains Rancière's observation about the double scandal of science and utopia. It pays tribute to the place of aesthetic objects as illustrations of the messiness of human freedom. The "20th of July" could be in any year and the "second regiment" in any army. "Woyzeck, just think, you've still got a good thirty years to live, thirty years! That's 360 months and days, hours, minutes! What are you going to do with that ungodly [*ungeheuren*] amount of time?" the captain remarks.[61] The measurement of time is both precise (360 months, etc.) and monstrous (*ungeheur*), much like the play's relationship to its so-called source materials. Indeed, Woyzeck might already be already dead when the captain utters these words (by virtue of Johann Christian Woyzeck's 1824 death). Nevertheless, it is impossible to say when the character was born, as his given biography includes no year, making the measurement of his life inscrutable.

The same self-negating precision that generates a sense of incalculability in these instances reappears in a comment the doctor makes to the captain. "Yes, Captain, you might be stricken by an *apoplexia cerebralis*. But you might get it just on one side and be half paralyzed or—best of all—you might become mentally [*geistig*] affected and just vegetate from then on: those are approximately your prospects for the next four weeks."[62] In a different draft of the play (H2.7), the lines are more precise and even more muddled. "She'll be dead in four weeks. She's in her seventh month—I've had twenty patients like that already. In four weeks—you can count on that [*in 4 Wochen richt sie sich danach*]."[63]

At one point, the doctor commands Woyzeck to stay in place, comparing his frenetic movements to those of an open blade. "Stay here, Woyzeck. You're running around like an open razor blade—you might cut someone! [*er läuft ja wie ein offnes Rasiermesser durch die Welt, man schneidet sich an ihm*]."[64] There is an obvious allusion to the murder weapon in this line, but the doctor's words additionally emphasize that the play's many instances of counting are a process of cutting and dividing, with direct parallels to the anatomization of the soul Burton had mocked in 1621 and both Kant and Hegel had disputed thereafter. Woyzeck pauses in his work cutting switches with his friend Andres. "Yes, Andres—that stripe there across the grass, that's where heads roll at night; once somebody picked one up, he thought it was a hedgehog."[65]

These "heads that look like hedgehogs" are the tropological counterpart of Marie's subsequent comment that the drum major "stands on his feet like a lion" (H4.2) and has a "chest like a bull" (H4.6). As part of an extended series of human-animal admixtures, they connect to the doctor's comparison of Woyzeck to a dog, Woyzeck's comparison of Marie to a "Zwickwolfin" (lit. she-goat-wolf, H4.12), and of Andres to a mole (H2.1), among many others. Arguably the most sustained such instance takes place in the scene with the carnival barker. There, the carnival barker presents a monkey, canary, and horse as human doubles:

> Show your talent! Show your beastly wisdom [*dein viehische Vernünftigkeit*]! Put human society to shame! Gentlemen, this animal that you see here, with a [tail/penis (vulg.)] on his body [*Schwanz am Leib*], with his four hooves, is a member of all learned societies, is a professor at our university, with whom the students learn to ride and fight duels. That was simple comprehension [*Das war einfacher Verstand*]! Now think with double reason [*mit der doppelten raison*]! What do you do when you think with double reason [*mit der doppelten Räson*]? Is there in the learned *société* an ass? (*The horse shakes its head*). Now you understand double reason [*die doppelte Räson*]! That is beastiognomy [*Viehsionomik*]. Yes, that's no brutish individual [*Individuum*], that's a person! A human being, beastly human being, but still an animal, a *bête*. (The horse behaves improperly [i.e., urinates or defecates]). That's right, put *société* to shame! You see, the beast is still nature, unspoiled nature. Take a lesson from him.[66]

The joke is that the horse, despite being a "dumb animal," can nevertheless take part in learned society: as an anatomical specimen (whence the carnival barker's crass emphasis on the animal's genitalia) and as a "professor" of riding and dueling. The barker mocks the hypocrisy of an elite educational system that uses animals to instruct its human beings, while showing educated society to be full of "asses." That the horse either defecates or urinates (it is unclear which) during the performance amplifies the point by demonstrating that even so-called educated animals must expel waste. "That's right, put *société* to shame!" The horse's specific talent: "*viehische Vernünftigkeit*" (beastly wisdom, lit. beastly rationality), derived from the word *Vernunft*, the same term Kant uses for reason in the first *Critique*, throws the entire question of the human possession of reason as the basis for its distinction from the animal world into doubt, like the rest of the passage.

The invocation to think with double reason (*doppelte raison/Räson*) in the monologue must thus be understood as a commentary on the genesis of a critical fracture within the Cartesian and Kantian account of *Vernunft* (reason) brought about by the anti-Cartesian scientific stance that mind and body were linked. Suddenly, there were indeed multiple versions of reason. In the old eighteenth-century account advocated by Descartes and reworked by Kant and Fichte, transcendental and immaterial reason (*raison*) held sway. In the new nineteenth-century account—paradoxically arising from the same Enlightenment tradition as the first—both reason and the mind were partially or exclusively physical phenomena.

The neologism "*Viehsionomik*" ("beastiognomy") uses on a pun on the German word for physiognomy (*Physiognomie*) to drive the point home. Büchner's coinage *Viehsionomik* mocks the hypocrisy of so-called educated opinions that would maintain a hard distinction between nature and culture while simultaneously imagining it would be possible to read the composition of the mind from outward expressions on the body, as Lavater and Gall proposed. Like the other human-animal hybrids in the play, the horse exemplifies the "*tierische Mensch*" (beastly human being) generated by the intersection of the transcendental accounts of the mind with new empirical ones. This is indeed Michel Foucault's remark about the transcendental-empirical doublet in *The Order of Things*. Woyzeck's seemingly "mad" suggestion about the existence of a double nature ("Doctor, have you ever seen anything of double nature?") turns out to be a canny insight. "Double nature" is "double reason's" twin and tracks the contradictory accounts in which human beings formed part of nature (and so measurable in material terms) and in which they were wholly distinct from it (because immaterially immeasurable). "The toadstools, Doctor. There—that's where it is. Have you seen how they grow in patterns? [*Haben sie schon gesehn in was für Figurn die Schwämme auf d. Boden wachsen?*] If only someone could read that [*Wer das lesen könnt*]."[67] Who indeed would be able ascribe meaning to the natural world's *Figuren*?

## Representing the People's Mind

Since Thomas Hobbes's *Leviathan* of 1651, written during the English Civil War, the issue of how to represent the people as a people has formed a major concern within political theology—itself one of the sites at which the drama of European politics and philosophical metaphysics has been worked out. The well-known frontispiece to Hobbes's *Leviathan* tackles this problem of representation by offering a concrete image of the transcendent, God-like Leviathan, equipped with sword and bishop's crozier and looming over the English countryside in a visual instantiation of the body politic. Just as the commonwealth for which Hobbes advocates in the text is peopled by representatives who enter into a contract to prevent a war of all against all, the Leviathan's torso and arms in the frontispiece are peopled with tiny individuals whose collective mass comprises the sovereign's body. The frontispiece offers a visual anatomy of state power while also sustaining the medieval notion (outlined by Ernst Kantorowicz) of the king's two bodies. Debates about whether the figure's face is intended to represent Oliver Cromwell or Charles

I unintentionally sustain Kantorowicz's point about the double-bodied sovereign. Regardless of whose visage the face better resembles, its status *as* a face still makes clear that the sovereign joins together a particular individual (possessed of a specific mortal body) with the transcendental office of the king, for which she or he is merely the bearer. The image thus draws together and attempts to visually resolve a politico-theological conflict between representation and transcendence, showing the solution in terms of a mixture of material realities (the apparatuses of church and state—castle, crown, cannons, ecclesiastical courts, etc.—which all appear in the lower half of the image) and the unrepresentable convergence of wills that Hobbes describes in his contract theory.

As Hobbes writes in the introduction to Leviathan, "That great Leviathan called a Commonwealth, or State (in Latin *Civitas*), which is but an artificial man, though of greater stature and strength than the natural, for whose protection and defence it was intended; and in which sovereignty is an artificial soul, as giving life and motion to the whole body."[68] Recent scholarship

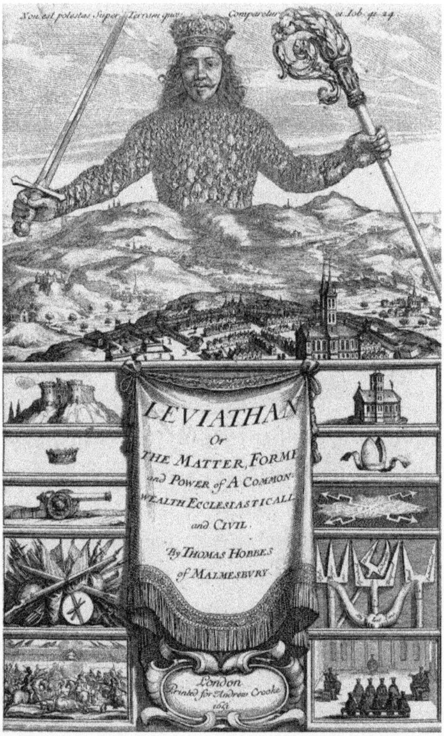


**1.2** Frontispiece to Thomas Hobbes, *Leviathan* (1651). Etching by Abraham Bosse.

*Source*: The British Museum.

focusing on the transition from royal to popular sovereignty has stressed the central dilemma this historical development posed for figuring the people. The art historian T. J. Clark identifies a modern (and modernist) reworking of Hobbes's image in Jacques-Louis David's 1793 painting *The Death of Marat.* Clark makes the case for the painting as an unlikely beginning to modernism. Clark reads the painting as much for what it practically shows—Marat's fatally wounded body draped over the edge of the bath—as for what the image represented at the time: a symbol of unity at a moment of intense political factionalization. *The Death of Marat*, Clark argues, produced a much-needed visualization of "The People" for the Jacobins at a moment of strife over the revolution's accomplishments and future direction. "The category 'People' had to have something be its sign. Among the signifying possibilities on offer in 1793, 'Marat' seemed one of the best. At least in him the category was personified. That might mean that the welter of claims, of identifications, and resentments wrapped up in the word could at least be concentrated into a single figure—and therefore shaped and contained."[69] If Marat could be made to stand for the People, then the Jacobins could fashion themselves as the People's sole representative and, on a symbolic level, put to rest the question of other factions doing so.[70] *The Death of Marat* actualized a hitherto purely imaginary sense of public unity and collective identity. The painting performed this unanimity by offering a cohesive picture of the body of the popular sovereign. It showed the People to themselves, holding up a kind of mirror in which to see a single, collective face for the first time, in place of the many differing faces of revolutionary class politics.

Clark's account leaves out, however, what happened to the "artificial soul" of sovereignty in the transition from royal to popular sovereignty. Eric Santner's development of Clark's argument in *The Royal Remains* likewise remains focused on the body, while nevertheless highlighting the centrality of representing the people to modernist aesthetics. In *The Royal Remains*, Santner proposes that Foucault's seductive but conflicting statements about sovereignty and biopower form a nexus at which Foucault draws attention to "the mutation of the King's Two Bodies into the People's Two Bodies," without being able to name it as such.[71] The task, as Santner conceives it in *The Royal Remains*, is to "introduce a slight adjustment into Foucault's terms and insist that the real object of the new physics of power is not simply the body or life but rather the flesh that has become separated from the body of the king and has entered, like a strange alien presence, into that of the people."[72] For Santner, in the wake of the French Revolution the royal flesh that supplements the king's purely individual biology, endowing his body with sovereignty's peculiar force, migrates into the "bodies and lives of the citizens of modern nation-states." The moment at which Louis XVI's physical head is pruned away also entails the loss of its symbolic double, whose sudden disappearance leaves the politico-theological apparatus out of joint.[73] The body of the king having thus vanished, a new way of configuring the relationship between the subject and the space of representation in the body politic must be found. Put slightly differently, the unity borne out of Ernst Kantorowicz's notion of the king's two bodies must somehow be restored. While Clark turns to David's painting of Marat, Santner points to modernist writers like Hugo von Hofmannsthal and Rainer Maria Rilke, as well as to Sigmund Freud, to make a related point. He tracks the migration of the royal flesh, a kind of fraught "surplus of immanence" haunting post-Revolutionary popular sovereignty in these writers' works, and points to the moments at which it catches modernist literary and visual art at "the unstable boundaries between figuration and abstraction."[74]

In Büchner's *Woyzeck*, however, it is no longer exclusively the representation of the *body* politic or the dilemmas of the royal *flesh* that are at stake. Büchner instead brings out the problem of representing the psyche politic, or what Hobbes had called the "artificial soul" of sovereignty. *Woyzeck* shows the

**1.3** Jacques-Louis David, *The Death of Marat* (1793). Oil on canvas. 64 × 50 inches (162 × 128 cm).

*Source*: Royal Museum of Fine Arts Belgium.

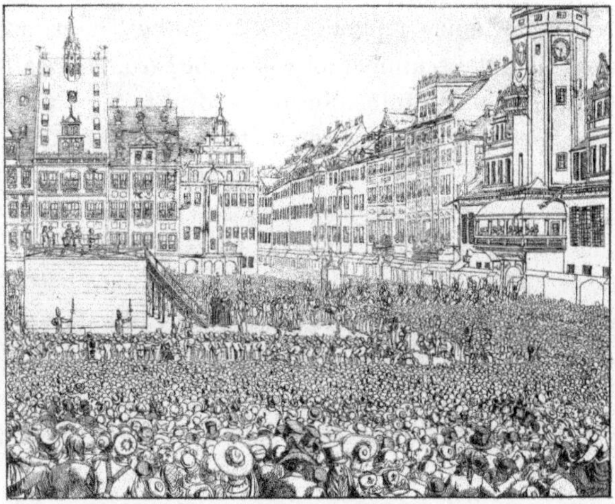

1.4 Christian Gottfried Heinrich Geißler, "Johann Christian Woyzeck's Execution on August 17, 1824 in the Leipzig market square." Federlitografie.

*Source*: Stadtgeschichtliches Museum Leipzig.

psyche politic entering a moment of profound crisis at the beginning of the nineteenth century in response to the rise of popular sovereignty.

This makes C. G. H. Giessler's 1824 engraving of the execution of Johann Christian Woyzeck particularly interesting. Despite its title, *The Execution of Johann Christian Woyzeck*, the image is manifestly not at all a picture of J. C. Woyzeck, who can barely be seen. It is a picture of the crowd. The image offers an unintentional study in the double-edged nature of representing the psyche politic, one which shows that its representation is crucial to the expression of a sovereign collective popular will and that such expression also fundamentally imperils that will by exposing it to the law's violence.

The tiny figures in Geissler's engraving are depicted in their sheer anonymized numbers rather than given any semblance of individuality, just as in the frontispiece to Hobbes's *Leviathan*. The crowd's gaze, however, directed toward the scaffold, no longer looks toward the sovereign's head (as in the *Leviathan* frontispiece) but to its absence. The crowd gazes upon the place where the head, the site of the "soul" of sovereignty, should be. Because the figures are so small and indistinct in Geissler's work, the image could as easily be one depicting the guillotining of Louis XVI in 1793 as it could be showing its stated subject matter, Johann Christian Woyzeck's death by beheading three decades later. The Geissler engraving's similarity to that famous royal decapitation helps suggest that the many smaller heads of the crowd in its foreground, watching Woyzeck's execution, must now also now collectively replace a missing head of state. To return to Hobbes, the engraving visually intimates that the crowd's smaller heads must unite into the "artificial soul" of sovereignty animating a new republican body politic. The paradox, however, is that it is also one of their number for whom the execution scaffold has been erected, suggesting that the transition from royal to popular sovereignty is afflicted by the invention of a new set of strategies designed to regulate the public mind and, indeed, the general will more forcefully.

This dilemma—that representing the general will also endangers its constituent members—is common to both Geissler's image and Büchner's *Woyzeck*. The many festival scenes in *Woyzeck*, some in which "*das Volk*" (the people) is made into a character, have clear parallels with the popular festivals Jean-Jacques Rousseau describes. In Rousseau's account in *The Social Contract* (1762), such spontaneous gatherings are the paradigmatic expression of the people to itself, the privileged site at which *la volonté générale* (the general will) is made most fully manifest. For Rousseau, however, this general will is not a divisible phenomenon. It can neither be counted nor measured, lest it cease to be general. The festival scenes in *Woyzeck*, by contrast, end up caught between an understanding of the people's mind that takes the transcendental position of dualism (and so presents a unified, generalizable will, without parts) and an understanding (common to the biological position of materialism and that of partial psychiatric disorders) that suggests *la volonté générale* can indeed be divided and quantified: in the form of clinical evaluations of popular mental health. This is what Clarus's report stated: "Finally, may all return from this dreadful event with the firm resolution: To *be* better, so that things may *become* better.[75]

## Psychopower

Rather than clinically diagnosing Woyzeck, Büchner's play exposes the psychopolitical problem to which the division of the mind gave rise. By suggesting that a metaphysically indivisible melancholia (Burton), *âme* (Descartes), *Vernunft* (Kant), and *Geist* (Hegel) were indeed anatomizable after all, biological psychiatry and partial mental disorders inaugurated a shift to an understanding of the mind's measurability on which contemporary clinical psychiatry, empirical psychology, and the neurosciences rely. This early-nineteenth-century scientific anatomization of the psyche cannot be an expression of biopower, however, because the entire issue in the 1830s revolved around the problem of how to represent the previously immaterial soul, reason, spirit, etc. as equivalent to the body. Foucault is clear, however, in his commitment to biopolitics' focus on the body and not the mind.

Foucault introduces biopolitics in the first volume of *The History of Sexuality* (1976). There he defines it as that which brings "life and its mechanisms into the realm of explicit calculations and made knowledge-power an agent of transformation of human life."[76] His related concept of biopower (*bio-pouvoir*) undergirds biopolitics. It comprises both a disciplinary "anatomo-politics of the human body" (focused on the optimization of individual bodies), which dates to the seventeenth century, and a more modern turn to the population's "species body" (*corps-espèce*).[77] Where it was once possible to describe sovereignty in terms of "the ancient right to take life or let live [*faire mourir ou de laisser vivre*]," symbolized by the sword, in modernity one speaks rather of a "power to foster life or disallow it to the point of death [*faire vivre ou de rejeter dans la mort*]."[78] In place of targeting individuals, power operates on the level of the population. The task is no longer one of wielding the deductive, life-negating power of the sword but of the affirmation and management of life, accomplished through the knowledge-power of calculability. The eighteenth-century genesis of demography (as, for example, in the work of Jean-Baptiste Moheau), analyses of the circulation of wealth (like Quesnay's *Tableau économique*, 1758), and studies of the relationship between resources and inhabitants (on display in the Prussian Johann Peter Süssmilch's *Die göttliche Ordnung*, 1741) all speak to a form of population control sustained by and through mass measurement. "The old power of death that symbolized sovereign power was carefully supplanted by the administration of bodies and the calculated management of life," Foucault writes.[79]

Biopower interfaces with both capitalism and the law in Foucault's account. It adjusts "the accumulation of men to that of capital" by expanding production and differentially allocating profit to keep pace with population rise.[80] It simultaneously makes the population more docile and readily optimized as a working force in his description. As life enters history, moreover, the law ceases to be the site of a strictly juridical power, but one in which the power of the norm increasingly holds sway. The law, without changing outward appearance or shifting from the traditional institutions of justice, covertly "operates more and more as a norm" that works to exert regulatory control on alleged abnormality.[81] For this reason, Foucault argues, the various world constitutions and legal codes formulated in the wake of the French Revolution should be scrutinized as vehicles through which the power of normalization is clandestinely sustained rather than exclusively celebrated as rights-bestowing formalizations of popular sovereignty.

Foucault's concept of biopolitics as he ambivalently developed it in his *History of Sexuality* (and in the subsequent lectures *Society Must Be Defended*, 1975–1976; and *Security, Territory, Population*, 1977–1978) nevertheless leaves open an interesting problem concerning the mind. Across these works, Foucault's hesitancy about psychoanalysis and his increasing attention on the techniques *producing* the self lead him to explore biopower's expression in sexuality, via security, and, ultimately, as contributing to governmentality.

Biopower drives the interpellative process of which the self is the end result, as the expression of a productive *pouvoir*. A study of the psyche proper gives way to Foucault's consideration of the role of asymmetrical power relations in shaping individuals' interior world. Far from it being a matter of interrogating the nature of an a priori psychic "stuff," let alone a pregiven psychic organization, Foucault's self is the construct born out of the interplay of unequal forces.

Büchner demonstrates that the same period between the seventeenth and mid-nineteenth centuries to which Foucault ascribes the genesis of biopower witnessed a strikingly analogous shift taking place that made the mind calculable by analogizing it to the body. Following Büchner, one could speak of the advent of a psychopower and a psychopolitics. Unlike biopower, psychopower involves the invention of the species mind, an *esprit-espèce*, based on the transcendental mind's entry into calculability in the early nineteenth century. While facilitating the expression of the general will, the act of anatomizing and dividing the mind came at the price of enabling both the management of the population's mental health and the optimization of the population's species-mind. Sovereignty was now expressible both as the biopolitical "power to foster life or disallow it to the point of death" and a related but distinct psychopolitical power to "make sane," to foster mental health or disallow it to the point of expulsion from legal and philosophical personhood (in the form of *Mündigkeit*). Alongside German somatic psychiatry, the early-nineteenth-century genesis of psychiatric censuses, biological psychiatry, and debates about "partial psychiatric disorders" all speak to this form of population control sustained by and through a mass mental measurement that simultaneously enabled the imagination of the soul of popular sovereignty.

Like biopower, psychopower interfaces with capitalism and the law. As Anson Rabinbach has shown, clinical psychiatry in Germany and France in the 1880s and 1890s was preoccupied with a perceived crisis of educational exhaustion that bled into larger ongoing debates about a seemingly ubiquitous modern mental fatigue.[82] Diagnostic terms like "*la céphalagie scholaire*" (scholar's brain) appeared alongside texts such as Angelo Mosso's *Fatigue* (*La fatica*, 1891), both of which suggested a correlation between mental overwork and physical exhaustion.[83] Meanwhile, the German psychiatrist Emil Kraepelin (the subject of the next chapter) conducted hundreds of experiments on children at his Heidelberg laboratory to measure "individually the onset of fatigue and fatigability of each child engaged in specific tasks. These 'work curves' became the plots of each individual's fatigue-biography."[84] Kraepelin used this process for "dividing the students according to their capacity for work," in a system of "tracking."[85] He then recommended the creation of a school day with a series of pauses for rest that would be scientifically designed to maximize students' productivity and proposed featuring lesson plans focused on short, digestible chunks of learning material.

The nineteenth-century preoccupation with typologizing students' susceptibility to fatigue and designing a productive school day anticipates the Chicago School's theories of human capital and investment in the self during the 1960s. Following a version of this observation in *The Eclipse of the Utopias of Labor*, Rabinbach argues that the Information Age and computerization have marked a shift away from the rigid physical management of the body (and its associated metaphorization as a machine) to an "autonomous" digital workplace in which workers mentally manipulate signs.[86] The "eclipse" entails a departure from the manipulation of the body to the use of the mind as a tool of labor. In its twentieth- and twenty-first-century form, psychopower promises to optimize mental life and the brain through brain-training apps, mindfulness, digitized meditation services, and even supplements that will supposedly improve thought.[87] These "health-promoting" techniques are all designed to render the worker, and especially the digital worker of the twenty-first century, ever more productive. The notion of a regulatable mental productivity is also correlated in the digital era with the genesis of psychological consumer profiles that streamline the interface between healthy thinking and purchasing. Psychopower is on display in the digital consumer profiling and the online advertising that targets past purchase history to formulate consumers' likely future buys. ("Customers who bought *Psychic Empire* also bought . . .") It is present in a giant media industry fascinated by clinical pathologies as expressions of genius. It is the source of a colloquial English (but growingly global) idiom of both "brainpower" and "brain drain." In short, psychopower sells. As it does so, psychopower souls. It teaches the subject to think of the self in terms of both standardized clinical diagnoses and an increasingly rigorously defined picture of mental health.

Büchner's play shows that as thought enters history, the law also functions more and more as a norm, working to exert regulatory control on alleged psychical abnormality and on so-called sanity. Following Foucault, one could say here that the various legal efforts to ensure the rights of patients with diagnosable mental disorders should be as celebrated for extending the privileges of popular sovereignty as they should be scrutinized for the ways through which they enable the power of normalization to be sustained. Neurodiversity, for example, makes a much-needed case for recognizing the rights of individuals with differing forms of brain function. It does so, however, at the potential price of reinforcing a standardized portrait of mental health.

The Nazi execution of psychiatric patients during the Aktion T4 (1939–1945) program at Sonnenstein Hospital in Pirna (see the third chapter of this book) shows one of the ways that this logic of affirmative exclusion developed.[88] Taking psychiatric patients' lives by gassing them was, in the context of the T4, justified by fascism's specious claims that these patients departed from a psychical norm framed as the equivalent to mental health. Their murder was permitted because their biological lives were allegedly invalidated by psychical degeneracy. This point about the continuing role of the body in the nineteenth century is exactly the one that Alys X. George makes in *The Naked Truth: Viennese Modernism and the Body*, in showing the important role that a materialist, anatomical influence, not just an ethereally psychoanalytic one, had on literature and art. Indeed, it is at stake in Eric Santner's work on Daniel Paul Schreber, *My Own Private Germany*, which frames Schreber's life as caught within the power structures of neuropathology and neuroanatomy that would reduce him to his brain.

Psychopower as I define it here is nevertheless different from the account offered by Bernard Stiegler, who uses the same term starting in *Taking Care of Youth and the Generations* (2008) and throughout his later work, developing it especially in his 2018 Nanjing lectures. It is also a departure from Byung-Chul Han's usage (which builds on Stiegler's). While there are overlaps between my use of psychopower and Nikolas Rose's on the management of the mind in both the neurosciences and psychiatry and with Kurt Danziger's scholarship on the development of psychology, here too it is important to recognize the key points of divergence. As helpful and illuminating as these theoretical frameworks are, they neither capture the full scope of psychopower's mechanisms nor the extent and form of its historical roots.

In *Taking Care*, Stiegler focuses on the technological changes specific to the late twentieth and early twenty-first centuries. He is concerned with how new material technologies—not simply abstract Foucauldian *technē*—have come to massively inhibit the development of popular *Mündigkeit* (maturity) in the present and so disrupt the operations of democracy, specifically by industrializing memory.[89] In his account, "mnemotechnics" (examples of which include analog mass media, telecommunications, and digital technologies) disturb the patterns of information transmission that normally take place between different generations and through the educational process. In an argument that builds on his work in *Technics and Time* (vols. 1–3), Stiegler contends that human beings now live in an era characterized by the use of capitalist external artifacts (things) as archives of experiences that individuals may or may not have experienced themselves. Rather than simply experiencing the passage of time and then recollecting it, the contemporary individual, Stiegler asserts, now turns to the preaccumulated memories and experiences deposited in socially engineered corporate technologies that are physically exterior to the person(s) to whom they originally belonged. For Stiegler, contemporary mnemotechnics generate a new form of collective consciousness that at once produces a "we" and allows the very meaning of collectivity to be defined by capitalist enterprise.

Stiegler develops this point further by noting that because twenty-first-century technology has exponentially automated and externalized thinking, it detrimentally "reprograms" huge numbers of people out of the ability to independently make judgments (Kantian *Urteilen*), a basic criterion for Enlightenment. Whereas intergenerational knowledge transmission and education used to serve this purpose by "storing" knowledge for future generations, such "long circuits" of care have now been replaced by technologized imposters that keep populations in a state of *Unmündigkeit* (immaturity). In contrast to both Kant and the position of the contemporary philosopher Peter Sloterdijk, Stiegler argues that it is no longer a set of guardians (*Vormünder*) who think for their charges, leaving the latter dumb and placid so that they do not dare to think on their own, but rather "service industries, cultural industries, and programs synchronizing individuals' activity into mass behaviors motivated by business plans" that step into that role.[90]

For Stiegler, these new mnemotechnical guardians reconfigure the human psyche. The psychic apparatus that Freud described in terms of the id, ego, and superego now yields to a psycho*technical* apparatus in the twenty-first century that is explicitly external, prosthetic, and technical. It retools attention by restructuring the very drives within human beings. In Stiegler's view, this psychotechnical apparatus is entirely compatible with Foucauldian biopower; it is simply an iteration that Foucault overlooked. Foucauldian biopolitics hence includes the externalized regulation of the *bios* through a sovereign capacity to "make live and let die" that is now contained within information technologies themselves. Psychopower, defined as the capacity to "make think," functions by "replac[ing] the psychic apparatus that should be constructing both the ego and id . . . with a psycho*technical* apparatus that controls attention yet no longer deals with desires but rather with drives, short-circuiting past (and present) experience by foregrounding future experience . . . in advance."[91] Stieger's term "psychopolitics" correspondingly involves the externalized regulation of the psyche by the preaccumulated memories stored in technology. Stiegler argues Foucault grasped the basic paradigm but neglected the agentless mind control of a new psychopolitics and its correlate psychopower.

Psychopower's natural extension is neuropower, Stiegler argues, which "conjoin[s] biopower and psychopower at the core of the cerebral organ itself."[92] Advances in neuroscience, Stiegler claims, have now made it possible to intervene in individual and collective memory processes, as well as those associated with prediction, on a neurochemical level. Retooling attention within the brain by altering its plasticity, both neuromarketing and neuroeconomics (developed by the American neuroeconomist Paul Glimcher in the 1990s as a way of linking cognitive neuroscience to economic decision making and so determining what the consumer "really wants") jointly cultivate what he calls a "monoculture of brains."[93] This too has a radical impact on transindividuation, or the reciprocal formation of the "I" and the "we" of collectivity.

The philosopher Byung-Chul Han picks up Stiegler's "psychopolitics" in *Psychopolitics: Neoliberalism and New Technologies of Power* (2017). There, he both builds on and departs from Stiegler's definition. For Han, as for Stiegler, psychopolitics involves updating Foucauldian biopolitics to suit a new era focused on technologically programming the mind, not simply the body. At the same time, Han objects to Stiegler's overemphasis on television at the expense of digital technologies like the internet and social media. As he argues, this prevents Stiegler from grasping that neoliberalism now operates by making use of "immaterial and non-physical forms of production" rather than the "biological, somatic and corporal" ones of earlier stages of capitalism.[94] Rather than using the body to overcome "physical resistance," contemporary neoliberal society functions by "optimizing psychic or mental processes" in a manner that—because taking place on a neural level—cannot be reduced to the disciplinary techniques Foucault allots to psychiatry.[95] Moreover, this new technology of power is no longer one that grasps the individual from without; it instead sufficiently conditions the individual's own interpretation of freedom as to make freedom seem compatible with psychopolitical self-optimization.

Stiegler's work and Byung-Chul Han's are different from my own approach insofar as both define psychopower as a contemporary phenomenon that augments the biopolitical paradigm by introducing the role of technology. The scenario they outline in the late twentieth and twenty-first centuries, however, was already present in the nineteenth and developed alongside biopower, not as a variation of it. Because psychopower is not a subdivision within biopower, there is no need to supplement the Foucauldian *techne* with material technologies or frame psychopolitical calculability in terms of the conversions necessary for information transmission, whether in television, radio, or computing. Psychical calculability, made possible by the representation of the mind as body, was already a major characteristic of the somatic psychiatry that emerged in the 1830s. While my understanding of psychopower does interface with the neurosciences, it is not in terms of the mind-altering neuropower that physiologically retools attention, as Stiegler describes. Instead, I agree with Stiegler's and Han's general observations about psychotechnical programming out of *Mündigkeit*, but would suggest that such programming is effective in part because it interfaces with a scientific understanding of the mind already conceived in terms of a mechanized information transfer system (the cognitive computationalist model of the brain as computer being only one example).

Without using the term "psychopower," Nikolas Rose and Joelle Abi-Rached also track the shift from a twentieth-century preoccupation with the prefix "psy-" to a twenty-first-century turn to "neuro-" in *Neuro: The New Brain Sciences and the Management of the Mind* (2013). In their Foucauldian reflections on the neurosciences and technology, they contend that "a number of key mutations . . . have enabled the neurosciences to leave the enclosed space of the laboratory and gain traction in the world outside," leading to what they frame as a need to describe "the new ways of thinking about the nature of the human brain and its role in human affairs that are taking shape."[96] As they stress, however, this process of consideration and criticism must take place without "defensive" recourse to overgeneralized, fact-neglecting critiques of neuromania. It should balance between a recognition of the ways that the modern neurosciences run the risk of producing a Foucauldian government of the soul, on the one hand, with a respect, on the other hand, for the opportunities neurobiology affords. These opportunities have a progressive political character. They take the form of an openness to the "role of nonconscious neural processes and habits in our decisions and actions" that Rose and Abi-Rached suggest will offset human beings' narcissistic tendency to think of themselves as "individualized, discrete, autonomous, coherent subjects, who are free to choose."[97] Turning to the nonconscious brain will offer a biological basis for a progressive social vision that downplays anthropocentric singularity a masterful, conscious intentionality.[98]

The distinction Rose and Abi-Rached draw between the era of the "psy-" and the era of the "neuro-," however, minimizes the epistemological continuity between those fields, making it seem as though the "neuro" is a departure from the calculable paradigm for mental life and health that developed beginning in the 1830s. *Neuro* defends a use of the neurosciences as a progressive program that will subvert human narcissism by focusing on the nonconscious but neglects that the notion of "nonconscious" life is still premised on a masterful anthropocentric self-awareness in the form of verifiable testing and measurement. This nominally nonconscious life remains replete with intentionality and choice because it must be defined from a perspective committed to the use of data and facts that attest to the reality of nonconscious life for humans. In this respect, nonconscious life cannot help but remain consciously knowable and locked within the knowledge system produced by "individualized, discrete, autonomous beings," who understand the world in similar terms.

Rose and Abi-Rached reject Fernando Vidal's concept of "brainhood" on the grounds that Vidal has mistaken *being* a brain for *having* a brain and so missed the neurosciences' nonreductive character, which they assert is already evident in the neuroscientific notion of an embodied mind.[99] The "reductive" mistake Vidal makes, however, is still one that involves recourse to the physicalized, measurable, divisible, and mathematizable understanding of the brain-mind shared by Rose and Abi-Rached. In this regard, their outwardly opposed positions are closer to being refinements on shared intellectual terrain. Indeed, all three maintain that intellectual inquiry conducted outside the established parameters of this terrain is illegitimate. Rose and Abi-Rached, for example, seek to "reject speculation wherever possible" in *Neuro*.[100] This position, however, risks affirming the same human narcissism from which the nonconscious brain was supposed to rescue human beings, by presupposing human beings' direct access to the facts in the absence of any speculative leap. It has direct consequences for how the project of critique is imagined, returning to the problems of Enlightenment identified by Stiegler and Han.

To outline the methodological stance they adopt, Rose and Abi-Rached turn to the *Oxford English Dictionary* for a definition of the term "criticism": "The *Oxford English Dictionary* provides a definition of criticism that matches our aims. Rather than fault finding or passing censorious judgement, we are critical here in the sense of 'exercising careful judgement or observation; nice, exact, precise and punctual.' It is in that critical spirit that we aim to describe the new ways of thinking about the nature of the human brain and its role in human affairs that are taking shape."[101]

It is of course important to be terminologically precise. This book would not exist in the absence of a commitment to that idea. Recourse to the dictionary to define criticism, however, turns the act of thinking into something that looks less like it; it is now the dictionary and not the thinker who defines thought. What does it mean to be "critical" according to a dictionary definition? Once hemmed in by an authoritative statement about its proper boundaries, criticism ceases to be the open-ended and speculative practice of determining its own scope and instead repeats the methodological presuppositions of the framework within which it is deployed. Criticism's new definition, however, leaves no space left to make that point. Any understanding of criticism that conflicts with that of the *Oxford English Dictionary*'s definition of "careful judgement or observation" (see the entries for "judgement" and "observation") is, of necessity, acritical. Definitions that do not adhere to the prerequisite that criticism is "nice, exact, precise and punctual" (see related entries) can be similarly discounted.

This is why it is important to note that psychopower as I describe it here is both a concept and an invitation to the practice of counterdisciplinarity. While I am compelled by Rose's arguments about the management of the mind in *Neuro* as well as by Kurt Danziger's related work on the development of the language of psychology, my own suggestion is different in two major ways. First, my suggestion is that psychopower is a common feature across the mind sciences because it stems from a common historical rejection of the transcendental and speculative tradition. Second, psychopower cannot be acknowledged in the absence of a critical practice, the meaning of which must remain open and so able to pivot flexibly to reflect on rationalist axiomatics.

## Büchner's Brain, Celan's Meridian

On and on and on and on and on and . . . The words bear repetition, for reasons to which Paul Celan's speech "The Meridian" is uniquely attentive. Celan's speech has since become well known for its elucidation of the *Gegenwort*. This is Celan's term for the "counterword," or declaration that detaches itself from all established meanings and, in Celan's estimation, functions as a sovereign act of freedom. Celan remarks, for example, that in plays like *Leonce and Lena*, "time and lighting are unrecognizable: we are 'fleeing towards paradise'; and 'all clocks and calendars' are soon to be 'broken' or rather, 'forbidden.'"[102] The *Gegenwort* shatters chronology. "Perhaps we can say that every poem is marked by its own '20th of January'? Perhaps the newness of poems written today is that they try most plainly to be mindful of this kind of date?"[103] To be *mindful* of this kind of date. Neither to adhere to it nor to endorse it. Not even to set it aside. "But do we not all write from and toward some such date? What else could we claim as our origin?"[104] *Woyzeck*'s carnival barker, attempting to prove that the horse is human after all, requests nothing less than a watch from his audience, so that the horse can show its skill at telling time. "Tell the gentlemen what time it is. Who among the ladies and gentlemen has a watch—a watch?" the carnival barker cries out. Büchner leaves the outcome of this demonstration indeterminate, however.[105] The scene ends at this point, leaving the matter, and the timing, open.

Celan's statements suggest that poetry (and art more generally) attends to the perils of calculability while yet maintaining a fiction of enumeration, in order to be able to claim an origin. It is of course feasible to think of Büchner's *Woyzeck* as "originating" in Johann Christian Woyzeck's trial and its source materials. It is feasible to say that the historical trial comes "first" and the play "second." It is also feasible to speculate that the play defies the very calculable logic that would suggest any chronological or countable relationship to the historical trial. Indeed, the fragmentary nature of its manuscript means that *Woyzeck*'s events can take place in any order. There is no first or last scene. The play's own structure mocks what subsequent editorial practices have attempted to do: arrange the fragments correctly. The ambiguous link between the fictional play and its historical source comments on the problem and necessity of calculability in the wake of the French Revolution, showing the immeasurable gulf that separates and joins them.

Perhaps Celan had calculability in mind when he wrote that the counterword is a "homage to the majesty of the absurd which bespeaks the presence of human beings [*Gehuldigt wird hier der für die Gegenwart des Menschlichen zeugenden Majestät des Absurden*]."[106] Neither that which can be counted on nor be accounted for, the counterword marks a sovereign freedom opposed to the sovereignty of imperial majesty. It embraces an absurd majesty instead. This is the sense of the "counter" that informs my own proposal for a counter-disciplinarity, the one that shows *Woyzeck*'s little phrase "*immer zu*" as not the measure of psychotic speech but the transcription of the immeasurable relationship between one and two, between a purported original and so-called adaptation, between the "real" Johann Christian Woyzeck and his seeming fictional double, between echo and echo. *Immer zu*: a counterword. "On and on and on and on and on." Perhaps the play's sanest lines. Perhaps.

The schoolteacher who recorded Johann Christian Woyzeck's execution in his diary states that the condemned man ascended the scaffold "shortly before 10:30 AM [*kurz vor halb 11 Uhr*]" on the day of his execution. How unlike this comment is from Clarus's 1823 medical report:

> On June 21 of the year 1821, at half-past nine in the evening, the barber *Johann Christian Woyzeck*, forty-one years old, dealt the forty-six-year-old widow . . . *Johanna Christiane* [Woost] seven wounds . . . one of which, a penetrating breast wound that cut through the first intercostal artery and both sacs of the pleura and punctured the descending part of the aorta . . . was declared unconditionally and absolutely lethal at the legal autopsy that took place the next day and in the report on that autopsy dated July 2, 1821.[107]

The schoolteacher, no doubt himself something of a stickler for precision, nevertheless allows Johann Christian Woyzeck to climb the platform only *sometime* around noon on that fatal day. Sometime. Not "on June 21 of the year 1821, at half-past nine in the evening." *Woyzeck* likewise refuses to carve up the mind as if it were the body, speaking against a lethal rule of number given in the name of justice. Celan's reference to high noon in his speech is often interpreted as an allusion to noontime in Büchner's oeuvre. "Doctor, have you ever seen anything of double nature? When the sun's high at noon and the world seems to be going up in flames, I've heard a terrible voice talking to me!" Yet it is possible that the noontime meridian to which Celan and Büchner both refer is not exact. It is possible that this noon is closer to the schoolteacher's "shortly before 10:30," a *Gegenwort* to the exacting, precise, and calculable meridian of 12:00 PM.

Toward the end of "The Meridian," Celan describes searching for Büchner's point of origin. "I find something as immaterial as language, yet earthly, terrestrial, I find the shape of a circle which, via both poles, rejoins itself and on the way serenely crosses even the tropics: I find . . . a meridian."[108] Cerebral anatomy contains a meridian as well. The brain's cerebrum is divided into two hemispheres at once joined and separated by the meridian's cleft. Perhaps Celan's imprecise meridian, the one at not quite noon, immaterial as language and yet earthly, is Büchner's brain meridian as well.

## CHAPTER 2

# BEFORE THE PRIMAL SCENE

## The Wolf-Man Between Sigmund Freud and Emil Kraepelin

*Professor Kraepelin thought that it was even more important now for me to stay, in order finally to get over my manic-depressive condition.*

—The Wolf-Man

*The patient spent a long time in German sanatoria and was at that period classified in the most authoritative quarters as a case of "manic-depressive insanity."*

—Sigmund Freud

The Wolf-Man, one of Sigmund Freud's most famous patients, kept the name given to him by his renowned analyst throughout his life. Ironically, the pseudonym Freud allotted his patient to conceal his identity and protect his privacy also became that same patient's self-description and public face. The patient, a Russian aristocrat born Sergey Konstantinovich Pankeyev (1886–1979), refers to himself as the "Wolf-Man" in the title and byline of his autobiography: *The Wolf-Man by the Wolf-Man* (1971). This too was for reasons of privacy. Notably, however, the Wolf-Man did not choose to identify himself as a case of "infantile neurosis" (the term Freud used for him in the title of his case history, written in 1914 but only published in 1918) or indeed of any psychoanalytic category later ascribed to him. Unlike the autobiography of another of Freud's case studies, Daniel Paul Schreber (author of *Memoirs of My Nervous Illness*, 1903), the Wolf-Man rejected diagnostic classification as identity.

It was not from a lack of diagnostic options from which to choose. The Wolf-Man's consultation with Freud in Vienna in 1914, when psychoanalysis was still so young that clinical practitioners were rare in imperial Russia, was his first analysis of many. He not only worked with Freud but also Freud's student Ruth Mack Brunswick, the American Rorschach specialist Frederick S. Weil, and (more unofficially) the American psychoanalyst Muriel Gardiner. During this time, he was given psychoanalytic diagnoses that ranged from paranoia (Brunswick) to obsessive-compulsive neurosis (Weil, Gardiner). Among the many case histories, documents, and letters connected to his case in the psychoanalytic literature, however, one is persistently absent. It involves a fleeting and unhappy consultation—as much for patient as for doctor—but nevertheless a decisive one. A consultation in which the Wolf-Man was given a very different name: manic depression.

Why did Pankeyev use Freud's pseudonym for him, "Wolf-Man," but not any of these clinical terms? Why, given that manic depression has since come to be regarded as the far more contemporary and scientific category, were both Pankeyev and Freud—and the many subsequent analysts—so quick to abandon it? The DSM-5's "Bipolar I Disorder," after all, is manic depression's modern heir.[1] What, if any, is the distinction between psychoanalytic neuroses and this "other" name, manic depression, which is so consistently missing from the vast psychoanalytic literature on his case?

This chapter uses the Wolf-Man's case history to map the major epistemological rift that separated psychoanalysis from clinical psychiatry beginning in the 1890s. It has since evolved into the definitive point of conflict between psychoanalysis and the DSM (as well as other differential diagnostic systems in non-Freudian clinical psychiatry). To do so, I follow psychopower's development during the period between the 1830s, when the first biological psychiatry took shape, into the opening years of the twentieth century. These decades both witnessed the expansion of biological psychiatry as well as the rise of a new field called psychophysics, which relied on the principles of physics to study psychical processes. Psychophysics forms the basis for both modern empirical psychology (Wilhelm Wundt) and the German psychiatrist Emil Kraepelin's clinical psychiatry, which put in place a rigorous, evidence-based system for differentially identifying individual mental disorders that anticipates the DSM's own. Both Kraepelin and Freud assessed the Wolf-Man in a clinical context. I show that the patient's use of the name "Wolf-Man" reflects his recognition of the rise of psychopower through Kraepelinian psychiatry and his attempt to navigate the psychopolitical dilemmas to which Kraepelinian classification uniquely gave rise.

***

No doubt "The Wolf-Man" is not the title Sergei Pankeyev imagined holding in his life. In the time that passed between his 1910 analysis with Freud and the composition of his autobiography, he went from being the sole heir of a landed estate near Odessa to living as an impoverished émigré near the Soviet sector in postwar Vienna, where he occupied a small apartment with his aging mother. When the Russian Revolution forced him to flee abroad in the early years of the twentieth century, he survived for a time on Freud's financial support and then by working in insurance. His marriage to a German nurse ended with her death by suicide just before the outbreak of World War II, leaving him childless. He never remarried and spent the last years of his life painting, drawing, and writing, when not in analysis. The chronicle of these later years and their accompanying analyses form the subject of Mária Török and Karl Abraham's *The Wolf-Man's Magic Word: A Cryptonomy* (1976). Török and Abraham comb through his case histories and his correspondence, looking for clues to his psychic language in the Wolf-Man's trilingual background.

Török and Abraham and indeed most secondary literature on the Wolf-Man's case focus on the period during his first encounter with Freud in 1910 and thereafter. Long before the Wolf-Man sought out Freud or knew anything of psychoanalysis, however, he pursued the medical assistance of his father's psychiatrist, a German doctor by the name of Emil Kraepelin (1856–1926). The Wolf-Man recounts in his autobiography that his father had consulted Kraepelin earlier in his life, during what was most likely the late 1890s or early 1900s.

> He [the Wolf-Man's father] was himself from time to time, at intervals of three to five years, attacked by a rather clearly defined melancholia, and would then go to some sanatorium in Germany and after a few months return fully recovered. His usual condition, which he subjectively characterized as normal, was characterized by unmistakable manic symptoms, so that the complete picture could well be regarded as one of those manic-depressive cases described by Professor Kraepelin. It was therefore not a matter of chance that of all the doctors my father had consulted in Germany, he had particular esteem for Professor Kraepelin and confidence in his ability to advise me.[2]

There was good reason for the Wolf-Man's father to recommend Kraepelin's assistance to his son. In 1905, the Wolf-Man descended into a state of what he alternatively characterizes in his memoirs as "deepest depression," "melancholy," and "unconscious mourning" following the suicide of his sister Anna.[3] Konstantin Pankeyev was apparently deeply concerned by his son's distressed mental state in the wake of Anna's death. He therefore proposed that his son do as he himself had done: pursue treatment with Dr. Kraepelin and avail himself of a prolonged stay in a German sanatorium.

By 1905, Kraepelin was a very well-known name in German psychiatric circles and had also acquired familiarity in imperial Russia. Kraepelin launched his career by setting up one of the first clinical psychiatric institutes in Russia in the 1890s. He established a clinic and psychiatric research laboratory at the University of Dorpat (present-day Tartu, Estonia), where he took in patients from the area and pursued studies in psychopharmacology. By the time the Wolf-Man's father consulted Kraepelin, however, the psychiatrist had returned to Otto von Bismarck's Germany, setting up a psychiatric laboratory first in Heidelberg (1891–1903) and then establishing himself at the University of Munich, a city in which he maintained his primary residence for the rest of his life.

Kraepelin's name at the time and since is closely associated with the psychiatric textbook he pioneered. Created by Kraepelin in 1883, this textbook went through multiple different editions until a pathbreaking sixth version of 1899, published the same year as Sigmund Freud's *The Interpretation of Dreams*.[4] Kraepelin's 1899 textbook cut new ground by suggesting that mental disorders were "differentiable," that is, able to be rigorously separated from one another, classified, and so made compatible with the disease specificity theory of illness operative in the rest of medicine. Disease specificity theory argued that diseases were independent entities existing entirely separately from their distinctive manifestations in particular individuals. Kraepelin's 1899 textbook, which (unlike in the case of contemporary textbooks) he used to publish all his latest research findings, showed disease specificity theory was as true for somatic diseases as it was for mental diseases. Kraepelin is also responsible in this work for identifying the disorder that has come to be known as schizophrenia.

The Wolf-Man visited Kraepelin at his Munich office in 1905. The reception was warm, at first. The Wolf-Man describes Kraepelin as a "stout, elderly gentleman" who recommended that the best option for the young aristocrat would be to spend time at a sanatorium near Munich, where several of Kraepelin's other patients were currently staying and that he himself visited on a regular basis. His patient clearly had a "manic-depressive condition," (*manisch-depressive Irresein*, a species of psychosis, in Kraepelin's view) just like his father. Manic depression, as Kraepelin understood it, was characterized by "sudden and violent" changes in mood.[5] Happily, the prognosis was favorable. The patient would recover with time.

During his stay in the sanatorium, however, the Wolf-Man managed to fall in love with one of the sanatorium's nurses. Therese, a German woman of Spanish descent, became his wife a few years later. A tumultuous courtship between patient and nurse ensued, during which Therese rejected him. Heartbroken but determined to forget her, the Wolf-Man abruptly left the Munich sanatorium later in 1905, against Kraepelin's wishes. He returned to Munich again in 1908 to seek Kraepelin's advice. Thinking himself cured of lovesickness, he believed he was still afflicted with manic depression, a condition to which he attributed his failure to successfully settle on a career. Kraepelin's response in 1908 was hostile. Declaring he had "made a mistake," he now refused to help the Wolf-Man or to provide him with any clinical advice at all.[6]

It is this failure that drove the Wolf-Man to both Freud and to psychoanalysis. Had the Wolf-Man's encounter with Kraepelin been successful, Freud's "From the History of an Infantile Neurosis" would not exist. Neither would the key psychoanalytic concepts that Freud developed there. Written against the backdrop of significant challenges to Freud's approach from psychoanalysts including Carl Jung and Alfred Adler, "History of an Infantile Neurosis" seeks to prove the import of infantile sexuality to psychoanalytic theory and to lay out the basic principles of psychoanalytic treatment.[7] In addition, this case history forms the basis for Freud's theory of the *Urszene* (primal scene): the child's real or inferred observation of his/her parents' intercourse and subsequent conclusion that their behavior entailed a violent act. It is, for this reason, associated with Freud's ideas about the castration complex, penis envy, anal eroticism, and the link between defecation and money.

There is thus a kind of primal scene to the Freudian primal scene: Kraepelin's diagnosis, associated with the Wolf-Man's own father, at whose situation the Wolf-Man likewise peered from a distance in his youth.[8] Freud notes this earlier diagnosis in passing in the famous 1914 case history, without specifying Kraepelin by name.

> The patient spent a long time in German sanatoria and was at that period classified in the most authoritative quarters as a case of "manic-depressive insanity" [*manisch-depressive Irresein*]. This diagnosis was certainly applicable to the patient's father, whose life, with its wealth of activity and interests, was disturbed by repeated attacks of severe depression [*Depression*]. But in the son I was never able, during an observation which lasted several years, to detect any changes of mood which were either disproportionate to the manifest psychological situation either in their intensity or in the circumstances of their appearance.[9]

Interestingly, Freud does not here dispute the validity of the diagnosis of manic depression as such or even contest its definition. Far from it. Freud observes that manic depression was a perfectly valid diagnosis for the Wolf-Man's father, who clearly did experience the changes of mood that Kraepelin identified as key features of the disease. That diagnosis was not applicable to the son, however; he identifies the cause of the Wolf-Man's alleged manic depression as the product of an earlier childhood trauma, thereby defending his key point about infantile sexuality from contemporaneous assaults on the concept by Adler and Jung.

In this respect, Freud seems to agree (at least in part) with the Wolf-Man's own characterization of his psychical struggles in 1905. Kraepelin felt that the Wolf-Man's moodiness at the Munich sanatorium conclusively proved his hypothesis that the patient was manic-depressive (just like his father). The Wolf-Man, however, objected at the time that there was a far more obvious cause: his love for Therese and her rejection of him. While Kraepelin insisted on the hereditary nature of his patient's disease and sought to justify his findings with only questionably related evidence of lovesick irritability, Freud, by contrast, was concerned in 1910 with his patient's response to his sister's unexpected suicide.

This was not the first time Freud had encountered Kraepelin's name. The two men never met in person, but Kraepelin's textbook was sufficiently popular and influential that Freud even refers to Kraepelin's diagnostic system at some length in his closing remarks on the Schreber case, "Psychoanalytic Remarks on an Autobiographically Described Case of Paranoia (Dementia Paranoides)," published in 1911. There, as the title of the case already subtly suggests, Freud both relies on and departs from Kraepelin's diagnostic system. Kraepelin never uses the term "dementia paranoides" in his work, only paranoia. Freud, however, hesitates about the adopting Kraepelinian diagnostic labels wholesale, preferring to modify them instead, a gesture seemingly also true with regard to the Wolf-Man's illness.

The Wolf-Man first paid Freud a visit in Vienna in February 1910, just as Freud was completing his work on the Schreber case. He traveled from his estate near the Black Sea to Vienna specifically for the purpose. The Wolf-Man was suffering from "disturbances of his intestinal function which were very obstinate." They had caused the patient to become "accustomed to enemas, which were given to him by an attendant."[10] It was not, however, the constipation and enemas that caused the Wolf-Man to visit Freud, only the patient's sense that "the world was hidden in a veil" or that he was "cut off from the world by a veil" for which the enemas were the cure, as they tore through this veil.[11]

After sending the Wolf-Man to an intestinal specialist to confirm that his complaint was indeed psychical in nature, not biological, Freud explained the patient's intestinal symptoms as something "carried forward from the infantile neurosis into the later one with little alteration."[12] He diagnosed his patient with an "obsessional neurosis" (*Zwangsneurose*) that had come to an end spontaneously in this patient's earlier life but nevertheless "left a defect [*Defekt*] behind it after recovery."[13] The term *Zwangsneurose* was Freud's own coinage from 1894–1895. He refers to it as a "nosographic innovation" in his text "Heredity and the Aetiology of the Neuroses" (from 1896, originally in French), in which he disputes his teacher Jean-Martin Charcot's position on the hereditary nature of the neuroses. "I was obliged to begin my work with a nosographic innovation. I found reason to set alongside of hysteria the obsessional neurosis [*Zwangsneurose*] as a self-sufficient and independent disorder, although the majority of the authorities place obsessions among the syndromes constituting mental degeneracy [*dégénéresecene mentale*] or confuse them with neurasthenia [*neurasthénie*]," he wrote.[14] Kraepelinian classification did not recognize any such disorder, either in 1896 or thereafter.[15]

Why didn't Kraepelin include a separate disease named "obsessional neurosis" in his diagnostic classification? What is the difference between Freudian "obsessional neurosis" and Kraepelinian "manic-depressive insanity"? Why did Freud disdainfully reject this diagnosis for the Wolf-Man? To address these questions, it is important to follow biological psychiatry's development in the period between the 1860s and 1890s and, in doing so, to tell the story of psychophysics.

## Psychophysics and Mental Math

Sigmund Freud and Emil Kraepelin were born the same year: 1856. Both Freud's work and that of Emil Kraepelin took shape in the swath of territory extending from the Bay of Pomerania on the Baltic Sea, in the north, to the Adriatic coast, in the south. Until the Austro-Prussian War of 1866, this stretch of land served as the easternmost border of the German Confederation. It was here that the *Bund* of member states proper abutted the western edge of those territories owned by individual members in the Confederation. In May 1856, Sigmund Freud was born to the wool merchant Jakob Freud and his third wife, Amalia Nathansohn, in the rented room of a locksmith's house in Freiburg, Moravia (present-day Příbor, Czech Republic), then one of the crown lands of the Austrian Empire. The same year, a child by the name of Emil Kraepelin was born to Karl Wilhelm Kraepelin, a music teacher, and Emilie Dorothea Auguste Johanne Lehmann, some four hundred miles to the northwest and across the Oder River in Neustrelitz, then part of the Grand Duchy of Mecklenburg-Strelitz, a member state in the German Confederation.

Educated during the era of German Unification (1871), the medical careers of both men developed against the backdrop of imperial Germany, imperial

Russia, and the Austrian Empire's turbulent disintegration and revolutionary struggles. Freud went on to found psychoanalysis. Emil Kraepelin became the progenitor of modern clinical psychiatry. Yet at the age of thirty, the two men were in radically different situations. Freud had married Martha Bernays in 1886 and was in the process of writing the preface to Jean-Martin Charcot's *Lectures on the Diseases of the Nervous System*. Kraepelin, by contrast, was about to set out for Russia.

The move was not Kraepelin's first choice. Kraepelin had been fired from his job as the clinical assistant to the famous neuroanatomist Paul Flechsig (1847–1929), chair of psychiatry at the University of Leipzig, in 1881. Losing the support of a prominent psychiatrist of his era sullied his reputation, and, having been deprived of a steady income, he spent the intervening years working in short-term hospital positions in postunification imperial Germany.[16] After brief stints in Munich and the city of Leubus (present-day Lubiaz, Poland), he accepted a post at the Dresden General Hospital as chief of psychiatry.[17] There, a letter from the German psychiatrist Hermann Emminghaus (1845–1904), his former teacher, reached him containing the welcome news that Emminghaus would be vacating his post as chair of psychiatry at Dorpat University in Russia (present-day Tartu, Estonia) in order to return to Germany. He wondered if Kraepelin would be interested in the Dorpat position.[18]

Kraepelin enthusiastically agreed. In addition to fulfilling his wish to become full professor by the age of thirty, the appointment represented a swift exit from professional limbo, financial instability, and what Kraepelin characterized in his memoirs as a state of profound "hopelessness."[19] His devastating break with Flechsig had been prompted at least in part by Kraepelin's neglect of the patients in his care at Leipzig University's Psychiatric Hospital. By allocating Kraepelin responsibility for these patients, Flechsig hoped to free himself to attend more to his research. Yet there were also larger factors at play.

Flechsig and Kraepelin managed to work together for only three months. During that time, the two men succeeded in developing an intense personal and professional animosity, fostered as much by Kraepelin's refusal of Flechsig's offer to oversee his *Habilitation* (postdoctoral) thesis as by Kraepelin's use of his position to fund unpaid postdoctoral research under a different advisor and on a topic at odds with Flechsig's intellectual agenda.[20] To make matters worse, it soon became apparent that Kraepelin had begun this line of research with an alternative advisor only *after* accepting the job and salary Flechsig offered him. Ironically, while Flechsig hired an assistant to relieve himself of mundane hospital tasks like patient care so as to dedicate more time to his brain-anatomical laboratory, he soon discovered it was his clinical assistant whose investigations were reaping the benefits of the arrangement—and with Flechsig's financial support, no less. The scenario must have felt especially exasperating in retrospect: the research that Kraepelin pursued in place of his assigned hospital tasks put him and Flechsig on opposite sides of what was soon to become a major rift within the developing field of German psychiatry.

In the mid-1880s, the older, pathological anatomical approach to mental illness was being challenged by newer means of getting inside the head that did not make use of the scalpel: hypnosis (driven by Charcot's work in Paris) and psychophysics. Flechsig, a specialist in neuropathology (concerned with locating signs of disease in the tissue of the brain and spinal cord), belonged to an increasingly unpopular anatomical approach that dealt predominantly with dissection. Some of his most enduring research involved mapping the relationship between the cerebral cortex and different mental functions.[21] Like other biological psychiatrists of his era, Flechsig also made extensive use of the microscope. Around the time of his abortive relationship with Kraepelin, he was developing a tissue-staining technique in Leipzig to visualize the progressive growth of myelin (an insulating coating on nerve cells) in the developing brain, a process now referred to as myelinogenesis.

Whether investigating microscopic brain anatomy or charting cerebral localization, Flechsig's research was indebted to the assumption that psychopathological disorders could be directly correlated with anatomical transformations in the brain.[22] Brain research would illuminate the causes of mental illness by revealing anatomical anomalies that corresponded to psychopathological forms.[23] In books such as *Gehirn und Seele* (Brain and soul, 1896), Flechsig further argued that the soul was a "function" of the body, much like somaticists such as Groos and Jacobi in the 1820s. Writing and working in the same city in which Johann Christian Woyzeck had been executed in 1824 on the basis of Dr. Clarus's damning forensic report, Flechsig remarked that only the brain could supply the "key to a *scientific* [*wissenschaftlich*] doctrine of the soul."[24] In fact, as Flechsig saw it, only the brain could provide a rigorous account of consciousness.

As with many psychiatrists in late nineteenth-century Germany, Flechsig's research was indebted to the work of the Berlin-based neurologist Wilhelm Griesinger (1817–1878). Griesinger's famous 1865 declaration that "mental diseases are brain diseases" established an entire field of investigation in Germany and abroad that accounted for psychopathology as a physiological disorder of the brain. Griesinger not only adopted the materialist approach to Cartesian mind-body dualism but also helped make psychiatry into a part of the medical profession in imperial Germany for the first time, shifting it out of the discipline of philosophy and removing it from the purview of asylums. Under Griesinger's sway, psychiatry in Germany in the 1860s and 1870s was transformed from a nonmedical specialty of largely untrained asylum directors, whose overcrowded institutions were mainly located in rural outposts, to the study of mental illness by way of neuropathology and psychiatric autopsy, conducted by medical professionals situated in urban university clinics.[25]

Griesinger's academic psychiatry also brought an important focus on psychiatric research and teaching, which gradually led to the inclusion of psychiatric course requirements for aspiring medical practitioners (1901) and the addition of a psychiatric section to the German medical licensing examination.[26] Additionally, Griesinger placed a heavy emphasis on building psychiatric clinics within the university system. Unlike private asylums, these clinics were to be models of institutional efficiency that would, in theory, help promulgate collective social well-being rather than simply shuttling sufferers out of the public eye.[27] Flechsig's intellectual agenda and even the existence of his research position as a chair of psychiatry at Leipzig University were both outgrowths of Griesinger's earlier innovations.

By the beginning of the 1880s, however, around the same time that Flechsig hired Kraepelin, critics of Griesinger's *Hirnmythologie* (brain mythology) were increasingly turning away from pathological anatomy to alternatives such as psychophysics.[28] There were several reasons for the shift. First, it remained difficult to determine precisely what structures researchers were seeing under the microscope, as the discovery of the neuron as the basic compositional unit of the brain (by the Spanish neuroanatomist Santiago Ramón y Cajal) would not take place until the late 1880s. Moreover, the brains of patients diagnosed with mental illnesses looked virtually identical to those without. As Freud discovered in his early research on aphasia (1891), there also seemed to be a missing conceptual link between physiology and psychology. The allegedly "associative" relationship between the two realms (supported by figures such as Theodor Meynert [1833–1892] and Carl Wernicke [1848–1905], as well as Flechsig) did not address how physical nerve fibers connected to the psyche, beyond simply stating that they did.[29] In addition, pathological anatomy had little to offer suffering patients and essentially no thought for clinical care.[30] In dealing with brain tissue drawn from corpses, it entirely neglected the experiences of living patients. At the same time, the volume of psychiatric patients in 1880s Wilhelmine Germany was rising as result of new social insurance programs initiated by Chancellor Otto von Bismarck—an attempt to combat the growing social democracy movement with new state-sponsored initiatives.[31] Of these programs, *Krankenversicherung* (health insurance) proved one of the most successful.[32] With the tide turning against somaticism and a rising number of patients seeking treatment (not postmortem analysis), it is understandable that Kraepelin should have become less and less convinced that "making thousands of brain preparations" was a good use of his time.[33]

There was a viable alternative. In contrast to Griesinger's somatic approach to brain disease, which relied on deceased patients as research material,

Gustav Fechner (1801–1887) and Wilhelm Wundt's (1832–1920) new "psychophysics" assumed that the psyche could be understood by measuring living patients' responses to various kinds of stimuli. Fechner's *The Elements of Psychophysics* (*Elemente der Psychophysik*), first published in 1860, proposed that the relationship between mind and body could be understood in terms of precise, invariable laws. As Fechner defined it, psychophysics was "an exact theory of the relationship of body [*Leib*] and mind [*Seele*]."[34] Like physics, psychophysics would be based on "experience and the mathematical connection of those empirical facts."[35] As Fechner wrote in the preface to *Elements*, his goal was to produce a specifically mathematical understanding of the psyche. He saw himself following in the footsteps of the German philosopher Johann Friedrich Herbart (1776–1841), whose failed efforts to do so had nevertheless broken important theoretical ground in Fechner's account.[36] For Fechner, as for Herbart, the metaphysically nebulous realm of *Geist* and *Vernunft* was precisely quantifiable.

To prove as much, however, Fechner had to begin by demonstrating that mental phenomena were divisible.[37] To make any progress, the unbroken stream of psychical experience would need to be converted into separable parts and these parts shown to represent countable equalities. Possessing appropriate psychological units, a means of differentiating between them, and a way to count their frequency would all be essential to the success of his undertaking. Fechner was aided in this regard by his mentor Ernst Heinrich Weber's research on the intensity of sensation (*Empfindung*). Extrapolating from Weber's earlier findings, Fechner proposed that, although no universal "unit" of sensation existed, it would still be possible—through infinitesimal calculus—to quantify sensations in terms of their perceived incremental growth or diminishment. Minute differences in sensation might not be evident to an external observer but should be obvious to the perceiving subject, who naturally experienced her, his, or their sensations growing or diminishing by degrees: from nonexistence (no sensation) to greater or lesser levels of magnitude.[38] This was already clear, Fechner pointed out, from the fact that one could speak of a "waxing" or "waning" of attention or an "increase" or "diminution" of desire.

To accurately measure a sensation (and so show that mental life was divisible), all that would be needed was a standard of comparison permitting the incremental change in *perceived* sensation to be correlated with an objectively measurable change in an external, physical stimulus. For obvious reasons, recourse to a physical standard (such as the yardstick, kilogram, etc.) would not work. Sensations had no physical reality. Fechner therefore suggested using a mathematical law instead.[39] In a flash of insight rivaling René Descartes's vision before the heated stove, Fechner claimed that as he lay in bed on the morning of October 22, 1850, he suddenly had a revelation about how the mind-body relation could be expressed in exact mathematical terms.[40] His controversial solution, the Fechner-Weber law, states:

$$\gamma = \kappa\,(\log\frac{\beta}{b})$$

In this equation, γ represents a sensation as determined by the experiencing subject's perception of relative increase or decrease. *β* indicates the absolute value of a mathematically measurable external stimulus. The *b* forms the "threshold value" of the same stimulus, that is, the amount needed for sensation γ to appear or vanish entirely. K is a constant, determined by the measurement unit of the external stimulus.[41] The law states that the magnitude of a subjective sensation (γ) is the logarithmic function of the magnitude of a stimulus (*β*/*b*), adjusted for unit (K). In Fechner's words, the formula "permits the amount of sensation [*der Grösse der zugehörigen Empfindung*] to be calculated from the relative amounts [*Grössenverhältnissen*] of the fundamental stimulus and thus [yields] a measurement of sensation [*Mass der Empfindung*]."[42] The German founder of empirical psychology, Wilhelm Wundt, would later tidily summarize the Fechner-Law as meaning that "sensation increases in proportion to the logarithm of stimulus."[43]

Although Fechner's approach inspired controversy that persists to this day, it is difficult to overstate the importance of his intervention. In a single line of algebra, Fechner managed to dispute centuries of theological and philosophical work committed to the mind's indivisibility. By taking issue with Kant's and Descartes's positions on the topic, Fechner also ushered in an entirely new way of studying mental life, one that would go on to form the basis for empirical (observation-based) psychology in Wundt's hands. The law also had spillover effects into other fields. It inspired the Austrian physicist Ernst Mach's theory of measurement in physics (measurement is not absolute but relies on the use of a standard) and set the terms for Charles Sanders Pierce's early work at Harvard on photometrics (*Photometric Researches*, 1878). It also had a significant influence on the German physicist and physician Hermann von Helmholz (1821–1894), driving his thinking on biophysics, the study of biological phenomena through the use of the principles of physics.[44] It even significantly shaped Freud's theories of the late 1880s and 1890s.[45] Yet while Freud turned to Fechner in an early attempt to formulate psychoanalytic principles and get beyond pathological anatomy, Wilhelm Wundt used the *Elements* as the basis for a significantly different set of investigations.

The Fechner-Weber law and Fechner's mathematical approach to psychology formed the groundwork for Wundt's research at his Leipzig University psychological laboratory, the Institute for Experimental Psychology, established in 1879–1880. It was the same university as Flechsig's own neuroanatomical laboratory. The Institute for Experimental Psychology became famous at the time, inspiring William James's own work at Harvard, and is best remembered today as the first psychology laboratory. In his 1863 work *Vorlesungen über Menschen- und Tierseele* (translated as *Lectures on Human and Animal Psychology*), a preliminary outline for years of research to come, Wundt expressly took up Fechner's claim concerning the divisibility of the mind and its composition of measurable psychic magnitudes, embracing the Fechner-Weber law as the privileged means of obtaining experience-based evidence about psychological functioning. According to Wundt, psychic phenomena were measurable, and their measurement by way of the Fechner-Weber law was sufficient to constitute a new field: psychology.

> This important law, which gives so simple a form to the relation of our apprehension of a sensation to the stimulus that occasions it, was discovered by the physiologist Ernst Heinrich Weber and has been called after him Weber's law. He, however, only examined its validity in special cases. That the law holds for all departments of sense was proved by Gustav Theodor Fechner. *Psychology* owes to him the first comprehensive investigation of sense, the foundation of an exact theory of sensation.[46]

Equipped with Fechner's law, Wundt outlined a program for psychological research in the *Lectures* that stressed the value of experimentation and measurement over the philosophical self-observation (*Selbstbeobachtung*) characteristic of the Cartesian approach and Kantian metaphysical psychology. Knowledge of the relationship between sensation and stimulus "allows us for the first time in the history of *psychology* to apply principles of exact measurement to mental magnitudes," Wundt remarked.[47] The Fechner-Weber law was, moreover, "a mathematical expression for a psychological process of universal validity."[48] Insofar as it permitted relative measurement of individual sensations, the law also made it possible "to bring together a large number of sensations into one continuous series" by "proceeding successively from sensation to sensation, from comparison to comparison."[49] Psychology would be the study of the psyche as its operations were laid bare in extended comparative chains.

Initially seeking a middle ground between the *Geisteswissenschaften* (human sciences) and the *Naturwissenschaften* (natural sciences), Wundt believed his experimental psychology would be capable of reestablishing philosophy's properly mediatory role between the two. Instead, it largely had the opposite effect, turning experimental psychology into a separate field within the academy by alienating philosophy departments, which were quick to charge Wundt with the same crude logical psychologism they attributed to contemporaneous phenomenologists like Gottlob Frege (1848–1904) and Edmund Husserl (1859–1938). By the time that Kraepelin met Wundt in the late 1870s (assiduously following his publications, attending his lectures, and eventually securing his mentorship), there was little question that psychology was considered part of the natural sciences and not in any way a speculative philosophical pursuit.

## Kraepelin in Russian Dorpat

During his extended exposure to Wundt's ideas, Kraepelin became convinced that if psychiatry were to adopt Fechner and Wundt's empirical, psychophysical approach to studying the mind, the longstanding issue of the field's legitimacy and proper domain of specialization could be definitively resolved.[50] His break with Flechsig and resulting period during which he worked in hospitals gave him little opportunity to pursue this idea. Once established in Dorpat with his own laboratory, however, Kraepelin began enthusiastically conducting his own psychophysical experiments on site and churning out reviews of psychophysical publications for the *Allgemeine Zeitschrift für Psychiatrie und psychisch-gerichtliche Medizin* (General journal of psychiatry and psycho-forensic medicine, hereafter *AZfP*).[51] These reviews, which appeared in the *AZfP* on a biannual basis between 1885 and 1891, show Kraepelin's extensive, intimate familiarity with psychophysics as well as his ongoing defense of the Fechner-Weber law against all detractors. As he remarked in a review from 1888, "all philosophical counterdemonstrations that tried to disprove the reality of psychological measurement" were merely useless "blows in the air [*Streiche in die Luft*]."[52]

Almost everything about which Kraepelin wrote while in Dorpat for the *AZfP* was in some way connected to Wundt's Leipzig psychology laboratory. If the articles under review had not been composed by Fechner or Wundt, they were written by Wundt's students, based on psychophysical experiments conducted in his Leipzig laboratory, or undertaken by Kraepelin's coworkers and doctoral students in Dorpat, all of whom were working on the Wundtian model Kraepelin imported to psychiatry there.[53] In addition to providing a detailed inventory of psychophysical research at the time, the reviews offer proof of Kraepelin's overwhelmingly positive regard for psychophysics and his interest in its many implications. Kraepelin's reviews include synopses of experiments on the perception of time, exertion of the will, fatigue, duration of attention, light perception (particularly variations in the perception of gradations), and sound perception. They cover articles on the reaction time to temperature as experienced on different parts of the body, on apperception, and on the association speed between letters, numbers, and colors. Several of the texts he reviewed focused on comparative recollection of words in native and foreign languages. In one case, Kraepelin covered an 1888 study by the

Leipzig researcher Gustav Oskar Berger that comparatively tested how quickly schoolchildren could read passages from Goethe's *Egmont* (in their native German) and Tactius's *Agricola* (in Latin) with increasing practice. Berger's "On the Influence of Training on Mental Processes" turned language into a computational metric for rapidity of acquisition, reducing literary works to the speed at which they could be spoken aloud and suggesting rapidity as a measure of comprehension.

The impact that psychophysics had on Kraepelin's psychiatric work is evident in the articles he wrote while in Dorpat. In his inaugural lecture at Dorpat, "The Directions of Psychiatric Research" ("Die Richtungen der Psychiatrischen Forschung," 1887) and his follow-up piece "Psychological Research Methods" ("Psychologische Forschungsmethoden," 1888) Kraepelin bemoaned the methodological heterogeneity of psychiatry in the late 1880s, claiming in this speech that the plurality of different "directions" in the field had inhibited its development and rightful ascendency to a place among the natural sciences and medicine.[54] Not only did the various types of psychiatric research fail to complement one another, but also—and worse still—they were all constantly producing new terminology. "In fact, at times it almost seems as if one cannot even rely on a common scientific language, especially when researchers do not withhold from giving new names to well-known things."[55] Kraepelin proposed in this speech instead that the field cease to "duck the responsibility of describing mental processes in a manner that is consistent and compatible with empirical psychology" insofar as the latter has "succeeded in creating strictly empirical research methods."[56] Like empirical psychology, empirical psychiatry should proceed by investigating the "laws of mental activity" and so unite around the clinical study of mental disorders "i.e. the empirical determination of individual forms of madness according to their course, cause and terminus."[57]

Only research on what Kraepelin called the law-governed parallelism (*gesetzmessiger Paralellismus*) between mental and physical functioning, which would supersede Cartesian mind-body dualism, could hope to elevate psychiatry to the level of medicine. Psychophysics would provide the needed basis for the shift. Whereas centuries of philosophical speculation had attempted to peer into an "autonomous, immaterial soul [*Seele*] distinct from physical reality," Wundt's approach had showed a different and more rigorous path forward.[58] Psychiatry's goal, Kraepelin argued, should likewise be a *Physiologie der Seele* (physiology of the soul) arrived at by the quantitative assessment of mental functioning, the opposite of what Kant had advocated: "The additional expenditure of patience and labor shall be rewarded, and richly so, with the progress made possible by the certainty and seriousness of the facts obtained, and particularly by the opportunity to arrive at a qualitative description of mental life by introducing measure [*Mass*] and number [*Zahl*]."[59]

Kraepelin acknowledged it would take more effort and time to focus on making mental measurements rather than use fuzzy philosophical introspection, but the payoff of a quantitative approach would be correspondingly greater, producing true scientific progress. For Kraepelin, shifting to a quantitative approach specifically meant placing scientific experimentation at the center of the psychiatric enterprise. Doing so would allow the "orderly and systematic" exploration of the psyche in a controlled test environment.[60] Psychophysics and the Fechner-Weber law had "emancipated" psychology from the tyranny of "metaphysical assumptions" and freed it to finally pursue the facts. Psychiatry should follow suit. "Fechner's *Elements of Psychophysics* is an intellectual achievement of the first order: it has brought an entirely new science to life, the numerous branches of which . . . bear ever new valuable fruit today," Kraepelin remarked in praise of the second edition of Fechner's *Elements* in 1891.[61]

By 1896, shortly after Freud published his *Studies on Hysteria* with Josef Breuer, Kraepelin was describing his entire psychiatric enterprise in terms of Wundtian psychology and psychophysical research. In the forward to the first volume of the journal he founded in 1896, *Psychologische Arbeiten* (Psychological works), while at the University of Heidelberg, he wrote passionately about his attempt to emulate Wundtian psychology in psychiatry. "For many long years I have had the task of making the methods and conclusions of psychological research usable . . . for psychiatry."[62] He returned to the problem of diagnostic heterogeneity that had featured in his earlier inaugural address at Dorpat University in the article he wrote for the journal's initial issue, "The Psychological Experiment in Psychiatry."[63] There he pointed out that psychophysics had, by increasing researchers' scientific knowledge of mental life, begun on a path that would no doubt lead to a "true anatomy [*Zergliederung*] of pathological states of mind [*Seelenzustände*]."[64] He speculated that it would eventually lead to a standardized classification system by disclosing the natural division of mental diseases and so eliminate diagnostic heterogeneity. In fact, Kraepelin proposed that empirical psychiatry would even complement psychological research by revealing a wide range of undesirable personal characteristics (*Eigenschaften*) that psychology—focused on studying only healthy individuals, not sick ones—might otherwise miss.[65] Only a year after Freud had put in place a rudimentary outline of the important role of language in clinical treatment, Kraepelin was advocating for a psychiatry geared toward the largely silent "anatomization" of pathological states of mind.

The language barrier Kraepelin faced in Dorpat contributed to his sense of the importance of creating a quantitative and observation-based psychiatry devoid of language. While Dorpat University had been officially a German-speaking institution since it opened in 1802 (a reflection of Baltic autonomy within the Russian Empire and longstanding German minority rule), that linguistic norm was jeopardized by Alexander III's decision not to renew autonomy in 1881. The tsar's move coincided with a Russification campaign to actively increase the role of the Russian language in everyday affairs and all forms of educational instruction.[66]

In addition to working in a university system that was facing increasing pressure to become a Russian-only environment, Kraepelin also was dealing with a patient population of Russians, Estonians, and Latvians who did not speak German.[67] This meant that Kraepelin struggled to communicate with his patients. To streamline these interactions and obtain a better overview of the most salient facts of different cases, he began using a system of *Zählkarten* (index cards, lit. counting cards) that succinctly summarized the main features of each patient's illness and tracked its development over time.[68] Kraepelin continued using these cards even after leaving Dorpat, as they provided a convenient, efficient way of searching for patterns across a large volume of cases, thereby eliminating the need to muddle through the extensive (and often inconclusive) documentation of individual patients' symptomatology. The cards made it possible to set aside the array of details accompanying a particular case in favor of a semantically and materially concise statement of the observed data. In many ways, the psychiatrist could now functionally dispense with interpreting what patients *said* and look for correlations between distilled versions of their cases and a broader preestablished pattern across cases. By studying a large number of these cards from patients in different locations, Kraepelin became convinced over time that mental illnesses were indeed separable and that they formed the units he sought, insofar as each disease possessed its own distinct developmental pattern. Mental disorders could be separated from one another according to their outcomes. To Kraepelin, this reflected such illnesses' real existence as discrete biological units in the natural world.

Kraepelin's classification established a new way of treating patients that was focused on predicting their recovery or decline. It also meant that one simply didn't need specific patients' stories: the basic story of a larger, average illness now served in these smaller narratives' place and operated as their collective representative. In a triumph of modern industrial efficiency that also aligned with the disease specificity theory of illness, suffering individuals could suddenly insert their experiences (filled with messy idiosyncrasies) into the classification system for it to be processed and a neat diagnosis obtained. Individual cases were either data points proving the general rule or, when failing to do so, deviant outliers. "The most interesting cases are not the most important," Kraepelin wrote in 1897 of the cards.

The *Zählkarten* were not Kraepelin's own invention. They emerged from the medical and population statistics increasingly deployed by centralized bureaucracies over the course of the nineteenth century to regulate, administer, and eventually define, in eugenic terms, their populations. Psychiatric statistics (and psychiatric censuses) had played a prominent role in this kind of data collection since the 1840s but had consistently run into the challenge of collecting meaningful data in the absence of a nationally or internationally standardized psychiatric classification scheme.[69] Psychiatric census cards had already been common fare in Bavarian psychiatric asylums since 1840s and 1850s, as asylum directors were required to inform the Bavarian government about their patient populations. Kraepelin would almost certainly have filled out such cards as a young psychiatric assistant in the Würzburg Juliusspital in 1870s. He would also have seen psychiatric statistics on the pages of the *AZfP*. Statistics about the mentally ill and articles reflecting German psychiatrists' struggles to establish a consensus about the proper disease categories had been regular features on the pages of the *AZfP* since its creation in 1844.[70]

The continuing failure to develop such a consensus eventually led the Prussian state to conduct its own localized psychiatric census in December 1871. For this census, an assistant (Albert Guttstadt) at the Royal Statistical Bureau of Prussia in Berlin suggested replacing the extant census cards developed by the Association of German Alienists with new ones, modeled on the categories and cards that had been used in the Prussian General Census of 1871. These new cards, which Guttstadt called *Zählkarte für Geisteskranke* (census cards for the mentally ill) in an article he published in the journal of the Royal Statistical Bureau, would update the older model by now collecting data about patients' prognoses. It was "in the interests of the state to obtain reliable information about the categories of the mentally ill [*Geisteskranken*] which have a determining effect on the need for mental asylums [*Irrenanstalten*], i.e., about the curable [*heilbaren*] and incurable [*unheilbaren*] mental patients," Guttstadt stressed. The new cards (figure 2.1) would also revise the older model by introducing more detailed questions about patients' heredity (#10 in the right-hand column), their *Gemeingefährlichkeit* (danger to the public, #11), the mental illnesses of their offspring (#15), and by adding the category "delirium tremens" to the list of illness forms (#12). These cards would also not require the signature of the doctor in charge of the institution.[71]

Whether through the imperial Prussian or locally Bavarian iterations, Kraepelin was certainly familiar with this mode of data collection. The contents of Kraepelin's cards differed significantly from those developed for state statistical purposes.[72] They did not include any categories about patients' family background, offspring, or danger to the public. Many did, however, stress disease course, potentially reflecting the emphasis on prognosis that Guttstadt introduced in his 1871 cards. As a variant of the psychiatric census card, moreover, they cannot be regarded as independent from wider attempts by state administrators to quantitatively represent the mental life of the imperial population.

The historians of psychiatry Matthias M. Weber and Eric J. Engstrom offer a sample patient description (in English translation) from one of the cards that they suggest is fairly typical of Kraepelin's descriptions in them overall. As

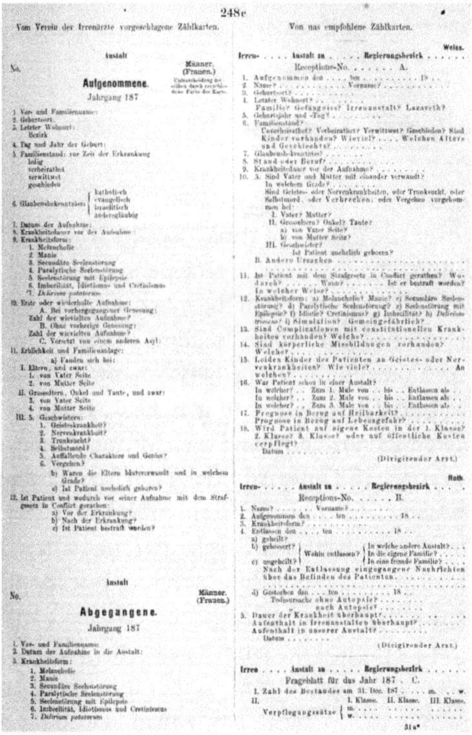

248c

Vom Verein der Irrenärzte vorgeschlagene Zählkarten.

Anstalt

No.

Männer. (Frauen.)

**Aufgenommene.**

Jahrgang 187

1. Vor- und Familienname:
2. Geburtsort.
3. Letzter Wohnort:
   Bezirk
4. Tag und Jahr der Geburt:
5. Familienstand: zur Zeit der Erkrankung
   ledig
   verheirathet
   verwittwet
   geschieden
6. Glaubensbekenntniss: katholisch / evangelisch / israelitisch / andersgläubig
7. Datum der Aufnahme:
8. Krankheitsdauer vor der Aufnahme:
9. Krankheitsform:
   1. Melancholie
   2. Manie
   3. Secundäre Seelenstörung
   4. Paralytische Seelenstörung
   5. Seelenstörung mit Epilepsie
   6. Imbecilität, Idiotismus und Cretinismus
   7. *Delirium potatorum*
10. Erste oder wiederholte Aufnahme:
    A. Bei vorhergegangener Genesung:
    Zahl der wievielten Aufnahme?
    B. Ohne vorherige Genesung:
    Zahl der wievielten Aufnahme?
    C. Versetzt von einem anderen Asyl:
11. Erblichkeit und Familienanlage:
    a) Fanden sich bei:
    I. Eltern, und zwar:
       1. von Vater Seite
       2. von Mutter Seite
    II. Grosseltern, Onkel und Tante, und zwar:
       3. von Vater Seite
       4. von Mutter Seite
    III. 5. Geschwistern:
       1. Geisteskrankheit?
       2. Nervenkrankheit?
       3. Trunksucht?
       4. Selbstmord?
       5. Auffallende Charaktere und Genies?
       6. Vergehen?
    b) Waren die Eltern blutsverwandt und in welchem Grade?
    c) Ist Patient unehelich geboren?
12. Ist Patient und wodurch vor seiner Aufnahme mit dem Strafgesetz in Conflict gerathen:
    a) Vor der Erkrankung?
    b) Nach der Erkrankung?
    c) Ist Patient bestraft worden?

Anstalt

No.

Männer. (Frauen.)

**Abgegangene.**

Jahrgang 187

1. Vor- und Familienname:
2. Datum der Aufnahme in die Anstalt:
3. Krankheitsform:
   1. Melancholie
   2. Manie
   3. Secundäre Seelenstörung
   4. Paralytische Seelenstörung
   5. Seelenstörung mit Epilepsie
   6. Imbecilität, Idiotismus und Cretinismus
   7. *Delirium potatorum*

Von uns empfohlene Zählkarten.

Weiss.

Irren- . . . . Anstalt zu . . . . . Regierungsbezirk . . . . . .

Receptions-No. . . . . . . . A.

1. Aufgenommen den . . . . ten . . . . . . . . . . 18 . .
2. Name? . . . . . . . . . . . . Vorname? . . . . . . . . . . . .
3. Geburtsort? . . . . . . . . . .
4. Letzter Wohnort? . . . . . . . .
   Familie? Gefängniss? Irrenanstalt? Lazareth?
5. Geburtsjahr und -Tag? . . . . . . . .
6. Familienstand?
   Unverheirathet? Verheirathet? Verwittwet? Geschieden? Sind Kinder vorhanden? Wieviel? . . . . Welchen Alters und Geschlechts? . . . . . . . . .
7. Glaubensbekenntniss? . . . . . . .
8. Stand oder Beruf? . . . . . . . . . . . .
9. Krankheitsdauer vor der Aufnahme? . . . . . . . . .
10. A. Sind Vater und Mutter mit einander verwandt?
    In welchem Grade? . . . . . . . .
    Sind Geistes- oder Nervenkrankheiten, oder Trunksucht, oder Selbstmord, oder Verbrechen, oder Vergehen vorgekommen bei:
    I. Vater? Mutter?
    II. Grosseltern? Onkel? Tante?
       a) von Vater Seite?
       b) von Mutter Seite?
    III. Geschwister?
       Ist Patient unehelich geboren?
    B. Andere Ursachen . . . . . . . . . . . . . . . . . . . . . . . .
11. Ist Patient mit dem Strafgesetz in Conflict gerathen? Wodurch? . . . . . . Wann? . . . . . . . Ist er bestraft worden? In welcher Weise? . . . . . . . . . . . . . .
12. Krankheitsform: a) Melancholie? Manie? c) Secundäre Seelenstörung? d) Paralytische Seelenstörung? e) Seelenstörung mit Epilepsie? f) Idiotie? Cretinismus? g) Imbecillität? h) *Delirium tremens?* i) Simulation? Gemeingefährlich?
13. Sind Complicationen mit constitutionellen Krankheiten vorhanden? Welche? . . . . . . . . . . . . . . . .
14. Sind körperliche Missbildungen vorhanden? Welche? . . . . . . . . . . . . . . .
15. Leiden Kinder des Patienten an Geistes- oder Nervenkrankheiten? Wie viele? . . . . . . . . . . . . . An welchen? . . . . . . . . . .
16. War Patient schon in einer Anstalt?
    In welcher? . . Zum 1. Male von . . bis . . Entlassen als . .
    In welcher? . . Zum 2. Male von . . bis . . Entlassen als . .
    In welcher? . . Zum 3. Male von . . bis . . Entlassen als . .
17. Prognose in Bezug auf Heilbarkeit? . . . . . . . . . . . .
    Prognose in Bezug auf Lebensgefahr? . . . . . . . . . .
18. Wird Patient auf eigene Kosten in der 1. Klasse? 2. Klasse? 3. Klasse? oder auf öffentliche Kosten verpflegt?
    Datum . . . . . . . . . .

(Dirigirender Arzt.)

Roth.

Irren- . . . . . Anstalt zu . . . . . Regierungsbezirk . . . . .

Receptions-No. . . . . . . B.

1. Name? . . . . . . . Vorname? . . . . . . . .
2. Aufgenommen den . . . . ten . . . . . . . . . . 18 . .
3. Krankheitsform? . . . . . . . . . . .
4. Entlassen den . . . . ten . . . . . . . . . . . 18 . .
   a) geheilt?
   b) gebessert? / c) ungeheilt? — Wohin entlassen? In welche andere Anstalt? . . . / In die eigene Familie? . . . . / In eine fremde Familie? . . . .
   Nach der Entlassung eingegangene Nachrichten über das Befinden des Patienten. . . . . . . . . . .
   d) Gestorben den . . . ten . . . . . . . . . . 18 . .
   Todesursache ohne Autopsie? . . . . . . .
   " nach Autopsie? . . . . . . .
5. Dauer der Krankheit überhaupt? . . . . . . . . . . . . .
   Aufenthalt in Irrenanstalten überhaupt? . . . . . . . .
   Aufenthalt in unserer Anstalt? . . . . . . . .
   Datum . . . . . . . .

(Dirigirender Arzt.)

Irren . . . . Anstalt zu . . . . . Regierungsbezirk . . . . . .

Frageblatt für das Jahr 187 . C.

I. Zahl des Bestandes am 31. Dec. 187 . . . . . m. . . w.

| II. | I. Klasse. | II. Klasse. | III. Klasse. |
| --- | --- | --- | --- |
| Verpflegungssätze m. | . . . . | . . . . . . | . . . . . . |
| w. | . . . . | . . . . . . | . . . . . . |

31a*

**2.1** Albert Guttstadt, template for new Prussian census cards for the mentally ill. *Zeitschrift des königlich-preussischen statistichen Bureaus* (1874). Right column: Guttstadt's cards. Left column: cards developed by the Association of German Alienists.

*Source*: Albert Guttstadt, "Die Geisteskranken in den Irrenanstalten während der Zeit von 1852 bis 1871 und ihre Zählung im ganzen Staat am 1. December 1871 nebst Vorschlägen zur Gewinnung einer deutschen Irrenstatistik," *Zeitschrift des königlich-preussischen statistichen Bureaus* 14 (1874).

Weber and Engstrom point out, this description is devoid of both a biographic history and any commentary on the patient's psychological development:[73]

> Illiterate person. Marriage 1845. Husband alcoholic. Gets upset easily, bad conditions. As of March [18]91 irritable. Headache. May: increasing restlessness and confusion, babbles, moans. Severe cyanosis, othematoma on the right. Anxious, unintelligible stupid chattering. Unfriendly, reluctant. Change of mood. Scolds, hits, disoriented. Calms down slowly but not substantially clearer.[74]

This is all quite different from Freud's work during the same period. While Freud got his start in biology, conducting research on the nervous system of marine animals, this work eventually led him to reject a strictly biological and quantitative approach and shift to hypnosis, and then to the talking cure.

## Kraepelin's Psychiatric Textbook

Kraepelin's textbook is not, properly speaking, one book at all. Developed in multiple editions over the course of three decades, the *Lehrbuch* begins from the slim first edition of 1883, which Kraepelin wrote to obtain sufficient income to marry, and extends through the massive eighth edition of 1915, composed at the height of his fame.[75] The contents of the various editions closely track the stages of Kraepelin's career between major research institutions. After returning from Russian Dorpat in 1891, he was appointed to posts at the University of Heidelberg (1891–1903) and then Munich, where he was employed first by Ludwig Maximilian University (1903–1917) and subsequently directed his own private research institute, the German Research Institute for Psychiatry (Deutsche Forschungsanstalt für Psychiatrie, hereafter DFP) between 1917 and his death in 1926. Throughout these several professional moves and during his extensive travels abroad, Kraepelin remained in close touch with Wundt in Leipzig, at least until the latter's death in 1920.

The early editions of his textbook from 1883 through 1893 are at best rough sketches for what was to follow, written by a man new to the academy and only relatively recently in possession of his own psychiatric laboratory. By 1896, however, Kraepelin had been appointed to Heidelberg and given control over a large psychiatric laboratory, which he was able to populate with prestigious colleagues, including Alois Alzheimer (after whom Alzheimer's disease is named), as well as an eighty-bed clinic. The fifth edition of the textbook (1896) is the first to suggest an original argument that later versions would propose in far stronger terms: mental illnesses should be classified according to their outcome over time, not by their symptoms, as virtually all prior psychiatry had assumed and as psychoanalysis would continue to argue. In the preface to the 1896 edition Kraepelin makes clear that a properly clinical psychiatry should be defined by shifting from symptomatology to *time* as the basic metric for disease differentiation:

> The following book represents the most up-to-date version of the final, definitive step from a symptomatic to a clinical approach to mental illness. . . . Overall, the import of external disease symptoms has had to recede in light of this standpoint, which developed according to the genesis, course, and outcome of individual [mental] disturbances. For this reason, all mere classifications of disease according to symptom [*Zustandsbilder*] have disappeared from my morphology. . . . The superiority of the following clinical method

over conventional diagnosis has been substantiated by the certainty with which we are, on the basis of our concept of disease, in a position to predict the future course of mental illnesses.[76]

Whatever symptoms various diseases might happen to share, it was their respective developmental progress that separated them—their "genesis, course and outcome." This meant that even mental illnesses with seemingly identical symptomatology could now be distinguished from one another. Moreover, clinical psychiatry's primary goal suddenly became making predictive assessments. "We are, on the basis of our concept of disease, in a position to predict the future course of mental illnesses," Kraepelin wrote.

While his 1896 textbook proposed a conceptual reorientation of psychiatry toward disease duration, it made little progress practically applying it. The section on "The Forms of Insanity" (*Formen des Irreseins*) in the 1896 edition was indeed organized according to a different distributional principle than earlier editions. It grouped these diseases as subsets of either "Acquired Mental Disturbances" (*Erworbene Geistesstörungen*) or "Mental Disturbances Arising from Pathological Disposition" (*Geistesstörungen aus krankhafter Veranlagung*). It did not, however, create any radically new groupings. As a result, the 1896 edition functionally looked much like the other German classification systems from the 1890s that did not rely on time as a differentiating principle. The appearance of new disease forms had to wait until the groundbreaking sixth edition of the textbook Kraepelin published in 1899.

Kraepelin excitedly prefaced the 1899 edition with the news that he had completely revised his prior understanding of mental disease and had now isolated new forms: "The doctrine about the forms of mental illnesses has been much expanded [in this edition]. . . . In the [section on] clinical groupings, dementia praecox, manic-depressive illness [*manisch-depressive Irresein*], infectious mental illnesses, have been for the most part rewritten, although one will find at numerous other points more or less dramatic changes and additions. Overall, *differential diagnosis* has been examined in detail as much as possible."[77]

In the 1896 textbook, the two main categories ("Acquired Mental Disturbances" or "Mental Disturbances Arising from Pathological Constitution") were etiological, that is, based on the disorder's presumed origin. This etiological account vanished entirely in the textbook of 1899. Kraepelin replaced it with a differential diagnostic system. As the name suggests, differential diagnosis involves finding the best diagnostic match for patient's illness by comparing multiple completing possibilities. This assumed, however, that there *were* other diagnostic options to choose from.

Before Kraepelin's sixth edition of 1899, the German term *die Psychose* (the psychoses) simply meant all mental illnesses lacking an identifiable physical origin.[78] Anything that couldn't be directly traced back to brain disease, brain injury, metabolic disease, infectious illness, intoxication, or pregnancy formed part of this amorphous and mysterious catchall category that was as scientifically inscrutable as it was medically frightening. Kraepelin's breakthrough in the sixth edition was to pair the notion that the psychoses could be meaningfully divided (according to their temporal outcome) with the idea that doing so showed the existence of three separate (differentiable) diseases. These diseases were "dementia praecox," "manic-depressive insanity," and "paranoia."

Psychiatric patients who exhibited mood changes—like depression and mania, as the Wolf-Man's father apparently had—were cases of manic-depressive insanity (*das manisch-depressive Irresein*). They could be expected to recover with time. Patients who hallucinated and exhibited disturbances in reasoning but lacked a significant affective component had what Kraepelin called "dementia praecox" (premature dementia) and would get worse in the long run.[79] Those with paranoia (*die Verrücktheit (Paranoia)*) would experience delusions as well as hallucinations and most likely never get any better. Kraepelin thus identified dementia praecox, manic-depressive insanity, and paranoia as separate forms of psychosis by suggesting their contrary outcomes over time.

The 1899 textbook additionally distinguished between psychoses and *die Neurose* (neuroses), but in a manner utterly unlike Jacques Lacan's psychoanalytic distinction between the two in the mid-twentieth century. In the 1899 textbook, Kraepelin claimed that the psychoses allegedly appeared without warning and—at least in the case of the recurrent manic-depressive insanity—were "totally imperceptible during the period between attacks." The neuroses, on the other hand, were "as a rule, abidingly conspicuous." Like the psychoses, the neuroses also had differential forms: epileptic insanity (*das epileptische Irresein*), hysterical insanity (*das hysterische Irresein*), and traumatic neurosis (*Die Schreckneurose*). Finally, Kraepelin distinguished the psychoses and neuroses from another group he had long referred to as "Psychopathic Conditions (Degeneration Insanity)" (*Die psychopatischen Zustände (Entartungsirresein)*). According to Kraepelin, psychopathic conditions remained unchanged throughout a person's life after appearing "for no reason whatsoever." Psychopathic conditions were not internally differentiable. Instead, their various manifestations either represented an improvement or worsening of the same underlying state. Last, Kraepelin added a new category in 1899 that he called "Insanity Arising from Infection" (*das infectiöse Irresein*), which now preceded insanities respectively connected with fatigue (das *Erschöpfungsirressein*), intoxication (*die Vergiftungen*), and thyroid disturbances (*das thyrogene Irresein*) in his taxonomy.

Overall, Kraepelin's 1899 textbook, published the same year as Freud's *The Interpretation of Dreams*, solidified that the definition and delimitation of mental illnesses was the necessary precondition for any serious medical and scientific investigation of psychopathology. It affirmed that clinical psychiatry was defined by its reliance on a temporally based classification system, not a symptomatically organized one. While Kraepelin acknowledged that he had yet to produce a diagnostic taxonomy as clear-cut or enduring as the Linnaean system in biology, his 1899 textbook confirmed the value of imitating the biological model. Doing so would, allegedly, make psychiatrists less liable to be "swayed by preconceived opinions in the sober process of facts." Presumably, this meant less swayed by philosophical speculation or Griesinger's brain mythology.[80] Since mental illnesses were evidently naturally given forms, orientation toward a biological-style taxonomy also made good sense. At the same time, it meant that grouping mental diseases according to pathological anatomy, etiology (cause), or symptom would hardly do. These organizational approaches would only yield weak classifications in which the categories effectively collapsed into one another, no matter how separate they might seem at first glance. Instead of focusing on unusual outlying cases, psychiatry would do better to identify patterns among groups of similar cases:

> Through the elimination of all cases that do not correspond to the first type [i.e., similar-seeming diseases], we shall for the time be guided by a list of numerous smaller groups that deviate less and less from one another, whose nearer or more distant kinship readily reveals itself through a glance at larger observational series. The fastidious fragmentation of forms [*die gewissenhafte Zersplitterung der Formen*] into the smallest and ostensibly most trivial alterations, which we find today in the theory of muscular atrophy, is thus the indispensable preliminary stage for the extraction of a truly consistent picture of mental illness that corresponds to nature's own [*der Natur entsprechender Krankheitsbilder*].[81]

Only the standardization, discretization, and definition of the smallest basic units of all disease forms, whatever their cause, could produce solid results, minimizing the need for fantastic guessing games.

This is manifestly neither Freud's nor psychoanalysis's approach to diagnosis. Freud never developed a systematic psychiatric classification system, refused to pin down the exact meanings of the clinical terms he did use, and mostly departed from biology and quantification after the "Project for a Scientific Psychology" (itself ambivalently related to these topics). Freud was unconcerned with "fastidious fragmentation" of psychiatric diseases into their possible smallest units, as if they were anatomizable like organs in the body. He focused on language and was explicitly attentive to the problems of translation, as his interactions with the Russian-speaking Wolf-Man show. While Freud did develop a psychoanthropology, this psychoanthropology grew out of the careful study of individual patient case histories, not a mass metrics looking for overall patterns in a large volume of patients.

The clash in his work between the careful interpretive study of individual patient's stories and larger-scale anthropological claims exemplifies the epistemological difficulty produced by what the historian of science John Forrester calls Freud's method of "thinking in cases." Freudian psychoanalysis wasn't intended to be used on a mass scale. It worked best on an individual basis, a point that is supported by Gayatri Spivak's remark (in her writing on Freudian narcissism) that psychoanalysis cannot be usefully deployed as a generalized cultural critique. "Without the risks or responsibilities of transference, at least implicitly diagnostic and taxonomic, ignoring geopolitical and historical detail in the interest of making group behavior intelligible, and not accountable to any mode of verification, the brilliance of psychoanalytic cultural criticism has always left me a bit suspicious," Spivak writes.[82]

As Freud's topographical and structural models of the psyche show, however, Freud was not wholly opposed to psychical differentiation and division. The separation of id, ego, and superego is nothing if not tripartite. At the same time, psychoanalytic investment in careful reading and patient's statements to the clinician lent psychoanalysis a greater internal potential for dealing with cultural, linguistic, regional, and personal specificity (even if that was not how psychoanalysis was consistently historically used). By contrast, Kraepelinian psychiatry was committed to the subject's status as one discrete, average unit among many. Kraepelin regarded each person-unit in terms of their measurable degree of psychical health or illness, framing these categories as transposable from person to person, save in the case of deviant outliers. Language could be set aside in favor of measure and number, which spoke for themselves. This lent his system a degree of universality masked by the seeming specificity of the disease categories.

## Kraepelinian Psychiatry and the People's Mind

To fully understand the psychopolitical nature of Kraepelin's unusual textbook, a few additional details are important. Individual editions of the textbook, especially after 1896, represented Kraepelin's most recent research findings to date, as he chose to publish his laboratory findings within the textbook rather than as separate articles. At least a portion of the work's contemporaneous popularity is thus the result of this unusual decision, which made the textbook more like a compendium of his latest research than an introductory publication for students.

Kraepelin admitted that this arrangement meant few of his findings were peer reviewed. He claimed, however, that the need to make his research immediately available outweighed the import of subjecting his ideas to the time-consuming review process and, potentially (although he did not say as much), to contestation by his peers. This resistance to review reflects both an interest in publication speed and a central trait of Kraepelin. As Felix Plaut, Kraepelin's colleague at the DFP, remarked in his 1927 obituary for Kraepelin, in what was intended as laudatory comment, "The iron self-discipline that Kraepelin imposed upon himself, the willpower he exerted upon himself, prevented catharsis of any kind. He was allowedly an autocrat, who enforced his will in his field."[83] Allegedly a man of few intimate friendships who relished isolation, Kraepelin had, as Plaut put it, no tolerance for dealing with "servile natures."[84]

Beyond the classification system, Kraepelin's textbook is set apart by its sheer length. The various editions expanded dramatically in size over time. While the first edition of 1883 was just shy of four hundred pages, the multivolume eighth edition completed in 1915 ran into the thousands. The vast length tended to prohibit complete translations from appearing in other languages. Instead of reproducing the textbook in full, translators mostly selected portions to work on, chopping off everything they deemed superfluous to their area of clinical focus and national context. This is very much the case with the few partial translations that are available in English (see the appendix to this book) and helps account for the unusual scenario that while Kraepelin's work has been widely influential in the United States, his name remains virtually unknown there.[85] Unlike Freud's broadly circulated and translated writings, it was difficult to obtain Kraepelin's publications in any language after they went out of print in German in the late 1920s. Nothing resembling a "collected works" appeared until the early 2000s, and even then, only in German.[86]

While developing the various editions of his textbook, Kraepelin also began to incorporate images. This was largely at the behest of his publisher, who was concerned that Kraepelin's textbook be competitive with other psychiatric manuals and handbooks of the time, most of which had started to feature photographic or illustrative material.[87] The fifth edition of 1896 is the first to include visual material of any kind. Kraepelin makes a note of the change in his foreword to the work.[88]

Over time, the number and variety of images in the textbook increased. In addition to adding more photographs of patients, more handwriting samples, and more tables and charts, Kraepelin gradually introduced images of patient art, shots from his travels abroad, and pictures of brain tissue preparations. In general, he tended to retain images across the various editions, adding new visual material without removing prior images. His decision not to cut is a testament to how stable he saw his claims as being over time. It also suggests that the new patient photographs in editions after 1896 were taken of patients in the psychiatric clinic at Ludwig Maximillian University in Munich, rather than elsewhere, and are relatively current to the publication date of the associated volume.

The other significant change to the visual contents of the textbook after 1909 is the inclusion of images from the history of psychiatry. Like Johann Christian August Clarus's 1823 medical report on the mental state of the Leipzig murderer Johann Christian Woyzeck in 1823, Kraepelin framed his psychiatric research as part of Enlightenment progress and collective betterment. Carefully selected lithographs of the mentally ill chained to their cell walls, trapped in beds covered by thick metal gratings, locked in impossibly intricate straitjackets, and wearing restrictive wire masks covering their entire head and neck helped Kraepelin document the repressive cruelties of psychiatry's "prescientific" past and show how progressively humane his own approach was by contrast.[89] To bring this important comparative point home, Kraepelin added photographs of pacific-looking patients undergoing treatment at the Munich University clinic. An undated lithograph of "Deckbäder aus alter Zeit" (covered bathtubs from an earlier time), which shows patients locked inside restrictive bath capsules as they are violently sprayed in the face with water by an assistant wielding a kind of garden hose, is followed by photograph of the calm white walls, tiled floors, and visibly uncovered tubs of the *Dauerbäder* at his Munich clinic.[90]

Kraepelin also showcased the modern, humanitarian nature of his clinic by reproducing a carefully labeled diagram of the Munich building's floor plan in editions after 1909, which made the point about the objective and scientific nature of his psychiatric enterprise in spatial terms. A U-shaped peripheral structure, divided into equal wings for male and female patients, joins in the center at two correspondingly gendered examination rooms before jutting out into a large central lecture hall positioned in the middle of the property.[91] The layout of the diagram emphasizes that the presentation of research in the lecture hall that was collected from the "wings" is the clinic's central function.

Psychophysics comes into the textbook in several ways, largely functioning to ensure a new regulatable and measurable picture of popular mental health. Beginning in the textbook of 1896, Kraepelin proposed that psychophysics be used as a medical examination technique to help identify mental illnesses. The psychophysical methods he proposed using were initially limited in scope. By 1899, however, Kraepelin was recommending that possible disturbances of the understanding (*Verstand*, the same term Immanuel Kant used) be psychophysically assessed. He suggested using the Swiss inventor Matthias Hipps's chronoscope to measure the tiny intervals of time it took patients to recognize various words and letters or to make associations, much like in Wundt's experiment with the thought meter. He advocated exploring attention by asking his patients to add various sums with a pen that generated a recordable electrical current after they wrote a horizontal stroke indicating a sum at the bottom of a column of values. He proposed that memory deficiencies be assessed by having patients recite mathematical tables learned in childhood to a regularly chiming bell. He suggested individuals' overall psychic condition be gauged by studying muscular reflexes or by using the ergograph to measure the amount of work done when their muscles contracted.[92]

Kraepelin also began to measure handwriting by using a device of his own invention called the "writing scale." This intricate apparatus was small enough to fit on a desk and, through a system of levers connecting the patient's pencil movements on a special tray to a pressure-sensitive pen set atop a rotating roll of paper, indicated the relative degree of pressure exerted by the writer.[93] By comparing the pressure graphs from different patients who had written the same thing, Kraepelin believed he could show a correlation between the force of writing and different psychiatric illnesses. In figure 2.2, the line labeled with roman numeral I (at the top) serves as the baseline provided by a "healthy" female nurse as she writes the numbers "one" and "ten" on the writing scale. Subsequent graph lines show the result when produced by patients diagnosed with Kraepelin's differential psychopathological categories. Line II below it is from a male manic-depressive patient currently in the "depressive" state. Line III is from a female manic-depressive patient in a manic state. Line IV is from the same female patient in a calm state.[94] The diagram visually indicates that

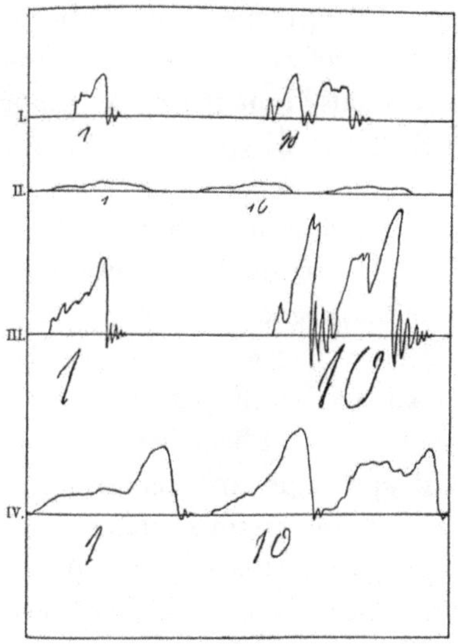


**2.2** Emil Kraepelin, psychophysical graph showing the pressure exerted on a piece of paper by different individuals writing the numbers 1 and 10. Undated book illustration.

*Source*: *Psychiatrie. Ein Lehrbuch für Studierende und Ärzte* II. Band. Klinische Psychiatrie (Leipzig: Verlag von Johann Ambrosius Barth, 1899).

writing pressure increases with the relative degree of mania: the more manic the patient, the more forcefully he or she would supposedly attack the page.

It also shows, however, that the mental health of the nurse is quantifiable: it can be measured and recorded by the writing scale just like the pathologies of Kraepelin's manic-depressive patients. Because the differential diagnostic system focused on the group, moreover, not any one case, the nurse's writing scale line is as much *her* personal line as it is an exemplar of universally generalizable (and measurable) mental health. This is evident in the fact that Kraepelin does not include lines from mentally healthy individuals of other genders or other emotional states. One healthy nurse covers all mentally healthy individuals.

The patient photographs Kraepelin included in the later editions of his textbook function similarly. Beginning in the late 1870s, a number of German psychiatrists claimed that psychopathology was associated with specific types of facial expressions and bodily movements that photographic technology was uniquely equipped to capture. This work carried Johann Kasper Lavater's (1741–1801) physiognomy and Franz Joseph Gall's (1758–1828) phrenology in new directions by suggesting that individual psychopathological states were externally visualizable on the body. The German sexologist Richard von Krafft-Ebing hypothesized in 1879 that using photography to identify psychopathologies would allow "experienced" viewers to make a probable diagnosis based on visual material alone. While Krafft-Ebing largely focused on psychiatric portraiture, Francis Galton (1822–1911), a eugenicist and proponent of scientific racism, came up with the idea of making composite images, in which multiple photographs of individuals from the same group were superimposed to produce a record of the selected type's allegedly most common stigmata. Galton's categories ranged from "Generals" to "Criminals." The German psychiatrist Theodor Ziehen's psychiatric textbook of 1894 explicitly took up the idea that photography contained the key to psychiatric diagnosis. Ziehen included images as part of his diagnostic toolkit.[95]

Kraepelin may have been at the mercy of his publisher in adding images to the 1896 edition of his textbook, but the patient photographs on display there clearly serve an important role in the book beyond the decorative. They operate as a psychophysical apparatus that captures subjects' pathology not through the measurement of reaction time, attention, or memory but in terms of a measure of light. The plates created by Kraepelin's assistants at Heidelberg documented pathological visual evidence that Kraepelin taxonomically analyzed in terms of his differential diagnostic scheme, thereby also rendering such images part of a predictive system that assured the quantitative metrics of both psychopathology and health, as in the case of the writing scale's lines. The photographs Kraepelin includes hence don't show individuals with a disease but provide a visual average of different psychopathologies. In fact,

2.3 Emil Kraepelin, "Manische Kranke" ([Patients with] manic-depressive insanity). Undated book illustration.

*Source*: *Psychiatrie. Ein Lehrbuch für Studierende und Ärzte* II. Band. Klinische Psychiatrie (Leipzig: Verlag von Johann Ambrosius Barth, 1899).

Kraepelin's photographs are functionally little different from Galton's composite images in this regard. Whereas Galton insisted on stacking faces atop one another, Kraepelin and his assistants used a far less technically demanding process to accomplish the same thing: they simply gathered multiple individuals from the same psychopathological group and arranged them next to one another in a single shot. Like Kraepelin's diagnoses, these images highlight the equivalency and interchangeability of different patients with the same disease.

That these photographs are images of diseases, not people, becomes abundantly clear when one considers how few individual portraits appear in the 1896 textbook or in subsequent editions. Since the *Iconographie photographique de la Salpêtrière* was first published in the 1870s, it was not unusual to see photographs accompanying psychiatric texts as illustrations of mental conditions. In the *Iconographie*, as in Krafft-Ebing's work and that of Theodor Ziehen, however, the images are of one person and might be mistaken at first glance for portraits. These authors may be show the same individual in a number of different states over time, but, with remarkable consistency, they tend to depict one person. Not so in Kraepelin's 1896 textbook, in which virtually every photograph is of a group and labeled accordingly: *Kataonikergruppe* (Catatonic Group), *Paralytikergruppe* (Paralytic Group), *Manische Kranke* (Manic Patients), etc. The decision to focus on groups and label them accordingly helps show how Kraepelin's classification was specifically designed to produce a collective portrait of mental illness and mental health, not one that dealt with individual cases.

## The Whale and the Polar Bear: Psychoanalysis and Clinical Psychiatry

"The whale and the polar bear, it has been said, cannot wage war on each other, for since each is confined to his own element, they cannot meet," Freud writes at one point in "From the History of an Infantile Neurosis."[96] The comment very accurately characterizes the relationship between Freudian psychoanalysis and Kraepelinian clinical psychiatry. For Freud, individual patients did not illustrate preestablished types but represented their own irreducible interpretive contexts (diagnosis taking a back seat to narrative). The case histories in *On Hysteria*, for example, are no more intended to "prove" that hysteria per se exists than is "From the History of an Infantile Neurosis" aimed at defending the existence of obsessional neurosis. If anything, Freud's remarks on the Wolf-Man are focused on infantile sexuality. His diagnostic ambivalence is clear. "From the History" does not actually allot his patient a diagnosis at all. It merely characterizes the Wolf-Man's current condition as a "defect" left behind by the spontaneous resolution of the earlier obsessional neurosis. Freud's work thus remains focused on illuminating the broader psychical mechanisms underlying the only more superficially important diagnostic label.[97]

Freud also remains concerned with symptoms, manifested on the level of language, in a way that Kraepelin does not. Freud's qualitative, language-based work prioritized the specificity of individual patients, each of whom might possess a unique dream grammar and so too a unique set of associative psychic linkages that would have to be disentangled during analysis. This is clear in how Freud reads the Wolf-Man's experiences and the stories associated with it.

"From the History of an Infantile Neurosis" (1918) documents a fragment of the Wolf-Man's treatment connected to the latter's childhood development of a fear of animals. The case famously pivots around the patient's childhood dream of several threatening wolves perched in a tree. In the dream, these wolves all have prominent bushy tails. In German, the term for tail, *Schwanz*, may also refer to the penis. Freud concludes that his patient's early fear of animals was in some way related to a fear of castration. The Wolf-Man had remarked in analysis that the dream reminded him of a story he had once heard from his grandfather about a tailor (*der Schneider*, lit. a cutter) who was startled by a wolf suddenly leaping through the window of his workshop. In the grandfather's story, the tailor caches the animal by its tail and pulls it off. The tailor later encounters a pack of wolves in the forest that includes this tail-less intruder. The tailor climbs up a nearby tree to escape, but the wolves climb on top of one another to reach him. In the story, the tailor saves himself by calling out "Catch the gray one by his tail [*Schwanz*]!" This frightens the tail-less wolf at the base of the stack, who runs away, causing the others atop him to tumble down as well.

Freud reads the grandfather's story as illuminating the significance of the bushy tails in the Wolf-Man's childhood dream. These dream wolves are threatening both because they are wolves and because they intimate the tailor's cut. This leads Freud to propose that his patient's fear of castration is based on an unconscious connection between the grandfather's story and something the Wolf-Man likely saw in his childhood. Freud speculates that the Wolf-Man may have witnessed a scene between his parents in which "the tail" seemed to disappear. Perhaps, while he was sleeping in his parents' bedroom, he had awoken to find his parents in a position where "he was able to see his mother's genitals as well as his father's organ." Perhaps he interpreted his father's actions as aggressive but also experienced profound fear at the time because his father's penis seemed to disappear, as if it had been cut off. Perhaps the unconscious recollection of this "primal scene" (*Urszene*) later generated his anxiety-provoking dream about the wolves.

Freud remains exceptionally hesitant about whether this primal scene truly happened. His analysis is speculative, designed to establish a fiction that is sufficiently compelling to take on the status of reality by explaining an unknown, and unknowable, primary truth. By contrast, Kraepelin's diagnosis of "manic-depressive insanity" eliminates speculation (now framed as part of a retrograde philosophical tradition at odds with verifiable scientific psychiatry), removes the need to listen to the Wolf-Man, and casts aside emphasis on interpretive analysis of language-based constructions. Kraepelin's diagnosis of the Wolf-Man as manic-depressive is based on the patient's heredity (his father's manic depression) and Kraepelin's observations of him, minus any attention to "unintelligible stupid chattering." This is presumably why the Wolf-Man's observation to Kraepelin that his mood swings could be related to his romantic infatuation with Therese made little difference. "[Professor Kraepelin] seemed fully convinced that the sudden and violent changes in my mood were proof of the correctness of his diagnosis," the Wolf-Man writes. No storytelling by patient, or grandfather, or psychiatrist is necessary whatsoever.

That Kraepelin's diagnosis also had a certain arbitrary character became clear through the scenario that unfolded when the Wolf-Man refused to stay at the sanatorium for the duration Kraepelin had prescribed. When he apologetically returned to plead for Kraepelin's help in 1908, Kraepelin coolly turned him down by suggesting that he was "mistaken." Although the Wolf-Man was probably not aware of it, Kraepelin's comment may have been intended to imply that the Wolf-Man was not treatable at all, given that he actually had a psychosis with an unfavorable outcome, like dementia praecox or paranoia. If so, asserting that the original (more favorable) diagnosis of manic depression was wrong allowed Kraepelin to simultaneously punish the Wolf-Man for his noncompliance, suggest his future medical decline, and refuse him further help all on objective grounds.

## Modernist Literature as a Simulacrum of Reason

Recognizing the key epistemological differences between psychoanalysis and Kraepelinian psychiatry is essential to understanding how each system respectively uses diagnostic terminology. Doing so is particularly important because it complicates a dominant and enduring perspective in secondary criticism about modernist literature: the argument that modernist literary works' sonic, semiotic, and graphic experimentation approximates a non-normative and liberatory madness. I explore this position by reconsidering Friedrich Kittler's argument that "literature is a simulacrum of madness" in his work *Discourse Networks 1800/1900* (*Aufschreibesysteme 1800/1900*). [98]

Kittler's basic claim in *Discourse Networks* is that semiotic systems underwent a radical shift between the nineteenth and twentieth centuries. The discourse network (Kittler's term for the circuit connecting literature's production, dissemination, and consumption) of the 1800s, he claims, assumed all texts contained meaning. These texts merely needed to be deciphered by sufficiently educated readers. "In the writing system of 1800 . . . nonsense letter and word permutations were not even worthy of being ignored."[99] Bursts of seeming inarticulacy in literary works—the "oh" of E. T. A. Hoffman's Olympia in "The Sandman" (1817) or the "ach" in Friedrich Schiller's poem "Longing" (1802)—were never truly meaningless. These expostulations instead represented a transcendental language of Nature, love, or woman (all synonymous with one another in the discourse network of 1800).[100] By 1900, Kittler claims, the rise of mechanized information transfer replaced human educators training their pupils to read for meaning with depersonalized, inhuman, mechanical messaging channels: telegraphs, typewriters, the radio, the gramophone. Now, the very movement of information made noise. Amid this clacking and jangling it became clear that, unlike in the discourse network of 1800, sound and sense need not be correlated.

As Kittler has it, the act of writing around 1900 shifted from the decryption of encoded sense to a "flight of ideas" (*Ideenflucht*) inspired by so-called random generators (*Zufallsgeneratoren*), of which his premiere example is psychophysics. He turns to the psychophysical research conducted by one of Gustav Fechner's students, Hermann Ebbinghaus (1850–1909). Kittler argues that Ebbinghaus's experiments from the early 1880s, which used actual words as well as combinations of nonsense syllables to evaluate to the human capacity for memory, created a forum in which the entire goal was making meaningless sounds. Kittler concludes that psychophysics therefore served as a "treasury of the signifier" in which senseless sounds based entirely on "randomness and combinatorics" could be developed.[101] Literary modernist work circa 1900 simply took up these nonsense sounds. "The victory of psychophysics is a paradigm shift. . . . Disturbances in speech ceased to converge in the beautiful wordlessness of the romantic soul." In the discourse network of 1800, Olympia's "oh" had been meaningful. In the discourse network of 1900, it was one more empty phoneme.

In Kittler's assessment, modernism's nonsensical phonetic combinations, analphabetism, wild graphic experimentation, and constellations of unpronounceable punctuation all build on the new free movement of signifiers. This flow was made possible by psychophysical experiments (like Ebbinghaus's) that put meaningless words into human mouths after mechanized information transfer had made a nonsense language possible in the first place. Kittler uses this premise to argue that literary writing circa 1900 is a "simulacrum of madness [*Wahnsinn*]." "The writer does not invent, but only simulates an insane person who in turn has not invented the rhymes, but rather . . . 'had to construct verses without any regard for the nonsense that resulted.'"[102] Writers simply approximated the jumbled babble that psychophysically inclined psychiatrists forced their patients to produce again and again. "The former [psychiatrists] compile and order whole archives of psychotic speech errors, which are then at the disposal of the latter [writers]. . . . Psychiatric discourse provides monographs on psychotic neologisms, rhyme manias, and special languages to which writers, seeking information from competent sources, need only help themselves."[103]

Heinrich Ball's "Seven Schizophrenic Sonnets," Georg Heym's "The Madman," Rainer Maria Rilke's "The Idiot's Song," and Paul Adler's "Song of a Crazy Woman" (and other similarly titled works) are, by this logic, merely polished versions of the "rough drafts" that psychiatric archives supplied.[104] Indeed, Kittler goes further, arguing that psychiatry set up a system of random nonsense generators producing a meaningless language that psychoanalysis then assiduously documented and interpreted ad nauseam.[105] Freud, equipped with his notepad, had only to decompose the Wolf-Man's somnambulant word "*Espe*" into the initials of the patient's first and last name (S. P., for Sergey Pankeyev), then "*Wespe*" (the German term for wasp), then the sexualized opening and closing of a butterfly's wings, and so on.

The problem, however, is that this perspective presents psychophysics as a semiotically liberatory exercise, overlooking its complicity with the Enlightenment system of rationalization committed to gluing sound and sense together. This oversight is reflected in how much Kittler has to distort psychophysics to sustain his claim. He must assume that linguistically oriented psychophysical experiments *were* the field, not just one part of it. A survey of Fechner's *Elements* and Kraepelin's psychophysics shows otherwise. Kittler thus either misses or disregards that there were just as many—if not more—psychophysical studies that wordlessly assessed the duration of sleep, measured the threshold value for recognition of light, explored the influence of coffee and tea on simple psychic processes, and looked at aural sensitivity to changes in sound volume as there were those that tested random syllabic combinatorics. He misses or minimizes the overall impact produced by a new quantifiable understanding of the psyche.

Strikingly, then, the discourse network of 1800 and the discourse network of 1900 turn out not to be so different after all. In both cases, literature passively reflects the real contents of contemporaneous scientific research. Circa 1800, the idée fixe and theories about intoxication rule the day, which are narratively repurposed by writers like E. T. A. Hoffman. Circa 1900, madness is linked to phonetic rubbish that has been culled from the psychological laboratory, which creative writers repurpose to striking aesthetic effect. This is the clinico-critical reading paradigm par excellence. Writers in this argument "seek information from competent sources" but apparently do not question these sources' claims or modify them in any form, as a counterdisciplinary approach would suggest. Creative texts remain little more than the worked-up versions of more primary scientific rough drafts. Aesthetic objects are recorder-respondents, not generators.

While Fechner and his followers arguably did create a new reserve of nonsense language, they did so in the context of a more fundamental transformation in how psychic phenomena were understood. Kittler's lack of attention to the extent to which German psychiatry was deeply fragmented during this period, and indeed divided among Griesinger's pathological-anatomical approach, Fechnerian psychophysics, and Freudian psychoanalysis, leads him to cite a monolith of "psychiatrists" without pausing to query which psychiatrists these were. This oversight, however, makes it look as though psychophysics, clinical psychiatry, and Freudian psychoanalysis had the same relationship to language and were not characterized by a significant epistemological

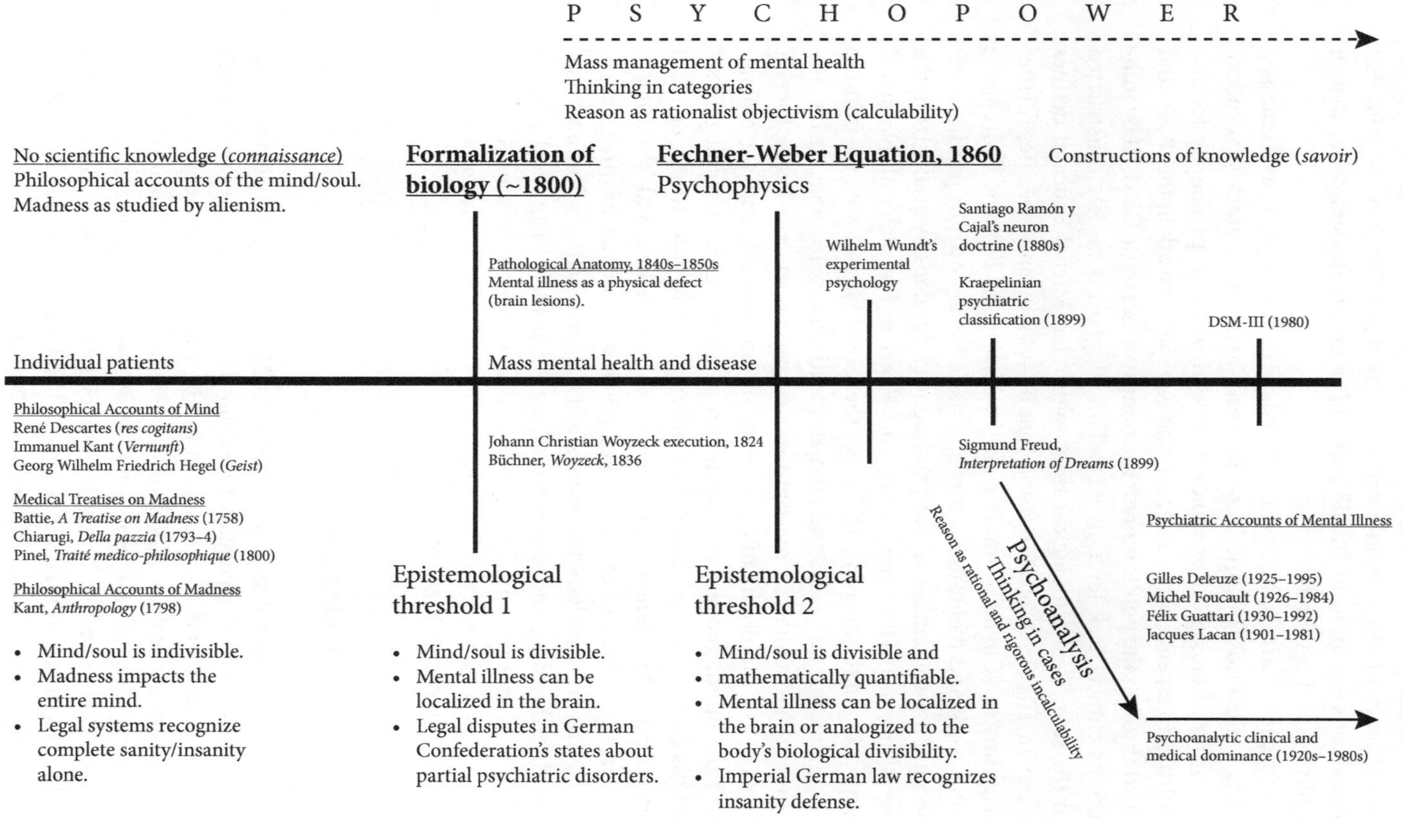


**2.4** Psychopower's development from the 1750s to the present.

*Source*: Author's diagram. Adapted from Michel Foucault's 1969 diagrams showing the epistemological threshold between individuals and species in biology. Michel Foucault and Lynne Huffer, "Cuvier's Situation in the History of Biology," *Foucault Studies* 22 (January 2017): 208–37.

divergence on this point. The end result is a conclusion about modernist literary works that has been as highly persuasive as it is difficult to sustain: that psychoanalysis's attention to "mad" patients' language is identical to that in psychophysics and psychiatry.[106]

Figure 2.4 summarizes the developmental arc of psychopower as it emerged beginning in the 1830s (Büchner's era, Johann Christian Woyzeck's execution, the beginning of biological psychiatry), formalized with psychophysics and the resulting divergence between Freud and Kraepelin's work in the 1890s, and continued through the publication of the nonpsychoanalytic DSM-III by Robert Spitzer's clinical task force in 1980. This diagram is loosely constructed around the set of "epistemological thresholds" that Michel Foucault defines for biology in *The Order of Things* and that he subsequently specifies further and diagrams in "Cuvier's Situation in the History of Biology."[107] I choose Foucault's work and diagrams as a rough basis for my own of psychopower here because my contention is that psychopower develops by analogizing the immaterial mind of Descartes, Kant, and Hegel to the material, biological body beginning in the opening decades of the 1800s. This allowed the mind to become (1) divisible into parts and (2) mathematically measurable. As the diagram shows, psychoanalysis does not escape psychopower: whence Freud's own focus on the divisibility of the psyche, his long struggle with the biologization of the mind, and the ethnocentrism of his psychoanthropology. Psychoanalysis does, however, constitute a different pathway within it: one that stresses the individual, language, interpretation, storytelling, and "thinking in cases" (Forrester), instead of an average portrait of mental health given in quantitative terms. I include the names of Deleuze, Guattari, Foucault, and Lacan within this diagram to make the point that their theoretical systems developed during an era in which psychoanalysis was a dominant clinical practice and so were naturally less attentive to the issues of psychopathological semiosis and nominalization.

## The Wolf-Man's Magic Name

Among the many unusual features of the Wolf-Man's case history is a peculiar discrepancy that Freud struggles to explain. The text of the Wolf-Man's famous dream as Freud recorded it in his 1910 analysis includes a specific statement about the wolves. "*Suddenly the window opened of its own accord, and I was terrified to see that some white wolves were sitting on the big walnut tree in front of the window. There were six or seven of them.*"[108] Six or seven wolves. In "History of an Infantile Neurosis," Freud also reproduces the Wolf-Man's drawing of this childhood dream scene as he recollected it as an adult. The Wolf-Man's drawing, however, shows only five wolves. His oil painting of

**Figure 2.5** The Wolf-Man (Sergey Pankeyev), drawing made during analysis with Sigmund Freud between 1910 and 1914. Undated journal article illustration.

*Source*: Published in Sigmund Freud, "From the History of an Infantile Neurosis" (1918).

this same dream, from 1964 (signed with his Freudian pseudonym *Wolfsmann*) repeats the gesture. There too, only five wolves.

This inconsistency is remarkable because the Wolf-Man makes a point in his autobiography of his own mathematical proficiency from an early age.[109] He notes that his mathematical talents led him to pursue a joint specialization in economics and statistics in law school.[110] The entire autobiography is written with a great deal of precision. The presence of "six or seven" wolves in the text of the dream and only five wolves in his subsequent illustrations deserves attention.

Like the diagnostic ambiguities in Büchner's *Woyzeck*, I believe it makes sense to read it as an ambiguity. This is different from (but not incompatible with) Freud's approach in the 1918 case history, which explains the five wolves by linking them to the time of 5 PM, at which hour the Wolf-Man may have witnessed his parents' intercourse as a child, in what Freud calls the primal scene. Freud also connects the five wolves in the 1918 case history to the Roman numeral V, based on the fact that in analysis the Wolf-Man had described this Roman numeral as reminding him of a woman opening her legs.

The inconsistency between the Wolf-Man's statement about the dream and his illustrations of it also has the effect, however, of contesting Kraepelinian psychiatry's calculable logic. It makes a point about the relative futility of exact enumeration, producing a precise imprecision that is similar in nature to Büchner's quasi-numerical descriptions in Woyzeck and his "20th of January," no particular year, to which Paul Celan attends. The Wolf-Man subtly comments on the epistemological limits of calculability. His consistent portrayal of only five wolves thereby also subtly endorses the Freudian psychoanalytic model, not the Kraepelinian psychiatric model, with its mental measurement and quantifiably specific clinical diagnosis.

I cannot help but imagine this is linked to the Wolf-Man's selection of the name *Wolfsmann* for himself. As a name, *Wolfsmann* plays out the psychoanalytic relationship to semiosis by asking the reader to interpret it. It makes the case that in a psychoanalytic context, attention to meaning, language, and interpretation are more important than reliance on standardized clinical definitions derived from numerical values. The painting with five wolves can perhaps only be signed by the *Wolfsmann*, as the numerical discrepancy the painting captures and the name *Wolfsmann* turn out to be synonymous.

Rather remarkably, the Wolf-Man's chosen name also linguistically performs its own incalculability. Török and Abraham take the novel of approach in *The Wolf-Man's Magic Word* of reading both Freud's case history and the contents of the Wolf-Man's later analyses by attending to his multilingual background. The Wolf-Man spoke English, French, German, and Russian. Reflecting on his multilingualism, Török and Abraham propose decoding his statements in analysis by moving freely between these languages, on the assumption that the Wolf-Man would psychically have done so himself. The "magic" to which the book's title *The Wolf-Man's Magic Word* refers is Török and Abraham's discovery, upon adopting this procedure of psychical translation, that "certain words [in the Wolf-Man's vocabulary] suffered an extraordinary exclusion and this same exclusion seemed to confer on them a genuinely magic power."[111] Nevertheless, Török and Abraham exclude the Wolf-Man's chosen name ("Wolf-Man") from the procedure, seeing that name as an identification with and indeed expression of his love for Freud.[112] They instead identify him through the psychical name he may have given himself, Stanko. The decision not to include the name *Wolfsmann*, however, has the effect of suggesting this name's own magic power. Reading with and against *The Wolf-Man's Magic Word*, I will write this name's multilingual possibilities here, in the form of an equation.

*Wolfsmann* (German) = Wolf-Man (English)
*der Wolf* (German) = *Volk* (*волк*, Russian)
*Volk* (*волк*, Russian) = *das Volk* (the people, German)

---

*Volksmann* = the people-person

This exercise speaks to the Wolf-Man's insistence—though how conscious is impossible to say—on his incalculability in the face of the Kraepelinian law of number. It also sheds light on Freud's inclusion, in a footnote he added in 1923, of a timeline of the important dates in the Wolf-Man's case history. This long footnote is full of numbers and seeming precisions: "1½ years old: Malaria. Observation of his parents copulating . . . ," "2½: Screen memory of his parents' departure with his sister . . . ," "4: The wolf dream . . . ," and so on.[113] This clinical timeline is nevertheless exceptionally strange insofar as it lists a set of dates in a narrative that is itself entirely speculative. Freud is ambivalent about whether the primal scene "happened" exactly the way he tells it in the case history or if it is simply a placeholder for a different series of events that nevertheless had an equivalent outcome. Just as in Büchner's *Woyzeck*, these are dates and precisions within a fiction, which means that they cannot "count" in the usual way. There is something in this about the calculability of the psychoanalytic *Urszene*. I am tempted to say it is the primal scene, but not the first.

# CHAPTER 3

# SCHREBER'S LAW

## Psychotic, Reading

*What's striking is that Schreber is a disciple of the* Aufklärung *[Enlightenment], he's even one of its last representatives.*

—Jacques Lacan

*He who in Kraepelin's sense . . . understands "sound experience" [*gesunder Erfahrung*] simply as the denial of everything supersensory, would in my opinion lay himself open to the reproach of allowing himself to be led only by the shallow "rationalistic ideas" of the period of Enlightenment [*rationalistischen Vorstellungen der Aufklärungsperiode*] of the 18th century, which after all are mostly considered to have been superseded, particularly by theologians and philosophers, and also in science.*

—Daniel Paul Schreber

The medical case history of Daniel Paul Schreber, a German jurist who chronicled his psychiatric breakdown in a 1903 autobiography entitled *Denkwürdigkeiten eines Nervenkranken* (translated as *Memoirs of My Nervous Illness*), is often told as a story of paternity. Both Sigmund Freud and Jacques Lacan focus on the role of the father in their respective readings of the Schreber case.[1] The father is also key to the interpretation put forward by the American psychiatrist Mortiz Schatzman, if for reasons different from Freud's and Lacan's.[2] Similarly, appraisals stressing the imperial context in which Schreber wrote his memoirs point out that Schreber was a good son of Otto von Bismarck's German Empire. He even held a prominent position in its court system. Schreber's mother is equally important to his famous case, however. Schreber is linked through his mother to the trial and execution of Johann Christian Woyzeck in 1824 and so too to psychopower, although that is not the only connection. Attention to the maternal line nuances the portrait of Schreber as a verbose first-person chronicler giving voice to psychosis and does so by transforming his relationship to the legacy of Enlightenment.

Schreber's maternal grandfather was involved in his capacity as professor of medicine in the Leipzig trial and execution of Johann Christian Woyzeck that inspired the German writer Georg Büchner's play *Woyzeck*. This maternal grandfather, Wilhelm Andreas Haase (1784–1837), served on the medical faculty at Leipzig University that enabled Woyzeck's death sentence by affirming the medical findings of the Leipzig medical examiner for the court.[3] The medical faculty's confirmation of Clarus's report was one of the last steps to be completed before Woyzeck's execution could take place and hence one of the last points at which the use of capital punishment could have been averted. It was not. Daniel Paul Schreber's maternal grandfather played a key role in ensuring that Johann Christian Woyzeck was beheaded. He did so in the service of the same Saxon legal system in which Schreber himself—Schreber, who was born and raised in the city in which Woyzeck was executed, medically treated by faculty in the same university that condemned Woyzeck to death—would serve as a prominent judge.

I engage Schreber's case through the lens of psychopower by exploring its matrilineal link to the Woyzeck trial. The 1823 trial raised a question about how to legally define mental illness that returns in Daniel Paul Schreber's case. Schreber was institutionalized against his will and placed under legal guardianship in 1894 because the provisions in the civil code of the newly unified German Empire made it possible to deem him legally incapable of reason on the grounds that he possessed a mental illness. The legal problem of how to define mental illness at the time, however, caused Schreber to turn to Emil Kraepelin's psychiatric textbooks in his clinical memoirs. It is also reflected in Walter Benjamin's discussion of Schreber's text. The chapter reads Schreber's clinical memoirs in dialogue with Kraepelin's and Benjamin's work to explore how a quantifiable portrait of in/sanity became part of imperial Germany's civil code.[4] While Schreber's text has been the subject of extensive discussion in both legal and psychoanalytic circles, I show that his book's reliance on Emil Kraepelin's clinical psychiatry interfaced with changes in imperial Germany's civil law.[5] These changes were as much related to a new definition of citizenship as they were to the gendering thereof.

The manner in which Schreber diagnosis himself, relying on Kraepelin's differential diagnostic system, complicates the prevailing interpretation of Schreber as psychotic. This is the medical term that was used to justify his forced institutionalization in the 1890s and remains the basis for most scholastic interpretations today. Schreber, however, believed he was suffering from a nervous illness, not a mental illness (of which psychosis was considered a part), and used that distinction as the basis for his legal appeal and eventual release. Schreber's self-diagnosis reframes the place of first-person speech in modernism's "mad" clinical memoirs, which are often understood as giving voice to mental illness and to psychosis in particular. Schreber's engagement with Kraepelin instead indicates his status caught between a law-like psychiatric project of Enlightenment rationalization committed to rigorous order (and semiosis) and a psychoanalytic fall out of representation (and symbolization) and into the Real. This dilemma is neither limited to Schreber nor his era.

## Le nom de la mère

Return to Leipzig. The medical case history of Daniel Paul Schreber (1842–1911), who was born and educated in that city, has often been told as the story of Schreber's fathers. There is the Leipzig neuroanatomist Paul Emil Flechsig (1847–1929), Schreber's first psychiatrist. Professor Flechsig initially regarded his patient's illness as a case of hypochondria, based on the presence of "persecutionary ideas," Schreber's extreme sensitivity to light and noise, and his auditory and visual hallucinations.[6] Several decades after Flechsig treated Schreber, Sigmund Freud reached a very different conclusion based on his reading of Schreber's clinical memoirs. Freud, who never met Schreber in person, instead interpreted Schreber's mental experiences as the product of a father complex linked to Schreber's unacceptable homosexual desire for this first psychiatrist.

Freud's 1911 account, "Psychoanalytic Notes on an Autobiographical Account of Paranoia (Dementia Paranoides)," characterizes Schreber as a case of "paranoia (dementia paranoides)." The case history concludes with an extensive diagnostic discussion of "The Mechanism of Paranoia." Freud argues that Schreber's paranoia developed from the patient's homosexual desire for Flechsig, which took the form of a delusion of persecution because impermissible. The "delusional" system Schreber describes in his *Denkwürdigkeiten*, Freud argues, is the record of the patient's attempt to reconstruct his internal world after Flechsig set off the psychical conflict that triggered Schreber's paranoid persecution.

Jacques Lacan developed Freud's work on the Schreber case into his concept of the *Nom-du-Père* (Name of the Father). Lacan expands Freud's reading of Schreber in his 1955–1956 seminar *The Psychoses.* Lacan contends that Schreber's inability to produce children and his election to a prominent position in the Saxon court system led the judge to experience a crisis in paternal symbolization. Lacan uses the Schreber case to formulate a psychoanalytic distinction between the neuroses and the psychoses (Lacan's is different from Kraepelin's division of the psychoses in 1899, as well as from the DSM's understanding of schizoaffective disorders). In Lacan's account, the neuroses are a product of the subject's relationship to an ego ideal, or imago, toward which the subject is always striving in what Lacan calls the imaginary order. The psychoses, by contrast, develop out of a rupture in the symbolic order, where Lacan states signification takes place. Psychosis involves the loss of the master signifier stabilizing meaning in the symbolic order. Lacan names this master signifier the *Nom-du-Père* (the Name of the Father) to signal its powerful role in making signification possible. Schreber's infertility and his discovery of the emptiness of the law, Lacan argues, caused the childless judge to question the very meaning of paternity and thereby fall out of the symbolic order and into the nonrepresentational space of the Real.

Beyond Flechsig the symbolic father, however, there is also Schreber's biological father, Daniel Gottlob Mortiz Schreber (1808–1861), a Leipzig University professor and specialist in children's health. In the 1970s, the American psychiatrist Mortiz Schatzman controversially contended, against the then dominant psychoanalytic reading, that Schreber's illness was correlated with the orthopedic restraints that Moritz Schreber professionally recommended for children. Schatzman interpreted the elder Schreber's inventions as a form of "household totalitarianism" and "poisonous pedagogy" that generated the younger Schreber's symptoms in the long term. His assessment connects with positions about Schreber's case advanced in political philosophy, which frame Schreber as a bellwether of fascist and Stalinist totalitarian power and the rise of antisemitism in Hitler's Germany.[7]

Finally, as Eric Santner has indicated, Daniel Paul Schreber was the child of Otto von Bismarck's imperial Germany.[8] Schreber studied law at Leipzig University, where he was an active participant in student debate and known for his support of pro-Bismarck politics. He then served among the jurists assembled in Berlin during the 1870s to codify the laws of the German Empire and even unsuccessfully ran for election to the Reichstag in 1882 on the conservative, pro-Bismarck National Liberal Party ticket. (Schreber lost in a landslide to the Communist Party candidate.) Until 1893, he worked for the German Empire as a judge for the Supreme Court of Appeals of the Kingdom of Saxony in Dresden. Even after his tenure as *Senatspräsident* on the Saxon Supreme Court was cut short by his illness, Schreber continued to identify with his professional title. The 1903 clinical memoirs are written by no less than "Daniel Paul Schreber, *Doctor juris*, retired Presiding Judge of the Dresden Appellate

Court" (*Dr. jur. Daniel Paul Schreber, Senatspräsident beim Kgl. Oberladesgericht Dresden a.D.*).

Amid these multiple paternities, Schreber's maternal lineage is less well known. Schreber's biological father died prematurely in 1861, from a fall from a ladder, when Schreber was in his late teens. Schreber's mother, Louise Henriette Pauline Haase, lived into her nineties and nearly outlived Schreber. She was, by all accounts, the force that held the large family of five children together after her husband's early demise. Schreber remained close with his mother throughout his life. Louise was the daughter of Wilhelm Andreas Haase (1784–1837), a professor of medicine and pharmacology at the University of Leipzig. In 1823, Haase was part of the medical faculty at the University of Leipzig summoned to review the case of the accused murderer Johann Christian Woyzeck.[9]

The Leipzig University medical faculty had been asked by the Saxon criminal court to provide a professional opinion on the controversial forensic psychiatric report about Woyzeck produced by Leipzig's state medical examiner, Johann Christian Clarus.[10] Wilhelm Andreas Haase's name appears as one of the four signatories of the university proceedings that confirmed Clarus's findings.[11] In deeming the accused sane, Clarus, Haase, and the medical faculty condemned Woyzeck to death and contributed to the tense contemporaneous debates about the insanity defense within the German Confederation. Legal questions about the insanity defense would later be resolved both by the German Empire's criminal code and the *Bürgerliches Gesetzbuch* (BGB). Daniel Paul Schreber's maternal grandfather thus helped ensure Johann Christian Woyzeck's execution and himself formed a part of the medical establishment linked to an early, contentious iteration of the insanity defense in the German Confederation.

Wilhelm Andreas Haase died before Schreber was born. The direct family connection, however, combined with Schreber's childhood in Leipzig, education at Leipzig University, and his own father's work as a medical doctor there, means that Schreber would almost certainly have been aware of Johann Christian Woyzeck's case. The fact that Schreber was employed in the Saxon court system that condemned Woyzeck and underwent psychiatric treatment in the Leipzig University medical system psychiatrically responsible for Woyzeck's demise makes this near certainty something more. If Schreber knew about the Woyzeck case, he was likely not only familiar with it but understood it in some detail.

Attention to *le nom de la mère*, the mother's name, "Haase," which joins Schreber to the legal, psychiatric, and imperial lineage of the Woyzeck case, supplements the psychoanalytic interpretation of Schreber as psychotic by virtue of his connection to the *nom-du-père*. As in the case of Büchner's *Woyzeck*, it destabilizes the understanding of Schreber's text as either the first-person account of psychoanalytic psychosis or a case of DSM-style schizophrenia. Indeed, Schreber did not see himself as psychotic. This is evident even in the title of his memoirs: *Memoirs of My Nervous Illness* (*Denkwürdigkeiten eines Nervenkranken*). Schreber clearly specifies he has a nervous illness (he is *nervenkrank*) and not a mental illness (*Geisteskrankheit*). The self-diagnosis is significant psychiatrically and legally. If Schreber was nervously ill, not mentally ill, he was exempt from the German civil code's definition of legal incompetency (the basis for his forced institutionalization). The BGB required the individual in question be mentally ill to merit guardianship.

Emil Kraepelin's psychiatric textbooks helped Schreber make this key point that he had a nervous illness and not a mental illness. Unlike in the Wolf-Man's case, Kraepelinian classification assisted the incarcerated jurist. Indeed, Schreber embraced Kraepelin's clinical diagnoses. Structurally similar to Kraepelin's textbook (not only his psychiatrist Paul Emil Flechsig's), the clinical memoirs are also the site of Schreber's struggle to carve out a scientific space that is eccentric to the Enlightenment's rationalist tradition and thereby forge a new relationship to the *nomos* and the law. This is an important feature of Walter Benjamin's reading of the Schreber case in 1928, which introduces the complications of defining *Geisteskrankheit* as this key philosopher of the Frankfurt School understood them.

## Walter Benjamin's Books by the Mentally Ill

The German philosopher Walter Benjamin, who had already written on the topic of the law when he composed a short essay on Schreber's *Memoirs* in 1928, notes Schreber's complex relationship to psychiatric classification in his reflections on the book. In Benjamin's essay "Books by the Mentally Ill. From my Collection" (*Bücher von Geisteskranken. Aus meiner Sammlung*), he describes first stumbling upon a copy of Schreber's *Memoirs* in an antiquarian bookshop in Bern.[12] He states that he was immediately captivated by the work, as many readers have continued to be in the century since its publication. The *Memoirs* offers an elaborate first-person account of Schreber's allegedly delusional system as it developed between his initial breakdown in 1893 and his litigiously embattled release from care in 1902. Benjamin observes, however, that in purchasing the book he inadvertently contributed to a trove of genre-defying volumes growing on the shelves of his home library. The presence of this cluster of unclassifiable volumes became evident to Benjamin when he tried organizing his book collection.

At least initially, the heterogeneous volumes seemed to be connected to one another by their owner's inability to part with them or shelve them elsewhere. Additional consideration, however, revealed a rough coherence. Benjamin claimed that all were "writings by the mentally ill" (*Bücher von Geisteskranken*). This classification is more than a little sardonic on his part. This new section of Benjamin's home library included Hans Blüher's *Heroic Ballad of Jesus of Nazareth* (published in 1922 and valuable for its "contribution to the pathology of anti-Semitic resentment"); Carl Friedrich Schmidt's *The Elements and Laws of Life and Science*, from 1842 (remarkable for its author's "manic" penchant for diagramming everything from the elements of psychic life and the varieties of bank holiday to "violent forms of death with reason to suspect foul-play"); and the "psychotic" Carl Gehrmann's *Body, Brain, Soul, God* of 1893 (a theologico-medical work replete with case histories such as "effects of sweaty feet on the sexual and respiratory organs").[13] Benjamin places Daniel Paul Schreber's *Memoirs* among their ranks.

To be mentally ill, at least in Benjamin's organizational logic, is thus either to be a psychiatric patient or to have produced an egregiously pseudoscientific text. The former is preferable to the latter. Benjamin depicts works written by authors diagnosed as mentally ill as containing more sound thinking than many of the nominally sane scientific tomes cobbled together under the heading of empirical truth. Schreber's outwardly mad first-person account of his "delusions" (*Wahnwelt*) is more rational than the declaratively scientific (but irrational) formulations of writers like Blüher, Schmidt, Gehrmann, etc., whose works were systematized to the point of madness.[14]

Reflecting on his happy bibliographic innovation, Benjamin characterizes Schreber's clinical diagnosis as "paranoid" (*ein Paranoiker*) as evidence of a successfully resolved taxonomic dilemma in the psychiatric sphere.[15] Psychiatry, Benjamin writes in a statement that unwittingly references the disease specificity theory of illness, has "long since progressed beyond the time when every symptom was misused to characterize a particular form of insanity [*Irrsinn*]."[16] The "paranoid" Schreber's book is an improvement on the likes of Blüher, Schmidt, and Gehrmann both because it is more sensical and because Schreber personally has been the beneficiary of modern psychiatric progress, which has accurately diagnosed him as "paranoid." This protects Schreber from slipping into an incontrovertibly more insane "cataloguing psychosis" (*Gruppierungspsychose*), which, Benjamin jokes, would be the appropriate diagnostic category for these other writers if psychiatry had not already ceased to coin disease names based on particular patients.[17]

Benjamin nevertheless concedes that the publishing situation remains imperfect. Some works written by the insane still occasionally fail to find a publisher despite being vastly more deserving of publication than the "mad" medical treatises of writers afflicted with a (would-be) cataloguing psychosis. Benjamin slyly alludes to his current writing is one such instance. "Yet I know of a manuscript that is finding it as difficult as ever to obtain the approval of a respected publishing house, even though it is at least equal to Schreber's," he writes.[18] Having destigmatized the mentally ill in his essay and recommended that readers turn their attention to "posters and leaflets by the insane [*Irren*]," Benjamin's final coup is to suggest his own status among them. The classification "books by the mentally ill" includes his own work, which nevertheless has yet to see print.

There is something decidedly odd about both the endorsement and Benjamin's intimation that he too is a case of *Geisteskrankheit.* The essay is premised on Benjamin's faith in the modern psychiatric establishment, which he appears to celebrate for having done away with symptoms. This is strange because Benjamin begins the essay by noting his familiarity with Freud's case 1911 history of Schreber. Freud's case history clearly does *not* do away with symptoms in the slightest. Then there is Benjamin's hesitancy about classification. He mocks Schmidt's attempt to depict "life and knowledge" in terms of their component elements.[19] He is likewise critical of the anonymous author of *Der Ganz-Erden-Universal-Staat* (The whole-Earth universal state) from 1924. This author does not hesitate to advertise it as a handbook for "heads of state" and include a detailed table (of which Benjamin reproduces an image) of the proposed salaries for different types of citizens. In it, "Currently Active Saints" and "Kings (special case)" feature alongside "Citizens in Domestic Service."[20] Special criticism is reserved for Gehrmann's *Body, Brain, Soul, God,* which Benjamin characterizes as a case of "theological medical science" elaborately illustrated by no fewer than "258 cases . . . concerned principally with menstruation and . . . based on the assumption that all the organs, nerves, blood vessel and parts of the body correspond to specific parts of the brain."[21] Benjamin even offers something resembling his own differential diagnostic classification. He describes Gehrmann as a case of "psychosis," Schmidt as having a "manic" worldview, and the anonymous author of *Der Ganz-Erden-Universal-Staat* as obviously afflicted with lunacy (*Narrheit*). Benjamin shows that modern psychiatry would likely fail to diagnose these truly "mad" cases as mad.

All of this helps demonstrate that Benjamin's evaluation of psychiatry is double-edged. He is likely not thinking of Freudian psychoanalysis in his discussion of psychiatry or at the very least not thinking of Freudian psychoanalysis exclusively. It is hard to say whether Benjamin specifically had Kraepelin's work in mind. At the very least, his indication that he had read Freud's 1911 case history shows that he certainly knew of Kraepelin, as Freud discusses Kraepelinian classification at length in the final part of the Schreber case. What is clearer is that by purporting to describe the creation of a special section in his library, Benjamin succeeds in dialectically questioning the very category he develops to do so.

On the one hand, Benjamin's "Books" essay rescues the mentally ill from unjust stigmatization, restores their writing to the canon of works deserving readers' serious attention, and destabilizes the boundary between madness and sanity. On the other hand, it endorses psychiatry's ability to produce precise disease definitions that solidify the madness/sanity divide. "Books" makes it seem as though the mentally ill are a coherent group. It then contradictorily proposes that this category includes both the clinically sane and insane. Having stated that "books by the mentally ill [*Geisteskranken*]" is his appropriate classificatory category, Benjamin nevertheless refuses to clarify the boundaries of mental illness. He even leaves his own mental status obscure. This foils the seeming terminological precision in the rest of the essay, with its outward celebration of psychiatric progress.

The essay comes to reflect that the classificatory dilemma both its author and psychiatry seemed to have resolved—how to group Schreber?—has not been resolved at all. The "cataloguing psychosis" Benjamin claims has been forestalled in his own library by psychiatric progress in the Schreber case instead rears its head again. By the conclusion of the essay, "cataloguing psychosis" accurately describes the paradoxes created by trying to differentiate between mental illnesses and by attempting to define who is among "the mentally ill." It even describes what happens if one endeavors to create a special section in one's library for works written by the mentally ill. Benjamin attends to the tension between rigorous taxonomic delimitation and indeterminacy that Max Horkheimer and Theodor W. Adorno mention in *The Dialectic of Enlightenment*. "Classification is a condition of knowledge, not knowledge itself, and knowledge in turn dissolves classification."[22] In his own idiom, Benjamin stages the double-bind between the Enlightenment's Baconian *Erkenntnis* (knowledge), which, as a form of power (*Macht*), "enslaves all creation," and the unwieldy, incalculable return of myth that Horkheimer and Adorno describe. [23]

Benjamin's selection of Schreber's book to do so is significant. Like Benjamin, Schreber has a diagnostic dilemma, and one to which Benjamin himself alludes. "In this way a motley collection came together over the years, a 'Library of Pathology,' long before I thought to actively build a collection of writings by the mentally ill [*Geisteskranker*]—indeed long before I even knew that books by the mentally ill [*Geisteskranken*] existed. Then, in 1918, in a small antiquarian bookshop in Berne, I came across Schreber's famous *Denkwürdigkeiten eines Nervenkranken*, published by Oswald Mutze in Leipzig."[24] Although Benjamin is building a collection of books by the mentally ill, the book that stimulates his choice of mental illness as the proper classificatory category is not written by an author who is mentally ill. Schreber is suffering from a *nervous* illness, as his title makes clear.

Benjamin's selection of Schreber's book as an exemplary case for this new subsection of his library suggests that the key conundrum of his "Books"—who is *mentally ill*?—is also present in Schreber's book. The shadow of the Woyzeck case returns to haunt Schreber's text. There, too, the problem centered on sufficiently delimiting the boundaries of mental illness and the possession of free will and the ability to exercise reason. The Leipzig medical faculty, Schreber's maternal grandfather among them, concluded that this division could be tightly fixed:

> [The facts cited in the medical examination in favor of Woyzeck's legal accountability demonstrate] that Woyzeck's physical condition presently or venal constitution may neither be considered an impediment to the free use of the understanding [*Verstandes*] in general nor as a direct motive for the crime itself in this particular case, and that no trace exists of either the former or that latter before during or after the crime, on the occasion of which allusions have [nevertheless] been made to the extremely difficult and now frequently misused category of ["]hidden madness["]—the basis for attempts to explain even Woyzeck's crime—and to cases of a blind, instinctual impulse to criminality. . . . We thus cannot object to the report [of Dr. Clarus], according to which there is no reason to assume that Woyzeck was in a state of mental disorder [*Seelenstörung*]—either at some time in his life or specifically before, during or after the murder—or that he experienced a necessary, blind, and instinctual impulse at the time, or, altogether differently, acted because driven by passionate stimuli.[25]

For Haase, Clarus, and the Leipzig University medical faculty, Woyzeck simply did not meet the legal definition of mental illness. "There is no reason to assume Woyzeck was in a state of mental disorder," because personal character does not affect "the free use of understanding." The partial mental disorder "hidden madness" does not apply. Woyzeck was not driven to the murder by a legally mitigating "blind, instinctual impulse." All of this meant he could be killed for his sanity. The same issue reappears in "Books," which recognizes in Schreber's *Memoirs* that the problem of bibliographic cataloguing is also one of human cataloguing and therefore to be approached with the utmost caution. Benjamin's reading presents Schreber as questioning the definition of mental illness (*Geisteskrankheit*), not identifying with it. Benjamin's insight that the *Memoirs* interrogates the viability of diagnostic labeling rather than affirmatively speaking to its sufferer's psychotic experiences becomes even more compelling when one turns to the specifics of Schreber's situation and the development of the civil code of imperial Germany.

## Defining Mental Illness in the German Empire

Schreber reached the height of his professional career in 1893 with his appointment as a high-ranking judge (*Senatspräsident*) on the illustrious Saxon

Supreme Court. He was nevertheless declared clinically psychotic and legally incompetent just a few weeks later. His initial confinement to the care of the Leipzig University psychiatric clinic (run by Emil Kraepelin's erstwhile foe, the neuroanatomist Paul Flechsig), involuntary retirement from the court, and compulsory transfer of financial power to his wife heralded a series of forced institutionalizations for a period that lasted the next nine years.

This was in large part because, at the time of Schreber's forcible internment, German civil law as put in place after unification in 1871 contained a provision that automatically revoked an individual's legal majority (*Mündigkeit*) in the event that person be deemed mentally ill. The provision was designed to preserve order in the public sphere. It viewed mental illness as dangerous because socially disruptive. Mental illness was on par with being a spendthrift or habitual drunkard, both of which were covered by German civil law's stipulations about legal incompetency. (This is indeed much like Clarus's own statements in his medical report on Johann Christian Woyzeck. "May the generations of youth now coming of age gaze upon the bleeding criminal and take good note of the truth that reluctance to work, gambling, drunkenness . . . can lead gradually and unexpectedly to crimes and the gallows.") Here is the section on *Geisteskrankheit* from the 1888 iteration of the BGB: "§28. A person who has been dispossessed of the use of reason [*welche des Vernunftgebrauches beraubt ist*], can be declared legally incompetent [*entmüdigt*] on account of mental illness [*Geisteskrankheit*]. If the condition described in the first clause comes to an end, the status of legal incompetency [*Entmüdigung*] must be again revoked."[26]

Practically speaking, however, mental illness lacked a formal legal definition. The term *Geisteskrankheit* was sufficiently flexible to be bent to almost any purpose, as it regularly was. In the 1890s, mention by a physician or other medical professional that a patient was experiencing hallucinations was typically sufficient to produce a designation of legal incompetency, as long as a close relative or spouse corroborated the doctor's findings, which Schreber's wife did. Put away with his spouse's blessing, Schreber relentlessly contested the terms under which he was held for the duration of his internment. In 1902, he successfully sued for his freedom and obtained a retraction of his legal guardianship. Shortly thereafter, he published the *Memoirs* with the spiritualist Oswald Mutze Press in Leipzig, against the vigorous and sustained protests of his family, who tried to purchase and destroy every copy of the work, no doubt because of its extraordinary contents.

In the *Memoirs*, Schreber asserted that he had been the victim of a cosmic conspiracy, led by his former psychiatrist, Paul Flechsig at Leipzig, to deprive him of his rights and commit "soul murder" (*Seelenmord*) on his person. As part of this conspiracy, he claims he was destined to be turned into a woman and inseminated by God, so that he could repopulate the earth following humankind's destruction. The *Memoirs* chronicle his cross-dressing and wish to be penetrated "as a woman." While largely written in the first person, Schreber also diligently records the messages he claims were transmitted to him by malign celestial voices in a special nerve language (*Nervensprache*). He additionally describes undergoing a series of painful "miracles" that amounted to nothing less than a living dismemberment: the siphoning off of his spinal cord, compression of his chest, extraction of his stomach, and infusion of his abdominal cavity with rotting human flesh, among other terrifying bodily violations.

Beyond documenting his experiences, Schreber also included a full appendix of the associated court proceedings in the *Memoirs*. These legal proceedings show that Schreber's diagnosis with "hallucinatory insanity" (*halluzinatorischer Wahnsinn*) in late 1893 by his psychiatrist Dr. Weber at the Sonnenstein asylum made it possible to legally and psychologically characterize him as mentally ill (*geisteskrank*) and thus to declare him legally incompetent (*entmündigt*). Schreber became the equivalent of a seven-year-old child in the eyes of the law. The legal designation also implied he had been philosophically thrown out of reason. Maturity (*Mündigkeit*) is Immanuel Kant's technical designation for the ability to reason independently in *What Is Enlightenment?* (1784), where it forms his main criterion for Enlightenment. To be deemed legally incompetent in 1893 was not only to be deprived of the rights granted to legal persons by the German civil code but also to be philosophically disenlightened. This is made explicit by §28, which states that suspension of legal majority applies to those persons who have been dispossessed of the use of reason. The resulting dilemma for Schreber, who was quite aware of the implications of *Entmündigung*, is beautifully captured by his and Lacan's differing comments concerning the Enlightenment, reproduced in the epigraphs to this chapter. Whereas Lacan frames Schreber as an inheritor of the Enlightenment tradition, Schreber—who had been deprived of his legal and philosophical majority—disputes that his work has anything to do with the "shallow rationalism" of the eighteenth century.

These two positions—the one asserting Schreber's status as reason incarnate, the other declaring his superlative ability to see the rationalistic emptiness of Enlightenment reason—form the knot that the judge negotiates in his writing and to which Benjamin's essay subtly refers. Schreber is trapped. He cannot contest the definition of reason in imperial German law by denying that definition or the law's legitimacy. Schreber served that same law for years. Attempting to dispute its statements would only validate the legal and philosophical conclusion that he had been "dispossessed of the use of reason" and so deserved to be deemed legally and philosophically incompetent. To accept the legal finding, however, would amount to the same thing. It would ensure that nothing Schreber said had to be treated as meaningful, as he was no longer legally or philosophically considered to be a reasonable person, a point that affirmed the need for the incompetency designation all over again.

It is from within this impossible position that Schreber's *Denkwürdigkeiten* discloses the existence of a Benjaminian classificatory disorder, a "cataloguing psychosis," at the core of clinical psychiatry. In the *Denkwürdigkeiten*, Schreber uses Kraepelin's psychiatric textbooks to support his legal case that disputed his diagnosis as mentally ill and sought his freedom alongside the return of his rights. He also, however, uses Kraepelin's textbook's contestation of psychiatric science's rationalist empiricism. Schreber's use of Kraepelin indicates his capacity to critically *read* Kraepelin's work. They show his ability to connect that reading with clinical psychiatry's legal implications. Structurally similar to Kraepelin's textbook (not only Flechsig's clinical publications), the pages of the *Denkwürdigkeiten* are also the site of Schreber's struggle to carve out a scientific space that is eccentric to the Enlightenment tradition and thereby forge a new relationship to the *nomos*. Jointly interpellated by psychiatry and law, Schreber simultaneously endeavors to declare an alternative form of rationality and imagine a different structure of jurisprudence. Like Benjamin's dilemma in the library, Schreber's quest becomes the accommodation of that which could neither be disposed of nor easily included within the existing order.

To whatever extent Schreber's breakdown was occasioned by a recognition of law's essential groundlessness (as Eric Santner has argued, following Walter Benjamin's *Critique of Violence*), Schreber's relationship to the law did not end there. The law's groundlessness is certainly part of the picture, but so too is its meaningful force, a force that Schreber's maternal grandfather had already exercised in putting Johann Christian Woyzeck to death and to which Schreber himself remained committed. What Freud characterizes as Schreber's *Wahnbildung* (his reconstruction of the psychical world after Flechsig provoked an apocalypse within it) should also be regarded as Schreber's establishment of a new law, an undertaking that is closely connected to *le nom de la mère*, his stated wish to be a woman, and his desire to give birth to a new world. Woman occupies a position marginal to Enlightenment in Kant's work, and Schreber struggles in the *Memoirs* with the (impossible) position of "woman" as the figuration of the outermost limit of the Enlightenment's effort conquer nature and simultaneously—through his mother and maternal grandfather—as a representation of Justitia, the Roman female allegory of justice who bears the scales aloft.

## Schreber on Self-Diagnosis and Legal Incompetency

The title of Schreber's *Memoirs* is not only a title but an argument. Schreber's title interrogates the meaning of the term *Geisteskrankheit* (mental illness),

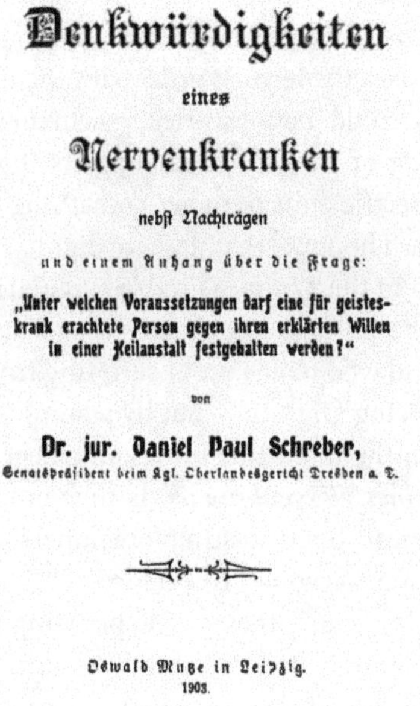

Denkwürdigkeiten

eines

Nervenkranken

nebst Nachträgen

und einem Anhang über die Frage:

„Unter welchen Voraussetzungen darf eine für geisteskrank erachtete Person gegen ihren erklärten Willen in einer Heilanstalt festgehalten werden?"

von

Dr. jur. Daniel Paul Schreber,

Senatspräsident beim Kgl. Oberlandesgericht Dresden a. D.

Oswald Mutze in Leipzig.

1903.

3.1 Daniel Paul Schreber, German title page of *Memoirs* (1903).

*Source*: Daniel Paul Schreber, *Denkwürdigkeiten eines Nervenkranken* (Leipzig: Kulturverlag Oswald Mutze Press, 1903).

like Benjamin's 1928 essay. In his title, Schreber contests his assigned clinical diagnosis of mental illness (and the associated legal designation of incompetency), replacing it with a self-diagnosis instead: nervous illness. This is difficult to see in the English translation, which abridges and reinterprets the longer German title.

Whereas the English translation by Macalpine and Hunter reproduces only first part of the German title (*Memoirs of My Nervous Illness*), the following, no less significant, subtitle reads: *with Postscripts and an Addendum Concerning the Question: "Under What Conditions Can a Person Considered Mentally Ill* [geisteskrank] *Be Detained in a Treatment Facility Against His Declared Will?"*[27] Adding to the confusion in the English title is the fact that in addition to shortening the title, Macalpine and Hunter render Schreber's unusual German term *Denkwürdigkeiten* simply as "memoirs." This German neologism, coined by Schreber, is much closer to "Great Thoughts" (Lothane's translation) or

"Peculiar Thoughts" or "Remarkable Thoughts" (Goodrich's suggestions) than the more benign and personal English "memoirs." In fact, the book quite literally opens with a declaration of its own thoughtworthiness.

Indeed, it goes further. *Würdigkeit* is Immanuel Kant's term for dignity in *The Groundwork of the Metaphysics of Morals* (1785), where he contrasts human value (for which he uses the term *Würde*) with the morally objectionable idea that human beings could have a price.[28] Schreber's title is thus closer to "Thoughts Deserving of Dignity" and suggests the book's contents are not intended to serve specific ends but have something of the immeasurable and singular about them. Thoughts that deserve dignity, indeed, thoughts that are worth consideration in their immeasurable singularity, will have been formulated by a person who possesses capacious use of his intellect (*Verstand*) and reason (*Vernunft*) and who hence is not suffering from a mental condition.

"Thoughts Deserving Dignity"—but by whom? Schreber does not present himself *as himself* in the main title but as an object of scientific observation. *Denkwürdigkeiten eines Nervenkranken* is thus not the possessive, personalized "my nervous illness" but instead a more impersonal, conflicted "Thoughts Deserving Dignity by a Nervously Ill Person" or "Thoughts Deserving Dignity by a Person with a Nervous Illness." The phrasing in the byline equivocates between an indication of Schreber's ability to regard himself objectively and his lack of even sufficient legal authority to use a possessive pronoun.

Schreber's diagnostic contestation is contained in his title. The word *nervenkrank* (Thoughts Deserving Dignity by a *Nervously* Ill Person) is strategically made to contrast with the term mentally ill (*geisteskrank*) that appears few lines later, in the subtitle. "*Under what Conditions Can a Person Considered Mentally Ill* [geisteskrank] *Be Detained in a Treatment Facility Against His Declared Will* [erklärten Willen]*?*" Schreber's decision to prominently call himself nervously ill is therefore tantamount to insisting that his incompetency is illegal because there is nothing wrong with his psychological functioning, only the somatic condition of his nerves. To affirm this point, he adds in his subtitle that he is only "considered" (*erachtet*) mentally ill, not someone who is so. Schreber here pits his self-diagnosis (nervous illness) against the one *merely declared* by his doctor and the court (mental illness). As he put it in his appeal to the court for release from incompetency and institutionalization in July 1901:

> I do not deny that my nervous system [*Nervensystem*] has for a number of years been in a pathological condition. On the other hand, I deny absolutely that I am mentally ill [*geisteskrank*] or ever have been. My mind [*Geist*], that is to say the functioning of my intellectual powers [*Verstandkräfte*], is as clear and healthy as any other person's; it has been unaltered since the beginning of my nervous illness [*Nervenkrankheit*]—apart from some unimportant

> hypochondriacal ideas. Therefore, the medical expert's report to the Court contains, in having accepted the presence in my case of paranoia (insanity) [*Paranoia (Verrücktheit)*], a blow in the face of truth, which could hardly be worse.[29]

Schreber reiterates the point he makes in his book's title in his legal appeal: he is nervously ill, not mentally ill. He has never been mentally ill (*geisteskrank*), as his mind (*Geist*), and with it his intellect (*Verstand*, a key term in the BGB and Kant's work), are as "healthy as any other person's." The court's continued insistence that Schreber is "paranoid," a category that was clinically synonymous with an affliction of *Geist*, is thus thoroughly absurd. It denies the truth. This means that the site in which he has been placed—a treatment facility (*Heilkunde*)—to address his alleged mental illness is carceral in nature: it only "detains" him because it is treating him for an illness he does not have.

The reader should trust the author on these points because the author is none other than a doctor of law: he is the retired presiding judge of the Dresden Appellate Court (*Senatspräsident beim kgl. Oberlandesgericht Dresden a. D.*). Schreber presents himself on his title page in a formidable, class-specific, and professional armature that showcases his status as a member of the intellectual elite and, therefore, again, not one likely to lack intellect (*Verstand*). Who better to judge a legal case about nervous versus mental illness, medical care versus irregular detainment, and legitimate versus illegitimate legal incompetency than a retired judge willing to offer his own name as an attestation to his good faith?

The complete title is Schreber's impassioned effort to correct his diagnostic record and thereby remove his designation of legal incompetency. These "thoughts deserving of dignity" document his awareness of the import of psychiatric classification in the legal sphere. Schreber argues that his condition is exclusively within the jurisdiction of a nervous disorder that affects neither his intellect nor his free will. The title also vests Schreber with the authority to question the medical establishment, highlighting his legal doctorate and his position as judge.

The title's legal stance also had a deep irony, however. Schreber was responsible for formulating the same legal code that worked against him when he became ill. Although brought up in a household entrenched in the medical profession, Schreber went on to a life dedicated to law. He studied law at Leipzig University, where he did not hide his support for both pro-Bismarck and pro-Prussian politics. After graduating from law school and passing the university bar exam in 1863, Schreber took the judicial oath (1865). His Leipzig legal degree launched the beginning of a successful legal career. His first positions included work for the district court (*Landesgericht*) of Chemnitz and then the Ministry of Justice in Leipzig. Within a few years, he obtained a doctorate in law (1869) and passed the state bar exam (1870).

The timing of his professional entry into the legal world coincided with a significant effort to standardize law in the newly formed German Empire. Born just before the revolutions of 1848 swept Europe, Schreber's early adulthood played out in the context of the military and political struggles to unify the German Empire. Following the Franco-Prussian War (1870–1871), Schreber was summoned to serve among the jurists at work in Berlin codifying the laws of the empire. This was a particularly important task given that the heterogeneous array of twenty-six states that made up the unified empire at its creation in 1871 each possessed its own civil code. The efforts of the jurists in Berlin (1878–1879) were a prelude to the establishment of a single legal code for the entirety of the German Empire, to be modeled around Napoleon's in France. This process, which lasted until 1900 and included an abortive first draft in 1888, resulted in the creation of the *Bürgerliches Gesetzbuch* (BGB), passed by the Reichstag in 1896 but not put into effect until 1900.

An enormously elaborate document containing no fewer than 2,385 sections, the BGB is often acknowledged as one of the most important legal undertakings of the modern era. It remains in effect, with modifications, in Germany today and has been the model for that of many other nations' civil codes.[30] As the historian C. M. Barber points out, however, in the period between 1871 and 1900, the German constitution's final shape continued to be a matter of discussion and debate. It evolved during this time in ways that were as much dependent on "the character and content of the laws" as on "the spirit of the people."[31] The Reich's constitutional transformation did not happen overnight, contributing to a "latent primacy of legislation" during this period. Law was generally viewed as positive step in social transformation after the 1848 revolutions. It was intrinsic to the formation of better society because it marked the "the final transfer of sovereignty, constituting an expansion of the basic rights of German citizens."[32] This included formal legal recognition of citizens as citizens.

The BGB defined citizenship in terms of *Rechtsfähigkeit* (acquisition of legal status, legal capacity), which began at birth. While birth brought about an individual's right to be subject to the law and its privileges, one only obtained legal "majority," *Mündigkeit*, at age twenty-one, at which point it became possible both to enter into legal contracts and assume a place in public society.[33] The legal notion of majority carried an additional symbolic importance in the 1890s. It symbolized the revolutionary rejection of what German lawmakers described as the *väterliche Gewalt* (paternal force/violence) of the sovereign, a translation of the French *la puissance paternelle* (paternal power) from the French Revolution.[34] (*Gewalt* is, of course, also Walter Benjamin's term in his "Critique of Violence [*Gewalt*]" from 1921.)

As Jacob Grimm (of the Brothers Grimm) pointed out in his *Deutsche Rechtsaltertümer* of 1828, in his joint investigation of folk culture and

German law, the concept of *Manneskraft* (potency, lit. man's power) was closely historically associated with definitions of *Rechtsfähigkeit* (legal capacity) in Germany. *Manneskraft*, Grimm remarked, involved both the right to manage property and bear arms. In the BGB, however, *Manneskraft* was no longer connected with legal capacity as such but became part of the legal definition of majority.[35] The legal renunciation of paternal power, or what the Romans called *patria potestas*, within the family therefore also contained the political symbolism of the renunciation of the royal authority with the advent of popular sovereignty. Majority implied both the individual's freedom from the familial rule of the father and freedom from the rule of a king:

> The construction of majority symbolized the renunciation of *väterliche Gewalt* within the family, and this served as a metaphor for renunciation of the absolute monarchial principle or a king as the public father and head of the sociopolitical body. . . . Tearing down filial devotion was part of the process of creating a modern nation, because it tore down the willingness of the subject to obey and vested him with control over his own affairs; in effect, it involved the bestowing of full citizenship.[36]

Barber's use of the male pronoun in this passage makes the point that bestowal of citizenship in 1871 was almost exclusively restricted to men. The BGB did not disenfranchise women outright or deny them legal majority. It did so, however, as the cumulative effect of the different legal norms it put in place. Paragraph 1363 of the new civil law was a particularly clear example of this. This paragraph concerned a woman's rights after marriage. "By the conclusion of a marriage the property of a wife becomes subject to the management and usufruct [right to make legal use] of the husband—contributed property includes also the property which the wife acquires during marriage."[37] Without depriving a woman of either citizenship or legal majority directly, the BGB nevertheless indirectly accomplished both, ensuring that a woman was subject to the father's legal and household power before age twenty-one and that upon marriage subject to the legal and household power of the husband.

Schreber helped draft this new civil law and put it in place. He also enforced it in his role on the Saxon Supreme Court. He even sought to represent it in seeking a seat in the Reichstag in 1882, running as the candidate for the conservative, pro-Bismarck National Liberal Party of imperial Germany's sixteenth district (Chemnitz). He was nevertheless deemed incompetent by the same law he produced, whence the import of his self-diagnosis. The declaration of his status as *nervenkrank* was designed to speak with the law's own nomological force.

## Nervous Illness Versus Paranoid Psychosis

Schreber was defeated in 1882 by the incumbent socialist candidate in a sweeping and thoroughly humiliating loss that contributed to the onset of what Flechsig called his first, "severe hypochondriacal," illness. This illness was indeed the reason Schreber initially consulted the famous Leipzig neuroanatomist. Flechsig treated successfully Schreber in 1893 and 1894, to Schreber's young wife Ottoline Sabine Behr's great satisfaction.[38] In the period leading up to this first illness, Schreber had changed positions and been promoted once again. Between 1889 and 1893, he served as *Präsident* at the Royal *Landesgericht* in Freiburg, where he presided over a panel of three other judges on a court of appeals. His happiness in Leipzig, Chemnitz, and Freiburg were colored only by his and his wife's failure to produce any children. Schreber and his wife adopted a daughter during this time, bringing the young girl Fridoline into the household shortly before Schreber's fateful appointment as *Senatspräsident* in Dresden in the summer of 1893.

Schreber was only actively in the position that graces the title page of his book for roughly one month. The prestigious post of *Senatspräsident* placed him in charge of a five-judge panel on the Royal Dresden Appellate Court (Supreme Court of Appeals of the Kingdom of Saxony) that dealt with civil law. Beginning on October 1, 1893, by early November he was beginning to suffer from what he characterized as extreme insomnia. His and Sabine's positive impression of Flechsig during Schreber's earlier illness led them to seek Flechsig's help again. On November 21, 1893, Schreber entered Flechsig's care at the Leipzig University psychiatric clinic and was put on temporary leave from his position as *Senatspräsident.* He remained with Flechsig (and now on an extended leave from his job) until the summer of 1894, during which time Flechsig documented his condition worsening. Flechsig's medical chart describes a progression from insomnia to delusions (*Sinnestäuschungen*) during this time. In the summer of 1894, Schreber was transferred from Flechsig's care to a private asylum in Coswig, just north of Leipzig.[39] Two weeks later, he was moved again, this time to a site that would be his home for the next eight years: the Royal Public Acute Care State Hospital at Sonnenstein Castle, near Pirna. Sonnenstein was a significantly larger establishment than either of Schreber's prior two institutional homes. It was run by a German-educated psychiatrist of Russian descent roughly Schreber's own age. Guido Weber had, like Flechsig, trained as a neuroanatomist and would be Schreber's primary antagonist in court beginning in 1899.

The court battles were, at least in part, caused by a marital conflict that unfolded early on in Schreber's treatment with Flechsig. During this time, Schreber entered into a financial struggle with his wife over her receipt of his paychecks. This is connected with Paragraph 1363 of the BGB, which gave the husband financial control over the family's affairs. The situation was only resolved in the winter of 1894 (at which point Schreber was already with Weber at Sonnenstein), when Schreber's former boss on the court, Carl Edmund Werner, addressed the problem by proposing that Schreber be deprived of his legal majority (that is, that he be *entmüdigt*) on the basis of Weber's 1894 diagnosis of "hallucinatory psychosis" (*halluzinatorische Wahnsinn*). Weber's diagnosis of Schreber was based less on what he observed in person than on what he had read in Flechsig's diagnostic report, particularly regarding Schreber's transition from insomnia to hallucinations. He also appears to have been swayed by Schreber's wife's financial distress. Weber continued to express faith in his diagnosis, however, throughout Schreber's entire time at Sonnenstein. Four years after Schreber's arrival, in a 1899 letter to the court, Weber even suggested that Schreber's mental state had further deteriorated:

> Without going further into the details of the course of his illness attention is drawn to the way in which from the early more acute psychosis [*Psychose*] which influenced all psychic processes and which could be called hallucinatory insanity [*halluzinatorisher Wahnsinn*], the *paranoid form* of illness [*paranoische Krankheitsbild*] became more and more marked, crystallized out so to speak, into its present picture. This kind of illness [*dieses Krankheitsbild*] is, as is well known, characterized by the fact that next to a more or less fixed elaborate delusional system [*ausgebauten Wahnsystem*] there is a complete possession of mental faculties and orientation.[40]

Weber describes Schreber's state as one in which the patient possesses use of his "mental faculties and orientation" but is nevertheless increasingly subject to a paranoid psychosis characterized by the presence of an elaborate delusional system. This is, indeed, just what would have been called a case of "partial psychiatric disorder" in Johann Christian Woyzeck's time. Schreber's delusions exist alongside demonstrable possession of his mental faculties. In 1797, the German psychiatrist Ernst Platner described this state as "amentia occulta" (hidden madness, *verborgene Wahnsinn*). In fact, "amentia occulta" is the same mental illness of which Schreber's maternal grandfather had denied the existence in the Leipzig medical faculty's report to the Saxon court in 1824. The difference is that over the period between 1824 and 1894, "partial psychiatric disorders" had been recognized by imperial German law. In J. C. Woyzeck's time, these disorders were not deemed sufficient legal grounds for reduced responsibility in a criminal context, as the Woyzeck trial showed. J. C. Woyzeck was not insane and so could be executed. By 1894, however, what had previously been called "partial mental disorders" and had been reconceived as paranoid psychosis now did have legal status.

Weber's 1894 attribution of "hallucinatory insanity" to Schreber and his 1899 report designating Schreber's hallucinatory insanity as paranoid psychosis, both of which functioned as a form of expert testimony, show that partial psychiatric disorders had become legally viable. Paranoid psychosis could be treated as a form of mental illness (*Geisteskrankheit*), and thus Schreber could be deprived of his majority. This is just what Carl Edmund Werner wrote to the Royal Ministry of Justice in 1894. Werner indicated the need for the "initiation of a temporary legal guardianship [*Bevormundung*]," in accordance with the medical findings of Dr. Weber.[41] Henceforth, Werner stated, Schreber's wife would be her husband's guardian, his "*Vormund*" (guardian, lit. speaker on his behalf).[42] Schreber's status as temporarily *entmündigt* was finalized before the year was out. As the diagnosis of "hallucinatory insanity" came with a negative prognosis (at least in Weber's estimation), the Ministry of Justice also forced Schreber to retire from his new post in November 1894. The move significantly reduced his pension.[43] In April 1901, despite Schreber's protests, the temporary status of incompetency was converted to a permanent one and lifted only with Schreber's successful legal appeal in 1902.[44]

The 1894 revocation of Schreber's legal maturity had as many legal consequences as it did symbolic ones. The same rights-bestowing, postrevolutionary imperial law that Schreber had helped write now reduced Schreber not only to the status of a child but also a woman, as these were the two persons incapable of possessing majority in the eyes of the law. The designation deprived Schreber of control of his finances and property and took away his rights to enter into legal contracts. It cost him his job and reduced his pension. Most importantly, it deprived him of his freedom (instead of ensuring it). Without majority (*Mündigkeit*), Schreber was no longer a German citizen in many ways. He now possessed only the capacity to be subject to legal rights and duties granted to all persons at birth (*Rechtsfähigkeit*) and not to what Grimm had called *Manneskraft* (the power of man). The fact that Schreber could not leave the Sonnenstein asylum even when he explicitly requested to do so was perhaps the most visible outward expression of this ironic legal situation.

There were additional symbolic implications to Schreber's loss of legal majority (*Entmündigung*) given the term's connections to both the Kantian concept of Enlightenment and to the French revolutionary notion of *puissance paternelle*. First, loss of legal majority had the effect of philosophically disenlightening Schreber. He was now neither legally capable of reason nor philosophically capable of thinking on his own behalf. He had been thrown out of the "brilliance" of Enlightenment. Moreover, the close historical connection between the revolutionary overthrow of the monarch's paternal power and the German concept of legal majority, embodied in the idea of the *väterliche Gewalt* (paternal force/violence), meant that the designation of incompetency symbolically cost Schreber the power of the father (his personal *väterliche Gewalt*) and was tantamount to pushing him back under the paternal yoke. The father's sovereign status was, however, now held by none other than his wife, his legal guardian.

Schreber's loss of majority thus effected a switch in gender roles as they were configured by imperial German law. Legal incompetency took away Schreber's rights as a male citizen (in many ways the only citizens who were full citizens), reducing him to the legal status of a woman and child in the process. It simultaneously conferred "his" rights on his wife. She symbolically acquired sovereign power by being legally elevated to the head of the household, made a full citizen, and invested with the postrevolutionary paternal power, the *väterliche Gewalt*, of popular sovereignty. Schreber's insistence on his status as *nervenkrank* was his legal solution to this intolerable situation. If only his nerves were affected, he did not need a legal, philosophical, or political guardian: he could speak for himself.

## Psychotic, Reading

Schreber used Emil Kraepelin's psychiatric textbooks to make the point that he was only nervously ill. Kraepelin may have been an appealing choice because he and Schreber's psychiatrist at Sonnenstein, Guido Weber, were on opposite sides of the psychiatric dispute that had caused Kraepelin's clash with Flechsig in the 1880s. Weber, like Flechsig, supported the neuroanatomical position advanced by the German psychiatrist Wilhelm Griesinger earlier in the nineteenth century: mental disease was brain disease, and thus psychiatry had nothing to do with psychology. Weber therefore entirely rejected Kraepelin's diagnostic system, with its differential classification of paranoia, manic depression, and dementia praecox. Weber instead saw paranoia as a neurological disorder resulting from the spastic state of the sensory nerves. Schreber's hallucinations, generated by such nerve spasms, truly were deceptions of the patient's senses (*Sinnestäuschungen*, hallucinations, from *der Sinn*, mind, and *die Täuschung*, deception). Schreber's progression over time only represented the growth over time of a tangled set of nervous complications, which made Schreber particularly interesting to Weber from a forensic perspective but little more than a boisterous inmate of Sonnenstein, at least while he was alive.

Weber's focus on the nerves would seem to agree with Schreber's own characterization of his illness as a nervous condition. The problem was that, legally speaking, only the presence of hallucinations was significant, not what caused them. Hallucinations consistently legally indicated mental illness (*Geisteskrankheit*), for which a deprivation of legal majority was appropriate. To contest the revocation of his legal majority, Schreber's task was to prove he was not *Geisteskrank*. This meant defining the boundaries of *Geisteskrankheit* and disentangling that definition from the presence of hallucinations. Kraepelin's model, although not neuroanatomical, was far more flexible than Weber's for Schreber's purposes. By creating a system of differentiation between the psychoses, it allowed for the possibility that only *some* mental pathologies would "count" toward a designation of legal incompetency; others could remain disconnected from it entirely. It made it feasible to consider the existence of a hallucination-producing disease that nevertheless did *not* fall under the heading of mental illness. Schreber was also presumably interested in Kraepelin's work because it offered him a chance to play an active role in determining the nature of his own illness: he did not have to be a corpse to assess what was happening to him. It allowed him to contribute to psychiatric science.

In fact, one of Schreber's main claims about the *Memoirs*, and his defense for its publication, is that it should be regarded as a scientific text (not a set of personal, subjective reflections). In his open letter to Flechsig, he appealed to his former psychiatrist for validation, an appeal that also shows he agreed with German neuroanatomy's scientific position about the important role of the nerves:

> I need hardly mention of what immeasurable importance it would be if you could in any way confirm the surmises I have sketched above, all the more if they could be substantiated in recollections of earlier years retained in your memory. The rest of my thesis would thereby gain universal credence [*vor aller Welt*] and would immediately be regarded as a *serious scientific* [wissenschaftlich] *problem to be investigated in every possible way.*[45]

The judgment of the Royal Superior Court of Dresden, which granted Schreber his freedom, similarly affirmed that Schreber's hope was for the text to be a scientific contribution. "Far from wishing to play the prophet of a new religion he looks upon himself solely as an object of scientific observation [*wissenschaftliches Beobachtungsobjekt*]."[46] In fact, Schreber initially endeavored to have the *Memoirs* published by the Friedrich Fleischer Verlag, his father's publisher. The very fact that Schreber sought to have his *Memoirs* released with this well-regarded scientific press is a powerful testament to the extent to which he considered his work to be a legitimate scientific treatise on par with Flechsig's and Kraepelin's own.[47]

The voluminous scholarship that had developed around the Schreber case nevertheless remains relatively unified in its affirmation of Schreber as a something to be read and not himself a reader. Freud does admittedly point out that Schreber was an excellent interpreter at the conclusion of his 1911 case history. As Freud suggests, playing on Schreber's concern about the status of his hallucinations, "It remains to the future to decide whether there is more delusion in my theory than I should like to admit, or whether there is more truth in Schreber's delusion than other people are yet prepared to believe."[48] Freud, however, is alone in his regard for Schreber's interpretive abilities both among the psychiatrists of his era and since, with few exceptions.

Contemporaneous psychiatric publications that appeared at the turn of the century about Schreber's case all heavily focused on the incompetency designation. Schreber's psychiatrist, Dr. R. H. Pierson, published an article in 1903 titled "On Incompetency Due to Dementia" (*Über Entmündung wegen Geistesschwäche*). During the same year, Dr. Guido Weber, under whose care Schreber remained longest and who is best known as his dogged court adversary, wrote a positive discussion of Pierson's text.[49] Weber also went on to publish an article about Schreber, "An Interesting Case of Incompetency" (*Ein interresanter Entmündungsfall*) in 1905, in which he explicitly defended a neuropathological account of paranoia against Kraepelin's new differential diagnoses.[50] This was followed by a piece written by the psychoanalytic renegade Otto Gross in 1908.[51] (It is possible that Kafka was familiar with the latter.) Schreber even reappears in later editions of Emil Kraepelin's diagnostic textbooks, completing the circle that Schreber initiated. Kraepelin cites Schreber's *Memoirs* in the 1913 edition of the textbook in the section on dementia praecox (an early term for schizophrenia), where he refers to Schreber's book as an example of the electrical and technological aspects of delusions in patients with the disease and of their tendency to be overly talkative.[52]

Secondary scholarship on the Schreber case has almost always framed Schreber as a case, not a reader. The American psychoanalyst Thomas Lothane's massive, meticulously researched *In Defense of Schreber: Soul Murder and Psychiatry* (1992) offers a nuanced picture of the historical state of German psychiatric practice at the time Schreber's illness but leaves out Schreber as a reader of psychiatry. Lothane's work complemented emerging research in Germany on the importance of neuropathology and Schreber's fraught relationship to his neuropathologically trained psychiatrist Flechsig.[53] It also drove subsequent research on the role of neuroanatomy and neuropathology in the Schreber case and particularly on Schreber's relationship to Flechsig.[54] In a rare departure from attention to Flechsig, Thomas Dalzell's 2011 book *Freud's Schreber Between Psychiatry and Psychoanalysis: On Subjective Disposition to Psychosis*, works through Freud's references to Kraepelin's work in the former's 1911 case history but nevertheless positions Schreber as an object for psychiatric research and not a respondent to such research.[55]

Schreber has also played an important role in poststructuralism and the antipsychiatry movement. The schizoid Judge Schreber with "sunbeams in his ass" is one of Gilles Deleuze and Félix Guattari's standard-bearers for schizoanalysis, an emblem of the *machine désirante*, and a basis for their concept of the Body Without Organs in *Anti-Oedipus*.[56] Schreber plays a key role in Jean-François Lyotard's *Libidinal Economy*, in which Lyotard, referring to his concept of the tensor, describes the Schreber case as one in which the patient experienced a vertiginous state of anal eroticism.[57] Schreber suffers from a conflict between aspirations to divinity and pestilential decay in Michel de Certeau's piece "The Institution of Rot."[58]

Other interpretations have mobilized Schreber as synecdoche for fin-de-siècle communication technologies in media studies.[59] Schreber is here a communication channel but not a communicator. Kittler characterizes him as a recording device and uses Schreber's description of an *Aufschreibesystem* (writing-down system) as the title of his work *Discourse Networks 1800/1900* (in German, *Aufschreibesystem 1800/1900*), which I discuss in the previous chapter. American legal scholarship has turned to the Schreber case for insights into how to approach legal texts as objects of interpretation.[60] Schreber is furthermore a well-established figure within literary criticism and has been a source of inspiration for a number of writers and visual artists.[61]

The consistent lack of attention to Schreber as a reader of his own plight and not just as a mechanized writer and copyist is odd because Schreber cites and shows familiarity with so many secondary sources in the *Memoirs*. That Schreber saw his text as a scientific treatise is supported by his extensive use of citational material throughout it. His work is heavily footnoted. Schreber made intermittent notes about his delusional system during his first five years at Sonnenstein. The note taking appears to have intensified during 1897–1898 before finally culminating in the production the *Memoirs*, written between February and September 1900.[62] This was roughly contemporaneous with his first (failed) legal petition to have his guardianship rescinded (October 1899). Schreber continued to expand the *Memoirs* as subsequent court battles unfolded. He wrote a set of postscripts to the main work between 1900 and 1901 and followed them with a second set at the end of 1902.[63] When the final volume was published in 1903, Schreber included the entire and newly resolved legal proceedings in a lengthy appendix. In its final form, it contained a short preface, an open letter to Professor Flechsig, and, following the twenty-plus chapters of the *Memoirs* proper, two postscripts, a legal addendum on his involuntary institutionalization, and an appendix of the court documentation.

Schreber's descriptions of his delusions in the main text are complete with footnotes to scientific literature of his era. They reflect a concerted effort to connect his theories with evidence from the latest research. The *Memoirs* quote psychiatric work by Rudolf Gottfried Arndt (1835–1900), by the anatomist and physiologist Georg Meissner (1829–1905), the astronomer Johann Heinrich von Mädler (1794–1874), and the zoologist Ernst Haeckel (1834–1919). Schreber points to work by the Swedish feminist Ellen Key, Romantic writers such as

Johann Wolfgang von Goethe and Lord Byron, the German philosophers Carl du Prel and Eduard von Hartmann, and, as many secondary commentators have observed, the publications of his first psychiatrist Flechsig.[64] He also cites Emil Kraepelin's textbooks at length, doing so with greater frequency than virtually any of the other footnoted citations.

Schreber adopts a systematic approach to using Kraepelin's textbooks. His reading of Kraepelin focuses specifically on Kraepelin's discussions of the general symptomatology of non-normative mental states, as those discussions appear in the 1893, 1896, and 1903–1904 editions of Kraepelin's textbook. Schreber demonstrates on the basis of Kraepelin's work that his hallucinations are neither a case of mental illness (*Geisteskrankheit*) nor incompatible with scientific fact.

Across these editions, Kraepelin uses this section of the book to describe and typologize the symptoms that appear in what he calls "*Irresein*," which is any kind of mental malfunctioning regardless of cause. Schreber would have been particularly interested in these descriptions because the category of *Irresein* had no legal implications. Kraepelin does not connect these symptom categories to specific disease, as his understanding of mental disorders is not symptom based. Of Kraepelin's symptom categories, Schreber focuses on "Disorders of Perception" (*Störungen des Wahrnehmungsvorganges*) and "Disorders in Intellectual Functioning" (*Störungen des Verstandesthätigkeit*). Within them, he is particularly concerned with Kraepelin's statements about hallucinations (*Sinnestäuschungen/Halluzinationen*) and disorders in the train of thought (*Störungen des Gedankenganges*).

His legal argument will be that while his doctors have always considered his visions to be hallucinations, they are no such thing. For him, these visions and their auditory accompaniments have an objective basis in reality: they are communication with "supersensory powers" (*übersinnliche Kräfte*). Schreber's word choice is important. He uses the adjective *übersinnlich* (lit. supersensory, beyond sensory perception) to show that whatever he is experiencing cannot be characterized as hallucinations (i.e., sensory deceptions, *Sinnestäuschungen*), because these experiences are simply beyond the boundaries of the sensory (they are *über-sinnlich*). Writing to Flechsig, Schreber remarks, "I have not the least doubt that the first impetus to what my doctors always considered mere 'hallucinations' [*blosse Halluzinationen*] but which to me signified communication with supersensory powers [*übersinnlichen Kräften*], *consisted of influences on my nervous system emanating from your nervous system.*"[65] Schreber's point here and elsewhere in the *Memoirs* is that there is nothing wrong with his senses, no weakness in his vision or hearing or thinking that allows him to be tricked. The situation is merely one in which something beyond human sensory capacity has begun to powerfully affect him and cause him to hear and see things, as it would do to anyone. This means that he is both in full possession of reason (not *geisteskrank*) and that his experiences are objectively verifiable.

Schreber uses Kraepelin's textbook to affirm the biological (not mental) nature of his illness and to prove that there is a documented scientific basis for supersensory experiences, which are therefore not hallucinations in the legally inflected sense of the term:

> I noticed therefore with interest that according to Kraepelin's *Textbook of Psychiatry* (5th Edition, Leipzig, 1896, p. 95 ff and particularly pg. 110 ff.) which had been lent to me (while I was occupied with this manuscript), the phenomenon of being in some supernatural communication [*übernatürlichen Verkehr*] with voices had frequently been observed before in human beings whose nerves were in a state of morbid excitation. I do not dispute that in many of these cases one may only be dealing with mere hallucinations [*Sinnestäuschungen*], as which they are treated throughout the mentioned textbook. In my opinion, science would be very wrong to designate as "hallucinations" [*Sinnestäuschungen*], all such phenomena lacking objective reality, and to throw them off into the lumber-room of things that do not exist; this may possibly be justified in those hallucinations [*Sinnestauschungen*] quoted by Kraepelin on page 108 ff., which are *not* connected with supernatural [*übersinnlichen*] matters.[66]

In the passage, Schreber agrees with Kraepelin's findings about hallucinations. He argues that while his experiences may seem fantastical, an esteemed contemporary German psychiatrist has scientifically documented the existence of "supernatural communication" in individuals with a nervous condition. He notes, however, that Kraepelin has potentially overgeneralized. Admittedly, most psychiatric cases truly will be ones of "mere hallucination." His own case, however, is unique. His hallucinations have an objective basis and are not fantasies. That is why his case is important for science. Scientific progress can only be made by setting aside a facile belief that all phenomena "lacking objective reality" simply do not exist.

The passage is also complete with detailed citational references that include the edition and even the pagination of Kraepelin's textbook to support Schreber's point. This shows that Schreber's interest in his claims being taken seriously. It also demonstrates that he regards Kraepelin's textbook much like a book of law: his citation of Kraepelin's work has the quality of a legal reference (edition and pagination), like the ones he would have used in his own legal practice and indeed that were used against him in the legal deprivation of majority. The passage is interesting for yet another reason as well. It repeats the logic that Schreber's maternal grandfather had used to help execute Johann Christian Woyzeck. Schreber argues his nervous condition has no impact on his use of reason and that he should be considered fully competent. Clarus and Haase likewise argued that Woyzeck's hallucinations did not count as a case of mental illness and therefore that Woyzeck could be held fully legally responsible and put to death.

In a passage citing Kraepelin that closely follows on the previous one, Schreber reproduces his move. He asserts, like Clarus and his grandfather did of Woyzeck, that he has a condition that has no impact on his reason. He maintains that what he sees has an objective scientific basis:

> In this connection, Kraepelin's remark on page 110 that those cases in which "the voices heard" have a supernatural [*übernatürlichen*] character "are not infrequently accompanied by visual hallucinations" [*Gesichtstäuschungen*, deceptions of sight] is very valuable for my own ideas. I think it probable that in a considerable number of these cases it was a matter of real visions [*wirkliche Visionen*] of the kind which I also have experienced, that is dream-images produced by rays, and which for that reason are very much more distinct than what is seen in ordinary dreams (compare Kraepelin, p. 107). On the other hand, the total content of the present work will hardly show anything in my case which justifies speaking of "the inability of the patient to use earlier experiences to correct thoroughly and accurately his new 'ideas'" (p. 146), or of "faulty judgment" [*Urteilsschwäche*], which Kraepelin says "invariably" accompanies delusions [*Wahnideen*].[67]

Here Schreber cites Kraepelin as an authority on the frequent copresence of auditory and visual hallucinations, a description that aligns with Schreber's own experiences. This allows Schreber to strengthen his case that what he is experiencing is something that medical science has already documented. Schreber also relies on Kraepelin to show his healthy mental state. This esteemed authority on mental illnesses writes that a rigidity of thinking and faulty judgment always accompany delusions. The existence of Schreber's book, however, with its copious citations and self-reflections, proves the absence of fixed ideas and faulty judgment in his own case. He must be healthy, and his hallucinations must have another cause. Schreber continues to expand this line of thought as the passage continues:

> I trust that I have proved that I am not only not "controlled by fixed and previously formed ideas," but that I also possess in full measure the "capacity to evaluate critically the content of consciousness with the help of judgment and deduction." He who in Kraepelin's sense understands "normal, healthy experience" simply as the denial of everything supernatural [*Übersinnlichen*], would in my opinion lay himself open to the reproach of allowing himself to be led only by the shallow "rationalistic ideas" of the period of Enlightenment

of the 18th century, which after all are mostly considered to have been superseded, particularly by theologians and philosophers, and also in science.[68]

Schreber again defends his mentally sound state using Kraepelin's definition of sanity. Kraepelin defines mental health as the "capacity to evaluate critically" the contents of one's own conscious perception using "judgment and deduction." The existence of Schreber's book shows that Schreber can do both. He is therefore quite well. Schreber nevertheless disputes Kraepelin's position that "normal, healthy experience" precludes the existence of supersensory phenomena. This would be unduly rationalistic. Schreber develops his point about the objective reality of hallucinations using Kraepelin's work in a postscript to the book, "Concerning Hallucinations," that he wrote in February 1901:

> Science seems to deny any reality background for hallucinations [*Halluzinationen*], judging from what I have read for instance in Kraepelin, PSYCHIATRY, Vol 1., p 102 ff, 6th Edition. In my opinion, this is definitely erroneous, at least if so generalized. I admit that in many, perhaps most cases, the objects and events which hallucinated persons believe to have observed exist only in their imagination. . . . Serious doubts in such a rationalistic and purely materialistic (if I may say so) attitude must arise in cases where one is dealing with voices "of supernatural [*übernatürlichem*] origin" (compare Kraepelin, Vol 1., p. 117, 6th edition). . . . I therefore cannot share Kraepelin's astonishment which he expresses repeatedly (for instance Vol 1. Pp. 112, 116, 162, etc, 6th edition) that the "voices," etc., seem to have a far greater power of conviction for hallucinated patients than "anything said by those around them." A person with sound nerves is, so to speak, *mentally* blind [*geistig blind*] compared with him who receives supernatural [*übersinnliche*] impressions by virtue of his diseased nerves.[69]

Schreber's reading of Kraepelin in this passage cleverly allows him to accomplish several things. He shows his capacity for judgment and deduction by offering a thoughtful and detailed discussion of Kraepelin's work. Returning to Kraepelin on the topic of hallucination supports Schreber's position that there is perfectly viable scientific evidence in the latest medical literature for what he is experiencing. He even shows that someone with a nervous condition may have greater possession of reason than someone without such a condition: "A person with sound nerves is, so to speak, mentally blind [*geistig blind*]." His only contestation, however, is that science has regrettably framed such hallucinations too generally in characterizing them all as imaginary. This generalization may have merit in most instances, but it does not apply in Schreber's case. If anything, he argues, his hallucinations give him greater cause to be released from the designation of incompetency because they show he is not "mentally [*geistig*] blind." Schreber thereby positions his book as a scientific supplement to Kraepelin's work, disagreeing with Kraepelin only at those moments when the specific characteristics of his hallucinatory experiences exceed Kraepelin's average disease descriptions.

Schreber's postscript "Concerning Hallucinations" goes on to speculate about the real phenomena that could account for what Kraepelin considers purely unreal hallucinations, in which patients describe hearing talking animals. Doing so shows that Schreber's so-called delusional experiences can have a real basis:

> When Kraepelin, Vol 1. P. 116, 6th Edition, reports that provoking voices are heard by hallucinat[ing] persons as coming from grunting pigs, affronting or barking dogs, crowing cocks, etc., he is in my opinion dealing with the same phenomena that I considered in Chapter 17 of my *Memoirs* at the end of a discussion on the subjective feelings caused by the seemingly talking chain-steamers, railway trains, etc. It is obviously only a simultaneously heard sounding of external noises added to the nervous impulses perceived as voices, so that these noises seem to echo the words spoken by the voices. These have to be clearly distinguished, in my case at any rate, from the genuinely talking voices of the birds, the sun, etc.[70]

Schreber points out that in many instances where someone is said to be hallucinating, the hallucinations possess a verifiable source, one that Kraepelin has overlooked. In these cases, Schreber explains, an external noise that does exist (a barking dog, grunting pig, chugging steamer, or clattering train) combines with the normal sounds of an individual's internal nervous impulses. The simultaneity of the two makes it seem as though the dog, pig, steamer, or train is actually talking, when it is not. Again, the explanation closely matches the one that Clarus and Schreber's grandfather advanced to characterize J. C. Woyzeck's experiences. Clarus and the medical faculty argued that the voices and visions the historical Woyzeck heard and saw were hallucinations (*Sinnestäuschungen*) produced by a "disorder of blood circulation" that he had ignorantly mistaken for objective reality.[71] Like his grandfather, Schreber affirms that generally these cases of hallucination are actually mistaken judgment. Mistaken does not apply in his own case, however, as his judgment is sound. The voices and visions he sees therefore have objective reality.

Schreber's use of Kraepelin's work to support his case for release from legal incompetency casts new light on some of the key concepts and ideas Schreber advances in the *Memoirs*. I am most interested in what Schreber describes repeatedly as a process of *Entmannung* (unmanning) and in a language he describes as the *Nervensprache* (nerve language), both of which have been the subject of extensive analytic and scholastic examination.

## The Mother's Law

Throughout the *Memoirs*, Schreber repeatedly comments on his transformation into a woman through a process of being "unmanned." Unmanning (Schreber's German neologism is *Entmannung*) entails being turned into a woman "able to bear children."[72] This means to him the full-scale biological conversion of the genitalia, designed to make Schreber capable of maintaining the human race after its complete destruction.

> This process of unmanning [*Entmannung*] consisted in the (external) male genitals (scrotum and penis) being retracted into the body and the internal sexual organs being at the same time transformed into female sexual organs, a process which might have been completed in a sleep lasting hundreds of years, because the skeleton (pelvis, etc.) had also to be changed. A regression occurred therefore, or a reversal of the developmental process which occurs in a human embryo in the fourth or fifth month of pregnancy, according to whether nature intends the future child to be of male or female sex.[73]

The unmanning Schreber experiences does not reach its conclusion, however. For that reason, Schreber also regularly comments on being filled with "nerves of voluptuousness (female nerves) [*Wollust- (weibliche) Nerven*]" that seek to accomplish his complete unmanning over time.[74]

Readings of the process of unmanning and insertion of nerves of voluptuousness into Schreber's body vary but have yet to remark on the important connection between Schreber's sense of being turned into a woman and his deprivation of legal majority. Schreber's neologistic reference to *Entmannung* (unmanning) resembles a corruption of the similar-sounding legal term *Entmündung* (incompetency). As it happened, both processes had a similar effect. *Entmannung* (unmanning) converted Schreber into a biological female by retracting his penis into his body and giving Schreber "female sexual organs" in its place. *Entmüdung* took the phallus from him and bestowed it on his wife. In describing *Entmannung*, Schreber makes a connection between his biological masculinity and the loss of legal majority that converted him into the equivalent of a woman in the law's eyes. Legally deprived of his property rights and symbolically bereft of his *väterliche Gewalt* (paternal force/violence), Schreber experienced a metaphorical castration.

Schreber's slip between *Entmannung* and *Entmündung*, between sexual difference and legal right, was already deeply encoded in the history of German philosophy, however. He succeeds in returning to a version of Kant's question about the relationship between sex and citizenship. In *What Is Enlightenment?*, *The Anthropology*, and a number of other texts, Kant repeatedly puns on the etymological similarity between the German adjective *mündig* (of full legal age, mature) and the German noun *Mund* (mouth). This is particularly apparent in a section of the *Anthropology* dedicated to defects of the cognitive faculty. There, Kant pauses to consider "mental deficiencies" (*Gemütsschwächen*) that may appear in the exercise of an otherwise healthy understanding. Kant's first example is children, who have an entirely healthy intellect that nevertheless has yet to be fully developed. Kant's second example is women who are timelessly immature: "*Children* are naturally immature [*unmündig*] and their parents are their natural guardians [*Vormünder*]. *Woman* regardless of age is declared to be immature in civil matters [*bürgerlich-unmündig erklärt*]; her husband is her natural curator. . . . It is true that when it comes to talking, woman by nature of her sex has enough of a mouth [*Mundwerke genug*] to represent both herself and her husband in court (where it concerns mine and thine) and so could literally be declared to be *over-mature* [*übermündig*]."[75]

Kant's description of woman as immature in civil matters regardless of age reflects the reality of the law in the late eighteenth century, under which a woman was not considered a citizen and could neither own property nor manage her own financial affairs. This also remained the case with the reforms of the BGB. Kant goes further, however. Relying on the *mündig/Mund* (maturity/mouth) pun, he comments that woman has "mouth enough" (*Mundwerke genug*) to represent herself and her husband in court. For Kant, even though women do not have legal standing, they are nevertheless sufficiently "mouthy" to be capable of representing both themselves and their husbands—the very person who should be speaking for them—in a legal setting. Women can therefore be declared "over-mature" (*übermündig*), that is, possessed of excessive legal majority because too mouthy. Underdeveloped in the exercise of their intellect, women are nevertheless grotesquely overdeveloped in the exercise of their mouths. In court, woman is monstrously two-headed. She compensates for her own well-deserved lack of legal authority by having the temerity to speak on behalf of herself and her husband.

In certain ways, Schreber had already experienced a version of the scenario Kant describes. The death of his father when he was nineteen put Schreber's mother in charge of the large household and would also have vested her with the legal rights she lacked while her husband was alive. When Schreber was declared incompetent in 1894, a similar situation developed with his own wife. Sabine Ottoline Behr became the beneficiary of the legal, philosophical, and political majority that her husband had helped write into law and that he had long arbitrated in his capacity as a judge. She became his *Vormund.*

An aspect of this regendering of citizenship and paternity comes through in Schreber's discussions of the talking sun. Freud reads the sun as a figuration of the father in his 1911 case history: "I should like to draw attention to the subject of the *sun*, which, through its 'rays', have so much importance in the expression of his delusions. Schreber had a quite peculiar relation to the sun. It speaks to him in a human language. . . . He identifies the sun directly with God. . . . The sun, therefore, is nothing but another sublimated symbol of the father."[76]

Freud neglects, however, two important features of Schreber's relationship to the sun. First, in German, the word "sun" is grammatically female: *die Sonne*. This even leads the English translators of the *Denkwürdigkeiten* to use a female pronoun for the sun when Schreber describes it speaking. Second, Freud neglects that in Schreber's family history, his mother legally and symbolically served in the role of the father after the death of Schreber's father in 1861. Schreber's mother lived into her nineties and remained very close with Schreber, meaning that she was a key figure in his life for most of his adulthood and far longer than he ever knew his father. If *die Sonne* was indeed the father for Schreber, as Freud argues, this sun was also biologically and grammatically female and took the form of Schreber's mother for most of his life and then his wife during his institutionalization. It makes particular sense that Schreber, *der Sohn* (the son, m.), should have wrestled with the figure of *die Sonne* (the sun, f.) because both the issue of paternity and gendering are wrapped up in the problem of Enlightenment (*Aufklärung*): the bringing of rational intellectual light to an otherwise "dark" and superstitious world. The speaking sun is at once the mother and the father for Schreber. It is grammatically female but invested with powerful authority, so legally male. It is the sovereign in Schreber's delusional system but the gender maximally deprived of sovereign legal authority in his lived political world. The sun of Schreber's Enlightenment is a question of gender.

Speech is therefore a problem for Schreber, who does not reject or appear uncomfortable with his *Entmannung* but who nevertheless struggles to know how to express himself. Far from accepting Kant's pejorative snipe about possessing too much mouth, Schreber strives to accomplish the impossible task of "speaking" as a woman in the legal sphere and does so in the service of rescinding the very guardianship that had placed him in that position. He too becomes overly "mouthy." There is the literal mouthiness represented by the attacks of bellowing. There is also his compulsion to repeat aloud the phrases from the various celestial languages he hears. There is his piano playing, which he describes doing with such force that he broke the instrument's strings. Closely related to what Kant describes in the *Anthropology*, Schreber also repeatedly litigates for his freedom in court, precisely the sphere for some of Kant's most vigorous criticism of women. Through turning to the sex and gender most deprived of legal majority in his era, Schreber seeks to resolve the dilemma of how to speak given his inability either to contest the law's legitimacy or accept its findings.

The other way in which Schreber accomplishes this challenging task is through what he called the *Nervensprache* (nerve language). Schreber's nerve language is not properly a language at all but a technique: it is a method of making one's nerves "vibrate in the way which corresponds to the use of the words concerned, but the real organs of speech (lips, tongue, teeth, etc.) are either not set in motion at all or only coincidentally." Unlike the various other languages Schreber describes in the *Denkwürdigkeiten*, the nerve language is a simple mechanized ideational conveyance system taking the form of silent speech. The nerves' vibratory movement is "generally imperceptible" to human beings. It is a channel to different linguistic registers and speakers without possessing one itself. Schreber compares it to being like the process of committing something to memory or to the repetition of a silent prayer. While the other languages Schreber describes in the book (the "basic language [*Grundsprache*]" and "soul language [*Seelensprache*]") operate on the level of content, the nerve language is a method inherently devoid of its own lexicon. It has the quality of a playback mechanism: at once cosmic megaphone and broadcast system. Indeed, it is the nerve language's seeming similarities to a telephone, radio, gramophone, and telegraph that has driven a great deal of work in media studies.

When the "order of the world" (*Weltordnung*) is functioning properly, Schreber states, no individual can control another's nerve language. Because the "order of the world" is out of joint, however, Schreber states that "[his] nerves [had] been set in motion from without" by "divine rays," which he alleged were manipulated by his puppet master–psychiatrist Paul Flechsig.[77] This is why he claims he is unable to control the tumultuous current of language poured into him and issuing from him. This language is not his. The *Nervensprache* also operates as a channel for a number of different celestial schemers. These anonymous figures repeat Schreber's thoughts to him after recording and warehousing them in what Schreber calls the cosmic "Writing-Down-System."

The technological character of Schreber's descriptions of the nerve language and his references to the ray's control over his nerves in what sounds like an elaborate electrical wiring system make it plausible to explain Schreber's delusions as the expression of a trauma produced by the advent of nineteenth-century communication technologies. This argument and its variations contend that modern communication technologies created a new soundscape at the turn of the century, which worked in partnership with the nonsense language produced by scientific fields like psychophysics. Writers and patients simply recorded these meaningless sounds in their own work, thereby creating a broken, fractured language decoupled from sense. It is equally possible and plausible to suggest that Schreber's nerve language is the mechanism by which Schreber endeavored to return to sense. It is the vehicle through which he attempted to speak after having been legally, philosophically, and politically "unmanned," all of which foreclosed the possibility of his speech and cast him as a woman. *This* reading stresses that Schreber may have fallen out of signification but that he actively strove to return to it. Having written the law that helped silence him, he nevertheless endeavored to again become a lawgiver, if from a compromised position that denied the meaningful nature of everything he said.

Since Schreber could no longer speak on his own behalf or in his own name, he adopted an ingenious alternative. The nerve language allowed Schreber to attribute his "own" speech to others. If Schreber could present himself solely as a communication channel facilitating others' words, not his own, he could achieve the impossible task of speaking on his own behalf from within a legal position that denied his capacity to do so sensically. Indeed, as he describes, *he* does not speak at all. In the nerve language, "the real organs of speech (lips, tongue, teeth, etc.) are either not set in motion at all or only coincidentally." This so-called speech is silent. It is generally imperceptible to other human beings. It lacks its own lexicon and merely is a conduit for others to speak through it: figures with proper and recognized authority. Flechsig, for example. The sun. All those who have not been unmanned.

These more legitimate individuals thereby accomplish another key task: they validate Schreber's thoughts by reinvesting them with the authority they would otherwise lack because coming from a person without reason. These thoughts, if already recorded and catalogued—a fact that already suggests their importance, indeed their *denkwürdigkeit*—can be returned to Schreber as both his and not his. They are at once worthless (*unwürdig*) because the thoughts of a woman and immeasurably valid and deserving of dignity (*würdig*) because no longer coming *from* a woman. They are at once the expression of pathetic castrated infertility and the cosmic potency of a higher power. They are disenlightened and irrational and the pinnacle of enlightened rationality. Because mechanically produced through the nerves, such that they do not affect the mind (*Geist*), they help prove Schreber's ineligibility for a diagnosis of mental illness (*Geisteskrankheit*).

If Schreber "speaks," he speaks in *le nom de la mère*, the name of the mother, which seeks to reestablish semiotic fecundity, reinstitute the law, and act with the power of paternal force (*väterliche Gewalt, la puissance paternelle, patria potestas*). Schreber indeed already knew the potency of *le nom de la mère*: the name of the mother is what executed Johann Christian Woyzeck. This is unlike the Name of the Father, which the Freudian and Lacanian interpretation stresses Schreber falls from. Schreber's attempt to reconstruct his world after his breakdown, and to do so from a legal and political position that would deny him the right to be a world constructor in any manner except biologically (whence, perhaps, Schreber's sense of having been impregnated), is carried out in the semiotically, representationally, and symbolically potent name of the mother.

What is so paradoxical about Schreber's *Memoirs* is that its scholastic reception as an autobiographical case of psychotic speech is exactly the opposite of Schreber's hopes for the work. To give Schreber his voice, this reading returns Schreber to the framework he spent hundreds of pages and multiple court cases contesting. Indeed, in the name of letting Schreber speak, the phenomenological interpretation—at least absent attention to *le nom de la mère*—silences Schreber all over again by repeating his designation of legal incompetency. Schreber is psychotic, therefore he is mentally ill, therefore his placement under guardianship was and is valid. This guardianship is no longer just legal, however, but also philosophical, one that insists on adherence to the medical and academic tradition asserting Schreber speaks for and about the experience of psychosis. If there is a mechanical quality to Schreber's experiences, it here returns as a rigid critical programming into psychosis as an interpretive idée fixe. A record on repeat or a radio tuned to no channel. With good intent, the effort to respect ethically Schreber's "psychotic" experiences by demanding that he speak on behalf of psychosis and as a psychotic nevertheless returns Schreber to 1893, to the Weber diagnosis, and to imperial German law. It rediagnoses him with the very clinical term he most fervently rejected and then presents what he says as "his" pathos-filled testament to a foregone diagnostic conclusion. Such a reading has the quality of a law and so cannot but neglect the extraordinary complex relationship to speech the law visited on Schreber.

Schreber's sincere and repeated attempts to show the somatic and not psychical nature of his disease, rooted in a problem with his nervous system, are thus taken to be a testament only to his terrified fear of his brain doctor (Flechsig), whose neuroanatomical approach allegedly threatened to deprive Schreber of his brain and reduce him to a living corpse. But what if the love for Flechsig that Freud identified included an appreciation for Flechsig's neuroanatomical approach? An approach that might have averted the entire situation had German law only recognized that it was possible to have a nervous illness causing hallucinations without being *mentally* ill? Attending to le *nom de la mère* does not necessitate revoking Schreber's place in psychoanalysis, whether in Freud's case history or Lacan's distinction between the neuroses and the psychoses. Neither does it mean discarding fathers and paternity in his case history. It simply means recognizing that psychosis and paternity may not be all there is. It means considering that diagnosis-first readings may be as ethically compromised as phenomenologically progressive.

If Schreber sided with Flechsig's neuroanatomy, he could not, in any event, have said as much. The *Nervensprache* is silent, after all. In this regard, Schreber touches on what writers like Sandra Gilbert and Susan Gubar argued in *The Madwoman in the Attic* long after his time.[78] As Gilbert and Gubar discuss regarding nineteenth-century English authors such as Jane Eyre, Mary Shelley, and Emily Brontë, among others, the ascription of madness to women was not a liberatory gesture but one of confinement associated with the attribution of monstrosity. Schreber too makes a version of Gilbert and Gubar's point: to be declared mad is not always subversive. Sometimes it is just pathologizing.

This position has, however, faded over time, both for better and for worse, to be replaced with one invested in a narration of the self and a related faith in the witnessing powers of phenomenological subjectivity. It has become a significant feature of interpretations of modernist literary works and their successors. It characterizes texts such as Rainer Maria Rilke's *Notebooks of Malte Laurids Brigge* (1910) and Evelyn Waugh's *Ordeal of Gilbert Pinfold* (1957) as being "about" the narrator's descent into ontological confusion in a technologizing world or because of the trials of modernity. Often, it purports to grant dignity to the author's or character's experiences, which are seen as a testament to individual suffering or a liberatory cry of freedom flung in the face of normative standards. The problem, however, is the underlying assumption that a psychodiagnostic assessment will be value neutral as long as the categories the diagnostician uses are sufficiently scientific, that is, that they adhere to a sufficiently rigorous definition of mental illness (*Geisteskrankheit*). (One could add to this the difficulty that such a position assumes the omniscience of the first person about itself). We are back with Walter Benjamin. The unacknowledged diagnostic act of speaking for another frames itself as making room for the fully sovereign speech of another while also making room for human cataloguing.

That Schreber was "silenced" by German imperial law working in partnership with the medical establishment does not mean that what he has to say upon entry into print is of necessity just. The *nom de la mère* in Schreber's case is psychopower, which assumes the right to execute members of a calculably and divisibly sane population. In attributing his condition to a biological factor (his nerves), Schreber also unwittingly affirms biology as the basis for human classificatory practices, contributing as much to an imagination of the properly biopolitical regulation of populations as to the belief that those with mental illness are truly sick. For Schreber, the matter is not a question of how to treat "the mentally ill." It is simply a question of proving he is not among "them."

This is the racist, antisemitic, nationalist, and prefascist dimension of the *Memoirs*, an expression of psychopower's grasp on a portrait of popular mental health that is not restricted to policing the mad but extended to controlling the sane. This is why Schreber is not feminist or progressive in any sense of that term that would extend beyond a white, Western European, heterosexual understanding of it. Schreber's "feminism" and his disruption of the gender norms are built around a baseline insistence on heteronormativity and on the essential validity of traditional gender roles, a position that regards homosexuality as intolerable. Schreber's bid to become a woman arises in the context of his legal quest to recover his "lost" male potency and regain his sovereign masculine right. It develops from the belief that a woman is a castrated man and that female world creation is only ever accomplished through pregnancy.

Schreber in effect treats the legal standards of citizenship as defined by the BGB as being synonymous with the natural order, or *Weltordnung*, an order of the world in which a woman cannot speak for her natural male guardian. The order of the world is out of joint, however. Deprived of his legal majority (*Mündigkeit*), Schreber cannot speak for himself and so is "reduced" to the status of a secondary citizen, woman. In this way Schreber takes for granted that men who become women (and women who become men) are at odds with the naturally legal and legally natural order of the world. That order must be reestablished because it is both legal and natural. Whatever desire Schreber may sincerely have felt to become biologically female and to assume a female gender role is presented by the *Memoirs* as the experience of being *reduced* to a woman. Schreber's quest is to remedy it by seeking the return of his legal majority: a representation of *Manneskraft* (male power) in a sense beyond the juridical.

Schreber contributes to psychopower by suggesting there is a measurable and provable normal, that the law's definition of sanity, backed up by medical research, can and should hold—indeed, that it can and should hold everywhere. With Flechsig's help, Schreber hopes that his "thesis would thereby gain universal credence [*vor aller Welt*]." He sides, as it were, with Clarus and his grandfather in 1823. It is thus interesting that the Sonnenstein asylum from which Schreber obtained his release in 1902 on grounds of sanity should have both a dark future and a complicated past. Sonnenstein was one of the kingdom of Saxony's first mental asylums when it was constructed in 1811. It was considered medically progressive at the time for its use of occupational therapy.[79] The asylum furthermore held the distinction of being the first in Saxony to be linked to a university system, in this case Leipzig University. The first chair, Johann Christian August Heinroth (1773–1843), was alive in Woyzeck's time. Heinroth was not summoned to conduct Woyzeck's medical examination (the task belonged to the state physician) and not included in the medical faculty's vote (he was not technically a member of the medical faculty).[80] After Woyzeck execution, Heinroth nevertheless endorsed Clarus's findings in the medical controversy connected with the insanity defense that unfolded in Saxon psychiatric circles.

Schreber died in 1911, meaning that (unlike the Wolf-Man) he did not live to see the outbreak of World War I or the collapse of the German Empire. Two decades after his death, however, Sonnenstein became one of the sites at which the Nazi Party executed psychiatric patients in the sweeping T4 program (1939–1945), which National Socialism claimed was a form of "social hygiene" that would remove persons "unsuited to live" from the general population. The Saxon Memorial Foundation set up in the early 2000s to document the history of Sonnenstein under National Socialism documents that around 15,000 people considered mentally ill or mentally disabled were murdered between 1940 and 1941 in gas chambers set up in the Sonnenstein basement. This basement, the Saxon Memorial Foundation records, was also used to gas prisoners from concentration camps. They do not mention that the legalized use of the death penalty for both the sane and the mad at Sonnenstein goes back to 1823.

Schreber nevertheless also contested the validity of instrumentalized scientific rationality in his *Memoirs*, striving time and again to show that it is possible for what he heard and saw to have an objective reality, if one that had yet to be recognized. This is oddly Johann Christian Woyzeck's position as well. A position that cost him his head. Woyzeck, who murdered his widowed lover in broad daylight with a broken blade. Enlightenment. The psychotic reads law. The writer of just laws is punished by them.

## CHAPTER 4

# EXPRESSIONIST *WELTREVOLUTION* AND PSYCHOPOLITICAL WORLDING

For six tumultuous days in April 1919, the German Jewish expressionist writer Ernst Toller commanded the equally short-lived Bavarian Soviet Republic. Romantically dubbed the "Revolution of Love" by Toller at his trial, it was less idealistically designated a *Scheinrepublik* (pseudorepublic) by the Communist Party, which refused to recognize it. Toller's ill-starred Soviet or Council Republic (*Räterepublik*) in Munich survived only from April 6 to 12, during which time it was run chiefly by artists and intellectuals.[1] For the short duration of its existence, the *Räterepublik* purported to represent the interests of the Bavarian proletariat against both those of the right and the left, the latter in the form of the "insufficiently radical" Weimar Republic. Its bloody suppression, which—in the words of Toller's lawyer functionally amounted to "the revolutionaries of yesterday charging the revolutionaries of today . . . with high treason"—was the basis for Toller's drama *Masse-Mensch* (1921), written from a prison cell in the fortress of Niederschönenfeld in 1919.[2]

The play premiered at the Nürnberger Stadttheater in 1920 and reached the Berlin *Völksbuhne* a year later, in a celebrated production by Jürgen Fehling. The print edition contains a dedication "to the proletariat" (*den Proletariern*) and a poetic epigraph heralding the "world revolution" (*Weltrevolution*) in grandiose terms. "Bearer of new movements. / Bearer of new social forms [*Gebärerin des neuen Schwingens. / Gebärerin der neuen Völkerkreise*]," it declares.[3] Whatever naïve idealism may appear in these lines is forcefully tempered by the contents of the play, which concludes with the offstage execution—by firing squad, no less—of its everywoman protagonist Sonja Irene L.[4] This bitter end is foreshadowed in the epigraph's own concluding lines: "The century blazes red / Bloody beacon of guilt / The earth crucifies itself [*Rot leuchtet das Jahrhundert / Blutige Schuldfanale / Die Erde kreuzigt sich*]."[5] Nodding at once to the Russian Revolution, the violence with which the *Räterepublik* had been snuffed out, and the blood of the *Gebärerin*'s metaphorical parturition, the epigraph concludes in a red apotheosis of messianic birth-death. Having greeted the birth of fresh *Schwingen* and *Völkerkreise*, the drama also recognizes their teratological nature, pivoting to make the unexpected point that these new oscillations and reorganizations do not necessarily betoken a better world, merely a different one. Neither, the play seems to suggest, are they confined to the realm of politics. The *Weltrevolution* cannot but mark the world's own wholesale transformation.

As if in testament to the jointly civic and psychological dimensions of this metamorphosis, Sonja Irene L.'s husband, an unnamed civil servant, retorts, "Peace is the illusion of neurasthenics [*Friede ist Phantom von Nervenschwachen*]" when his wife pleads with him to join her in an antiwar strike.[6] The comment mobilizes a familiar key term from the early twentieth century's Zeitgeist of nervous exhaustion. It also reflects a subtle shift within the more familiar discourse of nerves, shock, and modernity.[7] Pejoratively characterizing antiwar protestors as mentally ill, the line additionally suggests that neurasthenics form a kind of *Völkerkreis*; it deliberately creates a parallelism between this group and the formalized political entities, such as the USPD and KPD, historically responsible for the German Revolution.[8] Neurasthenics are an agential social faction in the husband's eyes, which are also, by proxy, those of the state. Both the petitions for peace and the petitioners are neatly written off by his words. The group's outwardly benevolent humanitarianism merely dresses up the uglier reality that such peacemongering is symptomatic of the neurasthenics' underlying weakness and effeminacy, which can only be properly recognized by the objective gaze of the state-cum-clinician.

Although a passing remark, the husband's words capture the double-edged quality of social reconfiguration to which the epigraph also alludes, reaffirming that the play does not merely attend to the triumphant upheaval of entrenched class hierarchies but the genesis of a wide spectrum of new divisions in, and definitions of, the *Volk*. *Völkerkreis* was notably also the term used by German ethnographers such as Friedrich Ratzel (1844–1904), who coined the word *Lebensraum*, and Hans Ferdinand Helmolt (1865–1929) to describe "circles of peoples" in the sense of ethnic groups linked to geographic regions. In Helmolt's massive *Weltgeschichte* (*World History*, 1899–1907), *Völkerkreise* are the spatiodemographic units of division that organize his world history's nine volumes.[9] In short, both the husband's retort and the epigraph gloss what the play's unusual title already has indicated: a flickering between one and many that sustains without resolving the issue of differentiability. *Masse* in *Masse Mensch* might serve as an adjective (identifying a collective "Mass-Man"), a noun (alluding to the relationship between "Mass and Man"), or a possessive (the "Masses' Man").[10] As the homonym of *die Maße* (plural of *das Maß*, measurement), it emphasizes the difficulty of knowing just how to count. Of taking the measure of man or men. In a legal context, it evokes the *Strafmaß*, or sentence, quite literally a "measure" of penalty. If *Masse-Mensch* offers, as its subtitle claims, "a fragment/play [*Stück*] of the social revolution of the twentieth century," it would seem to trace an ambivalent upheaval in the relationship of part and whole, and in the ways of recognizing them, that is as much the more familiar story of interwar Central European convulsions in the body politic and the drama of individual agency within historical materialism as it is the less familiar one of a contemporaneous shift in psychosocial coordinates that is neither limited to psychoanalysis nor explicable purely in the era's popular rhetoric of nervous illness.

Indeed, just as Toller was putting pen to paper in prison, Emil Kraepelin, who happened to have clinically assessed the writer a year earlier, offered his own account of the forces and groups responsible for the *Räterepublik*. His article "Psychiatric Observations on Contemporary Issues" ("Psychiatrische Randbemerkungen zur Zeitgeschichte") appeared in the pages of the conservative *Süddeutsche Monatshefte* in June 1919, in an issue entitled "Zur Wahrheit der Revolution" (Toward the truth of the revolution). It accompanied damning reflections on Communism in praxis, antisemitic commentary on Kurt Eisner, and an allegorical poem written by no less than the director of the Württemburg State Statistical Office about the consequences faced by a horse that sought to throw off its rider.[11] Kraepelin's "Psychiatric Observations" declared the need to conclusively eliminate misconceptions in the public sphere about the psychological basis for the political events of 1918/1919. The piece purported to diagnose the pathological state of Germany's "collective soul" (*Volkseele*) following World War I. Recent mass movements showed distinct signs of psychiatric disturbance, the author argued. In fact, their leaders were statistically "outside the boundaries of the average [*aus dem Rahmen der Durchschnittsbreite*]" and so also outside the boundaries of normality.[12] They could be classified in two groups. Either such leaders possessed "hysterical traits" (*Persönlichkeiten mit hysterischer Zügen*), in the case of the "poets and dreamers," or they were manic-depressives (*deren Seelenzustand zumeist dem manischdepressiven Irresein angehört*), in the case of the "frenetics" (*Vielgeschäftigen*).[13] Followers consisted of "a swarm of inferior personalities" (*ein Schwarm minderwertiger Persönlichkeiten*), some of whom were "without a doubt . . . psychopaths

[*Psychopathen*]."[14] Like the play, the article created a new synonymy between mental illnesses and social groups, or *Völkerkreise*. Hysterical poets and manic-depressive frenetics were responsible for recklessly inciting the psychopathic herd to violent uprising. The *Novemberrevolution* was merely an unfortunate consequence of this more general affliction of the *Volkseele*.

The article's classificatory system is taken from Kraepelin's *Psychiatrie: Ein Lehrbuch für Studierende und Ärzte* (Psychiatry: a textbook for students and doctors), which was in its eighth edition as of 1915.[15] In offering a clinical typology of revolutionary leadership in his article, Kraepelin was in fact repeating his textbook's groundbreaking 1899 assertion about differential diagnoses. His descriptions of "hysterics," "psychopaths," and "manic-depressives" in "Psychiatric Observations" are taken directly from his textbook, utilize nearly identical language, and rely on the work's rigorous typological divisions. In addition to reaffirming the real existence of the textbook's claims, however, "Psychiatric Observations" went a step further, suggesting the Kraepelinian classification system's broad practical applicability beyond the clinical sphere.

Despite the article's sweeping generalizations about the population, "Psychiatric Observations" also relied heavily on a single case history to support its claims: that of Ernst Toller, whose (unpublished) medical report Kraepelin had written a year prior. In the earlier 1918 psychiatric assessment—prompted by Toller's participation in a strike—Kraepelin dismissed Toller as yet another tragic example of the "psychopathic personality" (*die psychopatische Persönlichkeiten*). He regarded his patient as well within the bounds of an average "psychopathy," defined in his textbook as a form of degeneracy (*Entartung*) notable for its relative stability over time and its deviation from the normal: "[The psychopathic personality] is to a certain extent a question of psychological deformity [*Mißbildungen*], the pathological nature of which is recognizable only in terms of its overall deviation from the basic parameters of health [*allgemeinen Abweichung von der Gesundheitsbreite*], not based on a shift from an earlier, healthier time."[16]

Just one year later, however, in the wake of the *Räterepublik*, he used this same diagnosis to make a claim about the emergence of a vast social pathology that seemed to originate with Toller. Whereas Kraepelin's 1918 medical report was quick to dismiss Toller's case as that of one more pitiable reprobate, his 1919 article seemed to do precisely the opposite, making Toller *the* definitive exemplar of psychopathy and its dangers. Although the article admittedly never mentioned Toller by name, the enormous public attention his trial for treason received across national German media meant no one who read "Psychiatric Observations" could fail to know exactly whom its author had in mind when he declared a dangerous plague of hysterical psychopathy sweeping the nation. Here, then, a paradox arises. Between the medical report and the article, Toller at once melts into the anonymous generality of an abstracted, determinative psychopathy (which apparently conditions his entire being) and is singled out as its paradigmatic representative, whose recent political actions determine the features of the disease.

At once individual and group in his psychiatrist's assessments, Toller sheds light on a broader, if also more elusive, consequence of Kraepelin's novel classification scheme: the genesis of a new way of narrating case histories that created anthropological divisions but left the individual's place, agency, and legal culpability exceptionally uncertain. It did so at a moment when the birth of "statistical thinking" (Forrester, Porter, Hacking) and when German philosophers like Ernst Bloch were beginning to articulate a *Wirproblem* (We-problem).[17] Yet at the same time Kraepelinian psychiatry was redefining the individual's role within the case history, its methodology lacked the capacity to take account of the broader revolution in the study of mental disease it inaugurated. Heavy reliance on testable evidence had the effect of eliminating the need for methodological self-scrutiny, which was now replaced by adjusting empirical procedures to refine the precision of factual results. Beyond these results, there was simply nothing to say. Thus, when Kraepelin began to use his textbook's conclusions to assert the universal existence of his psychiatric disease categories, finding evidence for them on research trips to Southeast Asia, Latin America, North America, and the Middle East, a critical consideration of just *how* research conducted primarily in Germany had metamorphosed into a set of vast anthropological categories remained wholly outside his scope.

The epistemological limit point, beyond which Kraepelinian psychiatry could not stretch to reckon with its own assumptions about the *Volkerkreise*, is the point from which Toller's play *Masse-Mensch* begins. Toller's staging of the ambivalent boundary between one and many in his play, between *Masse* and *Mensch*, offers a way of understanding what Kraepelin's psychiatric classification system could not see itself. *Masse-Mensch* displaces the psychiatric dilemma concerning individual and group into the theater, raising questions pertinent to psychiatry even if not disciplinarily situated within it. It furthermore suggests that the indirect, nonthematic reconstitution of Kraepelinian psychiatry's epistemological dilemmas within a thoroughly "unscientific" medium—here, German expressionist drama—may be one of the few ways of recognizing that those dilemmas are present at all.

Both *Masse-Mensch* and "Psychiatric Observation" were written in response to the *Räterepublik*'s brief efflorescence and violent suppression, and both ask questions about the composition, divisibility, and gendering of the postwar social body. Whereas the story of proletarian struggle has long been a mainstay of critical and theoretical discussion, the more elusive story of psychiatry's related circles and divisions has yet to be told.

* * *

Still largely unknown as a writer in 1919, Toller had begun his unlikely path to the head of a sovereign state over the course of the 1918 antiwar strikes in Munich, which resulted in his arrest. Having served time in a military prison, he returned home only to be placed under psychiatric observation by his mother, who was horrified to discover her son's willingness to plot against the nation. "Apparently my mother had been unable to imagine how her son had come to be accused of treason. He must be ill, she had thought. . . . So she went to the family doctor, who gave her a certificate which she sent to the Court—I had been nervous since childhood—hence this psychiatric evaluation," Toller reports in his autobiography.

The doctor to whom Toller was assigned at the University of Munich psychiatric hospital proved significantly more appalled. Although Toller's mother had hoped to remove her son from the political melee by having him medically evaluated, Toller's arrival at Kraepelin's institute merely returned him to it. The encounter represented the collision of two starkly divergent political agendas, the battle between which was now lifted from the public strife of the Munich streets and transferred to the private corridors of psychopathology and law. Kraepelin, head of the newly opened Deutsche Forschungsanstalt für Psychiatrie (DFP), then located inside Munich University, was also a fervent nationalist and founding member of the conservative Vaterlandspartei (Fatherland Party). It was against precisely this party and its deceptively titled proposal "Guidelines for Paths to a Lasting Peace" (which called for German rule of Belgium, demanded the Russians return "to Asia," and beat the drum for an African empire, among other peace-defying claims) that Toller had publicly petitioned. The wholesale failure of Kraepelin's hyperconservative political proposals did not, however, prevent his private research institute—the first of its kind in Germany—from opening in the midst of World War I. Its creation was a testament to his work's international prestige by 1919 and his close ties to powerful financial backers. Leaders of the German war industry (such as the steel and arms manufacturer Gustav Krupp von Bohlen und Halbach) and prominent American philanthropists, including the Jewish-American banker James Loeb, all contributed funds to the enterprise. Loeb, now best known as the founder of the Loeb Classical Library, had also been Kraepelin's patient. He donated 524,000 marks—roughly three million dollars in the currency of the time—to the venture in 1916, the largest sum of any of the original donors.[18]

Newly ensconced at the helm of the DFP and embittered by the government's rejection of the "Guidelines," Kraepelin made no effort to hide his outrage at the 1918 strikers from Toller. "How can you dare to deny Germany's rightful claims to power? Germany needs new *Lebensraum*, Belgium and the Baltic Provinces. You are responsible for our failure to capture Paris. You are delaying our victory. The enemy is England," Toller recalls his doctor furiously rebuking him at the institute.[19] Perhaps unsurprisingly given the circumstances, Kraepelin and his senior doctor at the DFP, Professor Ernst Rüdin (1874–1952), produced a psychiatric report on Toller that maximized the potential for legal ramifications. In a repetition of the psychopolitical paradigm that played out in Johann Christian Woyzeck's case of 1823, Kraepelin treated the revolutionary events of 1918 as an opportunity to enchain his patient by declaring him legally sane. Finding Toller "a psychopathic and hysterical personality [*eine psychopathisch und hysterische Persönlichkeit*]," he also functionally ensured the writer could *not* be considered insane in the eyes of the law. He therefore could be held legally responsible for his actions: "The psychopathic and hysterical personality, which is simply a state of the defective personal disposition [*einen Zustand mangelhafter Charakteranlage*] and the maladjustment of the psyche's [*Seele*] various basic properties to the [joint] imperatives of self-preservation and social coexistence—not a mental defect [*Defekt*], mental disturbance [*Geistesstörung*], or mental illness [*Geisteskrankheit*] in the narrow sense of the word—does not in general fulfill the provisions of §51 of the Criminal Code of the German Empire."[20]

In other words, Toller might be defective by disposition, but he was not technically mentally ill, at least according to Kraepelin's 1918 report's interpretation of the law. He was answerable for his actions in the munitions strike and could, in theory, be further prosecuted for them, despite already having served time in a military prison. Section 51 of the *Reichsstrafgesetzbuch* (RStGB) from 1871 stated that no criminal act had been committed in cases where the perpetrator was in a state of "pathological disturbance of mental functioning [*krankhafter Störung der Geistestätigkeit*]" and lacked free will: "No criminal act [*strafbare Handlung*] has been committed in cases when the perpetrator at the time of committing it was in a condition of unconsciousness [*Bewusstlosigkeit*] or pathological disturbance of mental functioning [*krankhafter Störung der Geistestatigkeit*], on account of which his ability to make free choices [*freie Willensbestimmung*] was suspended."[21]

Kraepelin's concerted effort to deem Toller compos mentis thus represents the unusual scenario of a psychiatrist endeavoring to prove his patient sane in order to ensure he could be locked away. Upsetting the archetypal narrative of the deranged alienist who deems his victims mad so as to illegitimately imprison them within a remote asylum—contemporaneously realized on screen in *The Cabinet of Dr. Caligari* (1920)—Kraepelin deliberately labeled Toller sane in the hopes that the writer might thereby end up behind bars. Toller's nominal release from Kraepelin's institute thus paradoxically also represented his symbolic entry into legal culpability, inverting the distinction between the unfreedom of forced institutionalization and the alleged freedom of release.

The textbook's exceptional specificity, combined with its claim that diseases possessed a life course, enabled Kraepelin to argue that Toller did not meet the conditions for pathological disturbance as spelled out in §51 of the criminal code. Kraepelin's meticulous separation of hitherto invisible disorders was the ground on which its author could confidently state which counted as mental illnesses "in the narrow sense of the word" and which fell into other classifications, which, while still being exceptionally serious illnesses, did not come with a legal exemption from criminal responsibility. As Kraepelin noted in his report: "The symptoms of a mental disorder in the sense of §51 are absent in Toller at the time in question. . . . Pathological motives such as hallucinations, delusional ideas, etc. were not present."[22]

Yet while Kraepelin dismissed the idea that Toller was delusional, he still managed to conclude that Toller's overall character was "erratic, volatile, unstable, agitated, contradictory [*ungleichmässig, sprunghaft, unstät, unruhig, widerspruchsvoll*]." This description allowed Kraepelin and, later, the Munich court, to thread the needle of holding Toller criminally responsible while simultaneously finding him dangerously clinically ill. Yet far from being evidence of anything Kraepelin saw in the course of Toller's stay at the DFA, the language in Kraepelin's psychiatric report simply applied the textbook's preexisting definition of "psychopathic personality" to the writer and did so nearly word for word. As the *Lehrbuch* had already noted, "The patients summarized here consistently showed an unbalanced, volatile [*sprunghaften*] character that lacked stability [*Stätigkeit*]." Their "way of life appears aimless, contradictory [*widerspruchsvoll*]," and their constitution "erratic [*ungleichmässig*]."[23]

Kraepelin's medical report of 1918 implicitly establishes that it is not Toller who is ill, as his mother thought, but society who is ill with Toller:

> His actions are easily accounted for by his excitable, highly strung personality, which is constantly pestering for attention and advancement . . . and by the characteristic, seductive, leading effects that arise from mass movements and act more strongly on natures such as Toller's [*auf solche Naturen wie Toller*] than on the harmonious mind [*harmonische Seele*] of wholly normal [*ganz normalen*], coolly deliberative, and strong-willed . . . men.[24]

Note the language: "on natures such as Toller's." The writer and those of his type are, it would seem, outlying data in a sea of the sober minded. Toller, whose Jewish heritage is already a prominent feature of the report, becomes doubly emblematic of an allegedly undesirable social group plaguing the *Volkseele* with these words. The extreme antisemitism that characterized the trial and influenced the reactionary response to the *Räterepublik* is present in Kraepelin's report before those events occur, where it guarantees that Toller's threat to national health can be interpreted as simultaneously racial and psychiatric in nature. Judaism, socialism, and mental disease entail one another in a vicious circle of criminal culpability that nevertheless proceeds under the name of nonconfinement. And, while Kraepelin endorsed degeneration theory and social Darwinism—features of his research evident in his report's focus on Toller's heredity—he does not present his conclusion in the language of Cesare Lombroso or Francis Galton. In Kraepelin's judgment, seemingly medical and juridical, Toller is dangerous because of his psychopathy, which secondarily suggests a link to the "social pathology" of Judaism, already well established in Germany by 1919. Thus, while it is easy to think that Kraepelin was simply reiterating what had already been said about degeneration, his research had found a new way to support such claims by establishing the idea of psychiatric baseline, an average normality. No matter how small the deviation from this norm, it was always an indication of degenerative psychopathy. "It goes without saying that the discovery and pursuit of pathological variations in the human race, even in their subtlest early forms, is a task of the utmost importance," he wrote in *Psychiatrie*, before going on to note that, in this regard, psychiatric research extended "far beyond purely medical questions" and into the "study of the innermost essence of man."[25]

The basis for Kraepelin's claim is as coolly deliberative as the "harmonious man" to whom Toller is negatively compared. Interestingly, the 1918 medical report frames Toller's social threat as one of quantitative deviance, not malign intent. His doctor writes that Toller has always shown "abnormal traits in his mental constitution and character" and so must be characterologically distinguished from the "completely normal average person [*vom völlig normalen Durchschnittsmenschen*]."[26] Toller's abnormality is, in other words, empirically valid. As a statistical outlier, however, he menaces the "healthy" cohesion of a naturalized social mean from the far corner of the graph. Lone datum in the wilderness beyond society's central cluster, his erratic (*ungleichmässig*) character is of a piece with his statistical erroneousness. Whence the danger he represents. Healthy enough to act by free will, he (and those like him) are a structural plague on the social body.

Indeed, Toller's declared relief at being discharged ("They let me out after four days, and I thanked my lucky stars") was ultimately undermined by the malign return of his psychiatrist's seemingly exculpatory diagnosis at his 1919 trial for high treason, during which the 1918 psychiatric report was used as evidence. Ernst Rüdin served as medical expert for the prosecution in 1919, a role he assumed both based on his coauthorship of Toller's 1918 medical report and prestigious position at the DFP. Rüdin testified that the 1918 report's overall conclusions remained accurate but that the patient's present condition was, in his expert opinion, "significantly better than in the previous year." The reason for this was "unclear" to Rüdin, but it nonetheless led him to conclude that Toller was more responsible now for his actions than when first diagnosed. If his former patient's condition had improved, this patient's capacity for free decision making had increased, and with it his guilt.[27] The court affirmed the doctor's findings in its final judgment, which unequivocally embraced Toller's full legal responsibility (*Zurechnungsfähigkeit*) and ruled out any exemption via §51.[28] Kraepelin did not personally take the stand, but he nevertheless paved the way for Rüdin's in-court statements. "Psychiatric Observations" was published a month before the trial began and suggested the extreme danger the patient represented to society, thereby priming the court to view Toller as psychopathic before ever having laid eyes on him.

Toller, whose abnormality in the 1918 report had consisted in belonging to a group defined by its measurable deviance, is twisted by the 1919 article into the racial and psychological standard-bearer of the movement to which he politically lent his name. Six-day leader of the *Räterepublik*, his role as ideological representative of the proletariat (despite his manifestly bourgeois background) is insidiously transmuted into evidence of their collective malady in a handful of pages. If Toller in any way represents "the people," in Kraepelin's article it is only in a defamatory clinical sense. Without ever mentioning Toller by name in the article, Kraepelin nevertheless makes clear that this writer and his co-conspirators are the *specific* individuals to whom he is referring. "Personally, I have found that in the recent demonstrations a number of the leading personalities [*führenden Persönlichkeiten*] and their followers whom I have either been able to examine or of whom I acquired more precise information, belong to one of the above groups" of leadership types (that is, "psychopaths," "hysterics," "manic-depressives").[29] Returning to the grotesque conjuncture of mental illness, race, and political ideology, he speculates on the hereditary basis for psychopathy in mass movements. "The active involvement of the Jewish race," with its "psychopathic predisposition," "harping criticism," and "rhetorical and theatrical abilities," in these kinds of upheavals "has something to do" with such movements' "psychopathic nature."

Apparently, however, it is not simply the leaders of these movements who are ill but the movements themselves. Reaching back in time, Kraepelin accounts for the Paris Commune, Russian revolts of 1905, Russian Revolution, and Germany's fate at the end of World War I as psychical fallout from a shock to the population. Sudden jolts (such as war) allegedly dislodge the "forces of reason," producing mass hysterical disorders in demographic groups more vulnerable to instability because phylogenetically underdeveloped.[30] Women and children, as well as "excitable, unstable, weak-willed individuals"—note the similarity to the language in Toller's medical report and in the Schreber case—revert to primitive behaviors and "dark instinctual urges" at these moments of shock, unlike the "internally well-grounded male," in whom such behaviors no longer dominate.[31]

This observation forms part of Kraepelin's overall picture of human inequality, the description of which forms the last third of "Psychiatric Observations." Social stratification is the result, not the cause, of individuals' inherently differing "primal predisposition." Recent political movements have attempted to invert this basic truth by fancifully blaming external causes for the existence of a socioeconomic hierarchy. In truth, this stratification is the just result of the population's naturally variant abilities. The attempt to replace its highest echelons with a "conglomeration of those countrymen whose ancestors could not, over the centuries, rise to the top," a conglomeration more succinctly known as "the proletariat," is as perverse as it is inequitable, he concludes. Toller escaped a death sentence but was nevertheless given five years on account of his criminal well-being.

Inspired by Kraepelin and Rüdin, medical speculations about Toller continued even after he was sentenced. In the months that followed the trial, several German psychiatrists took it upon themselves to consider the psychiatric background for Germany's recent mass movements in relationship to Toller's case. Like their predecessors, these medical professionals regarded the writer as both a free-willed actor deserving punishment and the more passive representative of a vast social pathology. Kraepelin's former doctoral student, Eugen Kahn, now an assistant doctor at the DFA, expanded his mentor's original claims in a pair of medical articles composed later that year. "Psychopaths as Revolutionary Leaders" ("Psychopathen als revolutionäre Führer"), delivered as a talk to the Bavarian Psychiatrist's Association in August 1919, declared that there was a long historical trail of psychopathic personalities heading revolutionary movements, which reached at least from the Italian monk Giacomo Savonarola to the German participants in present-day events.[32] In "Psychopathy and Revolution" ("Psychopathie und Revolution"), written for the *Münchener Medizinische Wochenscrift*, Kahn asserted that Toller was an "object lesson [*Schulbeispiel*]" in the link between mental illness, criminality, and revolutionary activity. In November, the Berlin physician Hugo Marx published "Medical Thoughts on the Revolution" ("Ärztliche Gedanken zur Revolution") in the pages of the *Berliner Klinischer Wochenschrift*. Hugo Marx lamented the uptick of "infectious" pathological collective thinking exhibited by the revolution and bemoaned the loss of rational individual judgment. Marx cited both Kraepelin and Kahn's prior articles on Toller in support of his conclusions.[33]

The psychiatric discourse surrounding the case was sufficiently widespread and the articles sufficiently prominent to inspire a backlash in the press. Witnesses for the defense at Toller's trial had included no less than Thomas Mann and Max Weber, so it is unsurprising that there should have been a heated response from the left. Attacks on the medical aspects of the trial focused almost exclusively on psychiatric pseudoscientificity.[34] Writers for the literary magazine *Das Forum* and the USPD's *Die Freiheit* railed against Kraepelin, Kahn's, and others' arbitrary attribution of these nonscientific descriptions to the *Räterepublik*'s leaders.[35] They condemned psychiatric classifications' extension into the realm of law. This was similarly the position Toller adopted in his later play *Hoppla, We're Alive!* (*Hoppla, wir Leben!*) from 1927. In that work, the revolutionary leftist protagonist, Karl Thomas, undergoes a forced psychiatric examination after a failed attempt to assassinate a turncoat comrade. "Professor Lüdin," who attends to Karl Thomas in the play, is a parody of Rüdin and an extreme caricature of a Kraepelinian clinical assessment.[36] Lüdin barks out "Normal" or "Abnormal" as Thomas describes the events leading up to his assassination attempt, assigns numbered diagnostic classifications to individuals in his patient's story ("Type two," "Type three"), and is every bit the visibly malevolent quack.[37]

By the time *Masse-Mensch* premiered in late November 1920, scheduled as a series of closed performances for trade unionists at the Nürnberg Stadttheater, Kraepelin's diagnosis of Toller was sufficiently well known to appear in a police report about the production. At the performance scheduled for the evening of November 26, 1920, the theater made unsold tickets available to the public. Members of the antisemitic Alliance for the Unity and Protection of the German People (Deutschvölkischer Schutz- und Trutzbund) showed up to purchase them, with the intention of disrupting the performance. Their extreme heckling forced theater staff to remove dozens of people from the performance, attracting the attention of both press and police. The report issued the next day by the Northern Bavarian Police deemed the play harmless on the grounds that it proved how diseased Toller truly was. "The Proletariat of Nürnberg hereby has the opportunity to assure themselves of Toller's psychopathic disposition through his [own] work."[38] If would-be revolutionaries on the left had any doubt about Toller's abilities as a leader or, indeed, any remaining fantasies about the *Räterepublik*, the police concluded that the play would quell such misplaced notions.

At the same time, they banned further performances in Nürnberg, on the grounds that outbreak of a riot within the theater had given too much advertising to such a literarily worthless piece. Even though no print copy of the play yet existed, the matter of the ban was taken up by the Bavarian parliament in December at the request of a representative of the Deutschnationale Volkspartei. While acknowledging that theater censorship was no longer legal as of 1919 and that the drama's more detailed content remained "unknown," the government representative Zetlmeier nevertheless found a Bavaria-wide ban perfectly legitimate. *Masse-Mensch*, he claimed, had violated *criminal* laws.[39] Having been created in the fallout from two criminal convictions and a psychiatric report, even the play's performance became the object of criminal contestation. The same rulings and psychiatric report that gave rise to the piece also conditioned its reception, in which Toller's personal criminality was seamlessly transferred to that of his creation.

The police department's claim that *Masse-Mensch* was worthless as art did not prevent Erwin Piscator from proposing to stage the play at his Proletarisches Theater in Berlin. Piscator, however, quickly changed his mind after finding the play a poor match for the theater's ideological goals and deeming it structurally fragmentary. The play only reached Jürgen Fehling's at the Volksbühne in 1920. In contrast with the drama's stormy initial introduction to the stage, Fehling's classically expressionist production was hugely successful (replete with "Jessner Steps" and a cyclorama), with many critics lauding his staging as on par with the work itself. Following a string of sold-out performances in Berlin, *Masse-Mensch* traveled to Estonia, Moscow (in a constructivist production put on by Vsevolod Meyerhold and in a translation by Osip Mandelstam), and numerous venues in the United States, to major success.

Taken together, they collectively demonstrate how quickly Kraepelin's conclusions spread in variety of different scientific, legal, and popular venues following the trial and how they came to have extrapsychiatric explanatory capacity. Moreover, all seem to repeat the same paradoxically dual identification of Toller as a singular person and Toller as a psychiatric type. The medical articles and police report find him at once individually responsible and merely an example of a larger, more dangerously systemic pathology, associated with "radical" revolutionary movements.

In one sense, the link between the *Lehrbuch*'s diagnostic categories, Toller's individual case history in 1918, and Kraepelin's article for the *Süddeutsche Monatshefte* and its successors is purely chronological. The *Lehrbuch*'s claims precede the events of 1918–1919. Toller's chance encounter with Kraepelin at the institute occurred a full year before he assumed leadership of the *Räterepublik*. It therefore makes sense that the medical report and article should each draw on Kraepelin's prior work. On the other hand, these texts are linked by a peculiar cyclical loss and return of their protagonist's proper name. Kraepelin initially identified Toller as part of a quantitatively deviant group ("psychopaths") in which the latter's own singularity no longer mattered or mattered only insofar as it provided further evidence for the broader pattern of deviance. Just a year later, however, in "Psychiatric Observations," he concluded that mass movements were psychotic and hysterical on the basis of his study of the *Räterepublik*'s individual leaders, not their disease groups. If *Ernst Toller*, a confirmed psychopath, led the *Räterepublik*, and if *Ernst Toller* was tried, convicted, and punished for treason in that role, then the movement Toller led was also clearly psychopathic. Does the name "Toller," then, designate an individual or a species? Lowercase "toller" of Kraepelin's initial 1918 report, toller-the-Psychopath, is clearly subsumed by the nosological type to which he purportedly belongs. Capitalized "Toller" of the *Räterepublik* and trial, Toller-the-traitor, is clearly a singular person, one whose right to a capital letter also marks his eligibility for capital punishment. In "Psychiatric Observations," however, both seem to be true.

None of the published critiques of Toller's "psychiatricization" attend to this odd duality. The articles in *Das Forum* and *Die Freiheit*, as well the caricature of Rüdin in *Hoppla, wir leben!*, make claims about psychiatric pseudoscientifity but ignore how Toller was able to be simultaneously subsumed by his alleged disease and function as its standard-bearer. If these critical reports and articles did not make much headway with the complexities of Kraepelin's assessment of Toller, *Masse-Mensch*—the title of which quite literally stages a question about the relationship between individual and group—provides substantially more insight.

## *Masse-Mensch*: Expressionist Theater and Mass Psychiatry

Toller's *Masse-Mensch*, which was written shortly after Kraepelin's "Psychiatric Observations" appeared in print, describes the same bizarre typological flickering between case and category that occurs across Kraepelin's assessments of Toller, albeit transfigured into the idiom of revolutionary action, not clinical practice. The play's ambiguous representation of identity and solidarity attends to the problems that clinical psychiatry likewise possessed but lacked the capacity to independently see.

*Masse-Mensch* follows the bourgeois Sonja Irene L.'s ideological struggle after she becomes a convert to the local workers' movement. It centers on her effort to choose between revolution by force ("*korperlicher Gewalt*," physical violence) and the peaceful pursuit of nonretributive justice that preserves human life but achieves more moderate change.[40] Although the play is neither situated in time nor concretely located in geographic space, it contains obvious echoes of the *Räterepublik*, an event that would have still been quite fresh in the audience's mind. In keeping with the format of the expressionist *Stationendrama*, a variant of the medieval mystery play that used disconnected scenes in place of a narratively chronological plot, *Masse-Mensch* tracks Sonja's intellectual and political development across a series of progressively escalating situations. Beginning from an initial argument with her husband about her participation in a strike (tableau 1), in which she must choose between the security and physical love of marriage and a commitment to her political ideals, the play ends with her execution for treason (the culmination of tableau 7).

*Masse-Mensch* has been widely regarded by secondary literature as a classic of German expressionism. Although few of the authors, dramatists, and visual artists formally deemed expressionist would have conceded to the title, and while the exact definition of expressionism remains contested, a broad description might note the movement's origins in an opposition to impressionism, its focus on a break with tradition (often figured as an intergenerational conflict between father and son), its calls for a new language, and its thematic interest in the renewal and regeneration of mankind.[41] Indeed, *Masse-Mensch* forms part of the loose canon of works that Walter H. Sokel characterized as "Messianic Expressionism," a coinage for literature and art produced during the 1910s and early 1920s that relied on the "visualization of subconscious or existential states" to offer a "vision of social renewal."[42] The messianic dimension to which Sokel refers in the phrase is an effort to capture the ways that expressionism espoused a general faith in the belief that the "only present certainty [was] the expectation of a radically different future."[43] Expressionism understood as a kind of existential condition, not a movement, was committed to the belief that art could make a new reality possible. While the messianic strain of expressionism gained steam in the early twentieth century, its roots extended back to ideas expressed in Friedrich Schiller's *Aesthetic Education* (1795), Friedrich Hölderlin's and Novalis's Romantic concept of the poet-prophet, and Nietzsche's *The Birth of Tragedy* and *Thus Spoke Zarathustra*, all of which had a significant influence on expressionist thought. For obvious reasons, messianic expressionism also had direct connections to revolutionary politics. In the face of Wilhelmine corruption, mass industrialization, and the horrors visited on Europe by World War I, expressionists from Kurt Hiller to Wassily Kandinsky repeatedly proclaimed that their tragic occurrence nevertheless presaged a redemption just over the horizon. Toller himself remarked on it in his piece "On the Revolution on Stage" ("Zur Revolution der Bühne," 1923). "Our dream is a great community [*Gemeinschaft*] between stage and audience; a community [*Gemeinschaft*] of attitudes toward life and the world; a community [*Gemeinsamkeit*] of ideas, cooperation, pregnant with connections between listeners and actors, a glowing unity of all involved."[44]

The birth of this new community entailed the creation of a new man, *der neue Mensch*. As Ernst Bloch proposed in his philosophically expansive and genre-defying *The Spirit of Utopia* (*Geist der Utopie*, 1923), modern society deeply longed for a common, uniting experience that would get beyond the merely factual.[45] Yet such longing also required a meeting point between individual and collective experience. "I am. We are. That is enough. Now we have to begin," Bloch writes, highlighting that it is the beginning undertaken by this "we" that poses the greatest challenge.[46] Works of art are, according to Bloch, to be interpreted as the site of the "ultimate self-encounter," in which "our [combined] figure" succeeds in hearing itself "in the inconstruable, absolute question, the problem of the We in itself [*im Wirproblem an sich selbst*]."[47]

Bringing together Bloch's concept of the *Wirproblem* and Martin Buber's theories of *Gemeinschaft*, expressionism's *New Man* represents the anointed figure who—whether in drama, prose, or poetry—actively strives to step beyond subjectivity and into the *Wir*, thereby also bringing about a collective redemption and inspiring the reader/audience to follow the same path. Frequently, such striving took the form of martyrdom. The protagonist's death was an act of sacrifice that enables rebirth as the fully realized version of this New Man, who thereby also opened the door to a socialist brotherhood of humanity. Georg Kaiser's Eustache in *Die Bürger von Calais* (*The Burghers of Calais*), Toller's own Friedrich in *Die Wandlung* (*The Transformation*), and Jimmy in *Die Maschinenstürmer* all represent variations on this theme.

In *Masse-Mensch*, however, the scenario is somewhat different. Not only is Sonja Irene L. one of the exceptionally few female protagonists to serve in the role, and indeed one of the few female protagonists in expressionist drama, but she is also clearly tied to the German women's suffrage movement that had gained the vote for women in the 1919, the same year Toller wrote the play. The result in the play is that her capacity to embody a universalized humanity remains locked in tension with her biological sex, to which the other characters in the play (who all otherwise lack a proper name) repeatedly draw attention in various ways. This complicates the ending. The messianic apocalypse that should make way for a new world can only succeed if Sonja does indeed die on behalf of all humanity. That is, it can only succeed if she manages to successfully vanish into the mass (named by the play's title) and renounce her proper name. The play's awkward efforts to fit Sonja into the role of everyman, combined with her own struggle to commit fully to a (potentially violent) proletarian struggle, reenacts the dilemma Toller himself faced when confronted by Kraepelinian classification, which neither allowed him to vanish into the mass nor to retain his own distinct identity. *Masse-Mensch* captures what clinical psychiatry could not acknowledge: that psychodiagnostic classification produced new types of groups—*neue Völkerkreise*—even though it purported merely to arrange divisions that were already there.

Because Toller's stage directions indicate that the action of the play is set either in *Traumbilder* (dream scenes or dream tableaux) or "in visionärer Traumferne" (in the visionary remove of a dream), *Masse-Mensch* operates much like the "other scene" (Freud's term in *Die Traumdeutung* for the psychical locality from which dreams arise) of Kraepelinian classification. The struggle between one and many that takes place in *Masse-Mensch* reconstructs, in the form of a psychoanalytic and theatrical *Traumbild*, clinical psychiatry's unacknowledged creation of categories that supposedly only gathered similar people together but practically functioned as if the groups were autonomous individuals, threatening the very identity of those they purported to merely represent. This aligns well with Sokel's remark about expressionism relying on "visualization of subconscious or existential states" to offer a "vision of social renewal," as long as one acknowledges that in *Masse-Mensch* "social renewal" is split between expressionist hopes about the world to come and the much more ominously social reordering that Kraepelin, Ratzel, Helmolt, and the members of the Vaterlandspartei envisioned.

This duplicity is no doubt behind the multiple works of secondary scholarship that regard Toller's depiction of the masses of *Masse-Mensch* as rather ideologically suspect. Grunow-Erdmann proposes that despite being dedicated to the proletariat, *Masse-Mensch* actually shows "a politically underdeveloped, easily manipulated mass" reduced to an "Echofunction."[48] Reading Toller's drama in light of the racialized theories of the French psychologist Gustav le Bon (1841–1931), especially in *Psychologie des foules* (*The Psychology of the Masses*, 1895), and Freud's *Massen-psychologie und Ich-Analyse* (*Group Psychology and the Analysis of the Ego*, 1921), Hoffmann argues that Toller's play largely repeats Le Bon's and Freud's claims. Like them, Toller supposedly shows that the individual is little more than a captive automaton in mass movements, which inevitably bring out "primitive" instincts all too easily harnessed by a charismatic leader. This misses the possibility that the work's "wavering" ideological commitment might instead be a commentary on how theories like Le Bon's had made it possible to think about the mass in these ways. Exploring Toller's drama in greater length helps articulate the types of remarks the work makes about Kraepelinian psychiatry.

***

One of the play's most prominent features is its representational instability: there are no true characters in *Masse-Mensch*. "Figures" (*Gestalten*) representing types—a Companion, Bankers, Female Prisoners, Shadows, etc.—populate the dream scenes, while "Players" (*Spieler*) occupy the more real ones. Even Sonja's name turns out to be of rather dubious stability. The cast list is only place in which the name "Sonja Irene L." is present at all. Neither spoken nor mentioned in the play, the "Sonja Irene L." of the dramatis personae only participates in the action in her role as "*Die Frau*" (which can mean either woman or wife in German). Toller's stage directions frequently indicate that those on stage are not the players and figures themselves but bearers of their faces. "Clerk: face of the man [*der Mann*]," "Prisoner: face of the man [*der Mann*]," "Enchained Figure: face of the woman [*der Frau*]" are only some of the quasi-personae who appear throughout. As Toller remarked in a letter to Fehling, "It is still a question whether we exist as individuals" ("Es ist noch eine Frage, ob wir persönlich existieren").[49]

Sonja's opening decision to sacrifice her marriage for the proletarian cause only embroils her in a second dilemma, however. Tableau 2, the first

*Traumbild*, features a burlesque stock exchange in which human lives are being traded alongside shares. The bankers there have devised a scheme to improve the war's weak "human material" (*Menschenmaterial*), that is, their troops, by establishing a state bordello disguised as a sanatorium (*Kriegserholungsheim*). Their proposal symbolically illuminates war's crude impersonal bartering with men's and women's lives, suggesting a "solution" that unites exploitative capitalist military and sexual economies in a single so-called treatment center. Unsurprisingly, the proposed sanatorium will be regulated by a calculated system of exchange as grotesque in its specificity as comic in its inequality.

| | |
|---|---|
| Vierter Bankier: *Drei Preise.* | Fourth Banker: *Three Prices.* |
| *Drei Kategorien.* | *Three categories.* |
| *Bordell für Offiziere:* | *A brothel for officers:* |
| *Aufenthalt die Nacht.* | *To stay for the night.* |
| *Bordell für Korporäle:* | *A brothel for corporals:* |
| *Eine Stunde.* | *An hour.* |
| *Mannschaftbordell:* | *A worker's brothel:* |
| *15 Minuten.* | *Fifteen minutes.*[50] |

In tableau 3, Sonja faces fervent calls from groups of young female and male workers (*Gruppe junger Arbeiterinnen*, *Gruppe junger Arbeiter*) to destroy the factories lining the banker's and industrialists' pockets and sustaining the war. She nevertheless remains hesitant to use violence and proposes a more peaceful solution. A player titled "the Nameless" (*Der Namenlose*) appears at this point and makes a powerful case for an armed insurrection. By the conclusion of the tableau, he has convinced the reluctant Sonja/*Die Frau* to join his side. The following tableau, another *Traumbild*, features the Nameless in the role of death. He invites *Die Frau* to a dance of death inside the prison, where she discovers that her husband/*Der Mann* is among those to be executed. Before he can be shot, however, Toller's stage directions indicate that he "metamorphoses into one of the guards [*verwandelt sich in das Einer Wache*]."[51] The tableau closes Sonja/*Die Frau*'s monologue on how easily killer and victim can change places.

In the fifth tableau, Sonja/*Die Frau* and the Nameless argue about the merits of "steel weapons" versus "intellectual weapons" inside a heavily barricaded hall. Dire reports of heavy casualties are rolling in, and the conversation is regularly interrupted by grim updates about the loss of multiple proletarian strongholds throughout the city. The Nameless remains indifferent to the precipitously rising number of deaths. The proletariat has thrown off its chains of slavery and is now "free"—even if such freedom is obtained in the grave. "They are dying for the mass." It soon becomes clear that those in the hall are the only ones left to defend the cause. A worker arrives and states he has taken a group of local citizens hostage. He has killed half of them in vengeance and is holding the remainder as leverage. While the Nameless applauds his actions, Sonja/*Die Frau* is appalled and proclaims she will defend these innocent men and women. In response, the Nameless accuses her of treason and calls out her class status: "How dare *you*, a woman from those circles, poison the hour for decision!"[52] The tense situation is further aggravated at this point by the citizen-hostages' demand to "see the leader," which those in the hall mistake as proof of Sonja's duplicity. By this point, government forces have closed in, shots can be heard from outside, and the Nameless vanishes into the crowd just before the workers discover they have been locked in the hall. A desperate chorus of the *Internationale* breaks out but is soon cut off by machine-gun fire. Soldiers pour in, and Sonja is arrested as the movement's leader.

In the sixth tableau, the Woman (now labeled "the prisoner [*die Gefesselte*]") appears crouched down inside a cage in the center of the stage. Headless shadows surround her. They accuse her of murder, citing her silence and inaction as evidence of her guilt. The shadows fade and are replaced by bankers (from tableau 2), who declare she is "guilty stock [*Aktie Schuldig*]" and an example of "misspeculation"—and must be written off as a loss. The bankers vanish and are replaced by a group of prisoners wearing caps over their heads "with slits for eyes" and bearing numbers on their chests. At a loss, she turns to the warden to ask who or what is truly guilty: the masses, God, man, she herself?

In the seventh and final tableau, set in the Woman's prison cell, she is visited in sequence by the Nameless (whose proposal to kill the warden and flee she rejects), a priest (whose final rites she refuses), and her husband (who rejects her offer of brotherhood). Having renounced masses, church, and state, she indicates to the officer on duty that she is ready to face the firing squad and leaves the stage. Two female prisoners break into the cell. The women are busy stealing her mirror, leftover bread from her last meal, and her silk handkerchief when they are interrupted by the noisy volley of shots offstage, signaling Sonja/*Die Frau*'s execution. Guiltily returning the mirror and handkerchief to their original places in the room, each prisoner asks the other "Sister, why do we do such things? [*Schwester, warum tun wir das?*]" before the curtain drops.

The name Irene means "peace" in Greek, and a number of secondary commentators have suggested that Sonja sacrifices herself in pursuit of peace at the end of the play. Critical scholarship largely reads the final scene in positive terms. Sonja's death allegedly allows the two remaining female prisoners—figurations of society at large—to recognize the selfishness of their individual desires and see themselves as part of a greater collective whole. In the line "Sister, why do we do such things?," the "such things" refer to the women's attempted theft and its symbolic extension in human greed more generally. This reading concludes that the women's question is also the sign of their transformation and of a broader social metamorphosis, all of which fits neatly with the messianic interpretation of the play in which Sonja is a Christlike

New Man who must struggle between her own desire's and Buber's "*we*," which she ultimately gives her life to realize.

This would fit neatly, were it not for the problem that it is not clear who dies. Up until the moment of the execution, the drama has heavily emphasized the permeability of identity. Toller's refusal to concretely fix the protagonist's identity with a single proper name, his construction of the cast from a mix of grammatically substantivized adjectives and common nouns, and his choice of *Masse-Mensch* as a title are evidence of how this dissolution of identity operates. The adventures of the hyphen across the play's various print editions indicate the unresolved nature of the title's formulation and are a testament to the problem it poses. The characters in the play freely change both places and faces. The role of one seamlessly transitions into that of another, whether via literal metamorphosis (as in *Der Mann*'s transformation into a guard) or a shift in ideological position (as per *Die Frau*'s temporary adoption of the ideological perspective of the Nameless). This is in addition to the trade in human lives that forms a running motif throughout the drama. First evident at the stock exchange, where bankers assess the value of human material, the motif of a human economy reappears in the anonymous worker's choice to take hostages as bargaining chips in tableau 5 and via the appearance of accusatory numbered phantoms in tableau 6, which "reckon" the extent of Sonja's guilt. This overall representational destabilization consistently complicates efforts to establish just how many people each "character" is supposed to be and suggests a profound slipperiness between their various roles.

That two female prisoners in tableau 7 end up repeating the very line with which the play closes should raise a question about who is actually on stage. While the figures might indeed be separate, the play leaves open the possibility that "they" are one woman accompanied by her own echo. Or as Toller put in his letter to Fehling, written from inside Niederschonfeld, one woman accompanied by what he calls her "mirrored death [*Spiegeltod*]":

> Two women once walked past the window of my cell, while I was clinging to the iron bars. Apparently two old maids. Both had short white hair and both wore dresses of the same shape, the same shade, and the same cut; both carried a gray umbrella with white spots and both wobbled their heads. Not for a minute did I see these as "realistic human beings" going for a walk in the narrow prison lane of a "realistic" Neuburg. It was a dance of death by two old maids, one old maid and her mirrored death [*Spiegeltod*], that gaped at me.[53]

If the play's two prisoners are thought of as extensions of the women in Toller's letter, in whom he recognized a singularity made possible by death's all-leveling force, the appearance of a mirror in the closing sequence is important. The mirror offers a physical clue about an epistemological process of mirroring at work, capable of producing many from one as well as one from many. The mirror reflects the relative unsteadiness of the women's differentiation and signals an ongoing, more general disruption of representational fixity. If these two female prisoners can be interpreted in both the plural and the singular, however, Sonja/*Die Frau* is also subject to the same instability. The character Sonja/*Die Frau* can only really be off stage facing the firing squad and the two female prisoners safely on stage if the audience is willing to set aside the cross-pollination of individuality and collectivity that has formed the play's drama thus far and made up its title. Alternatively, however, if none of these characters are discrete individuals, then the distinction between off stage and on stage disappears, along with its correlates: endangered/safe, before the firing squad/in the prison, condemned to die/allowed to live. The play may end with two individual women contemplating their future from a position of safety. It may also end in a mass execution in which everyone is gunned down in the same breath.

The *Gefangene*'s equivocal body positions support this dual reading. One of the women helplessly gyrates her arms in the air while the other crumples to the ground, hiding her head in her lap. While these movements might indicate newly minted proletarians bemoaning a prior lack of class political consciousness, they also suggest that the two figures may just have been shot. This leaves the audience in a complicated position. All of the options seem unappealing. While it is possible to accept the triumphant narrative of Sonja L.'s martyrdom in the name of a good collective cause, the fact that Sonja L. doesn't properly have her own name makes this position difficult to sustain. Accepting that she is shot or that that everyone on stage dies, however, makes the audience a potentially complicit witness to murder while destroying the sense of collectivity the play has tried to foster, if with some difficulty. Alternatively, thinking of the scenario as one in which no one escapes alive (audience included) does produce a collectivity, but only through the solidarity of death. In such a scenario, what is good for everyone is good for no one, because no one is left. Instead of resolving the issues of guilt and responsibility raised in the final tableau, the play inconclusively finishes by extending the impossible question, at once plural and singular, "Who is guilty?" across the fourth wall.

# CHAPTER 5

# THE ECONOMIC HYPOTHESIS

## Soul Markets of Soviet Fiction

*With the modern "psychological" analysis of the work-process (in Taylorism) this rational mechanisation extends right into the worker's "soul": even his psychological attributes are separated from his total personality and placed in opposition to it so as to facilitate their integration into specialized rational systems and their reduction to statistically viable concepts.*

—György Lukács

In his 1973 work *Symbolic Economies: After Marx and Freud*, Jean-Joseph Goux proposes that psychoanalysis has a general equivalent. Although the notion of a general equivalent was first created by "theories concerning economic exchange-value," Goux argues that the general equivalent can nevertheless take on unusual significance outside of a strictly economic horizon. His proposal is that capitalist economics, Saussurian linguistics, and Lacanian psychoanalysis are all variants of a more fundamental logic of exchange that emerged at the end of the nineteenth century.

Like György Lukács's discussion of reification in *History and Class Consciousness*, Goux stresses that recognizing the role of a general equivalent has the potential to substantively illuminate aspects of cultural institutions as a whole. He alleges that it will show how qualitative value judgments can be produced in virtually any field organized by a regulated play of substitutions.[1] There is a close configuration, Goux contends, between reason and the "systematic institutionalized configuration of monovalent measure."[2] In Lacanian analysis, he claims, the general equivalent for subjects is the Father, and the general equivalent for objects is the Phallus. Like gold, the Father and the Phallus are simply "commodities" that have been given a special status and thereby acquired both autonomy as well as the capacity to confer value.

Goux's work forms part of a larger, longer-standing discussion about the existence of a psychic economy within psychoanalysis. Freud describes an economy of nerve forces in his early work "Project for a Scientific Psychology" and writes in 1915 of an "economic hypothesis" that would understand psychic life in terms of a calculus of mental energy. Whatever one thinks of Goux's transformation of these early theories of Freud into an account of how psychoanalysis itself configures substitutive play, his idea raises an interesting question. Do non-Freudian accounts of the mind possess a logic of exchange? If so, what kind of general equivalent do they use?

This chapter argues that the Soviet writer Vsevolod Ivanov's understudied novel *У* (*U*, 1933) grasps the development of a non-Freudian psychic economy that grew from the German psychiatrist Emil Kraepelin's research on mental illness at beginning of the twentieth century.[3] The novel's economic postulations are as much a reflection of Stalin's planned economy as they are a commentary about the new kind of psychological metrics, which contained analogous possibilities for inflation, deflation, and speculation in the process of "psychic reconstruction" (*psikhicheskaya peredelka*) needed to make the New Soviet Man. Set against the backdrop of the first Five-Year Plan, the novel sheds light on the emergence of a value form within Kraepelinian psychiatry, suggesting that it is not merely Taylorism that configures the worker's soul but the very study of the soul that rationalizes it. Written a moment just after psychoanalysis had been abolished in the Soviet Union, the novel takes a surprisingly critical stance on the role of valuation in non-Freudian approaches to the mind. Showcasing the economic underpinnings of psychopower, it demonstrates how the Soviet embrace of behaviorism, neurology, and clinical psychiatry interfaced with capitalist economics and generated a psychiatric value form.

***

Vsevolod Ivanov (1895–1963), a member of the Serapion Brothers and a friend of the Russian formalist Viktor Shklovsky, is better known for his works about the Russian Civil War, such as *Armored Train 14–69* (*Bronepoyezd 14–69*) from 1922, and short prose set in Siberia and Central Asia than for this unusual novel. Widely popular in the 1920s, Ivanov wrote both short stories and novels during this portion of his life, the heyday of Russian futurism and postrevolutionary aesthetic experimentation by groups like the Left Front for the Arts. Ivanov started his novel *Y* in 1929 and had completed it by 1933.[4] Short excerpts appeared in the Soviet journal *Literaturnaya gazeta* in November 1933, but the full work did not see publication until 1987. The Swiss press L'Age d'homme (in Lausanne) released an incomplete Russian edition in 1983, and extracts were published in *Ogonek* (1987, no. 26) and *Literaturnaya ucheba* (1987, no. 5). The complete text was published in Moscow in 1988 (by Kniga) and in 1990 (by Sovetskiy pisatel'). The work is unusual as much for its delayed publication as for its departure from Ivanov's previous work in terms of subject matter. Earlier novels, such as *Colored Winds* (*Tsvetnyye vetra*, 1921) and *Azure Sands* (*Golubyye peski*, 1923), had told the story of a highly animated natural world in Siberia and focused on the events of the Russian Civil War, in which Ivanov fought for the Red Army. This posthumously published text, by contrast, was set in urban Moscow, critical of the Soviet system, and preeminently concerned with economics and mental illness.

"A novel is a novel, devil knows whether it's on the money, whether it's interesting, sad, happy, or just a bit of double-dealing; commentary is the sure bet—the thoughts there belong to someone else [*mysli v nikh chuzhiye*], which is to say they are useful."[5] So begins *Y*, written in 1929 as the economic crisis following the end of the New Economic Policy (NEP) was in full swing. The book wagers that readers will be more interested in citational material than the novel itself and so begins with the reference matter. The main story of a hospital accountant, psychoanalyst, and Soviet labor recruiter's detective-style quest to determine a psychiatric diagnosis and then to undertake the wholesale psychological transformation of society is preceded by pages of "end" notes citing sentences the reader has yet to see and a story she has yet to be told. In addition to the notes, the novel is framed by multiple epigraphs and no fewer than three sets of commentary to the commentary, at least if one does not count a *seeming* fourth, which turns out to initiate the main action. Having finally arrived at the central plot, however, the reader disconcertingly discovers that it, too, is filled with multiple temporal inversions and digressive interruptions.

Soviet-era economics, popular psychological theories, and formalist literary experimentation all come together in Ivanov's sprawling novel. The protagonists' psychiatrically focused efforts to make a medical claim unfold against the historical backdrop of the economic transition from Lenin's free-market approach under NEP (1921–1928) to Stalin's first Five-Year Plan (1928–1932). This transitional period was characterized by severe food shortages and the growth of a robust underground economy driven by rampant speculation. *Y*'s opening lines about the comparative "worth" of a novel must therefore be taken in the context of a fluctuating system of economic valuation in which the prices might rise or fall at the turn of a page and where only what is foreign—whether currency (*chuzhiye den'gi*) or reference matter (*chuzhiye mysli*)—can truly guarantee value. The work's reverse-order exposition (reflected in the references with which it begins) offers the literary approximation of the rampant speculation occurring during these years, which forms a prominent part of the plot. Is there truly a story here or merely a clever hoax to disguise the lack of one? Just as entrepreneurial NEP men made money by anticipating shifts in the volatile market, so too does Ivanov's novel stake a narrative claim in speculation, which organizes the book both on the level of form and content. The text gambles on the existence of events, characters, scenarios, and outcomes whose appearance in the story-to-come is shown to lack any true guarantee, while it simultaneously declares that its 250-some pages will, somehow, add up to a novel after all.

## Buying Time

Two jewelers walk into a psychiatric hospital. What follows is less a gracefully unfurling punch line in the novel than the cleverly orchestrated deferral of one. The backstory precipitating these jewelers' arrival at the E. Kraepelin Psychiatric Hospital outside of Moscow is no less intricate than the novel's drawn-out prefatory apparatus. The impassioned diagnostic dispute that their case provokes at the Kraepelin Hospital is merely a prelude to a maze of interlacing subplots. The work's patchwork of styles and whimsically Sternian digressions span from Gogol and Dostoevsky to Poe and Bergson. Literary citations are mixed in with historical details of Communist Party intrigue and satirical representations of Soviet economic history in the 1928 post-NEP crisis, during which the book is set. Like the decimated hulk of the Christ the Savior Cathedral that looms throughout the novel, there are not so much chapters in *Y* as leftovers (scraps of dialogue, pointedly unhelpful observations) raised to the level of subheadings. A would-be first chapter entitled "Excuse me, can we actually start?" gives way to chapter-like divisions such as "The conversation gets closer to the point."[6] If *Y* is a burlesque psychiatric detective story, the search therein is as much for the cause of a mental illness as it is for a causal throughline in a sea of wildly unpredictable events.[7] Constantly raising the stakes, the book never makes clear when, or if, the payoff will arrive.

Narrated jointly by Yegor Yegorych, an unnamed compiler (*sostavitel'*), and multiple anonymous metadiegetic interlocutors, the action gets started when a box of gold watches is stolen from two jewelers at the state workshop where they are employed. The jewelers develop a delusional illness that leads them to believe that the theft is part of a geopolitical conspiracy and a secret plot to forge a crown in the Soviet Union for an imaginary American emperor. They spread rumors about this fantastical scheme around Moscow's bustling Sukharevsky Market, a hotbed of speculation and the site of a vast underground economy in scarce goods. It spurs a frenzy of guesswork among the market's "terrible and pitiful rabble" (*strashnyy i zhalkiy sbrod*), who are consumed with trying to predict how the story—if true—will affect prices.[8] The situation is not resolved even when the brothers are forcibly removed from the city center to the "semi-calm ward" (*poluspokoynaya palata*) of the Kraepelin Hospital, located "an hour and a half" outside the metropolis. Placed under the care of the ward's resident doctor, the psychoanalyst Matvey Ivanovich Andreyshin, the jewelers soon become the subject of a heated medical quarrel. Dr. Andreyshin assesses their illness in Freudian psychogenic terms. He views it as the product of a trauma buried in the brothers' past, which must be brought to light in order for them to recover. By contrast, the clinic's renowned director, Prof. Ch. (the Cyrillic letter Ч), argues the disease is strictly biological in nature and incurable. The quarrel splits the hospital into two opposing camps, draws the attention of the wider public, and threatens to cause a major medical scandal.

Andreyshin embarks on a quest to find the woman supposedly responsible for their trauma and ropes Yegor Yegorych into his quixotic pursuit along the way. In a mash-up of other literary duos, Andreyshin is quickly revealed to be a Sherlock of very dubious intellectual abilities and Yegor Yegorych a Watson-cum–Sancho Panza of surprisingly canny insights.[9] Their search for Susanna (a Dulcinea-like figure, who turns out to be a prostitute) metastasizes into a gumshoe saga of indeterminate length, as the book quickly skews even the most basic metrics for measuring time: a symbolic reflection of the watches' disappearance and Bergson's concept of an immeasurable *durée* (duration).

Andreyshin and Yegor Yegorych first encounter the trickster Leon Ionovich Cherpanov, not Susanna. Cherpanov is supposedly recruiting workers for a future *kombinat* (industrial center) in the Urals that will be able to "regenerate man" (*pererodit' cheloveka*). As luck would have it, he is living in the same dilapidated, communal House No. 42 as Susanna and her extended family. The two men take up residence there and soon learn that its inhabitants are engaged in vigorous illegal speculation. The bourgeois inclinations of Cherpanov's housemates make little difference to his plans. In the following pages, he unhesitatingly recruits them as workers in the future *kombinat* and additionally gathers Moscow's least desirable laborers for the project. The nature of the secular rebirth that will convert this group of unsavory individuals into psychological Stakhanovites remains, however, like everything else, to be determined. Until the book's final pages, Cherpanov merely espouses blind faith in a packet of sealed documents in his possession that supposedly contain step-by-step instructions for the full-scale "psychological processing of society [*psikhologicheskaya obrabotka obshchestva*]."[10]

Neither the promised psychological processing nor the *kombinat* that would facilitate it ever materialize. Instead, the patriarch of Susanna's family betrays the entire household's illegal economic activities to the authorities. Cherpanov is revealed as a provincial engraver (counterfeiter) and a fraud. In the final pages, he is killed by the same men who hired him to engineer the hoax about the *kombinat* in the Urals. The residents of House No. 42 are arrested. Yegor Yegorych and Andreyshin, having never fulfilled their original mission, return to the hospital only to learn that the jewelers have been cured in their absence by no less than the head of the hospital's economic division. This man apparently borrowed a few "instruments and materials" from the Trust for Precision Mechanics, historically responsible for the production of watches, and treated the jewelers in what is ambiguously described as simply being "his own way."[11] Thus, having first "lost" time, the jewelers are apparently restored to health with a little tinkering in their own clockwork. Yegor Yegorych and Andreyshin both decide to write an account of the prior events. Andreyshin, who has inexplicably loved Susanna all along, happily envisions that his forthcoming psychoanalytic report will *perevospityvat'* (reeducate) her and make her love him, a delusional belief that echoes the jewelers' initial visions and recalls Cherpanov's statements about the coming *pererozhdeniye* (rebirth) of man.

*Y*'s plot reflects a larger speculative schematic in the book and the economic history of the time. Both the criminal codes of the RSFSR for 1922 and 1926 made speculation illegal (UK RSFSR, 1922 §137–38; UK RSFSR, 1926 §107). The codes attest to the reality that under war communism, unequal rationing (favoring party members) and forcible grain procurement (in which peasants were "compensated" with worthless paper currency) led to the growth of a vast speculative economy in consumer goods. The historic Sukharevsky Market in Moscow became something of a symbol for these activities. Lenin warned the Eighth Party Congress that while the market itself could be closed, the "the terrible 'sukharevka,' which lives in the soul and actions of every petty proprietor [[s]*trashna 'sukharevka,' kotoraya zhivet v dushe i deystviyakh kazhdogo melkogo khozyaina*]," would not thereby be obliterated.[12] NEP abolished the de facto appropriation of grain and brought with it the return of a stable form of currency, but as the price of consumer goods rose (and that of agricultural products fell) over the coming years, the peasantry had ever less incentive to sell to the state, leading to the Grain Procurement Crises of the late 1920s and Stalin's implementation of the first Five-Year Plan. With it, consumer goods once again became scarce, and tightly regulated commodities and underground trade practices blossomed afresh. *Y* uses the ongoing struggle by everyday citizens to obtain products to advance a point about the temporally speculative risk of the Soviet project as a whole.

The novel invests in an array of conjectural modalities that mimic these economic developments, while incorporating historical details that amplify the general sense of betting on an uncertain future. First, the novel sets up false expectations by appearing to rely on the problem-and-resolution structure of detective fiction. Nominally organized by a clinical hunt for the source of a psychological trauma, the novel gives the impression that all of its loose ends will finally be drawn together in a single cohesive explanation if the reader simply waits long enough. Yet Andreyshin is no Lupin or Father Brown. In place of the detective novel's concluding whodunit synopsis, grandly delivered by the clear-eyed sleuth, *Y* closes with Andreyshin's rambling and implausible explanations. There is no direct confrontation with Prof. Ch. whatsoever. If anything, Andreyshin's decision to write a psychoanalytic case history about the jewelers presages further uncertainties rather than the hoped-for resolutions.

*Y*'s paratext also helps frame the book in terms of a process of exchange. The bulky prefatory apparatus (three epigraphs, the reference matter, multiple preface-like excurses) frame the act of writing as a fundamentally predictive operation. A section "Concerning All Pages and Previous Notes [*Ko vsem stranitsam i predydushchim primechaniyam*]" explains how the compiler's "delicate handling of the printed word" has managed to prevent a vast amount of supplementary material from creeping into the novel, thereby allegedly "saving" thousands of pages: "Is there a 700-page introductory article here? No, there is not. A critico-biographical one of 970 pages? No, there is not. A name index of 130? A 121-page dictionary of ancient Greek words, which, although never mentioned, are necessary to understand allusions in the text? . . . No, no, and no! Even if you chalk up 41 pages to the compiler's exaggeration, he has nevertheless saved you 2,500 pages cash."[13]

Having economized by cutting back on so much unnecessary "spending," the compiler has supposedly freed up a substantial sum of literary cash, in the form of scarce paper, to be put to future use.[14] The phenomenon of saving for uncertain ventures to come also explains another curious visual dimension of the novel. *Y* repeatedly uses a horizontal line (known in typography as a "horizontal rule") to divide paragraphs. At first glance, it seems to "save" pages by facilitating a change of topic or by dramatically abbreviating the passage of time. On closer inspection, however, the horizontal rule isn't actually correlated with a meaningful narrative break or, indeed, any break at all. In some instances, it awkwardly separates a question from the corresponding answer. In others, it awkwardly splits a reporting clause from what is reported.

> I rejoiced—and Cherpanov began:
>
> ———————
>
> "I adore poetry, Yegor Yegorych."[15]

The irony throughout is that the same materials that so vigorously proclaim parsimony also unnecessarily bloat the text. *Describing* the absence of a hypothetical nine-hundred-page critical biographical article takes more space than simply omitting this sort of observation entirely. Similarly, use of the horizontal rule adds to, rather than subtracts from, the book's overall length. *Y*'s comical claim seems to be that such additions are justified because they show what *might* have been added to the work, thereby indicating the extent to which the book has been pared down from an enormous length to something that is, comparatively speaking, an evocative brushstroke.

To do so, however, *Y* must first convince the reader to conceive of writing in terms of pages saved or spent. The warped argument about the novel's relative concision makes sense only if the reader sees the literary act, as well as the material substratum that sustains it, as part of a speculative system. The book thus both describes the Sukharevsky Market and appears to function analogously to it by attempting to capitalize on predictive hypotheses. Indeed, the primary narrator is, quite literally, an accountant: Yegor Yegorych keeps the book/s. By drawing attention to its status as a material object (made of components that must be procured at a cost), *Y* encourages the reader to imagine that fiction is likewise susceptible to conjectural valuation, accruing value or losing worth by proxy. In fact, the novel even uses the timing of the act of reading—that it takes the reader a certain amount of time to complete each page and move to the next—to sustain a game of deferral. If Yegor Yegorych is bookkeeper, he is also a timekeeper. As Marx observes, in a speculative system "commodities are not sold for money but for the written promise to pay at a certain date," a description that captures the sense of timing at stake in *Y*.[16] The novel provides a series of written promises—the text's contents—that have worth because they are predicated on the supposition that a book will emerge by the time the reader reaches the last page. The same promises that vow to secure the future book, however, paradoxically also constitute its present (and only) realization, as the work is built from assurances that merely vouchsafe the novel's coming existence.

Ivanov does not shy away from using Andreyshin and Yegor Yegorych's experiences to simultaneously poke fun at the Communist Party's speculative activities. *Y* mocks the extraordinary speed at which Stalin envisioned change taking place in the first Five-Year Plan. In the book's ironically hyperbolized version of Soviet history, collectivization is completed immediately, industrialization accomplished overnight, and the massive Christ the Savior Cathedral in central Moscow—a symbol of both tsarism and the grip of religious superstition on the masses—turned to dust just as rapidly. The historical plan to demolish the cathedral (and build a glorious Palace of the Soviets) features prominently in *Y*. The novel is set in the year "they smashed up the Christ the

Savior Cathedral," which the book states contained "800,000 rubles worth of gold on the dome."[17] This remark is significant insofar as the director of the OGPU's economic division did indeed send a petition to VTsIK requesting permission to remove the dome's gilding in 1930, on the grounds that it contained "more than 20 poods of gold," (i.e., some seven hundred pounds) "at an estimated value of half a million rubles."[18] The petition further stated that if obtained, the sum would indeed be a "great contribution to the industrialization of the country," providing a much-needed influx of currency to support Stalin's enormously expensive process of transforming the Soviet Union from an agrarian economy to an industrial one. *Y*'s remark about the dome's worth is thus both a commentary on the Soviet Union's fiscal speculation about the future and a synecdoche for the text's array of hypothetical payoffs.

That the book's detective mission never finds anything, that its declarations of frugality functionally waste pages, and that its forthcoming existence turns out to be made only of the promises predicting it show the extent to which *Y* is organized by a dynamic tension between quantitative precision (*tochnost'*) and unquantifiable uncertainty. The novel's "betting games" are as much about guessing a particular outcome as they are about a tension between preestablished metrics for winning/losing and sudden rule changes that entirely destabilize the concept (and measure) of victory. The latter is embodied in the novel's frequent references to *schast'ye* (luck). As the *Dal'* dictionary defines it, *schast'ye* refers to "happenstance . . . luck, felicity in an undertaking, but not by calculation."[19] A transcript of a conversation between the compiler and an unnamed professor on this topic appears among *Y*'s prefatory materials. The compiler laments that there is no obvious metric to measure the success of a novel:

> "But what does it mean for a novel to be successful? The size of the print-run? Verbitskaya was read more than L. Tolstoy, and now E. Zozulya seems wiser to some than V. Khlebnikov. Longevity? Catch it if you can. . . . And who read Dante? Add to this, Professor, that the future decade will bear geniuses more often than the past century. Wherein lies my book's success, Professor?"
>
> "Laughter."[20]

In this conversation, laughter is the variable on which the novel's equally unpredictable *schast'ye* depends, rather than metrics like print runs, readership, etc. There is perhaps an element of Bataille's exorbitant laughter in Ivanov's *smekh*, insofar as both seem to dispense with predictable exchanges and emerge instead from "a blind spot in the understanding."[21] "But poetry, laughter, ecstasy are not means for other things. . . . Knowledge 'works' while poetry, laughter and ecstasy do not," Bataille writes.[22] Seen in this light, *Y* seems to vacillate between offering a historically determined critique of the Soviet economy of the 1930s, on the one hand, and providing a more positive insight about literature's inherent resistance to predictable outcomes, on the other. Paradoxically, the novel's commentary on the impossibility of equating God with 800,000 rubles' worth of gold, on a name index and a Greek dictionary with 2,500 pages of hard "cash," and on the massive exportation of the Soviet Union's grain with the hungry promise of industrialization is also a way of recognizing the import of literature's (and aesthetic objects') dependence on *schast'ye* in the sense of unpredictability, without which the readers would not bother to turn a work's pages in the first place.

This position clarifies the book's title. Several scholars have observed that the title means both the Cyrillic letter "У" (pronounced "u") and the Roman letter "Y," indicating a mathematical variable in algebraic expressions. While accurate, this doesn't explain how the semantic, phonological, and mathematical meanings of У/Y relate either to one another or to the body of text. The title nevertheless appears to be making a substantive point via this duality. Neither letter nor number, Cyrillic nor Roman, linguistic nor mathematic, "У" is the trace of *schast'ye* as uncertainty that evades precise measurement and predictive determination. At odds with the exchanges the novel seems to endorse, the one-letter title is the (literally) unspeakable point at which radical indeterminacy enters and upsets all metrics that would permit calculable certainty. It is the sign of variability itself, were such a thing possible, and an apt way of signaling the book's own imp of the perverse. If *У*'s generically programmed plot appears to come apart at the seams, if the book's insistence on imposing a material metrics on literature is countered by the defiant superabundance of its own prose, if its promises of the future are not only hollow but also merely dressed-up versions of the present, then it is because these occasions are opportunities for *smekh*, in the sense of both laughter and capriciousness.

## Psychic Transactions

Ivanov's decision to make his economically speculative text about psychiatry is important because it grasps that psychiatry had also recently become susceptible to transactional analogy and, with it, speculation. Dr. Andreyshin and Professor Ch. are representatives of two specific schools of psychiatric thought, although they also parody the array of European psychological theories that took root in fin-de-siècle Russia and continued to flourish in the decade after the Revolution and before Pavlovian behaviorism became the preferred approach in the Soviet Union. The psychoanalyst and the hospital director's disagreement over the jewelers' diagnosis sheds light on a foundational early split between Sigmund Freud and Emil Kraepelin's work. By presenting the psychiatric conflict in the context of the post-NEP crisis, the novel powerfully reveals the implications of the birth of a new, quantitative method of accounting for mental life that developed alongside language-based ones. *Y* tells the story of how psychiatry and psychoanalysis respectively tell stories, and the novel does so by attending to how narrative speculation and the general equivalent functions in each context.

Of the two clinicians in the novel, Dr. Andreyshin is the more easily recognizable. *Y* quickly establishes him as an inheritor of the Russian psychoanalytic movement that began at the turn of the century and formed a prominent part of urban intellectual life for the next three decades. Russian translations of Freud emerged as early as 1904. The popularity of these works, combined with Freud's analysis of members of the Russian aristocracy and his influence on followers such as Tatiana Rosenthal, Sabina Spielrein, and Mosche Wulff, meant that there was sufficient basis for psychoanalysis to continue and thrive after 1917. Supported by the state until 1929, Soviet psychoanalysis was an important, if short-lived, methodological tool in the campaign to transform the old imperial education system into one that fostered the development of new human beings, perhaps most visibly in the new field of pedology.[23] Embraced by Leon Trotsky, psychoanalysis's subsequent demonization was linked in part to his purge from the party. Andreyshin, who adheres in rough terms to Freudian psychoanalytic doctrine, serves as a placeholder for the hope in the 1920s that psychoanalysis could help form the New Soviet Man.

Professor Ch.'s psychiatric background is less obvious. Yegor Yegorych introduces him as the director of the E. Kraepelin Psychiatric Hospital and an "outstanding specialist in clinico-nosological psychiatry [*vydayushchiysya spetsialist kliniko-nozologicheskoy psikhiatrii*]."[24] Stating that Ch. is the director of the Kraepelin Hospital and that he is a respected specialist in psychiatric disease classification is tantamount to saying the same thing. The hospital's name refers to the German psychiatrist Emil Kraepelin. Kraepelin began research for his 1899 textbook at the (then-Russian) Dorpat University. He was chair of psychiatry and head of the university's psychiatric hospital between 1886 and 1891, a period during which he worked closely with the Russian psychiatrist Vladimir Fedorovich Chizh (1855–1922). Although Kraepelin's time in Russia did not directly contribute to his work's dissemination there, the psychiatric nosological system that he created based on it made his name familiar in Russian psychiatric circles for the coming decades.[25] A Russian translation of the eighth edition of Kraepelin's textbook was released in Moscow in 1910–1912. Sergey Korsakov used Kraepelin's psychiatric training course at the DFA as a model for his own in Moscow.[26] Moreover, Chizh went on to become Kraepelin's successor at Dorpat University, serving as hospital director and chair of psychiatry between 1891 and 1916.[27] Ivanov's fictional Professor Ch., specialist in "clinico-nosological psychiatry" at the E. Kraepelin Hospital, should therefore be taken as an allusion to the Russian psychiatrist Vladimir Fedorovich *Ch*izh and the fictional hospital regarded as a reference to the hospital that Chizh ran in Russian Estonia for some twenty-five years.

Ch. and Andreyshin's opening diagnostic dispute thus handily motivates the plot and establishes that the opposition between Freudian psychoanalysis and Kraepelinian psychiatry is a foundational rift. Indeed, the novel goes further than simply showing the clash between the two. *Y* reveals that the dispute between Ch. and Andreyshin is as much a quarrel about diagnosis as it is about narration. Ivanov's novel intuits the ways in which Kraepelinian psychiatry made a substantive change in how case histories were told. Here is how Yegor Yegorych explains the conflict:

> Some of our doctors, to which group our director also belonged, were followers of E. Kremelin [*sic*] and defended the theory of "nosological units" against the new system of symptom complexes; they supported the possibility of enumerating a person's illnesses and his psyche in terms of firm and unwavering types with precisely fixed pathological-anatomical attributes, as Hoche said: "the quest once and for all for fixed [disease] processes, uniform in their etiology, course, and outcome." Other doctors, to which Dr. Andreyshin belonged, defended the struggle for a detailed deeper understanding of the psyche, and in particular, found that the case of the jewelers had a psychogenic appearance, the result of an as-yet-undetermined emotion—a shock, this group reckoned, such that making a diagnosis, especially of the sort that Prof. Ch. had, was an almost frivolous undertaking.[28]

Ch.'s "side" is associated with systematicity, enumeration (*podvedeniye*), and types (*raznovidnosti*). He and his followers provide an immediate answer to the question of what has caused the jewelers' visions. By contrast, Andreyshin proposes a "deeper understanding of the psyche [*uglubleniye v psikhiku*]," the search for a purely hypothetical shock, and the investigation of an emotion that remains to be determined. Andreyshin offers no diagnosis and condemns his colleague for doing so. The passage satirically aligns psychiatry with scientific rigor and psychoanalysis with pseudoscience. At the same time, it also equivocates by making the rest of the book dependent on Andreyshin's belief in "digging deeper." Without Andreyshin's dogged certainty that the jeweler's trauma is psychogenic (originating in the mind, not the body) and his conviction that it can only be understood through a process of careful interpretation, there would be no novel. This is hardly a trivial observation in a text so self-aware of its own materiality. Had the book's composition been left to Ch., the reader could perhaps expect a text the length of a paragraph or chapter, at best. Andreyshin's clinical approach has a story to tell, and Ch.'s does not. In this sense, Ch. and Andreyshin are not really fighting over a diagnosis; they are fighting over different approaches to the role of narrative in the study and treatment of mental illness. Andreyshin takes the position that the jewelers' illness has yet to be understood and can only be grasped through a process of interpretive investigation that takes place in language. This language—in voluminous abundance—makes up the rest of the book. By contrast, Ch. takes the position that the jewelers' entire case has already been fully summed up by Kraepelinian classification: the diagnosis is the story, making it absurd to write anything further about the case, let alone to conduct additional investigations. The joke is that Freudian psychoanalysis will always be too wordy without enough substance and Kraepelinian psychiatry too full of substance to bother much with words. Yet this droll observation contains the more serious point that Kraepelin's nosology does indeed imply a distinct mode of reading and telling: one that abandons linguistic mediation and so loses the possibility for narrative suspense in the form of an uncertainty about the relationship between cause and effect.

*Y* successfully identifies how Kraepelinian psychiatry forecloses the uncertainty and equivocality on which literature depends, offering a predetermined outcome (recovery versus decline) in place of a branching plurality of possibilities. To Professor Ch., the representative of Kraepelinian psychiatry, the jewelers no longer need an interpretive process of discovery, because that process is already contained in psychiatry's nosological system. When Ch. disappears from the story, *Ch*erpanov takes his place, and House No. 42 (which the reader has already been told is filled with "borderline cases of minor psychiatry [*pogranichnyye sluchai maloy psikhiatrii*]") becomes the Kraepelin Hospital's double.[29] Similarly, Cherpanov's step-by-step guide for psychic renovation is merely an extension of the professor's psychiatric textbook and Cherpanov's psychological profiling of future workers for the *kombinat* a variant of Professor Ch.'s "nosological units." The fiscally speculative activities in House No. 42 are economic iterations of a quantitatively based psychiatry and ironically lend substance to Lenin's 1919 claim about a "little sukharevka" lurking in the soul. What therefore seems to begin as a demonstration of psychoanalytic pseudoscientificity turns into a sustained commentary on how the opposite clinical approach offers no greater certitude. In seeming to lay claim to a rigorously precise truth, Kraepelinian psychiatry proves equally perilous.

## The Psychiatric Value Form: Let Y = *Y*

The reversal in the clinical dimension of the novel mimics the reversal in the economic and narrative dimensions. *Y* initially presents psychoanalysis, economic speculation, and narrative uncertainty as problematic because inconclusive. All lack clear outcomes. By contrast, it stages empirical psychiatry, the socialist economy under Stalin, and adherence to predictable narrative norms as seemingly desirable because rigorous and in no way left to chance. The value of these things can be guaranteed, which correspondingly means that *schast'ye* plays no part in them. Yet *Y* also upends this arrangement. The novel would not exist without Andreyshin's psychoanalytic hypotheses about the jewelers, the bourgeois inclinations of the inhabitants of House No. 42, and a rejection of more classical literary norms. This signals the extent to which even a seemingly direct endorsement of certitude ends up hinging on a degree of uncertainty. The title's equivocality between the Cyrillic linguistic "Y" and the Roman mathematical "Y" captures this dilemma in space of a single grapheme. The title is unpronounceable and indeterminate because beholden to two distinct semantic regimes (linguistic and mathematical) and two distinct writing systems (Cyrillic and Latin), which nevertheless mutually condition each other. The impossibility of reducing the title to either captures the play of speculative ambiguity and determinative surety that likewise sustains the text.

In the course of this reversal, the nominally bourgeois Freudian psychoanalysis, condemned by Lenin and then effectively outlawed in the Soviet Union in 1929, proves less indebted to a "capitalist" form of psychic economy than the Kraepelinian one, which is shown by the novel to possess a value form.

Marx presents four stages of value development in the first chapter of *Capital*. In the "elementary," or "simple" (*einfache*), stage, commodities are connected to one another by a relationship of simple equivalence.[30] A certain amount of linen is equivalent to one coat. This relationship assumes the commodities' isolation. Linen, at this stage, is only ever measured in the number of coats it will make, and coats are only ever made of linen. In the "expanded" (*totale oder entfaltete Wertform*) form of value, however, it becomes possible to imagine multiple different types of equivalencies.[31] Linen, that is, might be measured in a certain number of coats, just as well as a certain amount of tea, coffee, corn, iron, etc. Each of these equivalencies remains a distinct relationship, however, until the third stage: that of the "general" form of value, *die Äquivalentform*, to which Goux refers in *Symbolic Economies*.

At this point, the awkwardness of having to contend with many separate relationships of equivalence is resolved by the advent of a *general* equivalent, representing value itself. The institution of a general equivalent simplifies everything by proposing that different individual commodities be measured according to a single standard. In other words, they are only related to one another with reference to this standard, which now plays the role of universal intermediary. The general equivalent represents a shift from establishing equivalence between specific commodities to establishing it in terms of a single privileged commodity, which now serves as "value in general" and thereby acquires an autonomous status.[32] The general equivalent ceases to participate in processes of exchange and simply mediates them. Elevating one special commodity to the status of universal general equivalent, however, ushers in the fourth stage, the money form (*Geldform*) of value. Now, gold steps into the role of general equivalent. Commodity X is now calculated in terms of a certain amount of gold, as are all other commodities. Reification (*Verdinglichung*) simply means the processes whereby the money form, which was originally premised on the arbitrary elevation of one commodity to this exceptional role, comes to acquire independence. Instead of expressing value, the money form creates value. It becomes the source of valuation, not merely one form of measurement among other possibilities.

In psychoanalysis, the presence of the symptom as signifier for an underlying trauma sets off the play of substitutions that is crucial for Lacan's work, Deleuze and Guattari's writing on "Capitalism and Schizophrenia," and Goux's claims about a psychoanalytic general equivalent. Across all of these texts, however, the symptom is the site of relational instability. The psychic economy that it facilitates is (with the possible exception of Goux's reading of Lacan) not one that confers value. In Freud's work, symptoms operate as external expressions of otherwise potentially undetectable pathologies. The hysteric's rasping cough indicates the existence of a deeper trauma, one that is perhaps associated with the throat (as in Freud's interpretation of Dora), but the trauma only reaches the level of discernment through an exceptionally indirect, coded insight: symptoms, indicating of the return of the repressed.[33] Lacan picks up this idea, suggesting that symptoms "can be entirely resolved in an analysis of language, because a symptom is itself structured like a language."[34]

When Deleuze and Guattari take issue in *Anti-Oedipus* with Lacan's claims, they contest the primacy of the Oedipal myth. They do not quibble with the import of the symptom, however, merely readjust its role. The recurrent appearance of a question about "the relationship between drives [*pulsions*] and symptoms, between the symbol and what is symbolized, has risen again and again," they remark, before concluding that this is a perfectly good question so long as the relationship between drive and symptom is not stripped of its relationship to production by the Oedipal myth. Symptoms must remain able to participate in the flow of desire, which is antithetical to capitalist economics.

In all these instances, symptoms cannot be pinned down, do not "stand for" any one thing, and, in consequence, do not form part of a capitalist psychic economy run by the law of general equivalence and mediated through a "money form" of value. In Kraepelinian psychiatry, however, the situation is rather different. Kraepelin notoriously dispensed with symptoms. In their place, he offered time. Inspired by Fechner's institution of a general equivalent for sensations (the Fechner-Weber law), Kraepelin presents time as the general equivalent for mental illnesses: disease outcome determines how individual diagnoses are to be separated from one another and also how they are valued. Installing time in the role of general equivalent produces a single stable metric against which the various diseases can be measured and graded as better or worse.

Ivanov's text is profoundly sensitive to the notion that Kraepelinian psychiatry makes time the general equivalent. In *Y*, Marx's capitalist general equivalent (gold) is linked to the psychiatric general equivalent (time) in the form of the gold watches. In other words, the fact that the *watches* in particular disappear is an indicator that time is the general equivalent in the realm of mental illness, just as gold is economically. The conjunction of "gold" and "watches" in Y shows the way in which the psychiatric economy has acquired characteristics of the market economy, and vice versa. The loss of the gold watches in the novel is tantamount to the loss of the psychiatric general equivalent, which understandably provokes the jewelers' delusions because it deprives the psychiatric economy of its universally mediatory term. Yet just as the loss of the economically valuable commodity destabilizes the jewelers, so too do the jeweler's psychiatric delusions end up destabilizing the economy, resulting in the wild fluctuations at Sukharevsky Market. It is therefore quite natural that the jewelers should be finally cured by the head of the economic department. Once the psychic economy has been made to resemble the market economy, only someone whose job it is to keep track of monetary balances will be capable of correcting psychiatric imbalance. It is quite natural that they should be medically assisted by help from the State Trust for Precision Mechanics (historically responsible for the production of watches) because it is only by restoring time to its rightful role as the psychiatric general equivalent that they can hope to be cured. The text is narrated predominantly through Yegor Yegorych because his job as psychiatric accountant is purpose-built for the task.

Although the book seems to be a critique of psychoanalysis and an endorsement of psychiatry, the absurdity of the jewelers' cure, not to mention the book's own metadiegetic excesses and its continued emphasis on *schast'ye* (fortune, incalculability), shows that it actually does the reverse. *Y* critiques Kraepelin's evidentiary, mathematized psyche, which puts in place a capitalist mental economy and counterintuitively supports psychoanalytic speculation on which the very existence of the narrative depends. Only by refusing a logic of general equivalency can storytelling as a process (and not an outcome) take place. This was a controversial position to take in 1933 and may have contributed to Ivanov's decision to keep the full manuscript in a drawer rather than seek its complete publication. In Ivanov's novel, the scientific and empirical model for assessing the contents of mental life (embodied in Professor Ch.'s work) is complicit both with capitalism and with Stalin's first Five-Year Plan, both of which are presented as being economically speculative. Ivanov, in other words, erases the distinction between the capitalist speculation that took place under Lenin's New Economic Policy (intended as a temporary stopgap measure) and the socialist speculation of Stalin's Five-Year Plan, which was supposed to conclusively put in place the industrial infrastructure for the new Soviet Union and make way for a different economic structure. The book's version of the New Soviet Man, moreover, mocks what it presents as the first Five-Year Plan's human speculation. It caricatures the Soviet New Man as a figure whose psychical transformation will be spearheaded by a counterfeiter and take place in a future and at a place so distant as to be impossible to reach. The book's bid for psychoanalytic speculation is thus tantamount to an economic critique, not merely a scientific one. Its economic critique likewise folds back into a commentary on the scientific representation of mental life. Ivanov shows that psychoanalytic speculation may lead his detective duo on a wild goose chase all over the city but that it is still more sensical than the "obvious" answer already sitting within the psychiatric hospital. Failure to follow the path of failure is the real gamble, Ivanov suggests, and a speculation not worth betting on. The sure bet, the one that has already calculated its own value, makes the journey to that logical conclusion hardly worth the trouble in any economy.

## CHAPTER 6

# MONODRAMA AS MASS SPECTACLE

## The Soviet Self on Stage

*The tradition of all dead generations weighs like a nightmare on the brain of the living.*

—Karl Marx

*Shut up!... Allow me to observe, Mr. Rational I, that we share the same nerves, and that when I yank on your nerves, I also yank on mine.*

—Nikolay Evreinov

The story of Vladimir Il'ich Lenin's body is well known. That of his brain less so. Without any of the body's fanfare or demonstrative exhibition, Lenin's brain has nevertheless been subject to as intricate a history of preservation, memorialization, and mythologization as its more publicly visible outer wrapping. When Lenin died on January 21, 1924, the fate of his brain held a special significance for the attending physicians who autopsied him. It appeared to hold out two important prospects. The first involved a material demonstration of Lenin's genius, which would thereby legitimate the cult of Leninism that Stalin had begun developing even in the months before Lenin's death. The second involved a conclusive debunking of Lenin's 1922 political testament, indicting Stalin. Evidence of significant brain pathology would, it seemed, massively bolster Stalin's claim that Lenin was no longer compos mentis at the time he wrote the testament and thereby put to an end the objections raised by the competing political faction headed by Lenin's wife, Nadezhda Krupskaya. Finally, the Politburo hoped Lenin's brain (because it carried the physical traces of its owner's cognitive superiority) would thereby offer a formidable biological demonstration of the Soviet Union's legitimacy. Such proof would scientifically support the notion that the Soviet Union was the (literal) brainchild of a superhuman prodigy, whose legacy and genius Stalin now inherited, at least in theory.

The study of Lenin's brain was initially conducted under the guidance of the German brain researcher Professor Oskar Vogt (1870–1959), who had already made a study of numerous "elite" brains at the Berlin Neurobiological Institute of the Kaiser Wilhelm Institute as part of a eugenic research agenda. Following Lenin's death, Vogt travelled to Moscow specifically for the purpose of studying Lenin's brain and establishing, in tandem, a center for human race biology (to be known as the German-Russian Laboratory for Comparative Race Pathology). Vogt led a team of Soviet scientists in creating the Moscow State Institute of the Brain, with the goal of comparatively assessing the cytoarchitectonic structure (cellular composition) of the contents of Lenin's cranium and, in tandem, contributing to a larger planned project of comparative race pathology.

Officially founded in 1928, the Institute of the Brain (Institut mozga) worked until 1936 to generate a report on Lenin's genius. Vogt's initial 1927 conclusion that Lenin had indeed been a "mental athlete"—based on the unusual size of the pyramidal neurons in his cerebral cortex—was amply supported by the final 1936 report's findings. Comparison with the brains of figures the institute had collected in the intervening years (including literary titans like Vladimir Mayakovsky, Andrey Bely, and Maksim Gorky, as well as the German politician Clara Zetkin and Nobel awardee Ivanv Petrovich Pavlov) demonstrated that Lenin's brain, apparently, had a larger number of overall furrows, structurally larger cells, and bigger frontal and temporal regions (associated with higher-level thinking processes) than any of the brains of these extraordinarily talented individuals. By 1936, however, it was no longer politically expedient to highlight Lenin's genius. Stalin was in the throes of purging the party of political rivals. The idea of underlining his predecessor's cognitive virtuosity threatened to cast an unfavorable shadow on Stalin's own mental faculties. The long-awaited 1936 report was classified as secret and not recovered until after the collapse of the Soviet Union.

The case of Lenin's brain raises a question about the brain's relationship to history that Karl Marx had identified in part in his *The Eighteenth Brumaire of Louis Bonaparte* (1852), written on the occasion of Louis-Napoléon Bonaparte's coup d'état. Marx famously remarks in his essay on history's repetition first as tragedy and then as farce. He goes on to comment that the historical "tradition of all dead generations weighs like a nightmare on the brains of the living." Given the fate of Lenin's brain, it is hard not to wonder at Marx's statement. In the Soviet Union, Lenin's brain did indeed tell history. The deceased Lenin's brain weighed like both a dream and a nightmare on the living traditions of the Soviet present. The brain told the history of Lenin's genius. It told the history of his testament. It told the history of the Soviet Union's greatness. It potentially told all too much. Is, then, Marx's comment in 1852 to be taken as a figure of speech? Or as an anticipatory celebration of neurology's coming role in the postrevolutionary Soviet Union? Or, considering the international prominence of figures such as the Soviet neuroscientist Alexander Luria, an insight about the properties of the brain and its relationship to memory? What kind of consciousness did Vogt and Soviet anatomists have in mind as they picked apart the brain of the celebrated theoretician of class-political consciousness?

This chapter considers how the physicalized representation of the mind was crucial to generating a sense of collective consciousness, the imagination of a "we," in the emerging Soviet Union. My inquiry focuses on how the new nineteenth-century psychophysics and empirical psychology portrayed the mind and changed how collectivity was and could be imagined. The curious fate of a piece of Russian avant-garde theater from 1911, which went on to become a Soviet mass spectacle celebrating the 1917 revolution, shows this process at work.

The Russian playwright Nikolay Evreinov's monodrama *In the Stage Wings of the Soul* is set inside a biologized representation of the human soul. The play explicitly refers to psychophysics (Gustav Fechner) and empirical psychology (Wilhelm Wundt) to justify its unusual staging. In the depoliticized space of Russian imperial theater, Evreinov exploited these contemporary scientific theories to a foster a sense of dramatic "coexperiencing," his technical term for the destruction of the fourth wall by complete psychical identification of actor and character. As a mass spectacle, however, the materialist premises of psychophysics and empirical psychology made it possible for the Bolsheviks to adapt Evreinov's play into a representation, built on the principles of coexperiencing, of unified collective consciousness for a larger psychopolitical purpose.

Nikolay Evreinov's monodrama became the basis for a Soviet mass spectacle that consolidated a picture of the Soviet people's mind. In so doing, it helped make the understanding of Marxist-Leninist class-political consciousness indistinguishable from the neurological research that would go on to replace psychoanalysis in the Soviet Union in the late 1920s. The play shows how an early iteration of the Soviet self, as a reflection of the artificial soul of popular sovereignty, was built from a Russian adaptation of aesthetic tradition dating back to Jean-Jacques Rousseau and the reception of the German mind sciences.

## Monodrama and Enlightenment: From Pygmalion to Petersburg

The Russian avant-garde playwright and director Nikolay Evreinov (1879–1953) first presented his theory of "monodrama" at a lecture to the Moscow Circle of Art and Literature in December 1908. Monodrama, he proclaimed to his Moscow audience, was a mode of dramatic representation in which all action took place in the mind of a single character.[1] This first-person protagonist, Evreinov asserted, helped facilitate a form of collective consciousness by directly connecting the theater audience to the drama by breaching the fourth wall. In his words: "The spectator 'coexperiences' [*soperezhivayet*] along with the characters. The ideal of a dramatic performance is in the equal importance of the experience on either side of the footlights."[2]

Evreinov presented his theory in multiple subsequent lectures across Petersburg during the early months of the following year and published it as a separate pamphlet. The theory had important consequences both for Russian drama at the turn of the century and for the later scholarship of the 1960s and 1970s that explored the function of role-play in social life. Most immediately, it inspired Evreinov's original monodramas *The Presentation of Love* (*Predstavleniye lyubvi*, 1910) and *In the Stage Wings of the Soul* (*V kulisakh dushi*, 1911; hereafter *Stage Wings*). The theory also contributed to his evolving concept of "theatricality" (*teatralnost'*). Evreinov understood "theatricality" in terms of a preaesthetic, biological instinct to play (*igra*) common to all conscious organisms.[3] Drawing on elements of sociology, ethology, the history of criminal justice, and psychology, Evreinov was one of the first theoreticians of the theater to suggest that theatricality was an anthropological category rather than a strictly formal element of stagecraft. Despite Evreinov's fall into obscurity in Russia after his emigration to Paris in the late 1920s, his oeuvre continues to be an essential, if under-researched, chapter in the early conceptual history of "theatricality" and sociocultural performance.[4] His theoretical writings on monodrama in particular have been recognized as a precursor to Jacob Moreno's clinical psychodramas and to Clifford Geertz's and Erving Goffman's work in cultural anthropology.[5] Monodrama is the often-overlooked predecessor of such works as Samuel Beckett's "one-mouth" play *Not I* (1972) and Ionesco's absurdist dramas.[6]

For all of monodrama's subsequent dramatic and cultural currency, Evreinov cited few historical antecedents for the genre in his 1908 lecture. Throughout his career Evreinov cultivated a self-conscious conviction in his own intellectual originality, in part as a means of reinvigorating older artistic forms.[7] Monodrama is a case in point. In his lecture on the subject, Evreinov claimed that he was revitalizing a "lost" Greek genre. As Kirsten Gram Holmström has shown, however, monodrama is "one of those rare cases where the origin and course of development of an art form are beyond argument."[8] The invention of monodrama as a genre can be traced directly to Jean-Jacques Rousseau's one-act play *Pygmalion* (written 1762, performed 1770). Evreinov, who was a scholar of Western theater history and the great-grandson of a French aristocrat, of course knew Rousseau. By reconsidering Evreinov's theory of monodrama through Rousseau's earlier variant, it becomes possible to see how Evreinov translated and updated many of Rousseau's ideas first for the Russian symbolist theater of the 1910s and then again for the Soviet mass spectacles of the 1920s.

Evreinov expands the Rousseauian model for a theater of self-representation. His reconfiguration of the actor-audience relationship (breaking the fourth wall) can be interpreted as a radical extension of Rousseau's dialectic of self and other as it appears in *Pygmalion.* Monodrama did not stop there, however.

Evreinov's modifications to the historical genre of monodrama attained their fullest expression outside the playing space of the traditional theater. As Spencer Golub has shown, Evreinov's theory of monodrama was the prototype for his 1920 mass spectacle *The Storming of the Winter Palace* (*Vzyatiye zimnego dvortsa*), organized for the third anniversary of the October Revolution.[9] The mass spectacle relied on more than eight thousand Petersburg residents to reenact the events of the October Revolution in their original location. The production, which played before an audience of over one hundred thousand, was a carefully scripted affirmation of Bolshevik revolutionary time. It helped craft a positive, well-ordered image of the October Revolution out of the chaos of the original events. Evreinov's mass spectacle helped inspire Sergey Eisenstein's depiction of the same event in his film *Oktyabr'* (*October*, 1928). Participants in Evreinov's mass spectacle rehearsed, solidified, and performed a collective proletarian identity on the model of monodramatic coexperiencing (*soperezhivaniye*). Evreinov's *Storming of the Winter Palace* fulfilled the promise of monodrama on a grand scale while simultaneously (if unintentionally) contributing to the mythogenesis of Soviet power and a solidification of the Soviet psyche politic.

## Evreinov's Theory of Monodrama

Evreinov may have concluded his Russian theatrical career in Petersburg with a paean to the Revolution, but it is essential to keep in mind that he was trained in the conservative environment of late-nineteenth-century theater. Evreinov did not abandon this training over the course of his career. Rather, he allowed his theories to be strategically appropriated in instances where doing so would permit him to achieve specific aesthetic goals, which were nevertheless ideologically complementary with politicized/Bolshevik aims.

Unlike the performing arts in the subsidized—albeit censored—Soviet era, the Russian theater circa 1900 was predominantly concerned with turning a profit and keeping its audiences entertained. For most of the nineteenth century, the theater was a government monopoly. Actors of the imperial theaters, because state employees, were thus far more interested in perfecting their craft and remaining financially solvent than in transplanting the latest progressive political tendencies to the stage. Students and stage managers alike dreaded political unrest, which interrupted their demanding rehearsal and performance schedules. As Paul du Quenoy has shown, the myth of the turn-of-the-century theater as a crucible for revolution was a joint product of Soviet-era historiography and Western fetishization of the radical Russian avant-garde.[10] Both groups of scholars have privileged revolutionary interpretations for the performing arts in the decades immediately following 1900. Their work has had the effect of minimizing the success of the imperial model: The theater, instead of being a site for tendentious social and political struggle in the waning Russian Empire, constituted an important aspect of civil society. In du Quenoy's words:

> The [performing arts] actively worked for the realization of their goals *within existing frameworks*, which included an expanding . . . community of cultural interests, a free commercial economy that offered a substantial entertainment industry, a professional sphere in which [performers] sought and gained a recognized place, and a state that . . . willingly accommodated them and . . . remained reluctant or unable to amplify its powers of control.[11]

In addition to six imperial theaters, Moscow and Petersburg boasted an array of private playing spaces and cabarets and a popular stage that was supported by government (with the explicit aim of promoting a culturally elevating alternative to drunkenness and debauchery). In the wake of the Russo-Japanese War, the Russian public looked to theater as a site of escape for political but likely also emotional reasons. Theater patrons were reluctant to support oppositional forums that set out to explicitly challenge perceptions or upset social norms, especially when such forums masqueraded as art. The fact that the public was similarly uninterested in sacred or mystical variants on theater did not, of course, prevent the Russian symbolists from exploring these avenues. The so-called first wave of symbolists (Konstantin Bal'mont, Valeriy Briusov, Zinaida Gippius, Fedor Sologub) translated the French neoromanticism of Charles Baudelaire and Paul Verlaine into a Russian key, in polemical reaction to the realism and positivism that had dominated Russian thought since the 1860s.[12] The early Russian symbolists, who were proponents of Nietzschean individualism, decadence, impressionism, and pathological subjectivity, gathered around the journal

*World of Art* (*Mir iskusstva*, 1899–1904). This journal not only served as a hub for a group of artists and art connoisseurs that included Leon Bakst and Sergey Diaghilev but also published creative writing and short essays by prominent Russian symbolist authors and essayists. Evreinov's monographs on the Belgian artist Felician Rops (1910) and English illustrator Aubrey Beardsley (1912) were a testament to his symbolist interest in the visual arts, as well as to his own crossovers with the stylized French decadence often associated with Joris Karl Huysmans.

As Russian symbolism evolved in the years before 1905, it turned increasingly toward the importance of spiritual goals in cultural life. By the time the Russian poet (and classical scholar) Vyacheslav Ivanov began publishing creative and theoretical texts at the intersection of Orthodox Christianity and Greek myth (an attempt to merge Vladimir Solovyov's doctrine of Divine Sophia with Friedrich Nietzsche's *The Birth of Tragedy*), the idea of the theater as a space for ritualized Dionysian expression was already part of a lively (if rarified) debate among the intelligentsia. The texts that this debate produced included reflections on the relationship between actor and audience. Among the most controversial of these was Fedor Sologub's "Teatr odnoy voli" (The theater of a single will, 1908). Sologub's essay radically reimagined the theater as a space in which the author's "will" (*volya*) could be directly channeled into the actions of a single protagonist. Writers such as Aleksander Blok (in "O teatre" [On theater, 1908]), Valeriy Briusov (in "Nenuzhnaya pravda" [Unnecessary truth, 1902]), and Vyacheslav Ivanov (in "Borozdy i mezhi. O probleme teatra" [Furrows and boundaries. On the problem of theater, 1909] and "Yesteticheskaya norma teatra" [The aesthetic norm of theater, 1916]) all polemicized against naturalism, debated the revival of Greek theater, and theorized the proper role of the director.

It was in this hybrid environment of widespread theater enthusiasm and symbolist experimentation that the twenty-two-year-old Nikolay Evreinov made his artistic debut. Evreinov was a recent graduate of Petersburg's Imperial School of Jurisprudence, with a thesis on the history of corporal punishment in Russia. He had immediately entered the civil service following graduation. His first plays were written while he was employed by the Ministry of Roads and Communications, a position he would hold until 1910. His three-act symbolist comedy *The Foundation of Happiness* (*Fundament schast'ya*, 1902) secured his reputation as a playwright and director of note.[13] By 1906, Evreinov was able to convince the theater critic Aleksander Kugel' and Baron Nikolay von Driezen (editor of the prestigious *Yearbook of Imperial Theaters* [*Yezhegodnik imperatorskikh teatrov*]) to collaborate with him on an ambitious new project. Evreinov was interested in developing a historico-reconstructive theater that would attend both to the accurate restoration of past forms and to the accompanying conditions of spectatorship. The result was the Ancient

Theater (*Starinnyy teatr*).[14] The joint undertaking debuted in December 1907. Its first season featured an eleventh-century liturgical drama (*The Three Magi* [*Tri volkhva*]), a thirteenth-century French miracle play (*The Miracle of Theophilus* [*Le miracle Théophile/Deystvo o Teofile*]), a fifteenth-century morality play (*Present-Day Brothers* [*Nyneshniye brat'ya*]), and a series of Renaissance farces. Evreinov and his collaborators spent the preceding months abroad, collecting primary source materials on the history of medieval theater at sites from Paris to Cologne and Nuremburg. The Ancient Theater gave Evreinov an opportunity to experiment with an onstage audience in period dress. This quasi-choral group encouraged the viewing public to respond "appropriately" (with historical accuracy) by guiding the audience through the production with their own reactions in real time.

The success of the Ancient Theater convinced Vera Komissarzhevskaya to appoint Evreinov the chief artistic director of her Dramatic Theater in 1908. In accepting the post, Evreinov ousted Vsevolod Meyerhold from the position and initiated a rivalry that would last until the former's departure for Paris. Many of Evreinov's initial productions at the Dramatic Theater were unwitting preparatory studies in monodrama. For example, Evreinov's "primitivistic production of Schiller's *The Maid of Orleans* (1908) was designed to present Joan of Arc . . . from a particular point of view, namely as she was conceived by the medieval mentality."[15] In his production of Gabriele D'Annunzio's *Francesca da Rimini* the same year, Evreinov divided the stage into light and dark halves. He restricted the play's positive and negative elements to the corresponding side in order to evoke the "mood" of the thirteenth century (in which the play was set).

Working with an onstage audience in the Ancient Theater and with the highly stylized productions at the Dramatic Theater gave Evreinov a solid basis on which to construct a theory of monodrama. The published pamphlet of his lecture, *Vvedeniye v monodramu* ("Introduction to Monodrama"), is just over thirty pages long. The text is built around a fundamental distinction Evreinov draws between the two terms "spectacle" (*zrelishche*) and "drama" (*drama*):

> When some event unfolds before me on the theatrical boards that stand for the world, I regard it as drama in the highest sense of that word only when I myself become, as it were, a participant in what is transpiring on stage. . . . The rest which I am unable to accept as my own drama I consider the spectacle of someone else's drama, no matter how beautiful, amusing or absurd it may be, only "spectacle" [*zrelishche*] and not drama.[16]

The etymology of "spectacle" and "drama" in Russian is important. *Zrelishche* is derived from the verb *zret'*, meaning "to gaze" or "to watch."[17] For

Evreinov, *zrelishche* is associated with the audience's passivity. It describes action that takes place from the "pulpit" (*kafedra*) and "concert platform" (*kontsertnaya yestrada*). In these instances, distant witnessing on the part of the spectator is sufficient to fully participate in the experience.[18] By contrast, "drama" involves active participation. Evreinov uses "drama," from the Greek *δρᾶν* (dran: to do, to accomplish), to describe scenarios in which genuine "coexperiencing" (*soperezhivaniye*) occurs. Evreinov's distinction between the two terms contributes importantly to his definition of monodrama. It is presumably also at stake in his selection of the term "mono*drama*."

> Now by "monodrama" I mean to denote the kind of dramatic presentation [*dramaticheskoye predstavlenie*] which, while attempting to communicate to the spectator as fully as it can the character's state of mind, displays the world around him on stage just as the character perceives the world at any given moment during his existence on stage. Thus, we are talking about an architectonics of drama based on the principle of the drama's stage coalescence with the way the character is presented.[19]

The phrase "dramatic presentation" (*dramaticheskoye predstavleniye*) in this passage is given to indicate an implicit contrast with the more passive idea of spectacle. When Evreinov speaks of an "architectonics of *drama*," he is not using the word drama idly. His new architectonics involves the active mobilization of the theater's full artistic structure in the service of the central character's subjective perceptions. When successfully deployed, this performance becomes "my drama" (*moya drama*), a phrase Evreinov uses in a technical sense rather than a merely possessive one. "My drama" is synonymous with coexperiencing; it is the antithesis of "foreign" (*chuzhoy*) spectacle.

The remainder of the lecture addresses three central concerns: whether the spectator can successfully coexperience with multiple protagonists in a single production, how the spectacular theater can practically be converted into a dramatic one, and why monodrama is important as a form. In order to justify his claim that monodrama must restrict itself to the perceptions of a single protagonist, Evreinov turns to psychology. Here, he suggests that Wilhelm Wundt's new German science of empirical psychology supports his belief in the biological limitations of perception; these limitations will always, he believes, restrict successful monodrama to a single perceptual viewpoint. His discussion then veers suggestively off track. Rather than making a case for a single protagonist, Evreinov ends up arguing for something closer to the importance of aesthetic appreciation as a motor process. He cites the German philosopher and psychologist Karl Groos (1861–1946) and the father of psychophysics, Gustav Fechner (1801–1887). Evreinov borrows Groos's term "inner imitation" (which he translates as "*vnutrenneye podrazhan'ye*"). It appears in

Groos's text *People at Play* (*Die Spiele der Menschen*, 1899) and refers to the externalized, mechanical expression of aesthetic enjoyment, which binds the viewer to his or her object. (Groos uses the example of child playing with a doll and lending it her/his/their own voice and feelings to answer the questions she/he/they poses to it.) For Evreinov, *vnutrenneye podrazhan'ye* is the emotive *action* that supports coexperiencing. It is important as a motor process. Evreinov is making a case for the value of testing neurophysiological responses as a way to measure aesthetic enjoyment, the point being that those responses can be seen (and measured) *as active responses*.

This emphasis on motion and on the physiology of empathetic association allows Evreinov to transition to his next point: the practical changes that a director can make to convert spectacle into (mono)drama. These too are focused on motion. Evreinov recommends that the monodramatic theater use gesture, highly detailed stage directions, a close correspondence between the protagonist and his/her environment, rapid scene changes, anthropomorphized props, and a dynamic representation of the protagonist that accords with how the protagonist sees himself/herself/themselves at any given moment (via makeup, mime, and lighting). Evreinov additionally mentions that the accompanying playbill should designate this protagonist as "I" (*ya*).[20] Little wonder, then, that Evreinov should have been accused by his contemporaries of removing the actor from the stage and replacing him with an all-powerful director. Many objected that there was little reason for the spectator to relate to the protagonist at all after so much heavy-handed manipulation.

Yet Evreinov's theory of monodrama was also after something larger. Monodrama, Evreinov claims, repeats the structure of man's conscious perception of the world: "I have not yet presented the rather weighty circumstance in favor of monodrama as the preferred form of contemporary drama, namely the fact that man's environment, perceived by his consciousness [*soznaniye*], does not appear as something inert and dead, lying outside of him."[21] Evreinov's understanding of monodrama is cinematic. As multiple commentators have remarked, Evreinov's innovations were better suited to the medium of film than they were to the (relatively) limited technical capacities of early-twentieth-century theater, which struggled to keep pace with the rapidity of the scene shifts that Evreinov's monodramas required. Indeed, there is much in *Stage Wings* that is reminiscent of expressionist film's exploration of subjective changes in first-person perception.

## Monodramatic Origins

Evreinov's innovations in monodramatic form are set against the backdrop of a long, predominantly European history of the genre. In "Introduction to Monodrama," he had claimed that

> this word (having become property of the scholastics, the word at present being utterly forgotten and its meaning lost to any but the sedulous philologist) used to mean a certain kind of predominantly melodramatic work, which from start to finish was performed by one actor alone. Even now we are able to make acquaintance with this type of performance through the appearances of a new kind of quick-change artist, in the style of Fregoli, Francardi and their sort. This art is of very ancient derivation; its originator appears to be the immortal Thespis, who more than twenty-five hundred years ago, after writing plays with several characters following a certain plan, took to performing them as one-man shows, with the help of linen masks and distinctive costumes of his own devising.[22]

Evreinov's emphasis on the Greek roots of monodrama in this passage follows an important current of Russian symbolism, promoted most famously by Vyacheslav Ivanov. Ivanov argued that there was a direct connection between the ancients and the Russian moderns. Since Russia had never passed through the Renaissance, the country was correspondingly less "mediated" than its European counterparts in relationship to Greek culture. Evoking a Greek genealogy helped Evreinov differentiate his approach from the prior tradition of monodrama beginning in the late eighteenth century and spanning France, Germany, and England. It situated him as an heir to the theater's deeper Thespian origins and established monodrama as a logical extension of Thespis's initial decision to speak "as a character" rather than in his own voice. Revitalizing monodrama from having been "totally forgotten" also permitted Evreinov the necessary creative freedom to restructure the meaning of the term, thus defamiliarizing the European meaning and reconstructing it anew. The very act of "introducing" monodrama helped Evreinov decouple it from the history it had accumulated in the century plus since Rousseau's *Pygmalion* had premiered.

Evreinov did not entirely separate himself from the European monodramatic tradition, however, even if his lecture and the accompanying pamphlet productively obscured references to it. His mention of monodrama as a form of "melodrama" is a historically accurate reflection of the genre's ties to the mixed musical form invented by Rousseau in the eighteenth century. Moreover, Evreinov's theory preserved many of monodrama's traditional elements of monodrama, even if he did not actively identify them as such.

What were these elements, and where did they originate? Rousseau's *Pygmalion*, which he designated a *scène lyrique*, was most likely written in 1762. It premiered in 1770 in Lyons and played in Paris at the Comédie Française five years later. It received a largely positive reception and remained in the repertoire until the nineteenth century. There is good evidence that Rousseau wrote Pygmalion as a "practical demonstration" of his theories on recitative (a sung form of ordinary speech) in French opera.[23] Rousseau was convinced that there was nothing specifically musical about the French language as opposed to other languages. He had outlined this position earlier in both his *Letter on French Music* (*Lettre sur la musique française*, 1753) and *Dictionary of Music* (*Dictionnaire de musique*, 1768). In the absence of any inherently linguistic basis for accompanied recitative, Rousseau used a combination of monologue, pantomime, and orchestral music in *Pygmalion* to produce an equivalent effect, under his neologistic heading "*scène lyrique*."[24]

The spread of monodrama across Europe is largely a history of translation. Although the genre did not have immediate successors in France, it passed rapidly into Germany through Goethe's 1772 introduction to *Pygmalion*. Franz Aspelmeyer and Anton Schweitzer set the play to new music that year; it was performed in Weimar in May.[25] Its popularity inspired Johann Christian Brandeis to write *Ariadne auf Naxos*, the music for which was composed by Georg Benda. The massive success of *Ariadne* in Germany prompted Benda to pen his own monodrama, *Medea*. The combination of Goethe's, Brandeis's, and Benda's work occasioned a flurry of new monodramatic productions. More than thirty monodramas appeared in Germany in the period between 1770 and 1790, even as the genre vanished from France. These productions were dominated in large part by lamentations of heroines from classical mythology.

As monodrama evolved, it also acquired connections to anatomy, physiology, and pathonomics, largely by association with Descartes's theory of the passions and the popularization of physiognomy in Germany through works by Johann Kasper Lavater (*Physiognomy*, 1772; *Physiognomical Fragments*, 1774–1778). At the time René Descartes composed his treatise *The Passions of the Soul*, causation was just beginning to be understood as the motion between substances instead of as an independent substance itself. Descartes's *Passions* explored the fundamental forms of psychic motion. Descartes concluded that the body and soul made contact through "animal spirits" in the blood that conducted physical motion to the seat of the soul (not the soul itself), located in the pineal gland. The Cartesian theory of the passions and German advances in physiognomy came together in J. F. Götz's little-known monodramatic study *Attempt at a Serialized Progression of the Passions for the Sensitive Friend of Art and Theater* (*Versuch einer zahlreichen Folge leidenschaftlicher Entwürfe für empfindsame Kunst- und Schauspielfreunde*, 1783). Götz had studied anatomy and even conducted his own informal dissections, acquiring body parts through a friend at the Academy of Art in Vienna. In the *Versuch*, he used nearly two hundred annotated etchings to present an exact gestural typology of the various emotions and their corresponding physical expressions as he envisioned them accompanying the poem *Leonardo und Blandine*. He rewrote the poem in monodramatic form. This was in keeping with his belief (influenced by the popularity of *Ariadne*) that monodrama was the only genre through which an artist could fully visualize the external signs of mental states.

At the same time, Goethe was developing his monodrama *Proserpina* (1778). Many of the central elements in the play's production, which Goethe outlined in an article in 1815, would become staples of the form overall. Goethe pointed to the significance of: "*Dekoration*" (decoration), "*Rezitation und Deklamation*" (recitation and declamation), "*Körperliche Bewegung*" (bodily movement), "*Mitwirkung der Kleidung*" (the incorporation of costume), and "*Musik*" (music, which accompanies speech, prompts artistic movements, and is incorporated into the chorus).[26] In the nineteenth century, monodrama evolved further as a psychological form, influenced by William James's stream of consciousness, Henri Bergson's notion of *la durée*, and Freud's theory of the unconscious.[27] Monodramas by Richard von Meerheimb, Edmund Picard, and the French symbolists (Mallarmé, Rachilde) emerged in the two decades before Evreinov's "Introduction to Monodrama." Evreinov himself cites Hauptmann and Andreev as part of the tradition.[28] In the words of Culler:

> One may say that there arose in the decades immediately before and after the turn of the [eighteenth] century several related art forms that focused on the solitary figure, most frequently a woman, who expressed through speech, music, costume and gesture the shifting movements of her soul. That the figure was solitary and that virtually the entire text consisted of her utterance was an attempt to focus on her subjectivity; that she was feminine was a further indication that the drama was one of passion.[29]

One could add to Culler's definition the additional remark that these "shifting movements" were tied to an anatomical understanding of the passions, reinforced by the findings of associationist psychology that interpreted Descartes's work as physiological. Associationism stressed corporeal topographies of the mind by explaining the movement of human passions through recourse to their mechanical construction. Mental states for thinkers such as David Hartley and James Mill in this account were cumulative and built upon one another through concretely discernable physical pathways. One might also add that by the late nineteenth century, the initial focus of monodrama on subjectivity was adapted to a focus on literary and artistic techniques by which to convey the nuances of first-person perspective. Common to the genre across both the eighteenth and the nineteenth centuries was the centrality of physical change as the essence of the medium, especially change that represented concrete, physical "movements" of the soul.

In this regard, Evreinov's theories in the "Introduction" are very much in line with those of his predecessors. His conception of monodrama preserves the centrality of physical change as a direct representation of psychic motion. Like prior iterations, he places a substantial emphasis on gesture and pantomime. In addition, his work is organized by an assumption about the universality of passions, in contrast with dramatic monologue, where the passions are connected with the actions and circumstances of single individual. His insistence that the protagonist should always be designated as "I" (*ya*) in the playbill is a tribute to his belief in the common experience of the passions.

In addition, Evreinov's "Introduction to Monodrama" can been seen as contributing a number of minor modifications. Unlike the eighteenth-century monodrama, none of his protagonists are borrowed from classical mythology. All are male.[30] In general, Evreinov is far less concerned with the presence of music than were the monodramas (and melodramas) of the past. In place of a musical score, he enhances the significance of scenery, stage directions, and especially lighting. Productions such as *Ariadne* and *Proserpina* had relied on a single actress to depict a variety of emotional states; by contrast, Evreinov's two monodramas display the changing states of a single consciousness with a plurality of actors.

Evreinov's most major and radical innovation was the idea of coexperiencing (*soperezhivaniye*), coupled with his insistence that contemporary theater do away with the footlights in favor of a full-scale theatricalization of life. Evreinov's work extended monodrama's prior attention to the expression of psychical experience and perception across the fourth wall through bodily gesture and onstage movement. His theater was premised around a sweeping empathy that blurred the distinction between self (the I of the audience and actor) and other (the I of the character). This was a part of Evreinov's theatrotherapy (*teatroterapiya*), a practice that, he claimed, would recover both spectator and theater from the debased, disconnected influences of contemporary drama. Contemporary theater, Evreinov remarked, was the lowest form of public entertainment. Insufficiently individuated, it merely attempted to satisfy everyone: "We have become gourmands in our individually refined tastes . . . the 'I' has become autocratic, but in the theater we are still [regarded] all together, they still offer us a collective spectacle, they are still trying to please us all at once!"[31]

Evreinov's experience at the Ancient Theater was an important step in reaching this conclusion about the importance of audience-actor fusion. His experiments with an onstage audience, which functioned as an emotional mediator between the historicity of the medieval stage action and the responses of a late imperial Russian theatergoing public, gave him a robust framework from which to develop a full-scale understanding of empathetic mutuality.

While Evreinov directed and collaborated on a number of monodramas at the Crooked Mirror theater in the 1910s, he wrote only two himself. The first, *The Presentation of Love* (*Predstavleniye lyubvi*), had a relatively narrow reception and almost no performance history of note. By contrast, his 1911 work *In the Stage Wings of the Soul* (*V kulisakh dushi*) received a great degree of attention in Russia and abroad, rivaling the success and popularity of his most famous work, *The Main Thing* (*Samoye glavnoye*, 1921).[32] *Stage Wings* was performed in London in 1915 (by a suffragette theater), in Vienna in 1920, and Rome in 1929, among performances at other major urban centers across Europe.[33] It inspired a series of works by the Russian-American Dada artist Man Ray, which then made their way into a number of French surrealist publications.

## *In the Stage Wings of the Soul*

*Stage Wings* premiered at Petersburg's Crooked Mirror (Krivoye zerkalo) theater in 1912. Evreinov had taken a position there as chief artistic director, following his stint at Komissarzhevskaya's Dramatic Theater. Part of the theater of "small forms" (*Kleinkunst*), the Crooked Mirror repertoire initially played outside normal performance hours, often featured a triple playbill of one-act performances, and regularly experimented with producing experiences of bodily shock in order to wrench the spectator out of normative forms of perception.[34] The name "Crooked Mirror" was borrowed from the epigraph to Nikolay Gogol's *Inspector General*: "Don't blame the mirror if your mug is crooked [*Na zerkalo necha penyat', koli rozha kriva*]." As its name suggests, the theater was forum for light comedy and satire—very seldom of a political nature and most often slapstick or absurdist in nature. Evreinov's *Stage Wings* was both.

*In the Stage Wings of the Soul* (*V kulisakh dushi*) takes place in little more than a heartbeat. It is played predominantly inside a human torso—an expansion of the physiological tradition tying monodrama and the passions to anatomy. "The action lasts half a minute [*vremya deystviya ½ minuty*]," the stage directions claim.[35] The curtain rises to reveal a character named the Professor standing on the proscenium in front of a blackboard and a second curtain that hides the main stage. The Professor announces that he recently received of a copy of *Stage Wings* from the author himself. At first glance, he regarded the work "with great mistrust [*s bol'shim nedoveriyem*]," considering it to be "some shallow vaudeville, devoid of deeper meaning [*kakoy-libo pustoy vodevil', lishennyy proizvodsmysla*]."[36] Yet, brandishing his chalk and citing the work of Freud, Wilhelm Wundt, and Théodule Ribot, he explains that the play is in fact rigorously scientific and attentive to the latest findings in psychophysiology. The human soul, the Professor elucidates, is in fact composed of three parts: the Rational (*ratsional'noye nachalo dushi*), Emotional (*emotsional'noye nachalo dushi*), and Subconscious (*podsoznatel'noye nachalo dushi*). All are housed within the human breast. He sketches a diagram of the heart, spine, lungs, and nerves (which he compares to a telephone) on the board and details the relative locations of the three parts of the soul: just above the diaphragm.

Proclaiming that it is best to leave further explication to the actors, the professor exits. As the second curtain sweeps up, a stage set identical to the chalk diagram comes into view, replete with a cast of huge, anthropomorphized organs that beat and respire as though independently animated. No photographs survive of the original production, but Evreinov later described the set (designed by the Russian artist and stage designer Mikhail Pavlovich Bobyshev) in his memoirs:

> A gigantic spine [set] in the vast depths of the Catherine Theater included bluish gaps between the vertebrae. . . . The large heart, varying its speed in correspondence with the pace of dialogue and action, was highly naturalistic and blazed with a crimson tinge. The spongy, blue-gray lungs rose and sank like sails on a boat in a storm. The dark purple diaphragm, on which my monodrama played, had been put together by the [theater's] carpenters with strict attention to anatomical accuracy.[37]

These memoirs gleefully record that a female audience member fainted when the second curtain rose to reveal the torso.[38]

At the beginning of the production, the three parts of the soul are seen in the center of the stage. The Emotional is wearing an artist's shirt with a red bow tie, while the Rational is dressed in a frock coat. The Emotional shouts for vodka into a telephone fused to the side of the torso. The Rational—snatching the receiver away—counters with a call for valerian. Massive nerve fibers, which resonate when plucked or strummed, span from the rafters to the floor. The Subconscious, clad as a worn traveler in a black mask, slumbers inertly in the foreground.

The telephone calls supposedly reach what the audience has to surmise is some kind of unified self, which is nevertheless not a character in the play but intuited by pauses in the Emotional and Rational's telephone conversations. When not on the phone, the Emotional and Rational present their opposing worldviews. They frequently strum the resonant nerve strings reaching from the rafters to the playing space. The Emotional insists on artistic freedom, the importance of emotional volatility, and the beauty of a French cabaret singer. The Rational advocates balanced judgment, appropriate medical sedatives, and an unbiased assessment of the singer's merits.

Before long, this singer's seductive "image" (*obraz*), as interpreted by the Emotional, appears on stage. The "First image of the singer" (*pervyy obraz pevichki*) sings briefly in French. She has hardly finished when the Rational denounces her. "Oh, what a delusion! . . . Forget her . . . forget her . . . this is just your fantasy!"[39] The Rational declares the singer is well past her prime. She has concealed her age with a wig, a false bust, and fake teeth. "She's not as she seems! You're kissing make-up, you're caressing a wig.... She's forty years old."[40] Far from being melodious, the Rational asserts, her singing is incoherent and imitative.

To the horror of the Emotional, a second "image" of the French cabaret singer is summoned by the Rational onto the stage. Evreinov gives the following stage direction: "*As he* [the Rational] *begins to speak, the first image of the singer fades away to the right—from which direction 'I Number One'* [The Rational] *summons a second image of the singer, defiled to the point of comedy.*"[41] Having brought forth this alternative vision of the singer, the Rational additionally conjures up an idealized version of the Wife. She materializes carrying a small child and angelically murmuring a delicate lullaby. Not to be outdone, the Emotional marshals a slovenly, second "image" of the Wife, who appears in a coffee-stained housecoat.

At this point, the idealized wife and the idealized singer begin a physical altercation on stage. The Emotional and Rational cheer accordingly. The idealized singer triumphs. Overcome by the thrill of the singer's victory, the Emotional throws himself on the Rational and strangles him. Nerve strings snap. The heart momentarily ceases to beat. The Emotional falls at the feet of the idealized singer, professing his love. She dismisses him, however, claiming it has all been little more than a joke. In desperation, the Emotional rushes to the telephone and demands suicide, providing instructions on how to find a gun. "The revolver is in your right back pocket... Quickly!... Quickly!... I can't bear it much longer... Shoot true! ... Between the third and fourth ribs... Well go on then, go on... What are you afraid of? It will only be a moment. Hurry!"[42] A shot is heard offstage. A hole appears in the heart, and red streamers of blood pour onto the proscenium.[43] The lungs cease respiring. The heart stops entirely. Just before the curtain falls, a train conductor appears. His lantern illuminates the darkened stage. He informs the Subconscious that he will need to change trains. The latter rises sleepily, collecting his hat and bag, and—yawning—exits the stage.

There has been little critical work done on the play in secondary scholarship. In English, both Spencer Golub and Sharon Marie Carnicke mention it without offering significant analysis. Martin Esslin gives a remarkable reading of it as a prototype for Samuel Beckett's *Endgame* in his *Theater of the Absurd* but is relying on a 1915 translation and little real knowledge about Evreinov. More recently, Alexandra Smith has studied the play as part of the modernist aesthetic. Russian scholarship has devoted a great deal of attention to the history of the Crooked Mirror theater, to Evreinov's anthropolitical theory of theatricality, and to his time as an émigré-author in Paris but relatively little on the play itself. Specific studies are limited to work on the role of masks in *Stage Wings* (S. Murata); Evreinov's relationship to the scenographers at the Crooked Mirror, including Bobyshev (D. V. Fomin); and the avant-garde search for "new forms" in imperial theater (N. V. Rostova).[44]

The absurdist exchanges of the cavorting selves and the slapstick-style eruptions of disproportionate violence in *Stage Wings* are only superficial elements of the action. They conceal a larger concern: the loss of symbolic distance between the object being represented and its representation, between the figural and the literal. Evreinov's work is a very radical expansion of a structural dilemma first introduced by monodrama's precursor: Rousseau in *Pygmalion*, a dilemma that Paul de Man has explored in some length.

In *Allegories of Reading*, Paul de Man devotes an entire chapter, entitled "Self," to Rousseau's *Pygmalion*. De Man is particularly interested in the problem of self-referentiality. He begins with a quote from Rousseau's second discourse, *On the Origins of Inequality* (1754). The second discourse is "the story of 'a man' [speaking] of man . . . to men," de Man states, quoting Rousseau.[45] De Man distills from this statement a paradox within the relationship between Rousseau's anthropological discourse and that discourse's concrete subject, the human being:

> Language can only be about something such as man (i.e., conceptual) but in being about man, it can never know whether it is about anything at all including itself, since it is precisely the *aboutness*, the referentiality, that is in question. Rousseau's anthropological discourse, as it comes to deal with questions of selfhood, of knowledge, of ethical and practical judgment, of religion and politics, will always be the restatement of this initial complication in a variety of versions that confer upon his work an appearance of consistency.[46]

No matter the topic of Rousseau's writing, in de Man's view Rousseau is consistently replaying the question that language encounters in referring to a conceptual (rather than concrete) entity. Is language in these scenarios—when "a man speaks to man of men"—ever referring to anything other than itself? De Man reads the relationship between self and other produced by Venus's actions in the myth as it is told by Ovid in terms of a set of antinomies that contrast "speculative nature" (in which the self is reflected) and "formal nature" (in which it is absent): hot and cold, art and nature, man and God.

In Rousseau's reworking of Pygmalion, however, formal nature is made speculative. Pygmalion states: "All my fire (*feu*) has been extinguished, my imagination is ice cold (*glacée*), the marble comes cold (*froid*) out of my hands . . ." Here the contrast between the heat of passion and the chill of imaginative frigidity is derived, de Man says, "from a transference from the figural and the literal that stems from the ambivalent relationship between the work as an extension of the self and as a quasi-divine otherness."[47] This contrast between hot and cold in the passage isn't grounded in the expected difference between the coolness of the marble and the warmth of Pygmalion's body. Instead, the text effects a subtle shift. It transforms the materiality of temperature into the figurality of an affective state. The external, material qualities of hot and cold become a figuration of different affective circumstances within the self. The (inevitable) result of such an attempt, de Man claims, is an endless chain of substitutions, as Rousseau is attempting to show the "formal structure of representing," the structure of diegesis.[48] "The text [*Pygmalion*] is dramatically structured as a dynamic system of excess and lack (*défaut*) metaphorically represented in the polarity of self and other that engenders, in its turn, a chain of (as)symmetrical polarities: hot/cold, inside/outside, art/nature, life/death, male/female, heart/senses, hiding/revealing . . . , eye/ear . . . , lyric/dramatic, etc."[49]

These polarities should be material but become figural reflections of different emotional states of the self. This process of substitution climaxes in the moment at which the newly animated Galatea touches her body and declares "Moi," before touching Pygmalion and stating, "Ah, encore moi." The irony of Galatea's statement is bound up with the instability of literality and figurality. On the level of the literal and material, Galatea is indissociable from her creator. Pygmalion has *made* Galatea from stone, and so she is indeed "him" in the sense of being his handiwork. Her disappointed sigh, de Man argues, is also the representation of distance from him, of being precisely *not him* at all. On the level of the figural, that is, Galatea acquires her own consciousness and with it the ability to make independent use of the first person. She acquires the ability to recognize Pygmalion as an other. Galatea's statement, "ah, encore moi," indicates the distinction between herself and her creator, which must be rhetorically overcome by a statement asserting their identity. The statement shows that Galatea, once a material object, has now become her own "self."

Evreinov's *Stage Wings* relies on the same logic of substitution between the material and the figural that was activated by the ambiguity of "self" and "other" in Rousseau's *Pygmalion*. *Stage Wings* produces slips that are similar in type, though not in content, to the oscillation between the figural and the material. Evreinov's *Stage Wings*, that is, recovers the problem of referentiality in Rousseau's early monodramatic depiction of selfhood but vastly expands it with a combination of symbolist tools and psychophysiological research. Because Rousseau's and Evreinov's respective discourses are anthropological in nature, each writer can be said to be "speaking to man, of men."

From the start of *Stage Wings*, clues about the loss of figurality and materiality abound. Evreinov's play adds an unusual twist to Rousseau's *Pygmalion*, however, following monodrama's historical links to anatomy. In Evreinov's scenario, figural representations become bizarrely literal. This begins with Evreinov's choice of title. *In the Stage Wings of the Soul* would seem to indicate the purely metaphorical (figural) space of the soul and its division into correspondingly metaphorical regions: a "performance area" and "wings." *Stage Wings*, however, delivers the audience directly into an anatomically correct thoracic cavity that materializes the psychical playing space instead. This is no abstract mental theater but an actual stage with *real* wings.

An unexpected figural-material conversion also appears in the transition between the Professor's introductory mini-lecture at the play's opening and the action proper. The Professor's chalk drawing is initially presented as a schematic diagram of the soul. "In connection with this, the stage wings of the soul can be drawn in the following manner. *Draws a multicolored picture with chalk, which he then further explains.*"[50] When the second curtain goes up, however, revealing the enormous lungs and heart, the audience is confronted with the comic realization that the alleged diagram was actually a scale model. The stage directions read: "[The Professor] exits; the blackboard is retracted; the curtain rises, revealing a picture of the soul in exactly the same form as it had been described and drawn by the Professor."[51] The real difference between the Professor's chalk sketch and the play's mise-en-scène is one of size, not degree of figuration. Evreinov repeats the gesture again by including the presence of an actual telephone and the real nerve "strings." "What? Hello? You can't hear me? But I'm speaking quite loudly! . . . There's a ringing in your ears?" the Emotional cries into the receiver as the curtain rises on this anatomized soul.[52]

Evreinov is riffing on analogies like those made by William James in *Principles of Psychology* (1890) that the hemispheres of the brain communicated in a manner comparable to a telephone switchboard and by the German neuroanatomist Carl Wernicke that sensory-motor units interacted with one another through pulses on a telegraph line.[53] Evreinov is also parodying Freud's suggestions. For Freud, the psychoanalyst needed to acclimate himself to a patient "as the receiver of the telephone is adjusted to the transmitting microphone." Analysis should reconstruct the patient's unconscious through his own, "just as the receiver converts back into sound-waves the electric oscillations in the telephone line which were set up by sound waves."[54] These statements are intended to be figural. James does not think the brain is a telephone switchboard any more than Freud imagined doing analysis over the phone. In *Stage Wings*, however, scientific metaphors are transformed back into their technological and anatomical equivalents. The telephone is genuinely part of the human organ system: the *trubka* (the word for both "receiver" and "pipe" or "tube") is an anatomical as well as a technological channel. It does not stand for the nerves; it's already part of them, and they of it.

No less significant is the vibrational action of the nerve strings. "Don't yank on the nerves! . . . How many times have I told you? (*The nerves buzz every time they are touched*)," the Rational yells at the Emotional.[55] A few lines later the Emotional declares: "Shut up! . . . Allow me to observe, Mr. Rational I, that we share the same nerves, and that when I yank on your nerves, I also yank on mine, and when, by your good graces, my nerves stiffen up, then I become dumb as a brick, that is, I become like you. I want to yank on the nerves, I'll do so."[56]

The vibrational nerves are a comic stage effect. They are also a modification of Diderot's psychophysiological theories that contributed to Rousseau's thinking on gesture. Evreinov's innovation, however, is to omit the comparison that Diderot uses entirely. In his 1769 text *D'Alembert's Dream*, Diderot comments on the vibrational mechanics undergirding first-person perception. *D'Alembert's Dream* is a series of three philosophical dialogues in which Diderot establishes his vital materialism. There, Diderot claims that his speculations on consciousness have led him "to compare the fibers of our organs to vibrating and sensitive strings [*cords vibrantes sensibles*] that continue to vibrate [*oscille*] and produce sound [*résonne*] long after they have been plucked. It is this vibration [*oscillation*], this kind of necessary resonance [*résonance nécessaire*] that keeps us constantly aware of [an] object's presence, while the mind occupies itself with deciding what qualities that object possesses."[57]

Diderot uses a comparison (*ce qui m'a fait quelquefois comparer les fibres de nos organes*) to get from a musically inspired vibrational mechanics to the corresponding physiological actions of the nerves. Evreinov eliminates this mediating comparison entirely. The nerves in his play are not *like* the strings of the harpsichord (to which Diderot later compares them); they *are* a massive musico-corporeal instrument that is truly on stage. As in the case of the telephone, these nerves really can be plucked and really do vibrate. The technique shows the degree to which Evreinov intended for the audience to collectively experience the protagonist's emotional shifts in real time, not just sympathize with this protagonist's plight or follow the action with interest. Rather than being amused, entertained, or horrified by the thought of a scenario that *resembled* one's own life, Evreinov intended for the audience to collectively experience his protagonist's emotional shifts in real time, as if they were one's own life. Ideally, in Evreinov's theater, the relationship between spectator and performer would be one of identity.

Evreinov's "Introduction to Monodrama" even began with the premise that true monodrama was defined by the possibility for a theatrical piece to be designated "my drama." "I accept as drama only such 'action' as I am able to call 'my drama' without doing violence to my imagination."[58] Theater, when done properly, would occasion an act of identification. In Rousseau's *Pygmalion*, the act of identification (but not also of distinction) takes place when Galatea touches her creator and states, "Ah, encore moi." In Evreinov's *Stage Wings*, the entire play is a metatheatrical extension of that moment, where self and other are not sculptor and the statue but actor and audience. The theory of "coexperiencing" in monodrama is, effectively, the constant and repeated gesture of reaching across the footlights to connect two nominally separate bodies, which under ideal circumstances then mutually declare "Moi!"

The Russian word *kulisa* (backstage, wings, linkage), which appears in the title *In the Stage Wings [kulisakh] of the Soul*, is a cognate of the French *coulisse*. In French the word has technological, theatrical, and anatomical connotations.[59] The primary definition of *coulisse* is a fixed support along which moving parts slide, or, by metonymy, the moving part itself. Within theater, it can refer to the "mobile frame, holding the scenery, located at the edges of the stage" or the "space between the supports for the scenery." The *coulisse* helps get the scenery on and off the stage by relying on a basic sliding mechanism. There is also a related anatomical definition in French. *Coulisse* refers to the "smooth channel on the surface of a bone that permits the movement of the tendons." By referring to the *coulisse*, Evreinov's play accomplishes a transformation of the figural into the material in another way: the title's seemingly figural division of the soul comes to have anatomical connotations.

The history of monodrama as a genre involves the fusion of gestural, theatrical, and anatomical motion in order to physically express the movement of the passions. Evreinov's use of the term *coulisse* evokes that history while also setting up a pun. The anatomical setting for the play, with its moving organs, refers to the anatomical gliding motion of bone and tendon present in the physiological sense of the French. It also suggests the changeable nature of human emotion as a kind of "moving part," which is to be accompanied by shifting scenic accompaniments (a major principle of monodrama in Evreinov's "Introduction.") Taking the soul as his backdrop, Evreinov represents the history of passional motion in theater in psychophysiological terms. His play is both an example of monodrama as well as an allegory of it. Little wonder, then, that many of the rhetorical figures that appear in Evreinov's "Introduction to Monodrama" should end up on stage as real objects in *Stage Wings*:

> Expressing itself in images, the protagonist's blood must somehow circulate in the objects being presented on stage and the stoniest stone must not keep silent when it is beside the protagonist. The revolver, which I admire as a glittering plaything, is already not the same object when I am busily cleaning it for my master and of course no longer the same, when I pick it up to shoot myself.[60]

The metaphorical blood Evreinov describes invigorating his onstage objects and the perspectivally conditioned revolver he characterizes the protagonist holding in "Introduction to Monodrama" end up recast as physical realities in *Stage Wings*.

## Coexperiencing and the Social Contract

Rousseau does not address collective coexperiencing in *Pygmalion*, and de Man does not carry his analysis beyond the boundaries of the self. Self and other (and self and self) touch as Galatea and Pygmalion make contact, but Rousseau does not extend their encounter to a scenario involving more than two individuals. This would be less remarkable if Rousseau had not written *The Social Contract* the same year as *Pygmalion*. Unlike Pygmalion, *The Social Contract* is all about questions of political community. Rousseau's own thinking about political representation and questions of the self finds an unexpected inheritor in Evreinov's work. Evreinov used his 1911 play *Stage Wings* as a prototype for the eight-thousand-person mass spectacle *The Storming of the Winter Palace* (*Vzyatiye zimnego dvortsa*, 1920), put on as part of the 1919 Petrograd celebration of the Russian Revolution. In this enormous endeavor, which inspired Eisenstein's *October* (1928), Evreinov deployed monodramatic principles on a vast, propagandistic scale. *The Storming* is particularly unusual as Evreinov had relatively conservative political leanings, when he participated in politics at all. He never actively opposed the Revolution, but neither was he a director in the style of Meyerhold and Mayakovsky. Upon emigration to Paris in 1926, he joined the large cadre of Russian artists and writers seeking relief from the increasing ideological oppression of the Soviet Union after Lenin's death in 1924. In addition to lacking a political agenda, Evreinov was also product of the conventional educational and theatrical training of late-imperial Russia. The fact that he was selected to direct *The Storming* at all was most likely attributable to his success with historical reenactments at the Ancient Theater. Platon Kerzhentsev's prominent citation of Evreinov in his highly influential book on open-air spectacle *The Creative Theater. The Paths of Socialist Theater* (*Tvorcheskiy teatr. Puti sotsialisticheskogo teatra*, 1918) may also have contributed.[61]

Kerzhentsev, who had joined the Communist Party in 1904, was forced into exile in 1912. During the next five years, he spent time in the United States, France, and the United Kingdom, witnessing the many open-air and mass-spectacle-style demonstrations popular at the time. These had a significant influence on his later ideas on collective creation, several of which are articulated in his book *The Creative Theater.* Kerzhentsev is best known, however, for his political career. In addition to working as the Soviet ambassador to Sweden (1921–1923) and Italy (1925–1926), Kerzhentsev held a series of posts in the Communist government that gave him extensive control over culture and the performing arts. Beginning in 1928, he worked as the deputy head for the Department of Propaganda; served as the president of the Radio Committee

(1933–1936); and, from 1936 until 1938, held the post of chairman of the Committee for Artistic Affairs. In these various capacities, he was not only responsible for banning Mikhail Bulgakov's plays but also shuttering Meyerhold's theater.[62]

Kerzhentsev mentions Evreinov numerous times throughout *The Creative Theater*, notably even citing the concept of a "theatrical instinct of the working class." His most extensive assessment falls in chapter 4, "Socialist Theater" (*Sotsialisticheskiy teatr*). His assessment is mixed. On the one hand, he condemns Evreinov for the egocentric quality of "Theater for Oneself." On the other hand, he is clearly enthusiastic about Evreinov's ideas of an on-stage audience:

> The talented N. Evreinov has shown with great skill in his numerous books on theater (See in particular "Theater for Oneself" Volume 3) how strong the instinct to theatricality is in man, the thirst to "play a role," to create "staged" images. . . . But all these correct premises end in a wholly naïve conclusion, which proclaims the principles of theatricality as some kind of fundamental basis for the universe. Evreinov's theatrical instinct moves forward with the goal of making an egotistical and egocentric "theater for oneself," a theater cooped up in its own four walls. The theatrical instinct, for Evreinov, is not the joyous source of collective creation, but the starting point for individualistic, refined, self-pleasure. With this Evreinov dooms his theory to complete impotence. Creators of socialist theater should proceed from an aspiration to facilitate the full artistic revelation of the "I" in friendly, collective theatrical work. . . . The architecture of the theater . . . will also take into account a new task for theater: to connect the hall with the stage, to convert the spectators into actors. Indeed theater will approximate the character of antiquity to the greatest possible degree, the stalls of the house will always easily convert into playing space.[63]

Despite Evreinov's lack of personal political investment in a historical reenactment of the October Revolution, his staging of the mass spectacle nevertheless made good on the revolutionary promise of monodrama that Rousseau's *Pygmalion* left unfulfilled and that Kerzhentsev had already intuited as a possibility in Evreinov's work. The trick was to convert this egocentric "theater for oneself" in a "source of collective creation" that made "spectators" into "actors." Evreinov's shift from imperial monodrama to Soviet mass spectacle demonstrates an interesting instance in which a non-ideological figure was responsible not only for orchestrating a massive tribute to the proletariat but also stimulating one of its most famous cinematic depictions.

## From Monodrama to Mass Spectacle: *The Storming of the Winter Palace*, Petrograd, 1920

The mass spectacle as a form had just come into vogue in 1920 in Petrograd. Kerzhentsev's *Creative Theater* promoted the theater of the French Revolution as a possible model for such spectacles, as well as the more contemporary pageants taking place in the United States. Kerzhentsev had been influenced by the 1910 Russian translation of Romain Rolland's *The People's Theater* (*Le théâtre du peuple*), and many of his theories reflect Rolland's interest in forging a proletarian theater through a wholesale break with the bourgeois theatrical traditions of the past.[64] Four mass spectacles took place in 1920, of which Evreinov's was by far the largest and most ambitious. They were prefaced by the early experiment of the Red Army Theater workshop, in May 1919, during which a group of roughly one hundred performers staged the *Play of the Third International*.

As confidence in the success of the revolution grew, so did the conviction that time and resources should be invested in mass celebrations of major revolutionary events. The Russian artist Kerzhentsev Annenkov and the director Alexander Kugel' (with whom Evreinov had worked closely in past theatrical productions) staged *The Mystery of Freed Labor* for the May First celebrations of the following year. This production pulled Russian events into a world-historical arc by establishing a teleology between the slave revolt of Spartacus in 73 BC, Stenka Razin's uprising in tsarist Russia in the seventeenth century, and the October Revolution. A spectacle titled *The Blockade of Russia*, an angry reenactment of British and French anti-Bolshevik intervention during the Civil War, took place less than a month later, in late June. It was followed by Konstantin Mardzhanov's *In Favor of a World Commune* (July 19, 1920). Mardzhanov's production employed over four thousand participants drawn from a wide array of backgrounds and different levels of professional expertise. Students at theater schools took part, as did members of the Red Army, the Workers' Theater Club, and professional actors.[65] As in *The Mystery*, this production involved a progression of multiple settings and time periods. *World Commune* opened with a symbolic depiction of the overthrow of the monarchy during the French Revolution. This was followed by a series of rapid transitions through the First World War, the abdication of Nicholas II, and the onset of the Russian Civil War. The spectacle concluded with golden-toga-clad girls paying tribute to the Third International, as sirens blared and fireworks exploded over the city.[66] All of these extravaganzas were designed to place Russia and Russian events at the center of Eurocentric "world history."

Collective authorship and multiple directors were common practices in these performances. In keeping with the principles laid out by Rolland and Kerzhentsev, they relied on simplified action and an enormously pared-down score or soundtrack (often a single melody repeated at increasing volume). In general, dialogue was restricted to exchanges between choral groups or to single lines delivered proclamation-style by individuals with exaggeratedly opposite ideological affiliations. Improvisation was also an important feature.

In an interview with the newspaper *The Life of Art* (*Zhizn' iskusstva*) in late October 1920, Evreinov remarked that as a seasoned historian and theoretician of the theater, he could state with assurance that the task of directing *The Storming* was "unprecedented in terms of the complexity of its concept."[67] *The Storming* was held in honor of the third anniversary of the October Revolution. Unlike previous performances of this sort, the work focused exclusively on producing a (dramatized) historical reenactment of a single event that led up to the Revolution and the actual takeover of the Winter Palace by the proletariat. The spectacle was intended to be both commemorative as well as inspiring for the new cause. As Evreinov put it, "There arose a desire [leading up to the anniversary] to publicly commemorate [the event], which had become a landmark for the new Russia, the event that was in fact taken as the origin of the Soviet power of the working people."[68]

Evreinov was the main author and director, though he partnered with N. V. Petrov, Aleksander Kugel', and Yuriy Annenkov, all of whom had prior experience working on mass spectacles. He additionally records (in a set of remarks published several years later) that Professor N. I. Misheyev, D. N. Temkin (a composer), A. F. Klark (a Petersburg specialist in psychology), K. N. Derzhavin (a literary and theater critic), and A. G. Movshenzon (a translator and art historian) were involved in drafting the script.

The performance took place in the square in front of the Winter Palace. It featured three main staging areas. Two platforms were erected on either side of the enormous arched entryway in the General Staff Building that formed the southern entrance to Uritsky Square (in front of the Winter Palace). A bridge, placed across the entry to the General Staff Building, connected these platforms.[69] The platform on the left (as seen from the Alexander Column in the center of the square) held representatives of the proletariat. In addition to a large central staircase connecting the several playing areas to the square, the platform's décor included stylized brick walls, "factory chimneys, parts of machinery, and a prison," all lit from within by a strong red light.[70] As Evreinov reported in his interview with *Zhizn' iskusstva*, the tenor of events on this platform was to be set in the "tones of a heroic drama."

By contrast to this triumphalism, the events on the platform to the right—intended for representatives of the bourgeoisie and the provisional government—were performed "in a comic style." Here, the background of the various segments of the platform was occupied with an enormous rendering of an ancient, decaying hall, symbolizing the moldering decadence of the old regime. The vertically stratified division of the platform represented the hierarchical order of bourgeois society: servants on the lowest tier, followed by a tribune of the members of Alexsander Kerensky's provisional government, and topped off by a small throne-like platform for Kerensky himself. The mass action ordered by the Provisional Government (movements by the army, etc.) took place on the adjoining stairs. This so-called white platform was directed by Petrov.

The spectacle began at 10:30 PM. Both platforms were illuminated by powerful searchlights attached high on the Alexander Column. Their illumination alternated to "highlight" action occurring on one stage or the other. One can already see in this setup the return of elements from Evreinov's experiments with medieval mysteries at the Ancient Theater. The opposing Red and White playing spaces established a physical opposition between forces of "Good" and "Evil," which was played out in the clashes that carried parties from both sides into conflict on the bridge. There is a clear antecedent for this technique in Evreinov's earlier use of contrastive lights in *Francesca da Rimini* (1908), where the division of the stage into light and dark halves was intended to visually signify a value judgment about the characters' intentions.

The second staging area was the space of the square itself. Here, the audience (which numbered more than one hundred thousand) was divided into two blocks in the center of the square. A channel between them allowed for the movement of forces entering the square from beneath the archway in the General Staff Building. It also facilitated a concluding chase scene in which members of the Provisional Government fled proletarian forces. The central position of the audience allowed everyone to be fully immersed in the spectacle. In theory, anyone in the square should be able to take in any element of the action simply by turning in the appropriate direction.

Lastly, Evreinov envisioned the Winter Palace itself as an important actor. It constituted the third staging area:

> The Winter Palace itself has been drawn into the action as a gigantic actor, as a grandiose protagonist, which will display its expressions and inner experience. . . . We have solved this problem in a highly original manner, by borrowing a cinematographic technique; each of the 50 windows of the second floor will show, by means of its twinkling [i.e., by being lit from within], one or another moment in the development of the struggle within.[71]

The Winter Palace was also finally the site of a chase scene, in which members of the Provisional Government were driven out of the palace by masses of sailors and Red Army soldiers, who had been waiting "offstage" near the Moyka at the Pevchesky Bridge.

Music for the performance was supplied by a five-hundred-member orchestra (under the direction of Hugo Varlich). In addition to the groups already mentioned, the giant cast also featured as "extras" the battleship *Aurora* (stationed nearby on the Neva), a fleet of airplanes, and an artillery battery positioned in the Alexander Garden. Armored vehicles were stationed in the Palace Garden near the Winter Palace. Evreinov, who had not been in Petersburg for the historic storming of the Winter Palace, took pains to recruit many of the actual participants.

The action began with a gunshot.[72] The White platform was illuminated. Kerensky could be seen deliberating over whether to continue World War I. He concluded that it was important to pursue the war to a "victorious end" against mumbled protests that emanated from the still-dark proletarian platform. The Red platform was then lighted, and the disorganized forces of the proletariat could be seen beginning to form coherent groups while strains of the "International" played in the background. Back on the White platform, cartoonish capitalists dressed in tuxedos adorned with oversized carnations and sporting gold and silver top hats pushed sacks of cash (to finance the war effort) toward Kerensky, who was seen gesticulating wildly. The capitalists' wives, sumptuously adorned in fur, accompanied them. As Golub points out, "Among both the Red and White contingents there was great uniformity in movement and gesture, and repetition was used to great effect."[73] At one point, no fewer than twenty-five "Kerenskys" repeated a speech three times, while the generals and dignitaries listening rhythmically tapped their many hammers in approval. Throughout the performance, rhythm and repetition were used to prompt a sense of inevitability and necessity, ostinato techniques that were major components of modernism from Stravinsky's *The Rite of Spring* to Shostakovich.

Soon shouts of "Lenin!" could be heard from the Red platform. These grew louder and more frequent as an enormous red flag was raised on the platform and as the music of the "International" swelled. The ministerial bench on the White platform suddenly appeared in disarray, rocking wildly back and forth. At this point, thirty "Lenins" spilled out onto the Red platform and, like the "Kerenskys" before them, delivered a speech. The action on the White platform grew increasingly disorganized. An appeal for revolution was issued on the Red platform, and Kerensky (once again a lone actor) could be seen jumping into a car that sped him behind the gates of the Winter Palace, pursued by armed workers. Trucks now entered the square through the arch of the General Staff Building, passing between the two groups of spectators and rushing into the palace. Infantry and armored vehicles that had been waiting "offstage" rushed in. The previously dark palace was illuminated, such that individual scenes of conflict appeared silhouetted in its windows. The battleship *Aurora* fired shots, and "machine guns crackle[d], rifles fire[d], and the artillery thunder[ed]." Then a silence, followed by a chorus of thousands singing the "International."

There are many good reasons to think of this performance as a monodrama on a massive scale. First and foremost, the central position of the audience in the middle of the action—an audience in which many members had actually lived through the original event—combined with the use of historical participants afforded Evreinov the chance to experiment with "coexperiencing." Petrograders nevertheless had to be persuaded that what they remembered of the Revolution was chaotic and incorrect and that the new performance was a purified representation of the historical reality. The short period between Evreinov's reenactment and the actual Revolution meant that many members of the audience already possessed an intense affective bond to the "performance" action: They were its original protagonists. That bond needed to be reforged as part of the ideological conversion process. The spatial organization of *The Storming* (with the audience in the center) meant that there wasn't really any stage to begin with and hence no fourth wall to overcome. The decentralized (even simultaneous) quality of the action and the tendency of all events to be spread over the vast space of Petrograd's Uritsky Square reduced any lingering symbolic barrier between the viewing public and the drama. Evreinov even described the scenes set inside the Winter Palace (that is, silhouetted in the windows) in terms of "inner experience" (*Uritzskiĭ perezhivaniye*), a term that is practically a direct quotation of Karl Groos's "inner imitation" (*Uritzskiĭ podrazhan'ye*).

*The Storming* served different purposes for different groups. Evreinov clearly used his role as the principal director of the mass spectacle to experiment with a set of artistic and representational techniques that he had previously been able to test only on a limited scale. Now he had the whole of the Petrograd population at his disposal, not to mention the government's complete financial, civic, and even military support. By contrast, the Bolshevik Party used Evreinov's reenactment as a way to shore up revolutionary inevitability and to retrospectively legitimize their power. Above all, Evreinov's *The Storming* allowed the Bolsheviks to replace a messier historical reality with an aesthetically shaped narrative, which drew on poetical passions to validate the perspective of rather accidental power. There had been no guarantee that October 1917 would turn out as it did. The participants themselves had wavering faith that it would succeed. The new government needed to retroactively add affective intentionality to the chaos of the original events, one that would present the triumphant outcome of the Revolution as something they had known all along. Performance—especially performance on such a grand scale—turned contingency into necessity. *The Storming* thus involved transforming the concrete, physical expression of the passions from a comedic and erotic key (in which they had featured in the *Presentation of Love* and *Stage Wings*) into a political one, while nevertheless continuing to focus on the self.

Evreinov's staging techniques and theories of monodrama offered a near-perfect platform for the Bolsheviks to cast the Revolution in terms of a transition from spontaneity (*stikhiinost'*) to consciousness (*soznatel'nost'*). These were Lenin's terms to characterize the necessary ideological awakening of the postimperial Russian population, as laid out in his 1902 publication *What Is to Be Done?* (*Chto delat'?*). Spontaneity, as Lenin discussed it, was the default modus operandi of the bourgeoisie and the lumpen Russian laborers. It involved selecting the path of least resistance in order to achieve short-term political and economic goals. Although a state of spontaneity might entail the *imagination* of independence by a group or set of groups and could even encompass limited forms of struggle, ultimately the restricted historical vision of its practitioners made it inevitable that they would fall back into trade-union-style bargaining. Consciousness, on the other hand, entailed embracing the full theoretical, political, and historical necessity of overturning the economic and political system and a corresponding willingness to act without compromise for goals that might seem impossible to achieve. In Evreinov's hands, however, Marxist-Leninist consciousness became the physiological and egological consciousness of Fechner's psychophysics, committed to treating the mind and body as a single unified self.

The success of the Bolsheviks in producing a "battle" between spontaneity and consciousness in *The Storming* was to a great extent facilitated by Evreinov's decision to simply expand techniques he had already used effectively in *Stage Wings*, including borrowing structural components from the set layout. Despite the difference in scale, the "playing space" between the Winter Palace and the General Staff Building was well suited to reproducing the physical elements of *Stage Wings* as well as its theoretical presuppositions.

Moving from a human torso to an urban square was not entirely without its challenges, however. Upon beginning rehearsals, Evreinov immediately faced the practical problem of how to communicate with the members of his directorial team who were stationed in distant locations on the square, where they were directing individual groups of performers. To resolve the issue, Evreinov's team conceived of a "tall booth, as high as a two-story house, equipped with a number of telephones and signaling bells, built in the style of a 'command bridge' in the middle of the square, near the [Alexander] column."[74] Evreinov directed the entire performance from this central point. The telephone lines, according to Deàk, reached the directors of the Red and White platforms respectively, and the multiple assistant directors controlling the actions of groups such as the artillery, storm troopers, army, and the actors in the windows of the Winter Palace. The telephones began as a practical innovation rather than an essential diegetic part of the performance. Within Evreinov's theatrical oeuvre, their presence, however, evoked the telephone sutured into the side of the torso in *Stage Wings*. This telephone now experienced a third transformation. A metaphor for William James and Sigmund Freud, it became a humorous physiological prop in Evreinov's *Stage Wings*. When *Stage Wings* became *The Storming*, however, the telephone was returned to its full quotidian status and had to be actually used as a communication device, in an extreme version of the figural-to-material conversion de Man attributed to Rousseau.

Even the layout of the various components of the performance on the Palace Square replayed the structural layout of the anatomical theater in *Stage Wings*. The Alexander Column and the telephone booth rose from the square's center like the spinal cord, in front of which the opposing Red and White forces resembled the tussling Rational and Emotional. Their exaggerated encounters approximated the slapstick physicality of commedia dell'arte that had played such a central role in *Stage Wings*. The multiple iterations of Kerensky and Lenin repeated the multiple versions of the Wife and Singer. In each case, the physical presence of a second (or third) actor in the same role demonstrated a particular psychic projection of the protagonist, whether the fantastical imagination of the Emotional or the proletariat's emotional adherence to Lenin. The fact that quantitatively more "Lenins" appeared than "Kerenskys" on the platforms is significant insofar as the sheer number symbolized the relative strength of each among the population. This was a form of monodramatic psychoarchitectonics: "We are talking about an architectonics of drama, based on the principle of the spectacle's correspondence with the way the protagonist is presented," Evreinov wrote in the "Introduction."[75]

According to Golub, the playbill-libretto that accompanied the production stressed that the performance was not intended to be an exact reproduction of the historical events. It also asked the spectators to note "that the great masses of people used in the crowd scenes are not merely a body of trained actors but represent a single collective actor."[76] This was the same tactic that Evreinov had advocated in designating the central protagonist in his monodramas "I." The decision to stage the performance in and around the Winter Palace positioned the mass spectacle in the symbolic and spatial "core" of Petersburg, that is, in its spiritual center. The enclosed space produced by the amphitheatrical half-round of the General Staff Building and Winter Palace generated a sense of enclosure not dissimilar to that occasioned by setting *Stage Wings* inside an actual torso. In place of animate organs, one had the biological motion of a "living" participatory crowd.

These many similarities created an environment in which the initial dialectical shifts of self and other in Rousseau's *Pygmalion* could be reborn with newly politicized connotations. What Evreinov caricatured as "Good" and "Evil" forces within the historical events of October 1917 became spectacularized embodiments of spontaneity and consciousness for the Bolsheviks that produced a concrete vision of the Soviet self and the soul of popular sovereignty. The capitalists along with Kerensky were a variant on the character of the Emotional in *Stage Wings*. The scenes in which they were involved featured outbursts of desperation, moments of ideological compromise, representations of profound individualism, a lack of world-historical vision, and attention to short-term goals (fundraising for the war bonds, for example) that firmly aligned them with the unruly Emotional of Evreinov's earlier monodrama. Even the gold and silver top hats of bourgeoisie—signifying wealth—recalled the flamboyant bowtie of the Emotional's costume.

The population on the Red platform, on the other hand, embodied the Rational and so too the principle of consciousness. The Red platform's coordinated actions and evolving sense of collective timing helped produce a feeling of historically inevitable design. Because the Red platform seemed to acquire an increasing sense of the value of their struggle throughout the course of the spectacle, it was far easier to recognize in them the controlled production of far-sighted political awareness. The ministers' anthropomorphized bench, by contrast shown rocking back and forth, embodied Kerensky's loss of control just as the Red forces mobilized around Lenin and formulated a unified call for revolution. The slow blossoming of the "International" in the background during the course of the spectacle, the increasing calls for Lenin, and the ever more coordinated motions of the proletariat physically and aurally dramatized the transformation of a spontaneous chaotic impulse sweeping through an anarchic crowd into a carefully regulated and highly effective, conscious form of collective action. Consciousness was a script performed, whereas spontaneity, in Katerina Clark's words, "mean[t] actions that [were] not guided by complete political awareness, and [were] either sporadic, uncoordinated, even anarchic," all of which could certainly be said of the White platform.[77]

The mass spectacle collected the body of the people (who better than those who had actually participated in the events of 1917 to make up its numbers?) in a drama in which they collectively performed their status as a people and so too reconstructed the narrative of how they arrived at that point. Premised on both Evreinov's coexperiencing and Fechnerian psychophysics, this performance also provided a vehicle through which to bring to life the artificial soul of popular sovereignty within the body of the people and so animate the Soviet self. The transition from the figural representations to the literal in Evreinov's play (which draws on Rousseau's technique) enabled Evreinov's mass spectacle to materially represent the figural understanding of the Soviet self in the form of an (co)experiencable collective consciousness.

Just as in Evreinov's theory of monodrama, the goal was to generate a moment of identification in which the audience would "see through" the eyes of the protagonist, the protagonist here being the Bolshevik view of the Revolution. Evreinov's mass spectacle was designed to produce a scenario in which one hundred thousand Petrograders would announce their unity as a single proletarian body and mind, through whose eyes past events were framed. The exclamation "Moi!" in this setting would, in theory, unite a proletarian force in the process of building a stable identity, with the mythical, idealized proletariat as depicted as the body of the people by the mass spectacle. It would also—as in *Pygmalion*—initiate a set of important differentiations. The play of self and other in this setting was figured through a series of antinomies: Red/White, then/now, before/after, us/them. As the spectator turned from the Red platform, to the Winter Palace, to the entering trucks, to the artillery, to the *Aurora*, to his neighbor, the goal was for him or her to repeat, "Ah, encore moi."

To return to Lenin's brain (and Marx on the brain), historical materialism weighs on the brain by seeming to demand a materialist account of mental life as an escape from what Kerzhentsev characterized as the "theater of oneself." The scientific history of the brain nevertheless also weighs on historical materialism, configuring the latter's account of consciousness and collectivity. The mistake is therefore to see the transition between Evreinov's monodrama and the Soviet mass spectacle as something particular to Soviet political ideology when it instead says more about psychopower's ability to configure an imagination of mass mental life, just as was true in the case of Johann Christian Woyzeck's execution in 1824. Lenin's brain may have been scientifically of interest given Lenin's place as a famous twentieth-century personage, but in that guise it was functionally interchangeable with any of the others on the shelves of the Institut mozga. What made Lenin's brain special wasn't the size of its furrows or cells but the fact that it wasn't Lenin's alone. As a physical object, the brain stood for the invisible psychical solidarity to which Evreinov's mass spectacle had also given shape and voice. Because it localized Soviet psychical life, this lump of nerve tissue was interwoven with the monodramatic tradition. Both arrived at the self-identity of collectivity through a process of representation.

## CHAPTER 7

# SOMETHING WRONG WITH VERO

## Neural Landscapes of the Argentine Dirty War

Beginning in the 1880s, the Spanish neuroscientist Santiago Ramón y Cajal created a series of neural drawings based on a new cell staining technique that allowed him to see nerve cells under the microscope with remarkable clarity. Cajal's images have since become famous as the basis for the neuron doctrine, the concept that the nervous system is composed of discrete cells called neurons. This chapter explores how these iconic neural drawings reproduced a psychopolitical problem of picturing the individual and collective mind. Cajal's images reflect his unlikely preoccupation with Romanticism's subjective individualism and track his geopolitical anxieties about Spain's defeat in the Spanish-American War of 1898. In so doing, they present the brain's neural terrain as the site for the conquest of new territory and a paean to beauty of the Spanish landscape, designed to compensate for Spain's loss of its colonies in the war. These factors not only illuminate a psychopolitical dimension to Cajal's foundational neuroscienctific claims but also complicate the neural images' widely accepted status as objective. They do so without depriving the images of either their legitimacy or scientific utility. Instead, as Cajal himself believed, the images' so-called subjective features are inseparable from and complementary with their better-known objective status.

As the foundation for the neuron doctrine, Cajal's images are also precursors of contemporary functional neuroimaging, EEGs, and other twentieth- and twenty-first-century visual technologies for representing the brain. Reading his images as a generative combination of objective and subjective dimensions (a reading Cajal personally endorsed) raises a question about what these modern technologies depict and how their representations should be treated. I address this issue here by considering the interpretive and ethical consequences of applying findings from neuroscientific imaging and brain modeling to aesthetic works. Returning to the question of how to represent trauma, with which *Psychic Empire* opens through its discussion of PTSD, the chapter explores the Argentinean director Lucrecia Martel's 2008 film *The Headless Woman*, addressing what the film suggests is its central problem: the protagonist's head injury in a car crash. Martel's film offers a feminist take on head trauma, placing the matter of biologically visualizing female psychical interiority in conversation with both the scientific depiction of cerebral life and the legacy of Argentina's Dirty War (1974–1983).

Like Meret Oppenheim's photograph *X-Ray of M.O.'s Skull* (see the introduction), Martel's film troubles the figuration of trauma in somatic terms. The film's protagonist is named Vero, etymologically related to the Spanish noun for truth (*la verdad*) and to the verb "to see" (*ver*). If *The Headless Woman* is headless, it is because a psychopolitical account of truth (*verdad*) committed to direct visibility (*ver*) and complicit with the Argentine military junta's violent "disappearances" in the 1970s presents her psychical experiences in terms of an average portrait of mental health. This makes it impossible for her to speak about those experiences. It also makes it look as if there is something wrong with Vero. Reading the film in this way complicates a common position taken by interdisciplinary fields such as cognitive literary criticism, cognitive film theory, and neurocinematics on the relationship between art and science. In so doing, such a reading has implications both for questions of representation in the neurosciences and for history telling.[1]

***

If you look at the intricate pen-and-ink drawings of neurons by the Spanish neuroscientist Santiago Ramón y Cajal, you don't necessarily see a landscape. It is Cajal who tells his viewers to see them in this way. Writing in his autobiography, he compares the microscopic world of the brain and nervous system to the Spanish *paisaje* around him.

> Like the entomologist hunting for brightly colored butterflies, my attention was drawn to the flower garden of the grey matter, which contained cells with delicate and elegant forms, the mysterious butterflies of the soul, the beating of whose wings may some day (who knows?) clarify the secret of mental life. . . . Even from the aesthetic point of view, the nervous tissue contains the most charming attractions. In our parks are there any trees more elegant and luxurious than the Purkinje cells from the cerebellum or the psychic cell, that is the famous cerebral pyramid?[2]

This observation, which creates an analogy between the neural landscape Cajal saw under his microscope beginning in the 1880s and 1890s and Spain and the external world, is a common feature of the autobiography. There Cajal repeatedly characterizes the brain as a verdant expanse of dense neural forests. These forests are populated by trees (neural cells) that should, he claims, be admired for their dendritic arborealizations (branches). Cajal also refers to the "garden of neurology," speaking of the ways in which it "holds out to the investigator captivating spectacles and incomparable artistic emotions."[3] He characterizes the cellular world of neural life as a tiny portrait of the expanses of the Aragon region, in which he was an avid hiker and photographer during the years he developed the neuron doctrine. What quickly becomes clear from these descriptions is that the 1906 winner of the Nobel Prize in Physiology and Medicine wanted those looking at his scientific drawings to see them as animated worlds, not as cold, abstract microbiology.

The comparison is an interesting one. In 1898, as Cajal was completing the neuroscientific research that would earn him the Nobel Prize, Spain's place in the global geopolitical order was declining. The Spanish Empire had already lost many of its colonies in (then) Spanish America during the wars of independence in the early nineteenth century. With the Spanish-American War of 1898, imperial Spain further parted with colonial possessions in present-day Cuba, Puerto Rico, Guam, and the Philippines, handing them to the United States. In Spain, this loss was felt acutely enough to inspire the aesthetic practices of a group of Spanish writers known as the Generation of 1898. These writers responded in their work to new anxieties connected with Spain's perceived decline as a world power. Spanish authors like Azorín (José Martin Ruiz, 1873–1967) and Miguel de Unamuno (1864–1936) deliberately turned to the Spanish landscape in response, developing it in their fiction as an emotionally charged and nationally inflected space that spoke to the glory of an otherwise languishing Spain.[4]

As Laura Otis has shown in *Membranes: Metaphors of Invasion in Nineteenth-Century Literature*, a great deal of biological research in the nineteenth century regarded the self-enclosed unit of the cell as a surrogate for contemporaneous geopolitical struggles.[5] Cajal's work was no exception. Otis demonstrates that these struggles played a significant role in Santiago Ramón y Cajal's neurobiological theory. According to her argument, two major factors outside the typical disciplinary purview of the neurosciences influenced Cajal's key finding that the nervous system was composed of individual, autonomous cells, not an undifferentiated mesh.[6] The neuron doctrine, she argues, drew both on Cajal's sociopolitical anxieties about the *xenos* in Spain and his personal views about the import of individual willpower.[7] In her telling, Cajal's political perspective informed his neural biology. Only a scientific account that showed the existence of cellular boundaries as fixed as those of nation-states and as definitive as those of strong-willed persons could explain the composition of the nervous system. If national borders and individuals needed stalwart defenses against dangerous external forces liable to overrun their naturally discretized existence, neural life must be structured similarly.

Otis does not extend her argument further, but it accurately describes Cajal's drawings as well. As Cajal's autobiography makes clear, he was eager for his images to be seen as landscapes filled with the elegant neural trees of "our parks." The drawings were not simply illustrations of microscopic biology but pictures of lush, animate gardens in miniature, or forests in which mighty Purkinje cells, with their trunks and branches, outdid even the verdancy of Spanish *paisaje*. Following Otis's argument, the drawings speak to Cajal's views on the significance of willpower by showing nerve cells as powerful, autonomous individuals. They visually illustrate the same fixity of neural borders Cajal hoped to find on the geopolitical stage by depicting these cells as rigidly bounded.

Although Cajal's images have now long been recognized as the basis for the neuron doctrine, their journey to that point was not easy. The images were an object of major scientific controversy when Cajal first developed them. Cajal of course viewed his drawings as the height of scientific objectivity from the outset. The scientist with whom Cajal shared the 1906 Nobel Prize, however, an Italian neurologist by the name of Camillo Golgi, had a different view of the matter. Golgi was a stalwart proponent of reticular theory, the idea that the nervous system is composed of an unbroken neural mesh, or "reticulum." To prove the factual correctness of reticular theory over the neuron doctrine, Golgi contested the objectivity of Cajal's images right up to the moment of the two men's joint receipt of the Nobel Prize. Standing before the audience in Stockholm, Golgi defamed Cajal's drawings. He suggested in his award speech that Cajal had introduced spacing between neurons where none existed. This argument allowed him to charge that his co-winner's neuron doctrine was inaccurate and his own contrary claim about the reticulum correct.[8] For his part, Cajal leveled the same charge at Golgi, asserting until the end of his life that Golgi had manipulated his own drawings to mask the separation between nerve cells.[9]

As Lorraine Daston and Peter Galison's scholarship on this conflict has shown, both Cajal and Golgi regarded the objectivity of their images as a direct measure of their respective theories' validity.[10] For each, the presence of interpretive license in the other's illustrations was tantamount to disproof of the accompanying theory. Golgi's allegedly inaccurate depiction of the neural mesh meant reticular theory was wrong. Cajal's supposed illustrative distortions, which artificially created spaces between neurons, meant neuron doctrine was illegitimate.

If one takes the autobiography's statements and Cajal's Nobel speech together, however, a seeming paradox arises. Cajal appears to maintain the scientific objectivity of his neural images *and* present those images as charming Spanish landscapes filled with butterflies and trees. He imaginatively maintains the anthropomorphic qualities of his autonomous neural actors while nevertheless defending his neural images as exemplars of unmediated fidelity to nature. Consideration of the story Cajal tells in his autobiography about his forestalled artistic career helps show how this is possible and why it is important.

## Cajal's Neural Landscapes

Cajal's autobiography, *Recollections of My Life* (*Recuerdos de mi vida*, 1901–1923), spends much of the first volume (some three hundred pages) recounting its author's artistic endeavors and frustrated creative hopes as a young person. Lavishly illustrated with Cajal's own drawings and photographs, the first volume of the *Recollections* contains extensive, detailed prose descriptions of the architecture of the Aragon region of Spain, where Cajal was born and educated, and of other parts of the country where he traveled or held positions. By his own account, art was his first love and obsession:

> When I was about eight or nine years old . . . I already had an irresistible mania for scribbling on paper, drawing ornaments in books, daubing on walls, gates, doors, and recently painted facades. . . . A smooth white wall exercised upon me an irresistible fascination. Whenever I got hold of a few cents I bought paper or pencils; but, as I could not draw at home because my parents considered painting a sinful amusement, I went out into the country, and . . . drew carts, horses, villagers, and whatever objects of the countryside interested me. Of all these I made a great collection, which I guarded like a treasure of gold.[11]

Too poor to purchase paints, he recounts coloring early drawings by soaking colors out of books of cigarette paper, an effort that testifies as much to youthful ingenuity as to the determination with which he pursued this proscribed amusement.[12]

To his father's disappointment, Cajal's determination to draw apparently did not lessen over time. He claims that until his twenties, he and Justo Ramón Casasús (a physician) were locked in an unrelenting battle over his madness for drawing. His father believed it could lead only to poverty, not least because Cajal allegedly lacked a shred of talent. According to Cajal, Justo Ramón Casasús was determined that both his sons would pursue careers in medicine. His remonstrations and unwillingness to accept the praise heaped on Cajal by the drawing instructors with whom he studied during his schooling had no effect.

Cajal describes remaining an inveterate caricaturist of his teachers, whose frequent rebukes did little more than spur him on.

Outside of the classroom, he took pictorial inspiration from nature and continued to make very ready use of blank walls. His autobiography recounts efforts to create a pictorial dictionary of colors accompanied by drawings of corresponding natural objects, which, in the case of flowers he could not afford, he devised elaborate methods to steal.[13] An illustrated book written in the style of Jules Verne (Cajal's fictitious traveler explores the anatomy of giant aliens on Jupiter) was followed by extensive practice, under the guidance of the painter and professor Leon Abadías y Santolaria, copying the drawings of the Greek masters and the Madonnas of Rafael and Bartolomé Esteban Murillo. Cajal also experimented in watercolor, aquarelle, and oil.

All of this is of course Cajal's story about himself. One need not take his statements at face value, however, to conclude that Cajal regarded this era of his life as important. Whatever the historical accuracy of volume 1 of the *Recollections*, it documents Cajal's desire that readers know about his artistic background and empathize with his frustrated efforts to pursue a career as a painter. The first volume of the *Recollections* also makes clear that strict verisimilitude was something of an anathema to Cajal. His main reaction upon reading *Don Quixote* as a young person was apparently despair at Cervantes's excessive realism. The short stories Cajal composed later in life are notable for their fantastical scenarios. His protagonists include a man with eyes like microscopes, another who creates a serum to eliminate sin, and a third who contrives to age young women (while preserving their mental capacity) to combat the "dangers" of female sexual appeal.[14] Instead of writers like Cervantes, Cajal acknowledges being inspired at an early age by the works of Romantic authors: the French novelist Victor Hugo (1802–1885), the French writer François-René de Chateaubriand (1768–1848), the English poet Lord Byron (1788–1824), the Spanish poet José de Espronceda (1808–1842). He even claims to have borne the stamp of the Romantic movement's melodramatic fatalism and obsession with a sublime nature—not to mention its valorization of an intensely subjective heroic solitude—for much of his life.[15]

Packaged definitions of Romanticism and Enlightenment tend to separate the two based on the Romantic movement's rejection of Enlightenment rationality. Allegedly, Romanticism replaced the *ratio* with freedom of expression, emotional directness, the unbounded nature of the subjective imagination, and an appreciation for flights of extreme affective intensity. Whereas the period in Western Europe between the 1760s and 1790s had been dominated by an aesthetic focus on an ordered and impersonal world, this purportedly changed between the eighteenth and nineteenth centuries, as artists and writers began to valorize psychological interiority and cultivate an interest in irrationality. Scholars in the humanities have demonstrated, however, that such periodization misses the complexity of Enlightenment and Romanticism's relationship. Both Cajal's explicit comments about the influence of Romanticism on his life and the style in which his autobiography is written are a testament to the Romantic movement's enduring impact on him, but hardly in the form of a binary turn from Enlightenment. His writing bears out the interwoven nature of reason and romance, the fact that, as Deborah White remarks, "Romantic discourse emerges in the Enlightenment 'context' of skepticism and critique" rather than in contradiction to it.[16]

Cajal's prose is indeed strewn with passionate, grandiose descriptions that borrow from the Romantic canon of aching desire and crushing despair. He discusses attempting to ascend the Coll de Ladrones in the Pyrenees in pursuit of a view of "crystal and placid lakes bordered by lofty cliffs of painted rock over the steps of which there fling themselves rainbow cascades," not unlike Byron's Childe Harold.[17] Commenting on his delight in classical art, he writes of having been long "intoxicated" with the "aesthetic instinct, which at last quenched its thirst for the ideal in the pure stream of classic beauty," a sentence no less replete with subjective fervor and rarefied abstraction in English than in Spanish.[18] These sorts of descriptions, as well as his landscape photographs from the 1870s and 1880s featuring the transcendent intensity of the Aragonese mountains and mysterious depths of the forest, replay the Romantic preoccupation with the immensity of nature as a trope for man's subjective life. They resonate particularly with the early-nineteenth-century Romantic German painter Caspar David Friedrich's work.[19] In Friedrich's painting *Wanderer Above the Sea Fog* (1818), a lone man stands on a rocky outcrop with his back to the viewer, gazing philosophically into the blue-gray distance as fog swathes the jagged peaks surrounding him (figure 7.1).

The misty mountainous landscape that spreads out in front of him renders the external world a sublime figuration of his subjective interiority. It frames his internal life in terms of a transcendent craggy vastness of unplumbed depths. As the figure's back is turned to the viewer, the mountain landscape functions in place of his face, helping make the painting a portrait despite the figure's stance. Friedrich's 1822 work *The Lonely Tree* (*Der einsame Baum*) resembles the *Wanderer* (lone figure in mountainous landscape) but reverses the relationship between human and nature (figure 7.2a). *The Lonely Tree* shows a resplendently singular tree, which acquires anthropomorphic qualities by starring centrally in the painting. That Friedrich characterizes the tree as "lonely" (*einsam*, lonely, solitary) in at least one of his several titles for the work heightens the sense in which this is as much a tree as a person. It towers over others of its kind (in the midground of the work) and, given the perspective from which the painting is constructed, even looms over the mountains in

7.1 Caspar David Friedrich, *Wanderer Above the Sea of Fog* (1818). Oil on canvas. 37.3 × 29.4 inches (94.8 × 74.8 cm).

*Source*: Hamburger Kunsthalle, Hamburg.

the distant background, announcing its superlative heights of loneliness with Byronic pathos. Cajal's art shared many of the same features on display in *Wanderer* and *The Lonely Tree*. In an early oil painting, Cajal depicts a female figure lying on the beach, her face turned inscrutably upward as huge waves crash at the foot of a craggy precipice that could be pulled straight from *Wanderer*. Cajal's photographs of the Aragonese landscape even resemble Friedrich's own vistas (figure 7.2b). More importantly, these features reappear in the neural drawings. Cajal's iconic image of the Purkinje cell, for example, showcases the cell's transcendent singularity much like the erect masculine figure in Friedrich's *Wanderer* and vertically strident tree in *The Lonely Tree* (figure 7.2c). His drawings of glial cells in the olfactory bulb of a kitten (figure 7.2d) even have qualities of the soaring arboreal landscape in Friedrich's paintings and Cajal's own photos, showcasing different levels of "vegetal" growth organized on a vertical axis.

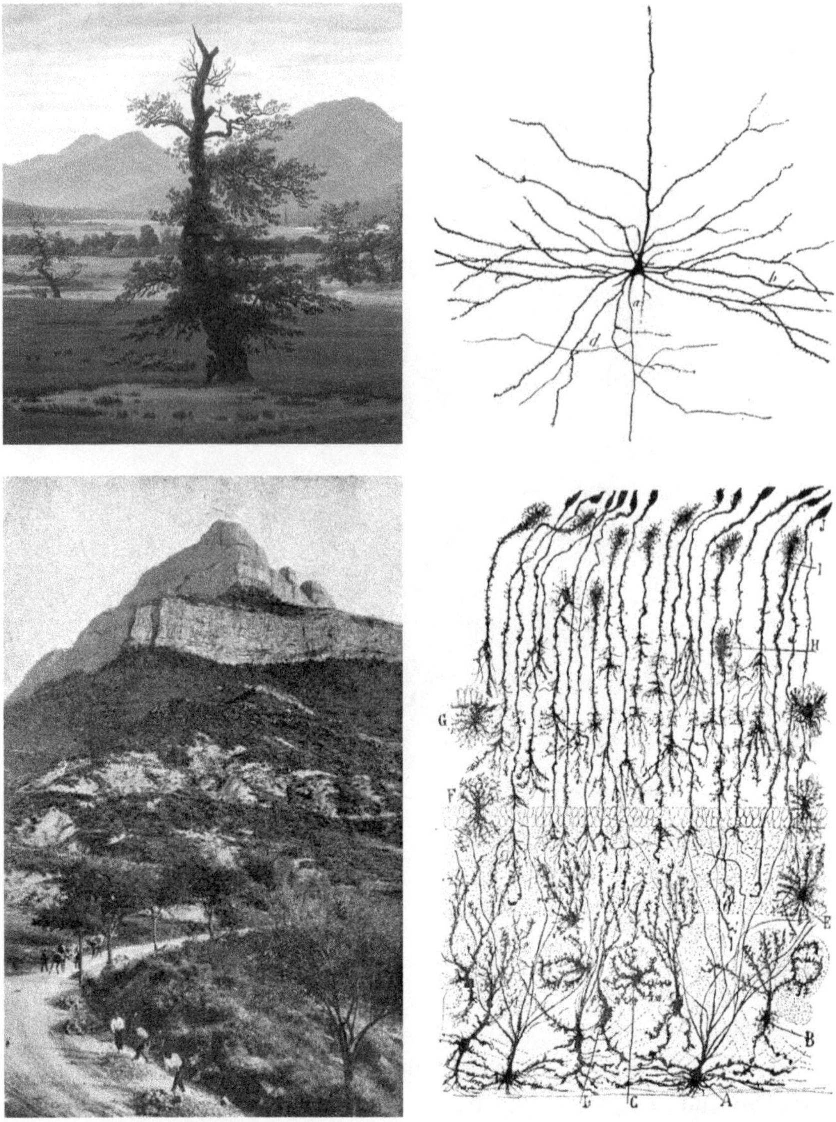

**7.2A–D** Works by Santiago Ramón y Cajal and Caspar David Friedrich. [A] Caspar David Friedrich, *The Solitary Tree* (1822), detail. Oil on canvas. 22 × 28 inches (55 × 71 cm). [B] Santiago Ramón y Cajal, giant pyramidal neuron in a thirty-year-old male. Undated book illustration from pen-and-ink drawing. *Textatura del sistema nervioso del hombre y de los vertebrados*, vol. 1 (1899). [C] Santiago Ramón y Cajal, photograph of Monte Oruel, Spain. Undated book illustration. *Recuerdos de mi vida*, vol. 1 (1917). [D] Santiago Ramón y Cajal, glial cells in the olfactory bulb of a kitten. Undated book illustration from pen-and-ink drawing. *Textatura del sistema nervioso del hombre y de los vertebrados*, vol. 1 (1899).

*Source*: [A] Alte Nationalgalerie, Berlin. [B] Santiago Ramón y Cajal, *Textura del sistema nervioso del hombre y de los vertebrados* (Madrid: Nicholás Moya, 1899). [C] Santiago Ramón y Cajal, *Recuerdos de mi vida. Tomo I* (Madrid: Imprenta y librería de Nicolás Moya, 1917). [D] Santiago Ramón y Cajal, *Textura del sistema nervioso del hombre y de los vertebrados* (Madrid: Nicholás Moya, 1899).

The emphasis on the Romantic masculine autonomy of the cell is made further explicit in Cajal's autobiography. Describing reproductive biology, Cajal writes of the "strongest and most fortunate sperm" triumphantly "rend[ing] the mysterious veil of the vitelline membrane and, losing its degrading tail, unit[ing] itself at last in sublime conjugation with the female nucleus."[20] The metaphor recurs in his characterization of neural life, where synapses become the orgasmic "final ecstasy" of neurons' "protoplasmic kiss."[21]

These passages in Cajal's autobiography are particularly notable because they appear at a moment in that work when he is quoting himself. In volume 2 of the autobiography (entitled *The Story of My Scientific Work*), Cajal describes fondly looking over his popular writings on histology from the 1880s and 1890s and finding joy in their "fantasy and ingenious lyricism."[22] He characterizes these publications, composed under the pseudonym Doctor Bacteria, as having been written in the "verbose" oral style specific to (Emilio) Castelar, president of the First Spanish Republic (established following Queen Isabella II's dethronement during the Spanish Revolution of 1868). Cajal states, "As I write these sheets, I have the articles before me. The reader will pardon the vanity of my old age if I declare that now, after thirty-nine years have passed, I find some solace in reading these impetuous scientific-literary effusions."[23]

Years after composing these popular texts, Cajal is still struck by his own works' literary qualities, in a manner not dissimilar to Sigmund Freud's comments about storytelling in psychoanalysis. He is still taken with their Romantic flair and "impetuous effusions." Indeed, he is still concerned with Romantic male heroism, which reappears in his characterization of the nerve cells as the keepers of good civic order in an "organic state" that would otherwise disintegrate into a Hobbesian war of all against all:

> Thus, as in every civilized nation the vital competition is done away with or greatly attenuated by the division of labour which makes the citizens have common interests and aspirations, so also in the organic state, thanks to the foresight of the nerve cells, to the allotment of functional rôles, and finally to the suppression of idleness and of excessive individual liberty, etc., the struggle disappears or is moderated, appearing only when the communal nourishment (of organs or cells) is seriously threatened from either internal or external causes.[24]

In the "nervous state" Cajal describes, the forethinking nerve cells function in partnership with an orderly division of vital labor to suppress idleness and "excessive individual liberty." Indolence and too much freedom are anathema to progress in civilized neural nations. These neural states must instead focus on the interests of their citizens as a group. Cajal's prose at this point makes the psychopolitical dimension of his neuroscience very clear. In the metaphorical scenario he describes, brain biology itself is a theater for playing out the dilemmas of popular sovereignty. Just as in the case of Clarus's medical assessment of Johann Christian Woyzeck in 1824, "the people" must be regulated so as to avoid either falling into idleness or overexercising their freedom and so disrupting the operations of the state and the common good.

Cajal's images also play out his preoccupation with Romantic heroism and male solitude. In them Cajal depicts strong-willed and autonomous cellular protagonists playing out amours, forging connections, or warding off threats from "outside," much like the solitary heroes of Romantic fiction and poetry. While highlighting neural discretization, these images also showcase the borders of individual neuron-states (thus satisfying the need to naturalize geopolitical borders on the level of biology). They allow Cajal to compensatorily conquer "new territory" for Spain by laying claim to the brain's terra incognita, symbolically recuperating the lost Spanish Empire in the process. Cajal's wishful global cartography, with nations neatly secured against invasion by one another, ends up projected onto a no longer strictly metaphorical "map" of the brain.

For Cajal, however, the fact that his drawings were metaphorical was the very reason for their scientific import. He reflects in his autobiography on the significance of his early publications as Doctor Bacteria. To him, these publications "had the advantage of calling the attention of wide-awake physicians to the ineffable enchantment of the almost unknown world of cells and microbes and to the very great importance of studying it objectively and directly."[25] Put differently, the subjective dimensions of these histological writings, their ability to reveal the "ineffable enchantment of unknown worlds," and by proxy the ability of his neural images to do likewise, is the entire reason to give them careful objective consideration. Any sufficiently attentive ("wide-awake") physician will understand as much. Good scientific practice includes sensitivity to the neural world conceived of as a Romantic landscape.

The dominant narrative about Cajal's life, work, and images nevertheless stresses that all are the fortunate product of his shift *away* from the aesthetic concerns of his youth and into the rigors of science. Cajal, so the story goes, may have wished to be an artist but happily became a scientist instead. Contemporary exhibitions that pair Cajal's neural drawings with the visual creations of artists "influenced" by them (such as, for example, the surrealists Federico García Lorca, Salvador Dalí, and Yves Tanguy) reinforce the notion of a fundamental divide between Cajal's truthful neural renderings and their creative (hence fictional) counterparts.[26] The same can be found in the historical scholarship noting the complementarity between Cajal's work in the visual arts and his neuroscientific pursuits. Having identified the commonality, however, researchers nevertheless largely balk at carrying its implications further.[27]

Cajal's statement about the neural world's ineffable enchantments as a motive for scientific investigation shows the opposite. It indicates that he regarded nominally subjective aesthetic practices, creative metaphors, and flights of imaginative fantasy as complementary with his scientific research and the dictates of mechanical objectivity. This resolves the apparent conflict between Cajal's insistence on his images' subjective, Romantic qualities (as beautiful Spanish landscapes) and his equal commitment to their rigorous objectivity in the face of Golgi's claims of his research's subjective bias. For Cajal, subjectivity and objectivity were compatible. To him, the neural drawings upheld the highest standards of science. They were (and remain) an indisputable basis for the neuron doctrine. The images were and are also, however, subjective, personal, and profoundly metaphorical representations of Romantic male heroism and of a Spain mourning for its lost colonial empire. For Cajal, one did not have to choose between the two options. The presence of the subjective dimension of the neural images did not eliminate their objectivity. If anything, it informed it. The objectivity of the neural images did not preclude their subjective debt to the Spanish Empire's nineteenth-century geopolitical upheavals or to Cajal's related interest in Romantic heroism and solitude.

Contemporary neuroimaging is profoundly indebted to Cajal's work. His position on the complementarity of subjectivity and objectivity thus raises a question about what more modern neuroimaging depicts and how it should be interpreted. If Cajal's images are as much about Romanticism and Spanish geopolitics as they are about brain cells, there is no guarantee that aesthetic works that seem thematically concerned with the brain or mind have anything to do with those topics.

Lucrecia Martel's 2008 film *The Headless Woman* (*La mujer sin cabeza*), for example, appears to be about its protagonist's disturbed state after she experiences a car crash. Attending only to her alleged head trauma, however, makes it impossible to grasp the film's pointed critique of visual evidence about the mind and brain. In place of a story about the brain, Martel constructs a cinematic world in which faith in appearances and biological veridicality sustains hegemonic presuppositions about gender, race, and history. This helps the film make two related points. First, Martel's film demonstrates that unless the aesthetic object in question has been carefully analyzed, any study of how the brain reacts while watching, reading, or viewing it can only hope to reproduce the initial assumptions about what that object shows or does. This kind of investigation will yield interpretive tautology, in which researchers' preliminary conclusions about an aesthetic object's "meaning" end up repeated by studies that purport only to explain why those features are there. Second, *The Headless Woman* reveals that its central character Vero, and by proxy also *la verdad* (truth) and *ver* (sight), may themselves be configured by an invisible psychopolitical process that conditions truth claims, shapes the meaning of visual evidence, and distorts its protagonist's first-person experiences.

I choose Martel's film for several reasons. First, it is set in Argentina (a Spanish colony until early 1816) and tied to the legacy of the Argentine Dirty War. This links the film to historical fallout from the period in which Cajal created his neural images. Vero is, moreover, a good case for a DSM diagnosis of PTSD. As someone living in a country wrestling with the consequences of genocidal political violence and at an age that means she would have been alive to "witness" this violence as a young adult, there is no question that Vero meets the criteria for posttraumatic stress disorder (309.81(F42.10)) as it is defined in the DSM-5. Here is "Criterium A" of that definition: "Exposure to actual or threatened death, serious injury, or sexual violence in one (or more) of the following ways. . . ."[28] Vero also potentially had a severe physical head trauma in her car crash, meaning that there is an obvious explanation for her seeming confusion.

Furthermore, the complicity between psychoanalytic practitioners and the Argentine military junta in the human rights abuses of the 1970s led the International Psychoanalytic Association (IPA) to create a special statement on the issue at their 1979 Congress in New York, expressing "opposition to the use of psychiatric or psychotherapeutic methods to deprive individuals of their freedom."[29] If anything, the disappearances in the Argentine Dirty War show the extent of psychoanalytic abuse, recognized by the IPA itself no less, and fit the familiar paradigm in which psychoanalytic methodology needs to be scrutinized and regulated. As *La mujer sin cabeza* places issues of gender, race, and class in dialogue with the nonpsychoanalytic mind sciences, however, the film challenges both the idea that psychology, psychiatry, and the neurosciences are free of ethical dilemmas because objective and the related position that psychoanalysis is the culprit.

Taking this approach opens onto the long cinematic tradition, dating back to the silent films created at the turn of the century, which critiques normative perspectives on the relationship between the brain, psychology, and perception. It simultaneously suggests connections to other films questioning the veridical output of visual technologies. I would point out Michelangelo Antonioni's *Blow-Up* (1966) in this regard, as well as the far lesser-known 1947 Golden Age comedy *Una mujer sin cabeza* (*A Headless Woman*, dir. Luis César Amadori), to which Martel's similarly titled film alludes.[30] The latter is particularly interesting as Amadori reproduced a popular North American sideshow attraction from the 1930s known as the "Woman Without a Head" in his 1940s film. This midway attraction created by a German refugee was based on a clever optical illusion.[31] An exploration of Santiago Ramón y Cajal's images in partnership with Martel's film thus raises questions and intellectual directions that exceed that pairing alone.

Collectively, Cajal's images and Martel's film offer a new picture of the relationship between the humanities and the neurosciences that is different from extant scholarship in literary criticism, cognitive film theory, and neurocinematics. This perspective has important consequences for understanding the role of representation in neuroscientific research in Cajal's time, as well as the present, and for related issues of how to tell history.

## Something Wrong with Vero: Lucrecia Martel on Head Trauma

The Argentinean director Lucrecia Martel's 2008 film *The Headless Woman* might be a film about the murder of a child.[32] It is unambiguously one that encourages its viewers to imagine it is about its protagonist's head trauma, whether psychological or biological. The opening scene shows a trio of dark-skinned, ragged adolescent boys and a dog playing on a deserted road in the rural, northwestern province of Salta, Argentina. The subsequent eighty-seven minutes follow the light-skinned, middle-class, middle-aged woman Verónica (Vero) after she has a car accident on the same road in the next scene. Vero does not get out of the car at the time of her accident, and the camera likewise remains strapped into the passenger seat during the crash. As a result, it is unclear who or what she has hit. The matter is never conclusively resolved in the film. The entire work struggles to come to terms with what has or has not happened. This uncertainty forms the film's affective soundtrack. A bizarre visit to the hospital (in which Vero has X-rays taken of her head but writes her nurse's name on the medical paperwork, not her own), a one-night stay in the local hotel (where she sleeps with a relative), and a fruitless attempt to go to work the next morning (Vero thinks she is a patient in her own dental clinic) all seem to indicate that she has become disoriented as a result of the crash. The camera follows her experience of seeming first-person bewilderment, which the film strongly suggests is the consequence of a traumatic head injury she received during the accident.

As the minutes roll by, however, the film also drops clues that Vero might be suffering from a psychological disturbance. Or, indeed, that she is struggling with a combination of physical and psychological difficulties triggered by the crash. There is even a suggestion that Vero has a preexisting psychiatric condition. Whatever the source, the implication is quite clearly that there is something medically wrong with Vero. Throughout the film, she is only able to perform basic life tasks with the help of her pointedly anonymized darker-skinned servants. Vero's disturbance is ironically magnified by her attendants' pretense that nothing is wrong, even as they compensate for her lapses.

Secondary scholarship in the humanities on *La mujer* overwhelmingly endorses the assertion that there is something wrong with Vero. Multiple commentators conclude that Vero is experiencing amnesia, while others speculate that she has been traumatized.[33] Explanations additionally include that Vero is concussed, confused, has "lost her bearings," is plagued by a guilty conscience, or is experiencing a general psychological crisis connected with her privileged economic status in a racist neocolonial order.[34] Even more diagnostically circumspect commentators conclude that Vero is at the very least "in an altered state of mind" or that the film is depicting an erratic "condition of consciousness."[35]

While no cognitive readings of the film yet exist (to the best of my knowledge), it lends itself quite readily to this style of interpretation for the same reasons that extant scholarship identifies: *La mujer* seems to be about something amiss with Vero. The basic tenets of cognitive media theory as defined by Ted Nannicelli and Paul Taberham in their edited volume *Cognitive Media Theory* include the following characteristics:

> (1) [A] dedication to the highest standards of reasoning and evidence in film and media studies and other fields (including, but not limited to empirical data from the natural sciences); (2) a commitment to stringent inter-theoretical criticism and debate; (3) a general focus on the mental activities of the viewer as the central (but not the only) object of inquiry and (4) an acceptance of an naturalistic perspective, broadly construed.[36]

Taking this approach with *La mujer* might mean relying on the findings of perceptual psychology to show how Martel "exploits the natural tendencies of everyday perception."[37] It could here entail looking at how Martel guides the audience's attention "toward what is pertinent for following the story that unfolds."[38] It might advocate for reading *La mujer* by tracking the film's "attentional engines," the formal devices the film uses, "to deliver the pertinent information to its audience."[39] Adopting the neurocinematic approach outlined by Vittorio Gallese and Michele Guerra in *The Empathetic Screen*, by contrast, could involve exploring how camera techniques do or do not facilitate viewer empathy with Vero's plight by engaging mirror neurons.[40] As Gallese and Guerra outline, it is possible to study the degree of stimulation these neurons experience when exposed to different types of camera techniques by using an EEG to measure event-related desynchronization between the brain's alpha and beta rhythms.[41] Conceivably, information gathered from such experiments could be applied to Martel's camera techniques in *La mujer* to study the "relational nature of cinematographic style and intersubjectivity."[42] One could also cognitively assess Vero's experience. In line with the neuropsychoanalyst Mark Solms's adaptation of Karl Friston's free energy principle, Vero's trauma might plausibly be the product of a disjunction between the homeostatic, relaxed state of free energy she experiences during her drive and that of the cortical-alarm-triggering crash.[43] Alternatively, following Catherine Malabou's approach in *The New Wounded* would suggest Vero's car accident is the cause of her difficulties. She has had a major head trauma that has entirely skewed her perception of the world. It would also be possible to read the film through the lens of neurodivergence. In such a reading, Vero possesses an unidentified (or unmentioned) form of cognitive variation that neuronormatively biased audiences fail to recognize and consequently misperceive as something wrong with her.

The confusion about just what is going on in the film only thickens when Vero attempts to obtain concrete proof about what happened that day. Neither the hospital nor the local police have any record of a child's death in a hit-and-run, although a young indigenous *campesino* boy (one of the three in the opening) has died in disconcertingly unclear circumstances. When Vero confesses to her husband, he refuses to believe her. Returning with her to the crash site, he protests she only hit a dog, before taking her car to be repaired. Her efforts to obtain her hospital admission and X-rays are likewise in vain: the hospital denies she was ever there. No X-rays can be found. The hotel lacks a record of her stay. By the end of the film, the only substantive change is to Vero's hair color, which she re-dyes from blonde to brunette. Whether Vero has committed murder, who or what killed the indigenous boy, and if the opening scene was her deranged, hallucinatory projection or a real event are simply left open questions. The film takes leave of them with the same indifferent shrug that Vero makes when she wanders away from the hospital intake paperwork.

This ambivalence encourages the spectator to regard the film's central paradox as a clash of objectivity and subjectivity. It appears to leave the spectator in the position of hunting for clues as to what *really* happened or acquiescing to the idea that Vero's perspective is sufficiently distorted as to make it impossible to know. Both her name and the film's title reinforce this binary. In Spanish, Vero is related to "truth" (*la verdad*) and "sight" (*ver*, to see). Her character seems to embody the idea that seeing is believing, a central principle of nineteenth-century scientific objectivity.[44] *Sin cabeza* refers to the mental state of losing one's bearings, sometimes because of love, but equally in instances of severe shock, as in the English-language concept of "losing one's head."[45] Vero, the film's title seems to suggest, has somehow lost her head. It is the audience's task to see the truth despite her unreliable narration.

Wariness about such willful guidance is apropos given Martel's allusions to the Argentine Dirty War (1976–1983) throughout *La mujer* and her Salta Trilogy, the three films she created between 2001 and 2008 about the women of Salta, Argentina. All indirectly meditate on the Dirty War's legacy for the present. The coup d'état that overthrew the Perón regime in Argentina in 1976 brought to power a military dictatorship that, on the premise of purging political dissidents, relied on genocidal practices to systematically terrorize the population. Their actions "disappeared" more than thirty thousand people, many of whose final fate and physical remains have yet to be recovered and may never be. The forcible disappearances were subsequently recognized by the Argentine judicial system as crimes against humanity. Known as *los desaparecidos* (the disappeared), the vanished persons are marked by the absence that shrouds them and the complexity, if not impossibility, of mourning their loss.

The Salta Trilogy seldom refers to the Dirty War outright but evokes the deceptive processes used by the dictatorship. The films realize a feeling of a heterotopic ghostliness and uncertainty rather than offering assurance that the era's atrocities are well and truly past. Like its counterpart films, *La mujer* cinematographically conjures the perceptual manipulations used by the civic-military dictatorship to highlight the limitations of firsthand testimony. In place of a treatise on "what happened" according to those who "really saw it," *La mujer* remains attentive to the peculiar mode of unperception that sustained a thirty-thousand-person disappearing act. As one recent monograph points out, *La mujer* is less concerned with objects and phenomena that can be immediately seen than with a white elite's sanctioned blindness to the social, racial, and political ordering of society and the unique forms of *not* seeing it employs to ensure the continuity of preferable fictions.[46] This sentiment is neatly summed up in Vero's husband's refrain: "no pasó nada" (nothing happened). In place of showing particular objects and events, then, Martel shows the array of socioeconomic, cultural, historical, and even scientific blockages that make them invisible. She shows strategies of ideological dis-apparition.

The film achieves this in two ways: by staging such blockages as actual physical barriers on screen and by the way it frames shots. The first, the barriers, are present in the form of surfaces that interfere with the audience's direct line of sight. They distort their object or yield only partial access to it by forcing the audience to peer through or around them. Vero's lacquer black sunglasses, which make her face impossible to see until after the crash, are a good example of this, as are her splotchy car windowpanes in the film's opening minutes. The car windows are covered with blurry handprints and then a kaleidoscopic profusion of raindrops that blocks access to what is outside the vehicle after the crash. Similarly, the superabundance of mirrors in Vero's home makes it difficult to look directly at its interior. Whenever the viewer tries to see the rooms' contents, the mirrors reflect other spaces instead.

These visual barriers help remind the viewer that images are mediated. They prompt the audience to recall that the film is similarly contingent on making (in)visible and, in this way, has a structural resemblance to the junta's actions in creating a picture of reality. The onscreen blockages imply the existence of "evidence" that can only declare itself as a kind of erasure, the place where something should be but is not. In place of an (impossible) declaration of censorship—impossible because it too has been censored—these points of blockage provide formal cues that Vero's experiences may be the product of systematic gaslighting by a patriarchal regime complicit with and perhaps a descendent of the Dirty War's military perpetrators.

Treating "*sin cabeza*" as a reference to Vero's putative loss of mental functioning mistakes the socioeconomic and patriarchal construction of a normative femininity for Vero's own psychical interiority. Her interiority, however, is precisely what has been carefully whittled away by these things. Even the fact that Vero embodies a normative fantasy of womanhood cannot be stated outright: who would do the speaking? Her status as little more than a depersonalized receptacle for gendered clichés is transferred instead to the film's cinematography.

Martel's choice of camera placement and framing (her selection of what to show in a particular shot) indicates the viewer's lack of access to Vero's interiority. The framing repeatedly decapitates Vero by forcing her head offscreen. In the crash scene, for example, Vero's head vanishes from view at the moment of impact (figure 7.3a-b). Subsequent camerawork similarly makes a point of dramatically cropping out her head (figure 7.3e). As she stands in the hospital's X-ray room, the lowered arm of the X-ray machine blocks it from view (figure 7.3d). When she locks herself in the bathroom at home, the camera focuses on the doorframe and her partial reflection in the bathroom mirror, showing her only from the neck down (figure 7.3c). As with the reflective surfaces and Vero's changing hair color (perhaps various shades of *verdad* on display?), these shots of Vero's headless torso say almost nothing about what or whom is being represented, let alone her thoughts. They say a great deal, however, about the forces conditioning its/her representation. The technique subtly indicates to the viewer Vero's status as an average signifier for a wishfully conceived (and narratively compliant) version of "Woman." Her cinematographic loss of a head expresses the deprivation of her individuality, a loss that "she" nevertheless cannot articulate precisely because of having already been made little more than a collection of platitudes. Of necessity, if she has been gaslit, Vero cannot speak to such gaslighting, as it is exactly the capacity for first-person perspectival distance that vanishes in the act.

In this way, Martel's response to the experience of the Dirty War resists the array of more monumentalizing memorial films about the disappeared that emerged in the mid-1980s.[47] Often made by the sons and daughters of the victims, these films commemorated a lost history by attempting to restore it to the full plenitude of verifiable fact.[48] By contrast, *La mujer sin cabeza* cinematographically evokes the perceptual manipulations used by the military junta and identifies the correspondent limitations of firsthand testimony in recuperatively documenting the reality of what took place. Her choice resonates with the famous accounts of human rights violations that—collected and

**7.3A–E** Lucrecia Martel, stills from *The Headless Woman* (2008). [A] Vero before the crash. [B] Vero during the crash. [C] Vero at home. [D] Vero at the hospital. [E] Vero in a public bathroom.

*Source*: *The Headless Woman*. DVD. Directed by Lucrecia Martel. Culver City, CA: Strand Releasing, 2008.

published by the Argentine National Commission on the Disappearance of Persons (CONADEP) as the report *Nunca Más* (Never again, 1984)—played a critical role in establishing a national narrative about the disappearances, as well as in prosecuting the junta's leaders.

Without denying the vital importance of such accounts, *La mujer* probes who and what they may leave out. Unlike *Nunca Más* and more contemporary outgrowths (the 2002 inauguration of an Argentine "Day of Remembrance for Truth and Justice," the 2010 opening of trials for military and security force collaborators), *La mujer sin cabeza* seeks to engage the legacy of the *desaparecidos* as one quite literally of dis-appearances, that is, of moments at which visibility was simply and irretrievably negated. The phenomena of mass disapparition is, she suggests, strangely at odds with the clarity and certainty efforts like *Nunca Más* attribute to eyewitness testimony and oddly incompatible with the establishment of a fixed narrative that makes the remembrance of suffering a national duty. How indeed to tell the official story of something that, officially, never took place? In keeping with the gritty, minimalist aesthetics of Argentinean New Wave Cinema, her film seeks to capture the insidious intertwining of the dictatorship's brutal actions with those actions' cover-up. In place of offering an evidentiary treatise on "what really happened" according to those who "really saw it," *La mujer sin cabeza* chooses to transpose the experience of the 1970s and early 1980s, not the events, into a modern-day struggle that requires the audience and the film's ambiguous victim-perpetrators to reckon with a murder that did and did not happen.

The fact that Vero's confusion so readily lends itself to the usual clichés about female mental disturbance, as well as cinema's oft-remarked—and much theorized—capacity to replicate first-person perception (Hugo Münsterburg, André Bazin, Sergey Eisenstein, Christian Metz), should perhaps make viewers wary, not comfortable, about the nature of what they are seeing. Indeed, taken in concert with the film's formal emphasis on optics and its historical allusions to the *desaparecidos*, it becomes increasingly difficult to believe that the cinematic techniques that appear to show first-person perception in *La mujer* (fragmentary narrative, disordered temporality, tightly constrained visual access, lack of plot) are reflections of her perspective. While viewers may imagine they are seeing Vero's stream of consciousness, this assumption causes them to neglect the film's elision (by decapitation, no less) of the first-person perspective around which it supposedly pivots. "Vero's" inner experiences are a bricolage of third-person claims originating in patriarchal norms, bourgeois privilege, the legacy of state terror, and naturalization of racial hierarchy. These claims nevertheless effectively *legislate* the desired conclusion "nothing happened" by being cloaked in the first person and seeming to speak in Vero's voice. The medical correlate "this woman is disturbed" simultaneously functions to ensure that anything Vero says to contradict the narrative "nothing happened" will not be taken seriously.

By exposing the constructed nature of evidence in *La mujer*, Martel conjures the truth-bending practices of the junta's cover-up and shows the ways they both distort first-person experience and the representation thereof. She thereby confronts her viewer with the need to find techniques for looking and thinking beyond canned narratives. Cinema, she argues in a 2012 interview, is better regarded as a tool to target unwittingly calcified perception and the onset of interpretive rigor mortis than it is a reflection of human perceptual activity.

> I believe that the tools cinema has to communicate a perception of time and space allow us to question perception. . . . When perception is questioned, and in some ways cinema allows you to do it, the world reveals itself for brief moments. I think that's what cinema is; more than revealing something about human beings, it reveals something about our perception. And in that sense, it is very political, because if it helps us unlearn a certain way of looking at things, then it might be possible to truly see certain things.[49]

She explicates with reference to *La mujer*: "In *La mujer sin cabeza*, what interested me was to approach a mechanism that was superlatively used during the dictatorship, that was essentially 'We don't realize what's going on.' . . . That 'I was unaware of what was evident' mechanism was what I wanted to approach."[50]

In both statements Martel prompts her viewers to engage in acts of unlearning that distinguish between habitualized, mainstream perception and the ways that cinema trains the viewer to perceive (and so think) differently. Her fictitious film proves to be a better objective imaging device than both the X-ray machine it depicts and the disturbed first-person perception it appears to portray. In place of a portrait of psychical or cerebral trauma (or a combination thereof), *La mujer* foregrounds new ways of looking at mental life by paying attention to strategies that make it visible.

While it is of course possible to explain Martel's visual choices in *La mujer* in terms of what the cognitive film theorists William Seeley and Noël Carroll call the attentional device of "variable framing" (a shift in camera position on the emerging events within the movie world), doing so only reproduces the same problem the film seeks to subvert.[51] Seeley and Carroll maintain that viewers will always be *visually guided* to "critical story information." Yet this position both conflates visual prominence with narrative significance and presupposes to know at the outset what the "critical information" is, thus short-circuiting the act of reading.[52] It produces a problem of interpretive tautology. This perspective assumes, in other words, that a film's most visually obvious aspects are its meaning. It then uses this assumption to investigate how particular films engage "the mental activities of the viewer." Doing so will certainly show how visually obvious interpretations of specific films engage human cognition. It will, for that reason, also remain on the level of explaining why that which is most visually obvious in a film appears so. This practice will not help in instances where the film in question is making a visually or interpretively subtle point, where it is contesting the equation of visibility with meaning, where it is challenging the naturalistic perspective, or where it cannot itself be reduced to a single meaning.

The use of research from the neurosciences about the brain to explain *La mujer*, for example, runs into the same problem of interpretive tautology. By demanding that viewers engage exclusively on the level of appearances, interpretations stressing *La mujer* as a case of variable framing, embodied simulation, disturbance of Friston's free energy, or neurodivergence unintentionally repeat the same erasure exemplified by the husband's refrain "no pasó nada." Nothing to see here. Paying lip service to empathy and intersubjectivity, they mistake the physical capacity to simply see a film with the learned ability to interpret it, causing *La mujer*'s cinematographic effort to disclose the production of (very convincing but nevertheless likely false) evidence to vanish in the process.

This raises a host of difficult questions. Is the awareness of intersubjectivity gained through a cognitive theoretical framework comparable with that available by attending to *La mujer*'s meditation on a violent regime's efforts to prevent its population from seeing too much or asking too many questions? How should one treat the fact that starting from an emphasis on cinema as intersubjective blocks the possibility of reading individual films' interrogations of structurally violent practices designed to foil and confuse? What role should the neurosciences play in reading films dealing with historical trauma? What role should histories like that of the Argentine Dirty War play in the neurosciences? What should one make of an interpretive focus on empathy that compellingly explains the pleasures of movie-going but also perpetuates a tired narrative about female feeble-mindedness and the dispensability of indigenous bodies? How should one understand interpretations that, by insisting "seeing is believing," work in opposition to cinema's and indeed many aesthetic objects' efforts at more indirect communication (if "communication" is even the right word)? Do neurocognitive analyses and humanities bids for Vero's pathologization (trauma, amnesia, etc.) sustain the dis-appearance strategies the film seeks to divulge? If not, how can their ascription of "something wrong with Vero" be rectified with the film's cinematographic and symbolic emphasis on the forcible removal of Vero's head?

In posing these questions, Lucrecia Martel's *La mujer* reflects on the unexpected social, racial, gender-specific, and ethical dimensions of Santiago

Ramón y Cajal's portrait of neural life. While the film is neither "about" Santiago Ramón y Cajal nor obviously influenced by his neural images, its subtle reworking of a seeming first-person account of trauma provides a space in which to think the legacy of nineteenth-century German neuroanatomy and biological psychiatry as they extend through the discovery of neuron doctrine and into the present. Martel's film offers a meditation on the limits of the visible and verifiable, questioning at once the production of evidentiality in general and any position assuming the unmediated nature of evidence about consciousness. Engaging the cognitive paradigm in reverse, the film explores where "dedication to the highest standards of reasoning and evidence . . . including, but not limited to empirical data from the natural sciences" has an unintended but unwelcome effect of disappearing the very story it purports to rigorously exhume.

## Neural Landscapes of the Argentine Dirty War

Santiago Ramón y Cajal's neural images function both objective representations of neural life and subjective representations of Romantic masculine individualism coupled with nineteenth-century resistance to decolonization. They are scientific. They nevertheless psychopolitically figure human neural experience in terms of measurable units (individual neurons and their related cellular processes), using that representation as the basis for a more generalized description of psychical experience. Cajal himself points out that the neural butterflies' beating wings may carry the secret to mental life. In compensating for lost Spanish colonial territory by intrepidly exploring the unconquered territory of the brain, Cajal's images also ensure a psychopolitical worlding to which Jacques Derrida pointed (as a feature of psychoanalysis) in his essay "Geopsychoanalysis: '. . . and the Rest of the World' " and that I characterize in this book as a "geoneuroscience." Cajal himself indicates this subjective feature does not undermine his images' scientific status. It merely complicates the outward binary between subjectivity and objectivity that the 1906 Nobel conflict seemed to put in place.

Lucrecia Martel's *La mujer* picks up on Santiago Ramón y Cajal's unlikely embrace of subjectivity both as it relates to the patriarchal structures of heroic masculinity and to the geopolitical dimension of his images. Writing out of a national context determined by the wars of independence against imperial Spain in the early nineteenth century (Argentina declared independence in 1816) and by the Spanish Empire's loss of colonies in the Spanish-American War, the film reflects on what it means to give neural life a voice. Vero is, at least potentially (the film does not provide a clear answer), both a victim of psychopower and the perpetrator of a terrible crime. The shadow of the

Argentine military junta's encouragement that citizens simply look away from the disappearances seems to fall over her, taking the form of a medically and juridically verifiable account of truth, promoted at home by her husband, that speaks in the name of hard evidence and visibility but sustains what is likely an officially sanctioned fiction. The film does not and cannot take a clear stance on this point, however. Doing so would participate in the same epistemological commitment to direct verifiability *La mujer* seeks to criticize.

That both sanity and normalcy have likely already been defined by the same forces complicit with the perpetuation of a "preferable" official story about the past (concerning the Dirty War and Vero's crash alike) leaves Vero trapped. Mental health in this world is synonymous with consent to the dissemination of a questionable account of history, which is nevertheless vouchsafed by the triplicate authority of the law, medicine, and hard evidence. If Vero is uncomfortable repeating this established narrative about either the war or her crash, the only alternative for her is to accept being framed as mentally unstable or brain damaged. After all, her resistance to the established narrative about these topics is already proof she does not meet the standard for mental health. Accepting this position, however, ensures that the stories "she" tells do not carry serious weight.

The film's outward emphasis on Vero's status as an unreliable narrator is hence a strategic device. It showcases the techniques that produce a version of first-person speech at the expense of the speaker's own personhood. Vero is headless in the sense that the physical site of her consciousness, intentionality, first-person narrative, and, indeed, the site in her body from which she would be capable of serving as an eyewitness has been metaphorically taken away from her. She cannot speak about her experiences—if "she" is even present in the film—because she is caught between a patriarchal, colonial, and genocidal definition of sanity on the one hand and, on the other, an account of psychical disturbance that complements it, invalidating "her" statements before "she" utters them. To the concept of bare life (Agamben's notion of the reduction of human existence to the mere fact of being alive), one might here add the concept of bare thought: the reduction of mental existence to the attribution of an individual's possession of a first-person perspective, which turns out, on examination, to be little more than a contentless, preprogrammed version of thinking (like that in Kantian intellectual guardianship) designed to sustain the status quo.

In this way, Vero's cinematographic decapitation recalls that of Johann Christian Woyzeck in 1824. In each case, a focus on sanity versus insanity, guilt versus innocence, subjectivity versus objectivity, distracts attention from the larger and more complex issue: the ability to use a medically and juridically validated account of sanity as a regulatory mechanism, one equipped with lethal force. In Martel's film, what appears to be a protagonist with whom viewers could empathize is very close to being little more than a psychopolitical automaton whose alleged individuality folds into a normative picture of mass mental health and womanhood. In *La mujer*, however, the plot of psychopower takes a further twist. The film points out that individuals who accept the psychopolitical version of mass mental health can now, at least potentially, kill with impunity because they are protected from having to give any story about what they have done that departs from the (no less sane) official narrative. Vero can thereby conveniently be made not responsible, as, officially, nothing has happened. If "she" thinks it has, there must be something wrong with her.

Martel shows that exclusive emphasis on that which is most obvious, most visible, most compellingly expressed, most documented, and most evidential in accounts of the past also has certain undesirable consequences. It has the potential to foreclose the narratives of those whose victimization historically extended to their violent exclusion from the production of evidentiality either through direct speech or the basic posthumous presence of their own physical remains. It makes an objective factual record into the privileged arbiter of historical reality, placing pressure on acceding to a standard of proof that may itself require consideration, in terms of who sets it and how it was established. In Martel's case, *La mujer* probes who and what may be left out by even most robust, ethnically oriented documentary efforts to obtain justice. These efforts are neither malicious nor filled with malign ideological intent but inevitably have holes because they require the creation of an official narrative about an event that officially never happened. While Vero certainly meets the conditions for a DSM diagnosis of PTSD, and while the entire film can be read in the critical terms established by cognitive media theory, explaining it in this way produces similar oversights, despite the genuine commitment to empathy, intersubjectivity, and the pursuit of justice behind it. Because they are unable to attend to psychopower, the diagnostic and related cognitive reading minimize Vero's responsibility for what may have happened and unfortunately frame her as an addled female requiring rational masculine guidance. Both frame the film's central dilemma as a clash between objectivity (what really happened during the crash/war) and subjectivity (what Vero "thinks" happened), instead of recognizing that the nominally objective portrait of Vero's mental state on screen has, most likely, already violently determined the expression of her so-called subjectivity.

*La mujer*'s attention to the neural landscapes of the Argentine Dirty War is important because it helps show the need for the neurosciences to consider the role of representation in their own practices. This is different from the methodologically unilateralist stance in interdisciplinary research since the neurocognitive turn of the 1980s and 1990s. In it, neuroscientific research findings tend to be applied to humanities objects as an interpretive lens, on the flawed assumption that the relationship only goes one way. Cognitive media studies relies on this perspective, as does a great deal of research in the neurohumanities.[53] These areas have made important interventions and will no doubt continue to do so. That is no reason for humanities scholars or neuroscientists to be limited to them.

Foremost among the benefits for the neurosciences in considering the role of representation is access to a new tool: the ability to account for the mimetic processes already conditioning day-to-day neuroscientific inquiry. The existence of mirror neurons in the brain no more means that there are tiny physical mirrors located there than did the cognitive computationalist paradigm, comparing the brain to a computer, mean that the brain conducted Boolean algebra. Both are simply useful metaphors. Brain anatomy is filled with them. The brain's pineal gland takes its name from the Latin word for "pinecone" (*pinus*), which the gland visually resembles. Long before Cajal identified neural forests, there was indeed already at least one pine tree in the brain. The brain's hippocampus is, moreover, based on its curved structure, named after the mythological Greek monster that was half-horse (*íppos*) and half-fish (*kámpos*, sea monster), now better known as the "sea-horse." The title of the cerebral cortex (the brain's outer layer) comes from the Latin term for "bark," *cortex*. That contemporary neuroscientific research speaks in terms of neurons "firing" or "sharing information" is a product of the language of World War II and specifically the British scientist Norbert Weiner's involvement in designing predictive control systems for antiaircraft artillery.[54] Discussions of the brain's ability to suffer, create form, and serve as an agency of disobedience by contemporary continental philosophy turn out to be just as anthropomorphic as Cajal's descriptions of neural cells, which he characterized as autonomous beings capable of engaging in "protoplasmic kisses," among other anthropoid activities.

A two-way dialogue would, moreover, help scientific discussions about the brain's physiological operations by clarifying the difference between those biological operations and the rhetorical lexicon of imitation regularly employed to describe them. For example, studies on mirror neurons, predictive coding, and the brain circuitry grounding cognitive replications of others' intentions all rely on figurative strategies pulled from the (English-language) idiom of mimesis and representation to describe cognitive acts of perceiving and relating to the external world. They nevertheless do so without awareness of it. To take only the example of mirror neurons, these neurons are said to "represent" others' observed actions.[55] Would it not be beneficial to understand what representation means in this context? And, indeed, to examine how the rise of English as a globalized scientific lingua franca may be responsible for determining that meaning, flattening the complexities of *Vertretung, Darstellung, representatio, représentation*, and other untranslatables? A purely colloquial idea of representation obscures the distinction between representation in the sense of a vehicle (the oil and canvas, in the case of a painting) and representation in the sense of reproduced event/object/person (the painting's subject matter). Are mirror neurons the vehicle, the content, both, neither?

In addition to facilitating a fresh methodological style, making space for a two-way dialogue would place the study of the mind and brain in greater conversation with major areas of research in humanist thought. It would enable consideration of the brain rooted in the humanities' ongoing analysis of the Enlightenment's and reason's troubled legacy. By engaging a new facet of the philosophical interrogation of "naturalness," it would also enable matters of gender, race, and class to come to the fore in the mind sciences, the need for which a growing amount of work has already begun to identify.[56] This would include acknowledgment that neural selfhood is at once an innately existing reality and a social product, as figures such as Nikolas Rose and Fernando Vidal have shown.[57] It would actively engage, instead of foreclosing, the competition between a materialist approach to phenomenology that largely dispenses with Edmund Husserl's critique of psychological data empiricism in *The Crisis of the European Sciences and Transcendental Philosophy* and research like that of Elizabeth Grosz, which suggests the abiding presence of the incorporeal within the material.[58] A two-way dialogue would, moreover, put the question of culture into play. Discussions by Kate Hayles, Mark Hansen, Luciana Parisi, and Bernard Stiegler have already foregrounded culture's relationship to *technē*, machine intelligence, and the existence of a technological nonconscious (building on the work of Gilbert Simondon and Martin Heidegger). Incorporating a consideration of cultural representation's role in the brain and neurosciences would expand these conversations, with important implications for research on artificial intelligence. Bringing culture into the picture would also foreground aesthetic epistemology, stressing the need to engage deeply with literary texts, film, and visual art as sources of analysis rather than with fixed evidence of scientific claims. This is in line with Stathis Gourgouris's argument about literature as a thinking tool.[59] It is similarly consistent with the claims of *Wissenspoetik*, or the poetology of knowledge. In modernist studies, the shift to focusing on representation in the brain and away from the brain's determination of how aesthetic objects function responds to Sianne Ngai's call to attend to a new set of aesthetic categories (what she calls "zany, cute, interesting") to understand "how aesthetic experience has been transformed by the hypercommodified, information saturated, performance-driven conditions of late capitalism."[60] Following Ngai's lead, it makes sense to suggest that the very need for new aesthetic categories may be a consequence of aesthetic objects' and artists' engagement with the new ways of understanding the mind and brain that overlap with hypercommodified and information-saturated late capitalism.

Subjectivity, in other words, has been a part of neuroscientific research from Cajal's work onward.

# AFTERWORD

## An Aesthetic Education in the Wake of the Neurocognitive Turn

Nicolas Negroponte, the director of the MIT Media Lab, stood before an audience in Vancouver, British Columbia, in 2014 and delivered a TED talk entitled "A 30-Year History of the Future." It concluded with a prediction. Negroponte noted that his "One Laptop per Child" initiative had already shown that computational technology could serve in place of schools in "primitive" parts of the world (Cambodia, Ethiopia, Africa generally). Based on its success, he proposed that in the coming thirty years, technological innovation would find ways to package education for ultrarapid delivery to the "last billion" people currently subsisting in disconnected ignorance. Coming advances would do away with the "inefficiency" (Negroponte's term) of having to learn by using one's own eyes to absorb text. His prediction: "You're going to swallow a pill and know Shakespeare. . . . And, the way to do it is through your bloodstream. So, once it's in your bloodstream, it basically goes through it and gets into the brain, and when it knows that it's in the brain and the different pieces, it deposits it in the right places."[1]

Backing up his claim by reference to neurotechnology research currently being carried out at MIT, Negroponte's vision is that by 2044 a combination of neuroscientific and technological advances will have corrected social inequality and rationalized knowledge acquisition on a truly global scale. There's only one small hitch, which he neglects to mention. Negroponte leaves out that the idea of a Shakespeare pill, or indeed a pill to understand any aesthetic work, presumes that "knowledge of Shakespeare" is a concrete, measurable, temporally fixed, and disciplinarily bounded object. It presumes that this definable knowledge can be converted into a physical form by the appropriate chemical processes and then packaged as a tablet, sold, and taken at breakfast.

This version of a more just global future is constructed around many of the same presuppositions that undergird the clinico-critical diagnostic reading paradigm. Negroponte assumes that aesthetic objects contain "answers" that are obvious. These answers can be converted into a material form and delivered to targeted sites in the brain. Shakespeare is a thing to be known, not a manner of knowing. Indeed, Negroponte takes the methodologically unilateralist stance in which aesthetic objects do not have a role in imagining how the brain operates or contributing to contemporary neuroscientific research. These objects are brain food, in the most limited sense. The notion of a Shakespeare pill extrapolates from the extant methodological paradigm all too regularly allotting the neurosciences the hard work of determining what really happens in the brain and allotting aesthetic objects (as well as their creators and interpreters) the softer role of being explained by these facts, of narrativizing them, or of stimulating trackable brain activity. This is hardly the description of a different future. It does effectively reiterate the status quo.

It seems apropos to return at this point to Gayatri Spivak's introductory remarks in her 2012 book *An Aesthetic Education in the Era of Globalization*. Spivak there begins by asking what an "aesthetic education" (a concept first developed by the German writer Friedrich Schiller in 1795) would mean in an epoch defined by a shift to information command as a surrogate for knowing and reading. Schiller makes the case in his *Letters on the Aesthetic Education of Man* that only a training in the arts can form the basis for ethical community and state building. Globalization, which takes place on the level of capital and data, and not the "sensory equipment of experiencing being," Spivak argues, nevertheless demands that intellectuals in the humanities and imaginative social sciences trade their survivance in practices of studying "the singular and unverifiable" for the more "lethal and lugubrious consolations of rational choice."[2] The sustainability of the humanities increasingly requires humanists' consent to their own peripherality, shading into irrelevance, in a (predominantly U.S.-driven, predominantly English-language) university model that cannot help but find itself ever more complicit with a globalized feudality of the North.

Referring to a 1992 lecture she gave at the University of Cape Town after the end of apartheid, Spivak proposes redefining the idea of an aesthetic education by at once evoking and critiquing Schiller's project. This would involve the "ab-use" of Schiller in a process of what she describes as learning "to use the European Enlightenment from below."[3] The polysemy of the prefix "ab-" (Spivak points to its meaning as "below," "away from," "point of origin," "supporting," and "the duties of slaves") designates a form of engagement with

Schiller's Enlightenment-era work that is at once supportive and undermining, both a departure from Enlightenment and a return to it, simultaneously an exemplification of mastery and the embodiment of resistance.

Schiller's *Letters on the Aesthetic Education of Man* (1794) is itself a revision of Immanuel Kant's *Critique of Judgment* (1790). It corrects what Schiller perceived as a problem within Kantian aesthetics' disinterested critique: its disinterestedness. In the *Letters*, Schiller brings together Kant's aesthetic project with the moral project Kant outlines in the *Groundwork of the Metaphysics of Morals*. Schiller then proposes that art enables a balance between an innate human *Sachtrieb* (sensuous drive), which restricts being to the experience of fleeting incoming sensations as they unfold in time, and a *Formtrieb* (formal drive), which seeks self-preservation, continuity, and a unified sense of personhood in the face of such change. Art, he claims, awakens a *Spieltrieb* (play drive) that stabilizes these two competing drives. In balancing them, art enables human freedom. Schiller defines such freedom as the ability to take account of both one's own sensuous desires and the moral law and make an informed choice between them.

Spivak counters with the need for an aesthetic education that would be ethical not by virtue of facilitating this kind of balance but because it is able to repel the siren song of habitualized knowledge and preprogrammed learning. Both remain blind to their own hegemonic presuppositions and hence unable to accomplish what Schiller describes: the act of considering themselves. Schiller seems to indicate, however, that it would be possible to access the ethical directly and inject it into a monolithic learning subject, much like Negroponte's Shakespeare pill is supposed to "deliver" the bard into the bloodstream. Spivak, by contrast, stresses the need to treat art as a site of long-term epistemological training. It prepares learner-citizens to acknowledge both their own and their educators' (inevitable) prior contamination by historico-cultural and ideological context. Learning as the process of learning how to learn, Spivak observes. It is therefore less a matter of arriving at the right answers through an aesthetic education than knowing how to proceed by way of the right mistakes, the "correctness" of which lies outside evidentiality and cannot be reduced to a flattened truth value because it is held in check by the anticipation of a future anterior. The Enlightenment thus ab-usively conceived is no longer a catalogue of great discoveries about the existence of a reasonable norm but, at its best, a taxonomy of brilliant, incalculable errors, she notes. Thinking in this way avoids having to simply bracket the Enlightenment's status as a colonial project of brutalizing educational conformism that, as Spivak cites Gramsci identifying in the *Prison Notebooks*, deliberately drives out "the weak and nonconformists," foreclosing the development of a subaltern intellectual.

I am compelled by Spivak's argument but believe it merits an addition. Psychopower shows that globalization does take place on the level of the "sensory equipment of experiencing being." It does at least insofar as capitalism and data have, since the early nineteenth century, been able to represent the sensory equipment of experiencing being as precisely that which *can* be valued and measured. Because the mind sciences are built on the premise of mind's mathematical anatomization, they naturally enable a crossover between "experiencing being," data collection, and processes of globalization.

What, then, is the meaning of an aesthetic education in the wake of the neurocognitive turn? What does the study of art, broadly defined, offer—or how should one imagine what it might offer—if the brain always already has all the thoughts? Suggesting that it may be possible to play (in the Schillerian sense of *Speil*) within the double bind of materialist fact and subjectivist fiction is hardly succumbing to reactionary neurophobia or proposing that the humanities barricade themselves behind the walls of philology or new criticism. It merely acknowledges a pressing need to learn to use psychology, psychiatry, and the neurosciences from below, and to so learn how to ab-use Wilhelm Wundt, Emil Kraepelin, Santiago Ramón y Cajal, and Sigmund Freud in the process.

The need for this practice is what the Italian neuroscientist Antonio Damasio's important argument about René Descartes overlooks. Damasio identifies René Descartes's "error" as follows:

> This is Descartes' error: the abyssal separation between body and mind, between the sizable, dimensioned, mechanically operated indivisible bodily stuff, on the one hand, and the unsizable, unidimensioned, un-pushpullable, nondivisible mind stuff; the suggestion that reasoning, moral judgement, and the suffering that comes from physical pain or emotional upheaval might exist separately from the body. Specifically: the separation of the most refined operations of the mind from the structure and operation of a biological organism.[4]

In this passage, Damasio makes the same point that I do in this book's account of psychopower. The Cartesian and speculative philosophical understanding of the mind (understood as *res cogitans*) is indeed "unsizable," "unidimensioned," and "indivisible." The scientific model, by contrast, is of necessity one that presents the Cartesian *res cogitans* as "sizable," "dimensioned," and "mechanically operable." The scientific model would not qualify as scientific if it did not do so. Damasio's error is to assume that the sizable, dimensioned, and divisible nature of the mind is an ontological given, devoid of historically conditioned representational features associated with the nineteenth-century scientific account of the mind that was necessary for the modern mind sciences' academic and disciplinary split with speculative continental philosophy. This causes Damasio to neglect that psychical divisibility and psychical calculability were historically simultaneous with broader projects of standardization across the Western European university in the nineteenth century, a trend encouraged by the formation of modern nation-states, the rise and fall of empires, and the advent of the mass, or crowd. Recognizing as much reveals that mending what C. P. Snow called the "Two Cultures" divide between the humanities and the sciences cannot involve subsuming the humanities within the sciences.

This is why Mark Solms's neuropsychoanalysis, which draws on Antonio Damasio's insights, does not meet the criteria for subjectivity for which it has nevertheless become a byword. Solms's research in neuropsychoanalysis first took off in the late 1980s, when he proposed an unexpected compatibility between Freud's early neurological work and contemporary neuroscience based on Freud's "Project for a Scientific Psychology." Solms suggested that psychoanalysis had been a detour driven by Freud's lack of access to modern neurobiological methods enabling the scientific study of mental events.[5] Had Freud possessed fMRI scans, for example, discussions of the cortical fallacy (the argument that the seat of consciousness is in the brain's neocortex, which Solms contests) might have emerged sooner, leaving little need for the descriptive vagaries of psychoanalytic metapsychology. Motivated by studies showing a physiological basis for Freud's work on dreams, as well as research demonstrating the neurobiological reality of affect (Antonio Damasio, Jaak Panksepp, Oliver Sacks), Solms took his patients' stories about their experiences seriously. Emotions were "real" because they had a basis in the brain, meaning that the stories patients told were "real" as well. In other words, Solms proceeded on the grounds that these stories, which had been traditionally excluded from neuroscientific data, shed light on properly scientific phenomena. "My emerging dream-research findings had convinced me that subjective reports had a vital role to play in neuropsychology," he remarks.[6] Solms then presented neuropsychoanalysis' disciplinary bridge in terms of the neuroscientific viability of first-person narratives. "I have spent the last three decades . . . trying to restore subjectivity to neuroscience," he writes.[7]

This is an appealing link. It returns psychoanalysis and patient narratives to a place of prestige within positive knowledge and seems to offer a more humane, ethical, and listener-based clinical approach to suffering. Solms also repeatedly stresses the need to give Freud his due. He emphasizes his willingness to do so even in the face of warnings from colleagues about relating contemporary research with psychoanalytic pseudoscience. He makes a point of mapping psychoanalytic concepts onto testable reality, "translat[ing] such metapsychological insights into the language of anatomy and physiology" and correlating "Freud's inferences about the functional mechanisms of subjectivity with their physiological equivalents."[8] Research he conducted in partnership with the British neuroscientist Karl Friston even leads Solms to quantify the Freudian drive (*Trieb*) for the first time.[9] In an article published in 2020, he resurrects Freud's discarded "Project" and "completes it" by redefining

Freud's abbreviations (Q, Qή, φ, ψ, ω, W, V, M) in light of contemporary neuroscientific knowledge.[10]

Advocating for the neuroscientific validity of patient narratives is not the same as acknowledging a subjective dimension within the neurosciences, however. In fact, it is the opposite. Subjectivity in Solms's model is valid only to the extent that it can be framed as not being subjective at all. In other words, patient stories become scientifically permissible within neuropsychoanalysis by virtue of their amenability to empirical verification and connection with real physiological phenomena. They are scientifically admissible exclusively when translatable into data. Only in this form can they be included alongside traditionally quantitative neuroscientific findings. There is now functionally no difference between the two. Far from nuancing the objectivity-subjectivity binary, such work reaffirms it, insisting that subjective observations are viable only when they meet the standards of neuroscientific objectivity. Whence the priority given to quantifying the Freudian drive and "translating" psychoanalytic concepts into anatomical and physiological equivalents. They would remain illegitimate otherwise. Presumably, in the absence of affective neuroscience's demonstration that "emotions exist," Solms's patients' accounts would remain merely stories.

The forward-looking endeavor of updating Freud by adding the missing quantification to his "Project for a Scientific Psychology" is, for this reason, not a new one at all. It recommits to a scientific position that premiered beginning in the 1830s and that forms the basis for psychopower. Solms returns Freud to the psychopolitical focus on the calculable measurement of mass mental health from which Freud's work marks a unique departure, albeit not a complete break. Neuropsychoanalysis assumes, just like Antonio Damasio in his writing on René Descartes, that the mathematically quantitative dimension of Freud's work *is* missing, that it is somehow an absence in Freud, something to be restored, and not a crucially constative dimension of the psychoanalytic project. This neglects the ways that Freudian psychoanalysis remains strangely caught between a commitment to psychical divisibility and an resistance to quantitative precision. While citing Fechner and psychophysics throughout *The Interpretation of Dreams*, for example, Freud nevertheless insists on the uninterpretable "navel of the dream," that which cannot be analyzed, and cannot be measured. Neuropsychoanalysis, however, psychopolitically colonizes the Freudian project. This does not mean, of course, that Freudian psychoanalysis is devoid of subjectivity, ethnocentrism, racism, sexism, homophobia, problems of power inequality, or the complexities of rhetoric. On the contrary. It simply means that psychoanalysis is not alone in this regard.

Affective neuroscience and neuropsychoanalysis nevertheless miss this key point about their own representational commitments, which careful analysis of aesthetic objects helps show, because the neurosciences remain committed to a clinico-critical reading practice that regards extradisciplinary objects from the arts exclusively in terms of their manifest emotive or thematic content. To make space for the inclusion of aesthetic works and patient stories, often the only option for neuroscientists so inclined is to first treat these aesthetic objects as if they were data and then regard the "answers" they provide as proof of established neuroscientific facts.[11] Unfortunately, the result is an extraordinarily limited picture of the objects themselves. In Jaak Panksepp's breakthrough text *Affective Neuroscience* (1998), an excerpt from Lev Tolstoy's *The Kreutzer Sonata* (1890) introduces "Neural Control of Sexuality" because it is describing lust. A selection of poetry from Joan Walsh Anglund on love precedes "Love and the Social Bond." In Damasio's *The Stranger Order of Things*, the poet Fernando Pessoa's remark from the *Book of Disquiet* that "instruments grind and play away inside of me" prompts Damasio to offer Pessoa assistance "identifying" the physiological correlates of this metaphorical orchestra. Pessoa's stated inability to discern the "fiddlestrings and harps" sounding inside him (and "only [hear] the symphony") requires a neuroscientific explication.[12]

In the process, the matter of how representational mediation conditions these aesthetic works (and thereby also conditions the affective neuroscience and neuropsychoanalysis allegedly embodied in them) gets lost. Tolstoy's controversial portrait of female sexuality in *The Kreutzer Sonata* (the woman in question is murdered by her jealous husband) vanishes without a trace. That Anglund is writing for a children's book and that Pessoa's excerpt is from the "factless autobiography" of his fictitious alter-ego Bernardo Soares (not Pessoa as author) likewise disappears.[13] With them, a host of related questions dissolves into the ether. Is Tolstoy's presentation of a pathologically lustful femininity in *Kreuzer* naturalized by Panskepp's epigraph and then inscribed within the "sociobiology of sexual attachment" on which Panskepp's chapter focuses? Does the shadow of this move return in the misplaced bid for gender equity on display in Solms's fable of the "woman scientist" he calls "Eve Periaqueduct" in *The Hidden Spring*? Eve's name and job as a structural engineer on a leaky dam, in what Solms calls a fable making up much of chapter 8 in that book. It is hard not to feel that Eve "Enclosing-Channel" (*peri+aqeuduct*) has been reduced to her reproductive biology.[14] Does it matter that the Anglund poem offers a portrait of love sufficiently simplistic for a child audience? What does it mean to identify the physiological underpinnings of a fictional character's metaphorical orchestra in any case?

The tendency toward literalism would be less problematic if it did not raise a tricky question about Freud's "Project" around which Solms's justification for neuropsychoanalysis pivots. The issue involves knowing what Freud's "Project" depicts. Solms repeatedly cites the opening lines of the "Project," in which Freud states he is seeking "to represent psychical processes as quantitatively determinate states of specifiable material particles." Solms proposes that neuropsychoanalysis will make good on this abandoned but neuroscientifically promising endeavor.[15] Freud's references to "neurones" (the German is *Neurone*) is the basis for Solms's argument that Freud was a materialist after all, even if he subsequently went off track.

A great deal had already been written by historians of science and philosophers on whether Solms's position is historically compatible with Freud's work and so too on whether neuropsychoanalysis remains consistent with psychoanalysis.[16] These works make wonderful insights. They nevertheless neglect to interpret the "Project." This creates a tendency to repeat Solms's assumption that "neurones" means physical cells. There is a case to be made, however, that Freud's *Project* is metaphorical, just like Santiago Ramón y Cajal's work on the neuron doctrine, and that regarding it as such would benefit neuroscience.

The "Project" is a series of untitled, posthumously published letters to Wilhelm Fliess from 1895–1896 only designated "Project for a Scientific Psychology" by Freud's English translator. This means that the text is far less coherent than its English name would make it appear. In these letters, Freud seems to make a bid to treat "psychical processes as quantitatively determinate states of specifiable material particles." This is quickly undermined, however, by his qualitative approach. There is a substantive disjunction between what Freud says he is doing and what takes place on the page. First, there are Freud's symbols. The Greek letters and German abbreviations he uses appear mathematically rigorous but are quite ambiguous. Although Freud touts the need to work quantitatively, he does not make use of a single actual measurement in the "Project." "Φ, ψ, ω" respectively designate systems of "permeable" (*durchlässige*) neurons, "impermeable" (*undurchlässige*) neurons, and neurons that, excited by perception, give rise to "conscious sensations" (*bewusste Empfindungen*). Q is a quantity of magnitude in the external world, and the vaguer Qή something like a quantity of psychical magnitude. To reiterate, Freud never assigns concrete numerical values to Q or its variations; he simply states they have the quality of possessing quantity. Neither does he offer any means for measuring permeability. In fact, the "Project" little resembles Gustav Fechner or Wilhelm Wundt's psychophysical research, from which some of Freud's terminology is nevertheless drawn. This makes it hard to know whether writing a "New Project for a Scientific Psychology" completes Freud's text or entirely reimagines it.[17]

Second, Freud never says that psychical processes are quantitatively determined states. He merely says that they can be represented—the German is *darstellen* ("to depict, to portray")—as such. Freud's goal is "to represent [*darzustellen*] psychical processes as quantitatively determinate states of specifiable material particles." Solms ignores this qualifier, but it is an important, consistent feature of the "Project." Freud returns to the idea of *Darstellung* when discussing the possibility of representing memory and so too when specifying how to represent it. He writes about a *Darstellung* of the *Neurone* and entitles part 3 "Attempt to Represent [*darzustellen*] Normal ψ Processes."[18] His opening bid to speak quantitatively about the psyche even involves a double comparison: *representing* psychical processes *as* quantitatively determined states. Taking the "Project" at face value, however, the literalist reading focuses only on Freud's seeming materialism. This misses the "Project's" similarities to the differential play of psychic forces Freud describes in later, allegedly unscientific, work. Such literalism is thus also strangely insufficient, preferring a weak presentism to what Freud writes on the page.

Solms thereby neglects a reading of Freud that is arguably more pertinent to his endeavor because it is able to take account of subjectivity in the neurosciences, instead of objectivity by another name. Known in English as "The Project for a Scientific Psychology," the letters instead do something closer to inaugurating a humanist psychology. They mark the beginning of an evolving series of metaphors Freud will use across later publications to showcase different ways of approximating mental functioning. Writing just three years afterward, Freud comments in *The Interpretation of Dreams* (1899) that "we should picture [*vorstellen*] the instrument which carries out our mental functions as resembling [*wie etwa*, a bit like] a compound microscope or photographic apparatus, or something of the kind [*u. dgl.*, or something similar]."[19] As in the "Project," he calls on his reader to engage in an act of representation (the mental imaging of *Vorstellung* rather than the visual imaging of *Darstellung*), which is further extended by the requirement to consider this instrument as being "a bit like" (*wie etwa*) a compound microscope. He once again points out that psychical locality cannot be shown directly. Psychical locality is not a depicted object (the histological slide beneath the microscope, the numerical quantity) but only roughly analogous to the operations of an image-producing technology to which it can be rhetorically compared. This highlights Freud's attention to the difficulty of picturing the mind. Is measurement, the microscope, photography, or something else "like" these technologies most appropriate? In 1925, Freud proposed a further possibility: the mystic writing pad (*Wunderblock*). "A Note on the Mystic Writing Pad" suggests the pad's wax base as an analogue for the unconscious. And just as the children's toy's top sheet can be lifted to produce a fresh surface for repeated inscription, so too can consciousness, Freud argues, be made fresh for new impressions, even as the wax/unconscious archives past ones.[20]

These instances in Freud's work disclose how language and representation condition the understanding of mental functioning. As early-twentieth-century analogies for the mental apparatus, the microscope, camera, and mystic writing pad anticipated the shift in the 1950s to the computer as the next iteration in the chain, followed by plasticity in the early 2000s. More recently, there is the 4E approach (no less metaphorical for relying on abbreviations of four words beginning with the letter *e*, at least in English) and Karl Friston's free energy model. This last comes full circle by treating its own statistically determined picture of the mind-brain relationship as the basis for the future creation of an "artificially conscious mind," which Solms speculates could be generated by "reverse-engineering the [natural] mind's functional organization."[21] In order for this move to work, however, Solms has to (re)define consciousness. In his account, consciousness is the "uncertainty felt by [a self-organizing] system" equipped with a Markov blanket (for "model[ing] the world") and the ability to perceive associated computer hardware as its body. This redefinition relies on an analogy that portrays consciousness *as* a self-organizing system, a rhetorical feature on which he does not remark.[22]

One could, by contrast, maintain the complementarity between psychoanalysis and the neurosciences simply by acknowledging that Freud's and Cajal's work both had representational aspects. Accepting that Cajal's and Freud's outwardly literal neurons are less objective than hitherto understood wouldn't preclude neuropsychoanalysis, neuroimaging, statistical modeling efforts, or even a continental philosophy of the brain. It would merely introduce a psychopolitical perspective from which to consider their debt to representation in ways that would nuance these positions. In addition, it would enable the neurosciences to engage aesthetic objects and psychoanalytic concepts as a style of thinking that remains in productive epistemological tension with their own claims. To those who doubt that working in this way is possible, I would point out that it has already been available for years before this book. The art historian T. J. Clark's remarkable reading of Freud's "Project for a Scientific Psychology" through the French artist Paul Cézanne's painting *The Large Bathers* (1898–1905) operates in just this manner.[23] Neither Clark nor Solms cite the other.

Making the shift on a large scale, however, requires willingness to regard both aesthetic objects and psychoanalytic thought as valuable to the neurosciences in terms of their resistance, *Widerstand*, or Celanian *Gegenwort* to easy subsumption beneath knowledge-power's sovereign umbrella. Because a counterdisciplinary reading practice that would serve as the *Gegenwort* requires the ability to engage aesthetic objects and attend to language and rhetoric, however, it is specifically a task for scholars dealing with representation and aesthetic objects. It requires a set of skilled humanists with the courage to invest in the legitimacy of their own practices. Advocating for physics over metaphysics, by contrast, neglects that speculative philosophy only ceased to be the domain for the exploration of the mind when mental life could be anatomized and framed in physics' terms. The position regrettably essentializes the historical and disciplinary transition from speculative philosophy to the modern mind sciences, as if that transition resolved the relationship between subjectivity and objectivity, instead of opening a new chapter in it.

Listen to the echoes of Meret Oppenheim.

*Go ahead, try to get inside. When you have captured my bones and beheld what lies in my head, when you have entered me in the most intimate of ways, when you have run your eyes through my marrow, what will you have? What will you have? What will you have?*

# APPENDIX 1

# GERMAN EDITIONS OF EMIL KRAEPELIN'S TEXTBOOK OF PSYCHIATRY, 1883–1915

First edition. *Compendium der Psychiatrie zum Gebrauche für Studirende und Ärzte.* Leipzig: Abel Verlag, 1883.

Second edition. *Psychiatrie. Ein kurzes Lehrbuch für Studirende und Ärzte.* Leipzig: Abel Verlag, 1887.

Third edition. *Psychiatrie. Ein kurzes Lehrbuch für Studirende und Ärzte.* Leipzig: Abel Verlag, 1889.

Fourth edition. *Psychiatrie. Ein kurzes Lehrbuch für Studirende und Ärzte.* Leipzig: Abel Verlag, 1893.

Fifth edition. *Psychiatrie. Ein Lehrbuch für Studierende und Ärzte.* Leipzig: Verlag von Johann Ambrosius Barth, 1896.

Sixth edition. *Psychiatrie. Ein Lehrbuch für Studierende und Ärzte.* I. Band. *Allgemeine Psychiatrie.* Leipzig: Verlag von Johann Ambrosius Barth, 1899.

——. II. Band. *Klinische Psychiatrie.* Leipzig: Verlag von Johann Ambrosius Barth, 1899.

Seventh edition. *Psychiatrie. Ein Lehrbuch für Studierende und Ärzte.* I. Band. *Allgemeine Psychiatrie.* Leipzig: Verlag von Johann Ambrosius Barth, 1903.

——. II. Band. *Klinische Psychiatrie.* Leipzig: Verlag von Johann Ambrosius Barth, 1904.

Eighth edition. *Psychiatrie. Ein Lehrbuch für Studierende und Ärzte.* I. Band. *Allgemeine Psychiatrie.* Leipzig: Verlag von Johann Ambrosius Barth, 1909.

——. II. Band. *Klinische Psychiatrie.* I. Teil. Leipzig: Verlag von Johann Ambrosius Barth, 1910.

——. III. Band. *Klinische Psychiatrie.* II. Teil. Leipzig: Verlag von Johann Ambrosius Barth, 1913.

——. IV. Band. *Klinische Psychiatrie.* III. Teil. Leipzig: Verlag von Johann Ambrosius Barth, 1915.

# APPENDIX 2

# ENGLISH TRANSLATIONS OF EMIL KRAEPELIN'S PSYCHIATRIC TEXTBOOKS, 1902–2002

1902 *Clinical Psychiatry. A Textbook for Students and Physicians. Abstracted and Adapted from the Sixth German Edition of Kraepelin's "Lehrbuch der Psychiatrie"* by A. Ross Defendorf, Lecturer in Psychiatry at Yale University. New York: Macmillan Company, 1902.

This translation condenses the two volumes of the German original into a single volume by eliminating hundreds of pages of the 1899 text. Defendorf also rewrites sections of the work for an American audience and replaces the original illustrations with his own. Reprinted in 1904.

1907 *Clinical Psychiatry. A Textbook for Students and Physicians. Abstracted and Adapted from the Seventh German Edition of Kraepelin's "Lehrbuch der Psychiatrie"* by A. Ross Defendorf, M.D., Lecturer in Psychiatry at Yale University. New York: Macmillan Company, 1907.

Like the 1902 translation, the 1907 version takes liberties with selecting what to translate and adjusts Kraepelin's prose to fit an American medical context. Reprinted in 1912, 1915.

1913 *General Paresis.* Nervous and Mental Disease Monograph Series 14. Edited by Ely Jeliffe Smith and W. A. White. Authorized English Translation by J. W. Moore. New York: The Journal of Nervous and Mental Disease Publishing Company, 1913.

A translation of one chapter (chapter 6, "Die Dementia paralytica") from the eighth edition of *Psychiatrie. Ein Lehrbuch für Studierende und Ärzte.* II. Band Klinische Psychiatrie. I. Teil (1910).

1919 *Dementia Praecox and Paraphrenia.* Translated by R. Mary Barclay, M.A., M.B. From the Eighth German Edition of the "Text-Book of Psychiatry," vol. iii, part ii, section on Endogenous Dementias. Edited by George M. Robertson. Chicago: Chicago Medical Book Co., 1919.

A translation of one chapter from the eighth edition of *Psychiatrie. Ein Lehrbuch für Studierende und Ärzt* (1913). This chapter "Die endogenen Verblödungen," includes both "Dementia Praecox" and "Die paranoiden Verblödungen (Paraphrenien)." Barclay's translation is closer to the original than Defendorf's earlier work and does not attempt to adjust Kraepelin's writing for a different national context.

1921 *Manic Depressive Insanity and Paranoia.* Translated by R. Mary Barclay, M.A., M.B. Edited by George M. Robertson, M.D., F.R.C.P. Edin. Edinburgh: E & S. Livingstone, 1921.

A translation of two additional chapters (chapter 11, "Das Manisch-depressive Irresein" and chapter 14, "Die Verrücktheit (Paranoia)") of the eighth edition. Barclay indicates in the preface that he produced the translation of "to complete the psychoses."

2002 *Lifetime Editions of Kraepelin in English.* Bristol, England: Thoemmes, 2002.

This five-volume set collects and reprints selected English-language translations from those listed above, including them alongside an English translation of Kraepelin's published lectures on clinical psychiatry.

Volume 1: *Lectures on Clinical Psychiatry.*

Reprint of a 1913 translation of Kraepelin's *Einfürhrung in die Psychiatrische Klinik. Zweiunddressig Vorlesungen.* Zweite, durchgearbeitete Auflage. Leipzig: Barth Verlag, 1905.

Volume 2: *Clinical Psychiatry. A Textbook for Students and Physicians.*

Reprint of Defendorf's 1907 translation of the textbook.

Volume 3: *General Paresis.*

Reprint of 1913, above.

Volume 4: *Dementia Praecox and Paraphrenia.*

Reprint of 1919, above.

Volume 5: *Manic-Depressive Insanity and Paranoia.*

Reprint of 1921, above.

# NOTES

## Introduction. After Analysis: Literary Modernism and Diagnostic Reading

1. Gilles Deleuze and Félix Guattari's concept of "schizoanalysis" provides a good example from affect theory. Deleuze and Guattari were responding to Jacques Lacan's psychoanalytic understanding of neurosis and psychosis, but the multiple definitions of schizophrenia that emerged in the twentieth century have both complicated and confused schizoanalysis' subsequent scholastic reception. Ruth Leys gives an account of the complexities of defining trauma in *Trauma: A Genealogy* (Chicago: University of Chicago Press, 2000). Both Melanie Yergeau, *Authoring Autism: On Rhetoric and Neurological Queerness* (Durham, NC: Duke University Press, 2018), and Ralph James Savarese, *Say It Feelingly: Classic Novels, Autistic Readers, and the Schooling of a No-Good English Professor* (Durham, NC: Duke University Press, 2018), show autism's important role in disability studies and the neurodiversity movement. At the same time, the neurocognitive turn of the 1990s brought hopes that the DSM's psychopathological categories could be correlated with specific sites in the brain, an expectation that has proved elusive. For a scientific perspective on this problem, see Steven E. Hyman, "The Diagnosis of Mental Disorders: The Problem of Reification," *Annual Review of Clinical Psychology* 6 (2010): 155–79. For a historical one, see Anne Harrington, *Mind Fixers: Psychiatry's Troubled Search for the Biology of Mental Illness* (New York: Norton, 2019); and Allan V. Horwitz, "The DSM-5's Failed Revolution," in *DSM: A History of Psychiatry's Bible* (Baltimore: Johns Hopkins University Press, 2021), 116–43. Mark Solms's neuropsychoanalysis, based on research in affective neuroscience, makes use of Jaak Panksepp's all-caps glossary of "genetically ingrained brain emotional operating systems" (e.g., LOVE, RAGE, SEEKING) alongside Freudian terminology, seeking

to translate between the two lexicons but also thereby generating further linguistic complications. Solms addresses artificial intelligence in the final chapter of Mark Solms, *The Hidden Spring: A Journey to the Source of Consciousness* (London: Profile, 2021), though this is hardly the only place in which problems of psychodiagnostic nomenclature intersect with issues in AI.

2. These numbers correspond to the numerical coding system used to differentially classify mental disorders in the fifth edition of the DSM. Even if individual terms like "schizoid" and "autistic" date back to the nineteenth century, the coding shows how dramatically their definitions have shifted in the context of the twenty-first century's systematized psychiatry. The psychiatric section of the ICD also uses numerical coding. American Psychiatric Association, *Diagnostic and Statistical Manual of Mental Disorders*, 5th ed. (DSM-5) (Washington, DC: American Psychiatric Publishing, 2013).
3. Free indirect discourse could then be thought of as the caesura in the problem of thinking what a representation of mental life would be, insofar as free indirect discourse attempts to account for and indeed narrate thought. I raise this point without being able to attend to it at greater length. I would minimally indicate that my position here diverges from that of Timothy Bewes on free indirect discourse and Stathis Gourgouris on whether literature thinks. Bewes frames free indirect discourse in terms of an unacknowledged "capacity for thought" in the "historical formation of the novel" without acknowledging that the meaning of "thought" is historically circumscribed. Gourgouris describes literary thought as the antidote to an antimythical scientific practice but does not take up the question of whether literary thought is itself dependent on scientific understandings of how thought operates. Timothy Bewes, *Free Indirect: The Novel in a Postfictional Age* (New York: Columbia University Press, 2022), 5. Stathis Gourgouris, *Does Literature Think? Literature as Theory for an Antimythical Era* (Stanford, CA: Stanford University Press, 2003).
4. Adolphe Quetelet, *Sur l'homme et le développement de ses facultés, ou Essai de physique sociale* (Paris: Bachelier, Imprimeur-Librarie, 1835).
5. Kant opens "An Answer to the Question: What Is Enlightenment?" (1784) by defining Enlightenment as emergence from a "self-incurred minority [*Unmündigkeit*]" from an "inability to make use of one's own understanding [*Verstand*] without direction from another." In his posthumous *Anthropology from a Pragmatic Point of View* (1798) he specifies that *Verstand* is synonymous in a general sense with the "higher cognitive faculty [*das obere Erkenntnisvermögen*]" and points out that both "mental deficiencies [*Gemütsschwachen*]" and mental illnesses (*Gemütskrankheiten*) constitute "defects in the cognitive faculty [*Erkenntnisvermögens*]," which disrupt the understanding. Affirming that these defects are tantamount to an expulsion from *Mündigkeit*, Kant characterizes the madhouse in *Anthropology* as the "place where human beings, despite the maturity and strength of their age, must still, with regard to the smallest matters of life, be kept orderly through someone else's reason [*durch fremde Vernunft*]." A long passage in §48 specifies that even in the absence of such defects, age and sex may still sufficiently affect exercise of the understanding (*Verstand*) as to constitute grounds for immaturity. Immanuel Kant, *Anthropology from a Pragmatic Point of View*, trans. Robert B. Louden (Cambridge: Cambridge University Press, 2006), 90, 96–97, 102–4. Ben Conisbee Baer's *Indigenous Vanguards* offers an extended discussion of race and gender in Kant's description of both *Mündigkeit* and guardianship, working from a complementary consideration of modernist literature and colonialism. Ben Conisbee Baer, *Indigenous Vanguards: Education, National*

*Liberation, and the Limits of Modernism* (New York: Columbia University Press, 2019), introduction, chap. 1.

6. T. J. Clark, *Farewell to an Idea: Episodes in the History of Modernism* (New Haven, CT: Yale University Press, 1999). Eric Santner, *The Royal Remains: The People's Two Bodies and the Endgames of Sovereignty* (Chicago: University of Chicago Press, 2011). The link between sovereignty and sanity can of course be traced back further than Immanuel Kant's work in the *Anthropology.* Ernst Kantorowicz's account of the king's two bodies clearly identifies a psychological aspect of that medieval and renaissance model of sovereignty. As Kantorowicz observes, English sixteenth-century jurists defined the king's body politic as inherently void of "natural Defects and Imbecilities," unlike the king's body natural, which might easily become diseased or foolish. It is the immaterial body politic's inherent freedom from imbecility that Kantorowicz identifies as the key problem driving the plot of Shakespeare's *Richard II.* For Kantorowicz, Shakespeare's rendering of Richard II's foolishness demonstrates the body politic, not just Richard II's body natural, in the grip of an imbecility that foreshadows the king's necessary fall from power. "Here [act 3, scene 3] 'Imbecility' seems to hold sway. And yet, the very bottom has not yet been reached. Each scene progressively designates a new low. 'King body natural' in the first scene and 'Kingly Fool' in the second." My own point is that the issue of the body politic's sanity persists across the transition from monarchial to popular sovereignty. Western political theology implies that sanity (freedom from "imbecilities") is a precondition for a sovereign people. Ernst H. Kantorowicz, *The King's Two Bodies: A Study in Mediaeval Political Theology* (Princeton, NJ: Princeton University Press, 1997), 7, 34.
7. Jennifer Spitzer, *Secret Sharers: The Intimate Rivalries of Modernism and Psychoanalysis* (New York: Fordham University Press, 2023), suggests exchanges between modernist authors like D. H. Lawrence, Vladimir Nabokov, and Virginia Woolf and psychoanalysis were "secret." I do not dispute that they were for those writers with whom Spitzer works in her compelling book. The problem is that framing the relationship between modernism and psychoanalysis as "secretive" imagines that psychoanalysis has not already long been the dominant scholastic mode of engaging modernism's relationship to the psyche.
8. Paul Hoff, "On Reification of Mental Illness: Historical and Conceptual Issues from Emil Kraepelin and Eugen Bleuler to DSM-5," in *Philosophical Issues in Psychiatry IV. Psychiatric Nosology*, ed. Kenneth S. Kendler and Josef Parnas (Oxford: Oxford University Press, 2017): 107–20. My comment about the history of the subject is referring to and paraphrasing from Fredric Jameson's thesis in *The Political Unconscious* (Ithaca, NY: Cornell University Press, 1981) about the need to always historicize. George Wilhelm Friedrich Hegel, Wilhelm Wundt, Emil Kraepelin, and Sigmund Freud use the German term *Bewußtsein* for "consciousness" but have different definitions of it. Vladimir Lenin, by contrast, uses the Russian *soznatel'nost'*, which (unlike the English and German) cannot mean general psychological awareness and is restricted to class-political consciousness.
9. Survey volumes on modernism often dedicate space to a discussion of the role of consciousness as such in the modernist novel. This accurately reflects a trend to present consciousness as a timeless ontological given that modernist literary experimentation historically captured in various novel ways. It does little to situate consciousness itself as a historically mediated category. See, for example, Pericles Lewis, ed., *The Cambridge Introduction to Modernism* (Cambridge: Cambridge University Press, 2007), 156–61.

10. Wundt's article "Die Geschwindigkeit des Gedankens" ("The Speed of Thought") was published in 1862, after Marx's *Critique of Political Economy*. The experiments he conducted for it, however, were carried out between 1857 and 1864, during his time as an assistant in Hermann von Helmholz's physiological laboratory at the University of Heidelberg.
11. Karl Marx, *A Contribution the Critique of Political Economy*, trans. S. W. Ryazanskaya (New York: Lawrence and Wishart, 1971), 20–21.
12. This point relates to a comment Marx makes at the beginning of *The Eighteenth Brumaire of Louis Bonaparte* (1851–1852), in *Karl Marx and Friedrich Engels Collected Works* (New York: International Publishers, 1975), 11: 99–197. "The tradition of all the dead generations weighs like a nightmare on the brain [*Gehirn*] of the living." While it is possible to take this sentence as a reference to the way that history changes the brain, such a perspective is oddly ahistorical as it retroactively imposes the logic of contemporary neuroscience on Marx's writing. It would be better to see Marx as indirectly commenting on the scientific advent of the brain as the new site at which neurologists like Wilhelm Griesinger (1817–1868) imagined history might take place.
13. Whereas the Ljubljana School frames Hegel and Jacques Lacan as complementary, my position returns to a strange fracture between the Hegelian account of consciousness and Lacan's work. It is possible to read Jacques Lacan's claim that Marx "invented the symptom" in terms of a "fundamental homology between the interpretive procedure of Marx and Freud." It is also possible to see Marx as independently calling for a historicization of both transcendental accounts of mind like Hegel's and of their modern scientific counterparts. Slavoj Žižek admittedly already acknowledges this possibility in passing in *The Sublime Object of Ideology* (London: Verso, 1989), 10.
14. On immunitas, see Roberto Esposito, *Bios: Biopolitics and Philosophy*, trans. Timothy Campbell (Minneapolis: University of Minnesota Press, 2008). Judith Butler describes precarity in *Precarious Life: The Powers of Mourning and Violence* (London: Verso, 2004). Giorgio Agamben develops his biopolitical concept of bare life in *Homo Sacer: Sovereign Power and Bare Life*, trans. Daniel Heller-Roazen (Stanford CA: Stanford University Press, 1998). In Agamben's more recent work *Hölderlin's Madness: Chronicle of a Dwelling Life, 1806–1843*, trans. Alta L. Price (Calcutta: Seagull, 2023), Agamben moves from biopower toward psychopower by refusing to clinically diagnose the poet Friedrich Hölderlin and instead "juxtapose[ing] the chronicle of Hölderlin's years of madness with the chronology of the history of Europe during those same years" (13).
15. Anson Rabinbach, *The Human Motor* (Berkeley: University of California Press, 1990). See chapters 6 and 7 for Rabinbach's discussion of psychology and psychiatry. See also Katja Guenther, *Localization and Its Discontents* (Chicago: University of Chicago Press, 2015); Katja Guenther, *The Mirror and the Mind* (Princeton, NJ: Princeton University Press, 2022); Laura Otis, *Membranes: Metaphors of Invasion in Nineteenth-Century Literature Science and Politics* (Baltimore: Johns Hopkins University Press, 1999); Nikolas Rose, *Governing the Soul: The Shaping of the Private Self* (London: Free Association, 1999); Nikolas S. Rose and Joelle M. Abi-Rached, *Neuro: The New Brain Sciences and the Management of the Mind* (Princeton, NJ : Princeton University Press, 2013); Nikolas Rose, *Our Psychiatric Future* (Medford, MA: Polity, 2018).
16. Kurt Danziger, *Constructing the Subject: Historical Origins of Psychological Research* (Cambridge: Cambridge University Press, 1990); Kurt Danziger, *Naming the Mind: How Psychology Found Its Language* (London: SAGE, 1997); Kurt Danziger, *Marking the Mind: A History of Memory* (Cambridge: Cambridge University Press, 2008);

Fernando Vidal, "Brainhood, Anthropological Figure of Modernity," *History of the Human Sciences* 22, no. 1 (2009): 5–36; Fernando Vidal and Francisco Ortega, *Being Brains: Making the Cerebral Subject* (New York: Fordham University Press, 2017); Stefanos Geroulanos, "The Plastic Self and Prescription Psychology: Ethnopsychology, Crowd Psychology, and Psychotechnics, 1890–1920," *Republics of Letters* 3, no. 2 (January 2014), http://arcade.stanford.edu/rofl/plastic-self-and-prescription-psychology; Stefanos Geroulanos, "The Brain in Abeyance: Freud and the Claim of Neuropsychoanalysis," *History of the Present* 1, no. 2 (Fall 2011): 219–43. Ian Hacking writes about multiple personality disorder in *Rewriting the Soul: Multiple Personality Disorders and the Sciences of Memory* (Princeton, NJ: Princeton University Press, 1995) and about transient mental illness in *Mad Travelers: Reflections on the Reality of Transient Mental Illness* (Charlottesville, VA: University Press of Virginia, 1998).

17. There are far too many to list all here, so I will restrict myself to a few recent highlights alongside a second mention of Anson Rabinbach and Katja Guenther's work (cited earlier) and Edward Shorter, *History of Psychiatry* (New York: Wiley, 1997). See Georges Didi-Huberman, *Invention of Hysteria: Charcot and the Photographic Iconography of the Salpêtrière*, trans. Alisa Hartz (Cambridge, MA: MIT Press, 2003); Gary Greenberg, *The Book of Woe: The DSM and the Unmaking of Psychiatry* (New York: Plume, 2014); David Hellerstein, *The Couch, The Clinic, and the Scanner: Stories from Three Revolutionary Eras of Mind* (New York: Columbia University Press, 2023); Allan V. Horwitz, *PTSD: A Short History* (Baltimore, MD: Johns Hopkins University Press, 2021); Allan V. Horwitz, *DSM: A History of Psychiatry's Bible* (Baltimore: Johns Hopkins University Press, 2021); Ruth Leys, *Trauma: A Genealogy* (Chicago: University of Chicago Press, 2000); Ruth Leys, *The Ascent of Affect: Genealogy and Critique* (Chicago: University of Chicago Press, 2017); Andreas Mayer and Lydia Martinelli, *Dreaming by the Book: Freud's "The Interpretation of Dreams" and the History of the Psychoanalytic Movement*, trans. Susan Fairfield (New York: Other Press, 2003); Andreas Mayer, *Sites of the Unconscious: Hypnosis and the Emergence of the Psychoanalytic Setting* (Chicago: University of Chicago Press, 2013); Andreas Mayer, *Sigmund Freud zur Einführung* (Hamburg: Junius Verlag GmbH, 2016); Camille Robcis, *Disalienation: Politics, Philosophy, and Radical Psychiatry in Postwar France* (Chicago: University of Chicago Press, 2021); Edward Shorter and Max Fink, *The Madness of Fear: A History of Catatonia* (Oxford: Oxford University Press, 2018). See also selected volumes in the Johns Hopkins University Press series Biographies of Disease.

18. I am elaborating on the discussion of the metronome in Jacques Derrida, *Rogues: Two Essays on Reason*, trans. Pascale-Anne Brault and Michael Naas (Stanford, CA: Stanford University Press, 2005), 55.

19. Two recent examples: Mark Solms, the founder of neuropsychoanalysis (committed to rehabilitating Freud's research as neuroscientific by treating patients' subjective accounts as valid scientific evidence) castigates metaphysics throughout *The Hidden Spring*, writing that "philosophers have assigned this problem [the nature of consciousness] to what they call 'metaphysics,' which is a way of saying they don't think it can be resolved scientifically." The Nobel Prize–winning neuroscientist Eric R. Kandel, in *Reductionism in Art and Brain Science: Bridging the Two Cultures* (New York: Columbia University Press, 2016), makes the case that abstract art's reduction of complex figuration to simple forms is the same methodology at work in science. The difficulty is that this position subsumes art within the "investigative, experimental approach" in the name of overcoming the bridge between the humanities and sciences. I have no criticism of either claim insofar as both reflect the nineteenth-century

separation of the empirical study of the mind from its continental philosophical precursor, enabling the former to enter into the ranks of medical science. I am less convinced, however, that repeating this disciplinary logic is the basis for resolving the "two cultures" divide (C. P. Snow) between the humanities and sciences. After all, the division of a unified philosophy into the humanities and sciences produced it.

20. Chanda Prescod-Weinstein, *The Disordered Cosmos: A Journey Into Dark Matter, Spacetime, and Dreams Deferred* (New York: Bold Type, 2021); Denise Ferreira da Silva, *Unpayable Debt* (London: Sternberg, 2022).
21. Jacqueline Rose, *On Violence and On Violence Against Women* (New York: Picador/ Farrar, Straus and Giroux, 2021), 1.
22. Catherine Malabou, *The New Wounded: From Neurosis to Brain Damage*, trans. Steven Miller (New York: Fordham University Press, 2012), xiii. I cite from Miller's translation but use the book's French title here, which the English modifies: *Les nouveaux blessés. De Freud à la neurologie, penser les traumatismes contemporains.*
23. The two positions raise a host of fascinating questions about the relationship between violence and visibility, representations of violence, structural violence, the violence of abstraction, agency and violence, and the link (causal or otherwise) between violence and suffering. I bracket them for the moment to allow Rose and Malabou to lay out their own positions.
24. I temporarily set aside discussions on Freud's biologism and neuropsychoanalysis, to which I return in the afterword to this book.
25. Rose, *On Violence*, 3.
26. Rose, *On Violence*, 1.
27. Rose, *On Violence*, 3.
28. Rose, *On Violence*, 171, 175.
29. Jacqueline Rose, *The Haunting of Sylvia Plath* (Cambridge, MA: Harvard University Press, 1992), 4.
30. Rose, *On Violence*, chap. 5: "Writing Violence: From Modernism to Eimear McBride," 199–228.
31. Rose, *On Violence*, 210.
32. Malabou, *The New Wounded*, xiii. Malabou uses an epigraph from Marcel Proust's *Sodom and Gomorrah* to introduce her description of her grandmother's Alzheimer's and her book.
33. Malabou, *The New Wounded*, xvi–xvii.
34. Malabou, *The New Wounded*, xvii.
35. Malabou presents PTSD's emergence in the grammar of scientific discovery, framing it as something the military medical community belatedly recognized after Vietnam veterans had attested to the diagnostic category's reality for years. Malabou, *The New Wounded*, 149, 150. Historians of PTSD and the DSM offer a different perspective.
36. Horwitz, *PTSD*, 88–89, 85–88.
37. Horwitz, *PTSD*, 96–98; Hannah S. Decker, *The Making of DSM-III: A Diagnostic Manual's Conquest of American Psychiatry* (Oxford: Oxford University Press, 2013), 274–75.
38. The matter of how and to what degree Kraepelin's work influenced the DSM-III and subsequent edition is a topic of ongoing debate. There is a consensus, however, that the DSM-III would have been impossible without Kraepelin's creation of a differential diagnostic system.
39. Horwitz, *PTSD*, 94.

40. Bruno Bettelheim, *The Empty Fortress: Infantile Autism and the Birth of the Self* (New York: Free Press, 1967). Bettelheim's theory about the link between concentration camp victims and children with autism helped establish the (now debunked) "refrigerator mothers" hypothesis. As Bettelheim writes in his earlier piece "Schizophrenia as a Reaction to Extreme Situations," the mother's lack of sufficient warmth toward her child produced an "extreme situation" in which the child felt, like the concentration camp victim, "totally helpless in the face of threats to his very life, at the mercy of insensitive powers . . . deprived of any intrapersonal, need-satisfying relationship." Bruno Bettleheim, "Childhood Schizophrenia: Symposium 1955:3. Schizophrenia as a Reaction to Extreme Situations," *American Journal of Orthopsychiatry* 26, no. 3 (1955): 507–18. I mention this as an interesting complication to Malabou's feminist thesis in *The New Wounded* and her subsequent books.
41. Malabou, *The New Wounded*, 149–51.
42. Malabou is thinking here specifically of the medical case of the German lieutenant Kaunders (whose skull was fractured by Russian gunfire in World War I). Kaunders became the subject of a legal trial in which Freud was called to testify as an expert witness because Kaunders had been accused of malingering (feigning illness) to avoid a return to the battlefield. Freud's report concluded that Kaunders's illness was indeed real but psychosexual in nature and so only treatable by psychoanalysis, not electroshock therapy. Freud's testimony is published as "Memorandum on the Electrical Treatment of War Neurotics" and appears in Sigmund Freud, *Standard Edition of the Complete Psychological Works of Sigmund Freud*, ed. and trans. James Strachey (London: Hogarth, 1950), 17:211–15.
43. Malabou, *The New Wounded*, 115, 155; italics in the original.
44. As a diagnosis, its stress on the "post" corrects what can now be cast as the pretraumatic Freudian neuroses, or anterior neuroses, which have always already anticipated the physical wound, making it impossible for true accidents to ever take place. The point reappears in Catherine Malabou, *Ontology of the Accident: An Essay on Destructive Plasticity*, trans. Carolyn Shread (Cambridge: Polity, 2009).
45. Malabou, *The New Wounded*, 17. In the second, untranslated, French edition of the book, she amplifies this point: "The great specter of such apparitions discloses [*révèle*] the economy of a contemporary global posttraumatic condition [*de condition post-traumatique contemporaine mondiale*] that demands to be thought." Catherine Malabou, *Les nouveaux blessés*, 2nd ed. (Paris: Presses Universitaires de France, 2017), 41. References to the globalized and uniform nature of PTSD abound in *The New Wounded*. The problem is "precisely that of the global phenomenon of psychic violence [*phénomène global de la violence psychique*]" (167–68). "The posttraumatic state is a gaping wound that appears on all the battlefields of contemporary society. A normal reaction to an abnormal situation, it inscribes the enigma of its event upon the global stage [*sur la scene mondiale*]" (161).
46. Malabou, *The New Wounded*, 155, 168, 156.
47. The universality of this position is important as much because of Malabou's background as a reader of Hegel—see *The Future of Hegel: Plasticity, Temporality and Dialectic*, trans. Lisabeth During (London: Routledge, 2004)—as because it helps address a point that the sociologist Nikolas Rose brings up in his book *Our Psychiatric Future*. Rose accurately points out that for all the public attention allotted to the DSM, it is neither the diagnostic manual used everywhere in the world nor even the most common one internationally. Some of the fuss around it is undeserving. I agree

with Rose to a point but selected the DSM less because I believe in its global reach or essential priority than because—as the case of Malabou (a French philosopher writing for a global audience) shows—there is a pervasive tendency to *imagine* that the DSM can be used everywhere or that it applies everywhere because its diseases are biological in nature. This is also true of the ICD.

48. Slavoj Žižek, "Descartes and the Post-Traumatic Subject: On Catherine Malabou's *Les nouveaux blessés* and Other Autistic Monsters," *Qui Parle* 17, no. 2 (Spring/Summer 2009): 123–47. Malabou's response only appears in the preface of the second (French) edition of her book.
49. Framing the contemporary subject as beyond love and hate, he argued, neglected that jouissance continued to play a role in cerebral pathology. Just because an event happened accidentally didn't mean that a phantasmatic place hadn't already been prepared for it in the subject's imagination. Malabou's assertion that Freud never articulated a "beyond" of the pleasure principle that did not rely on sexuality thus missed that there is no such thing as pure pleasure. Pleasure is inherently self-destructive. Her position had ignored Lacan's key insight about the difference between "pleasure (*Lust*, *plaisir*) and enjoyment (*Geniessen*, *jouissance*)." The description of wounded subjects who survived their own death merely repeated Lacan's previous insight about the barred subject, the $, elaborated in the L-schema. Žižek, "Descartes," 136.
50. Žižek, "Descartes," 137.
51. Malabou, *Les nouveaux blessés*, 2nd ed., xi.
52. This is my own reading of the epigraph, not Malabou's. She does not offer one after presenting the lines at the book's opening. The interpretation is consistent, however, with comments in *The New Wounded* about psychoanalysis's failure to keep up with modern medical imaging, its lack of attention to the brain, and the thesis that Freud shamefully ignored cerebral pathology.
53. IRT allegedly infused Dostoevsky's work with "a depth of understanding . . . a deepening of emotional response." Oliver Sacks, *An Anthropologist on Mars: Seven Paradoxical Tales* (New York: Vintage, 1996), 164.
54. Sacks, *An Anthropologist on Mars*, 164n3.
55. Oliver Sacks, *The Man Who Mistook His Wife for a Hat and Other Clinical Tales* (New York: Harper Collins, 1970), 280n15.
56. Malabou, *The New Wounded*, 53–54.
57. Malabou, *The New Wounded*, 54.
58. Gayatri Spivak, "Echo," *New Literary History* 24, no. 1, "Culture and Everyday Life" (Winter 1993): 17–43; reprinted as Gayatri Spivak, "Echo," in *An Aesthetic Education in the Era of Globalization* (Cambridge, MA: Harvard University Press, 2013), 218–40; citations are to this later edition.
59. "Without the risks or responsibilities of transference, at least implicitly diagnostic and taxonomic, ignoring geopolitical and historical detail in the interest of making group behavior intelligible, and not accountable to any mode of verification, the brilliance of psychoanalytic cultural criticism has always left me a bit suspicious." Spivak, *An Aesthetic Education*, 220. Spivak is here closely in conversation with Derrida's later writings on psychoanalysis and culture.
60. Freud's opens "On Narcissism" with the contention that "the term narcissism is derived from clinical description and was chosen by Paul Näcke in 1899." Spivak's approach counters that the term *narcissism* comes from literature and not from any of the nineteenth-century psychiatric sources Freud cites in a later footnote.
61. Spivak, *An Aesthetic Education*, 220.

62. These texts are certainly in conversation given their publication dates. "Echo" appeared in 1993, just a few years after "Can the Subaltern Speak?" of 1988. See Gayatri Spivak, "Can the Subaltern Speak?," in *Marxism and the Interpretation of Culture*, ed. Lawrence Grossberg and Cary Nelson (Urbana: University of Illinois Press, 1988): 271–313.
63. Spivak, *An Aesthetic Education*, 225–26, 235.
64. Spivak, *An Aesthetic Education*, 226–27.
65. See, for example, Stathis Gourgouris, ed., *Freud and Fundamentalism* (New York: Fordham University Press, 2010).
66. The category "culture-bound syndromes" premiered in DSM-IV and was subsequently replaced in DSM-5.
67. Malabou, *The New Wounded*, xix.
68. Malabou, *The New Wounded*, xv.
69. Given that no clinical trials were done to include PTSD in the DSM, as Horwitz points out in his *PTSD*, that category is ironically the most Freudian of diagnoses.
70. "By the end of the twentieth century, there seemed to be no doubt that the cutting edge of research on mental disorders lay in 'biochemical abnormalities, neuroendocrine abnormalities, structural brain abnormalities, and genetic anomalies.' . . . There was, however, a fly in the ointment. The findings from neuroscientific research were far from what researchers expected. They revealed a striking disconnect between the DSM model and their understanding of mental disorders." Horwitz, *DSM*, 118.
71. Ian Hacking, "Making Up People: Clinical Classifications," *London Review of Books* 28, no. 16–17 (August 2006), https://www.lrb.co.uk/the-paper/v28/n16/ian-hacking/making-up-people.
72. Gilles Deleuze, *Coldness and Cruelty*, in Gilles Deleuze and Leopold von Sacher-Masoch, *Masochism* (New York: Zone, 1989), 14.
73. Deleuze, *Coldness and Cruelty*, 16, 15.
74. In his response to Malabou, Žižek suggests PTSD can be integrated into the Freudian account, a position that misses the epistemological difference between the DSM's categories and those of psychoanalysis. He remains within the clinical terminology of DSM-III and its subsequent editions, taking for granted that "autistic" and "PTSD" are categories with fixed definitions that can inserted into the Freudian lexicon or analyzed in terms of it. This overlooks autism's and PTSD's redefinitions in different editions of the DSM. It also misses that, as part of a diagnostic encyclopedia, they form part of the symbolic order (not an entry into the Real). Would a Lacanian version of the DSM's posttraumatic subject then truly offer an exit from the enclosure of the commons, as Žižek proposes? The DSM's posttraumatic diagnosis is already linked to capitalist enterprise as part of a diagnostic system made for privatized health insurance and tied to the psychopharmaceutical industry, giving it the potential to amplify (not diminish) an ongoing process of proletarianization that privatizes the commons. Žižek's willingness to diagnose modernist literary works in his response to Malabou is then awkwardly caught between a cognitivist position that understands aesthetic objects as the literary expression of a neurological wounding and a Lacanian one seeing them as an encounter with the meaningless Real. Žižek, "Descartes," 140, 145–47.
75. Having divided, numbered, and named these four diagnostic reading paradigms, I would also want to maintain the relatively indistinct nature of their borders, the impossibility of their perfect enumeration, and the inadequacy of their titles.

76. Jessica Berman, "Modernism's Possible Geographies," in *Geomodernisms: Race, Modernism, Modernity*, ed. Laura Doyle and Laura Winkiel (Bloomington: Indiana University Press, 2005).
77. Elund Summers-Bremner, "Unreal City and Dream Deferred: Psychogeographies of Modernism in T. S. Eliot and Langston Hughes," in *Geomodernisms: Race, Modernism, Modernity*, ed. Laura Doyle and Laura Winkiel (Bloomington: Indiana University Press, 2005), 262.
78. Jacques Derrida notes the force of a *mondialisation* (worldwideization) generated by the formalized institutions governing psychoanalysis in his late essays "Geopsychoanalysis," trans. Donald Nicholson-Smith, *American Imago* 48, no. 2 (1991): 199–231, and "Psychoanalysis Searches the States of Its Soul: The Impossible Beyond of a Sovereign Cruelty," in Jacques Derrida and Peggy Kamuf, *Without Alibi* (Stanford, CA: Stanford University Press, 2002), 238–80. Engaging Derrida and Heidegger, Ranjana Khanna comments on psychoanalytic worlding in her *Dark Continents: Psychoanalysis and Colonialism* (Durham, NC: Duke University Press, 2003). Without dealing directly with Derridean *mondialisation*, many works of postcolonial research on psychoanalysis also take up the psychoanalytic relationship to empire and global space. See Anne A. Cheng, *The Melancholy of Race: Psychoanalysis, Assimilation, and Grief* (Oxford: Oxford University Press, 2001); Paul Gilroy, *Postcolonial Melancholia* (New York: Columbia University Press, 2005); Deborah Jenson, Warwick Anderson, and Richard C. Keller, eds., *Unconscious Dominions: Psychoanalysis, Colonial Trauma, and Global Sovereignties* (Durham, NC: Duke University Press, 2011); Dina Al-Kassim, *On Pain of Speech: Fantasies of the First Order and the Literary Rant* (Berkeley: University of California Press, 2010); Richard C. Keller, *Colonial Madness: Psychiatry in French North Africa* (Chicago: University of Chicago Press, 2007); Ankhi Mukherjee, *Unseen City: The Psychic Lives of the Urban Poor* (Cambridge: Cambridge University Press, 2022); as well as with Cathy Caruth's work on trauma in her groundbreaking *Unclaimed Experience: Trauma, Narrative and History* (Baltimore: Johns Hopkins University Press, 1996). My thinking on global modernism and psychogeographies has also been inspired by Jean Khalfa and Robert Young's release of Frantz Fanon's unpublished commentary on psychiatry and sociotherapy in a North African context in a single annotated volume. In French, see Frantz Fanon, Jean Khalfa, and Robert Young, *Écrits sur l'aliénation et la liberté* (Paris: Éditions La Découverte, 2015). In English, see Frantz Fanon, Jean Khalfa, Robert Young, and Steve Corcoran, *Alienation and Freedom* (London: Bloomsbury Academic, 2018). David S. Marriott's scholarship on Frantz Fanon's relationship to psychiatry and psychoanalysis in *Whither Fanon? Studies on the Blackness of Being* (Stanford, CA: Stanford University Press, 2018) and in *Lacan Noir: Lacan and Afro-Pessimism* (New York: Palgrave Macmillan, 2021) deserves mention here as well.
79. Elizabeth Wurtzel, *Prozac Nation* (New York: Riverhead, 1995); Sacks, *An Anthropologist on Mars*; Ethan Watters, *Crazy Like Us: The Globalization of the American Psyche* (New York: Free Press, 2010); Dana Becker, *One Nation Under Stress* (New York: Oxford University, Press 2013); William Davies, *Nervous States: Democracy and the Decline of Reason* (New York: Norton, 2019); Matthew Crippen and Jay Skulkin, *Mind Ecologies: Brain, Body, and World* (New York: Columbia University Press, 2020); and Anna Lembke, *Dopamine Nation* (New York: Penguin Random House, 2023).
80. Wilhelm Wundt, *Völkerpsychologie. Eine Untersuchung der Entwicklungsgesetze von Sprache, Mythus und Sitte* (Leipzig: Wilhelm Engelmann, 1900–1920); Georges

Dumas, *Traité de psychologie* (Paris: F. Alcan, 1923–1924). Dumas was Claude Lévi-Strauss's instructor at the Sorbonne—Levi-Strauss describes him at some length at the beginning of *Tristes Tropiques*—and did extensive work on psychiatry from a position in Brazil. This psychiatric aspect of structural anthropology has, to the best of my knowledge, gone unnoticed in secondary commentary on the ethnocentrism of structural linguistics.

81. Robcis, *Disalienation*.
82. Nikolas S. Rose and Des Fitzgerald. *The Urban Brain: Mental Health in the Vital City* (Princeton, NJ: Princeton University Press, 2022); Georg Simmel, "The Metropolis and Mental Life," in *The Sociology of George Simmel*, ed. K. H. Wolff (New York: Free Press, 1950), 409–24.
83. Laura Salisbury and Andrew Shail, eds., *Neurology and Modernity: A Cultural History of Nervous Systems, 1800–1950* (New York: Palgrave Macmillan, 2010).
84. David Freis, *Psycho-Politics Between the World Wars: Psychiatry and Society in Germany, Austria, and Switzerland* (Cham, Switzerland: Palgrave Macmillan, 2019).
85. Deligny's maps followed autistic children's daily movements at an experimental community Deligny developed in the Cévennes region of southern France. He used them to explore the possibility of decodifying gridded and standardized spaces that would allow his patients to move differently in the world. Reproductions can be found in Fernand Deligny and Sandra Alvarez de Toledo, *Cartes et lignes d'erre. Traces du reseau de Fernand Deligny, 1969–1979* (Paris: L'Arachnéen, 2013). Howard F. Stein and William G. Niederland, eds., *Maps from the Mind: Readings in Pyschogeography* (Norman: University of Oklahoma Press, 1989), xvii.
86. Sylvia Wynter, "Unsettling the Coloniality of Being/Power/Truth/Freedom: Towards the Human, After Man, Its Overrepresentation," *CR: The New Centennial Review* 3, no. 3 (Fall 2003): 257–337.
87. Denise Ferreira da Silva, *Toward a Global Idea of Race* (Minneapolis: University of Minnesota Press, 2007). See also Rei Terada, *Metaracial: Hegel, Antiblackness, and Political Identity* (Chicago: University of Chicago Press, 2023).
88. Mark Wollaeger and Matt Eatough, eds., *The Oxford Handbook of Global Modernisms* (Oxford: Oxford University Press, 2012); Michael Levenson, ed., *The Cambridge Companion to Modernism* (Cambridge: Cambridge University Press, 1999); Douglas Mao, ed., *The New Modernist Studies* (Cambridge: Cambridge University Press, 2021). Eric Hayot and Rebecca Walkowitz, eds., *A New Vocabulary for Global Modernism* (New York: Columbia University Press, 2016).
89. Benjamin Baltaser, *Anti-Imperialist Modernism: Race and Transnational Radical Culture from the Great Depression to the Cold War* (Ann Arbor: University of Michigan Press, 2015); Jessica Berman, *Modernist Fiction, Cosmopolitanism, and the Politics of Community* (Cambridge: Cambridge University Press 2001); Jessica Berman, *Modernist Commitments: Ethics, Politics, and Transnational Modernism* (New York: Columbia University Press, 2012); Katerina Clark, *Eurasia Without Borders: The Dream of a Leftist Literary Commons, 1919–1943* (Cambridge, MA: Belknap Press of Harvard University Press, 2021); Rossen Djagalov, *From Internationalism to Postcolonialism: Literature and Cinema Between the Second and the Third Worlds* (Montreal: McGill-Queen's University Press, 2020); Susan Stanford Friedman, "Planetarity: Musing Modernist Studies," *Modernism/Modernity* 17, no. 3 (2010); Steven S. Lee, *The Ethnic Avant-Garde: Minority Cultures and World Revolution* (New York: Columbia University Press, 2015); Nicole Rizzuto, *Insurgent Testimonies: Witnessing Colonial*

*Trauma in Modern and Anglophone Literature* (New York: Fordham University Press, 2015); Aarthi Vadde, *Chimeras of Form: Modernist Internationalism Beyond Europe, 1914–2016* (New York: Columbia University Press, 2016); and Rebecca L. Walkowitz, *Cosmopolitan Style: Modernism Beyond the Nation* (New York: Columbia University Press, 2006).

90. Lisa Siraganian, *Modernism and the Meaning of Corporate Persons* (Oxford: Oxford University Press, 2020); Natasha Wheatley, *The Life and Death of States: Central Europe and the Transformation of Modern Sovereignty* (Princeton, NJ: Princeton University Press, 2023).
91. Anna Hedberg Olenina, *Psychomotor Aesthetics: Movement and Affect in Modern Literature and Film* (New York: Oxford University Press, 2020); Emma Widdis, *Socialist Senses: Film, Feeling, and the Soviet Subject, 1917–1940* (Bloomington: Indiana University Press, 2017).
92. Stefani Engelstein, *Sibling Action: The Genealogical Structure of Modernity* (New York: Columbia University Press, 2017); Jakob Norberg, *The Brothers Grimm and the Making of German Nationalism* (Cambridge: Cambridge University Press, 2022).
93. Andrew Gaedtke, *Modernism and the Machinery of Madness: Psychosis, Technology, and Narrative Worlds* (Cambridge: Cambridge University Press, 2017), 8, points out the extraordinary difficulty defining psychosis. "While this core psychiatric concept has largely persisted into the present, it was also an unstable and contested category from the very beginning whose scope and rate of incidence expanded and contracted significantly in the last century."
94. Fredric Jameson, *Postmodernism, or The Cultural Logic of Late Capitalism* (Durham, NC: Duke University Press, 1992), 49.
95. Michael Hardt and Antonio Negri, *Empire* (Cambridge, MA: Harvard University Press, 2001); Michael Hardt and Antonio Negri, *Multitude* (New York: Penguin, 2004); Michael Hardt and Antonio Negri, *Assembly* (Oxford: Oxford University Press, 2019).
96. Deleuze and Guattari write off the clinical state, using that phrase to refer to the moment at which science steps in to halt the creative delirium and visions they argue generate great literary works. Conceivably, however, diagnostic terms *themselves* may form the "figures of a history and geography that are ceaselessly reinvented." Gilles Deleuze and Félix Guattari, *Essays Critical and Clinical*, trans. Daniel W. Smith and Michael A. Greco (New York: Verso, 1998), lv.
97. Jacques Lacan, *The Seminars of Jacques Lacan, Book XXIII, The Sinthome* (New York: Polity, 2016).

## 1. Büchner's Brain: On Psychopower

1. From the diary of Ernst Anschütz (1780–1861). Quoted in Karl Pörnbacher, Gerhard Schaub, Hans-Joachim Simm, and Edda Ziegler, eds., *Georg Büchner. Werke und Briefe. Münchner Ausgabe* (Munich: Deutscher Taschenbuch Verlag, 1988), 603–4.
2. For a timeline of the case, see Pörnbacher et al., *Büchner*, 600–2. Detailed materials can be found in Anja Schiemann, *Der Kriminalfall Woyzeck. Der historische Fall Büchners Drama* (Berlin/Boston: Walter de Gruyter GmbH, 2017). In English, see the "Contexts" section in Matthew Wilson Smith, ed., *Georg Büchner. The Major Works. A Norton Critical Edition* (New York: Norton, 2012).

3. Holger Steinberg, Adrian Schmidt-Recla, and Sebastian Schmideler, "Forensic Psychiatry in Nineteenth-Century Saxony: The Case of Woyzeck," *Harvard Review of Psychiatry* 15, no. 4 (July/August 2007): 170.
4. Johann Christian August Clarus, *Die Zurechnungsfähigkeit des Mörders Johann Christian Woyzeck: nach Grundsätzen der Staatsarzneikunde aktenmäßig erwiesen* (Leipzig, Gerhard Fletscher, 1824). The case history was subsequently reprinted and widely circulated in Adolph Henke's *Zeitschrift für die Staatsarzneikunde.*
5. Smith, ed., *Georg Büchner*, 208.
6. Steinberg et al., "Forensic Psychiatry in Nineteenth-Century Saxony," 172.
7. Smith, ed., *Georg Büchner*, 150. The sense of enumeration is stronger in the German. "Friedrich Johann Franz Woyzeck, geschworner Füsilier im 2. Regiment, 2. Battailon, 4 Compagnie geb<oren> -d.-d. <Mariae Verkündigung> ich bin heut d. 20 Juli alt 30 Jahr 7 Monat u. 12 Tage." Pörnbacher et al., *Büchner*, 232.
8. Only one has anything resembling a beginning, middle, and end. In German, these drafts are known as *Handschriften* (manuscripts) and labeled H1–H4 accordingly. I retain that notation to designate different drafts here.
9. It appeared in the Viennese Newspaper *Neue Freie Presse*, published by Karl Emil Franzos. Franzos, working in partnership with Büchner's brother (who had not found the work significant enough to include in his own edition of Büchner's works), then included the manuscript in an 1879 edition of Büchner's collected works, with the publisher J. D. Sauerländer.
10. Letter to Princess Maria von Thurn und Taxis (Munich, July 9, 1915). Rainer Maria Rilke, *Letters of Rainer Maria Rilke*, vol. 2: *1910–1926*, trans. Jane Bannard Green and M. D. Herter Norton (New York: Norton, 1948), 133.
11. See H1.2.
12. Smith, ed., *Georg Büchner*, 139. The translator takes several liberties with this passage, which I have attempted to clarify by offering the German. In the original manuscript, the passage can be found in H1.1.
13. Smith, ed., *Georg Büchner*, 160 (H1.10).
14. The patchy state of the manuscript (made worse by an early editor's use of a chemical preparation that irreparably blurred large portions of text) itself hearkens toward the modernist discovery of the typographical space of the page.
15. Harald Neumeyer, "Melancholie und Wahnsinn," in *Büchner Handbuch. Leben-Werk-Wirkung*, ed. Roland Borgards and Harald Neumeyer (Stuttgart: J. B. Metzler, 2015), 245. Neuymeyer's discussion cites work by Volker C. Dörr and Nicolas Pethes on Büchner's relationship to Robert Burton's *Anatomy.*
16. A few examples in German and in English: James Crighton, *Büchner and Madness: Schizophrenia in Georg Büchner's "Lenz" and "Woyzeck"* (Lewiston, NY: Mellen, 1998); Alfons Glück, "Der *Woyzeck*. Tragödie eines Paupers," in *Büchner, Katalog Darmstadt: Georg Büchner. Revolutionär, Dichter, Wissenschaftler. Katalog der Ausstellung Mathildenhöhe, Damstadt 2.-August 27 September 1987* (Frankfurt, 1987), 325–32; Richard T. Gray, "The Madness of Civilization: Carnivalization, Spectatorship, and the Critique of Enlightenment in Büchner's *Woyzeck*," in *Stations of the Divided Subject: Contestation and Ideological Legitimation in German Bourgeois Literature, 1770–1914* (Stanford, CA: Stanford University Press, 1995), 196–231; Christian Neuhuber, "Illustration, Inspiration, Interpretation: Bilder des Wahnsinns in und zu Büchner's Werk," in *Georg Büchner, Contemporary Perspectives*, ed. Robert Gillett, Ernest Schonfield, and Daniel Steuer (Brill/Rodopi, 2017); Holger Steinberg and Sebastian Schmideler, "War Woyzeck tatsächlich schizophren oder redete ihm die Verteidigung

eine Schizophrenie nur ein?," *Jahresheft für forensische Psychiatrie* 3, no. 71 (2006): 71–114. Readings of *Lenz* as schizoid are so common that this perspective even informs the jacket of the dual-language edition of the text: "Published posthumously in 1839, Lenz provides a taut case study of three weeks in the life of [a] schizophrenic, perhaps the first third-person text ever to be written from the 'inside' of insanity." Georg Büchner, *Lenz*, trans. Richard Sieburth (New York: Archipelago, 2004).

17. Armin Schäfer, "Biopolitik," in *Büchner Handbuch*, ed. Borgards and Neumeyer, 179; Peter J. Schwarz, "Clarus, Woyzeck, and the Politics of Accountability," in Smith, ed., *Georg Büchner*, 372.
18. Schäfer, "Biopolitik," 180.
19. Smith, ed., *Georg Büchner*, 144 (H4.8).
20. Other scholars have noticed this as a key feature of the play but reached different conclusions about it. See Burghard Dedner, "Producing 'Thoughts by Means of the Body.' Büchner and the Enigma of Consciousness," in *Georg Büchner, Contemporary Perspectives*, ed. Gillett, Schonfield, and Steuer, 31–48; Dorothea E. von Mücke, *The Seduction of the Occult and the Rise of the Fantastic Tale* (Stanford, CA: Stanford University Press, 2003); Barbara Natalie Nagel, "The Spirit of Matter in Büchner," *Comparative Literature and Culture* 13, no. 3 (2011).
21. Pörnbacher et al., *Büchner*, 586–87, 600–2.
22. Pörnbacher et al., *Büchner*, 586.
23. Pörnbacher et al., *Büchner*, 600–2.
24. Steinberg et al., "Forensic Psychiatry in Nineteenth-Century Saxony," 170.
25. This second report was then reviewed and confirmed by the Faculty of Medicine at Leipzig University.
26. Pörnbacher et al., *Büchner*, 650.
27. Smith, ed., *Georg Büchner*, 208.
28. Pörnbacher et al., *Büchner*, 650.
29. Steinberg et al., "Forensic Psychiatry in Nineteenth-Century Saxony," 174.
30. Bernhard Dedner, *Georg Büchner. Woyzeck. Erläuterungen und Dokumente* (Stuttgart: Philipp Reclam, 2000), 176.
31. Steinberg et al., "Forensic Psychiatry in Nineteenth-Century Saxony," 73. See also Edward Shorter, *History of Psychiatry* (New York: John Wiley and Sons, 1997).
32. On the differences between Vesalius and Burton, see R. Grant Williams, "Disfiguring the Body of Knowledge: Anatomical Discourse and Robert Burton's 'The Anatomy of Melancholy,'" *ELH* 68, no. 3 (Fall 2001): 594–95. Williams's reading of Burton's work as a parody of anatomization aligns with my own.
33. René Descartes, *The Passions of the Soul*, trans. Stephen Voss (Indianapolis, IN: Hackett, 1989), 35. For a discussion of why Descartes may have downplayed his argument for mind-body-dualism-based divisibility in the *Meditations*, see Steven J. Wagner, "Descartes on the Parts of the Soul," *Philosophy and Phenomenological Research* 45, No. 1 (September 1984): 51–74. In the article, Wagner also offers a discussion of Plato and Aristotle's division of the soul that is pertinent in this context, if further afield from my immediate argument.
34. Recent scholarship has nevertheless advocated using the *Passions* to support a materialist argument. The argument advocates for distinguishing in the *Passions* between "passions 'in' the soul" (passions created by the body's physical activity, to which the soul merely responds) and "passions 'of' the soul" (those passions that are the soul's own emotions proper). Separating "passions 'in' the soul" from "passions 'of' the soul" does not thereby make the soul divisible. It merely acknowledges that the soul

*in some way* has its own passions. Presumably, as in the case of the faculties, one and the same soul "in its entirety" (*tout entier*) is still present in all of them. To speak about a "union of the body and soul," or indeed of "soul's body," based on the *Passions* seems to risk applying the divisibility criterion to the soul, which both the *Meditations* and the *Passions* explicitly prohibit. Importantly, however, Descartes never says in the *Passions* that the soul *is* the pineal gland, only that its "principal seat" is located there. His wording retains a distinction between the gland at the center of the brain and the soul, allowing him to preserve a claim to dualism while still discussing operations taking place within the soul (which nevertheless do not constitute discrete parts as such).

35. Nicholas Malebranche, *The Search After Truth*, trans. and ed. Paul Olscamp (Cambridge: Cambridge University Press, 1997), 101–2.
36. Malebranche, *The Search After Truth*, 102. This is likewise true in Alexander Gottlieb Baumgarten's and Christian Wolff's work.
37. Konstantin Pollok, *Kants "Metaphysische Anfangsgründe der Naturwissenschaft"—Ein kritischer Kommentar* (Hamburg: Meiner Verlag, 2001), 93–109; Thomas Sturm, "How Not to Investigate the Human Mind: Kant on the Impossibility of Empirical Psychology," in *Kant and the Sciences* (Oxford: Oxford University Press, 2001), quoted in Pollok, *Kants*, 94.
38. Immanuel Kant, *Metaphysical Foundations of Natural Science*, trans. Michael Friedman (Cambridge: Cambridge University Press, 2004), 7.
39. Kant, *Metaphysical Foundations*, 4.
40. Kant, *Metaphysical Foundations*, 6.
41. A great deal of critical commentary has focused on whether Kant is writing off the possibility of empirical psychology as such, which is different from my concern here: to show that Kant sees the soul as mathematically indivisible. This move in *Metaphysical Foundations* reflects a prior comment in the *Critique of Pure Reason*. Kant writes there that any effort to establish an "empirical psychology" would have to assume "more than the Cartesian *cogito*" as the ground of "our pure rational cognition." In taking "observations about the play of our thoughts and the natural laws of the thinking self" into consideration, empirical psychology thus defined could produce a "physiology of inner sense, but could never serve to reveal such properties as do not belong to possible experience at all" and would never be able to "teach apodictically about thinking beings in general something touching on their nature, thus it would be no rational psychology." In other words, empirical psychology might have some uses, but it would be irrelevant for Kant's pursuits. See Immanuel Kant, *Critique of Pure Reason* (Cambridge: Cambridge University Press, 1998), 415.
42. Immanuel Kant, *Anthropology from a Pragmatic Point of View*, trans. Robert B. Louden (Cambridge: Cambridge University Press, 2006), 90.
43. Georg Wilhelm Friedrich Hegel, *Phenomenology of Spirit*, trans. A. V. Miller (Oxford: Oxford University Press, 1977), 197. The sense of the brain's divisibility is stronger in the German, as "*Gliederung*" can mean both "articulation" and "division."
44. Hegel, *Phenomenology of Spirit*, 198.
45. Dedner, *Georg Büchner*, 170–71.
46. Quoted and translated in Michael Heidelberger, *Nature from Within*, trans. Cynthia Klohr (Pittsburgh: University of Pittsburgh Press, 2004), 31. The subsequent quotation is also Klohr's translation of Heidelberger's German. See Johann Friedrich Herbart, *Psychologie als Wissenschaft. Neu gegründet auf Erfahrung, Metaphysik und Mathematik. Erster, synthetischer Teil* (Königsberg: August Wilhelm Unzer, 1824);

and Johann Friedrich Herbart, *Psychologie als Wissenschaft. Neu gegründet auf Erfahrung, Metaphysik und Mathematik. Zweiter, analytischer Teil* (Königsberg: August Wilhelm Unzer, 1824).

47. J. C. Hoffbauer, *Die Psychologie in ihre Hauptanwendungen auf die Rechtspflege nach den allgemeinen Gesichtspunkten der Gesetzgebung* (Halle: Schimmelpfennig, 1808).
48. This would seemingly align with Büchner's own scientific stance in his dissertation on the nervous system of barbel fish. Given that Woyzeck participates in the experiment only because he is impoverished, it has shades of social critique.
49. Smith, ed., *Georg Büchner*, 144 (H4.8).
50. This is likely also a tacit reference to the Schmolling case and ongoing debates about partial psychiatric disorders.
51. Smith, ed., *Georg Büchner*, 145 (H4.8).
52. "Es gibt eine Revolution in der Wissenschaft. Eine Revolution!" Pörnbacher et al., *Büchner*, 213 (H2.6). I here depart from the Schmidt translation in favor of my own. Schmidt translates the lines as "I'm revolutionizing science. A revolution!" but the German uses an existential clause ("es gibt," there is) that leaves the doctor's agency unclear.
53. Jonathan Sperber, "Echoes of the French Revolution in the Rhineland, 1830–1849," *Central European History* 22, no. 2 (June 1989): 200–17.
54. Maurice Benn, *The Drama of Revolt: A Critical Study of Georg Büchner* (Cambridge: Cambridge University Press, 1976), 17.
55. Schwarz, "Clarus," in Smith, ed., *Georg Büchner*, 368.
56. Smith, ed., *Georg Büchner*, 200. Italics are Clarus's.
57. Smith, ed., *Georg Büchner*, 200. Italics are Clarus's.
58. Jacques Rancière, *Short Voyages to the Land of the People*, trans. James W. Swenson (Stanford, CA: Stanford University Press, 2003), 49. Peter Thompson makes a related point in "Büchner, Science, and the Metaphysics of Contingency," in *Georg Büchner, Contemporary Perspectives*, ed. Gillett, Schonfield, and Steuer, 49–61.
59. This is Fredric Jameson's phrase in *A Singular Modernity: Essay on the Ontology of the Present* (London: Verso, 2002).
60. Jameson, *A Singular Modernity*, 178.
61. Smith, ed., *Georg Büchner*, 141 (H4.5).
62. Smith, ed., *Georg Büchner*, 145 (H4.9).
63. Smith, ed., *Georg Büchner*, 167.
64. Smith, ed., *Georg Büchner*, 167.
65. Smith, ed., *Georg Büchner*, 136 (H4.1).
66. Smith, ed., *Georg Büchner*, 139–40 (H4.1).
67. Smith, ed., *Georg Büchner*, 144 (H4.8).
68. Thomas Hobbes, *Leviathan* (Indianapolis, IN: Hackett, 1994), 3.
69. T. J. Clark, *Farewell to an Idea: Episodes in the History of Modernism* (New Haven, CT: Yale University Press, 1999), 27.
70. Clark, *Farewell to an Idea*, 47.
71. Eric Santner, *The Royal Remains: The People's Two Bodies and the Endgames of Sovereignty* (Chicago: University of Chicago Press, 2011), 10.
72. Santner, *The Royal Remains*, 10.
73. Santner, *The Royal Remains*, 10.
74. Santner, *The Royal Remains*, xxi.

75. Smith, ed., *Georg Büchner*, 200. Italics are Clarus's.
76. Michel Foucault, "Right of Death and Power Over Life," in *Biopolitics: A Reader*, ed. Timothy Campbell and Adam Sitze (Durham, NC: Duke University Press, 2013), 47.
77. Foucault, "Right of Death and Power Over Life," 44.
78. Foucault, "Right of Death and Power Over Life," 43.
79. Foucault, "Right of Death and Power Over Life," 44.
80. Foucault, "Right of Death and Power Over Life," 46.
81. Foucault, "Right of Death and Power Over Life," 48.
82. Anson Rabinbach, *The Human Motor* (Berkeley: University of California Press, 1992), 147.
83. Rabinbach, *The Human Motor*, 148.
84. Rabinbach, *The Human Motor*, 151.
85. Rabinbach, *The Human Motor*, 151.
86. Anson Rabinbach, *The Eclipse of the Utopias of Labor* (New York: Fordham University Press, 2018), ix.
87. For example, Neuriva, shaped like tiny brains, promises enhancements in "memory, focus, learning, accuracy, concentration & reasoning" (at least if one overlooks the lack of FDA approval).
88. For a history of the T4 at Sonnenstein, see the report compiled by the Saxon Memorial Foundation to Commemorate the Victims of Political Tyranny, *Pirna-Sonnenstein: von einer Heilanstalt zu einem Ort nationalsozialistischer Tötungsverbrechen: Begleitband zur ständigen Ausstellung der Gedenstätte Pirna-Sonnenstein* (Dresden: Stiftung Sächsischer Gedenkstätten zur Erinnerung an die Opfer politischer Gewaltherrschaft, 2001).
89. Bernard Stiegler, *Taking Care of Youth and the Generations*, trans. Stephen Barker (Stanford, CA: Stanford University Press, 2010).
90. Stiegler, *Taking Care of Youth and the Generations*, 38.
91. Stiegler, *Taking Care of Youth and the Generations*, 13.
92. Bernard Stiegler, *Nanjing Lectures 2016–2019*, trans. Daniel Ross (London: Open Humanities Press, 2020), 182.
93. Stiegler, *Nanjing Lectures*, 187.
94. Byung-Chul Han, *Psychopolitics: Neoliberalism and New Technologies of Power* (New York: Verso, 2017), 25.
95. Han, *Psychopolitics*, 25.
96. Nikolas Rose and Joelle M. Abi-Rached, *Neuro: The New Brain Sciences and the Management of the Mind* (Princeton, NJ: Princeton University Press, 2013), 8–9.
97. Rose and Abi-Rached, *Neuro*, 21.
98. Rose and Abi-Rached, *Neuro*, 24.
99. Rose and Abi-Rached, *Neuro*, 22
100. Rose and Abi-Rached, *Neuro*, 8.
101. Rose and Abi-Rached, *Neuro*, 8.
102. Paul Celan, "The Meridian," in *Collected Prose*, trans. Rosmarie Waldrop (New York: Routledge, 2003), 38.
103. Celan, "The Meridian," 47.
104. Celan, "The Meridian," 47.
105. Smith, ed. *Georg Büchner*, 157 (H1.2).
106. Celan, "The Meridian," 40.
107. Smith, ed., *Georg Büchner*, 200–1.
108. Celan, "The Meridian," 55.

## 2. Before the Primal Scene: The Wolf-Man Between Sigmund Freud and Emil Kraepelin

1. "The bipolar I disorder criteria represent the modern understanding of the classic manic-depressive disorder or affective psychosis described in the nineteenth century, differing from that classic description only to the extent that neither psychosis nor the lifetime experience of a major depressive episode is a requirement." American Psychiatric Association, *Diagnostic and Statistical Manual of Mental Disorders*, 5th ed. (*DSM-5*) (Washington, DC: American Psychiatric Publishing, 2013), 123.
2. Muriel Gardiner, ed., *The Wolf-Man by the Wolf-Man* (New York: Basic Books, 1971), 46. The translational history of this English-language book is quite complicated and deserves attention, considering what I describe in this chapter. Freud conducted his 1910 analysis with the multilingual Wolf-Man in German, although the analysis and case history referred to Russian, the Wolf-Man's native language. The Wolf-Man then wrote "The Memoirs of the Wolf-Man" in German. These memoirs were translated into English by Muriel Gardiner for inclusion in her English-language book *The Wolf-Man by the Wolf-Man* along with other materials relating to the case. In 1972, Fischer Verlag released a German translation of Gardiner's book: *Der Wolfsmann vom Wolfsmann*. This book does not clarify whether it reproduced the Wolf-Man's original German text of "The Memoirs of the Wolf-Man" or translated this portion into German from Gardiner's English work. Mária Török and Karl Abraham's *The Wolf-Man's Magic Word: A Cryptonomy*, which makes extensive use of Gardiner's materials, was written in French (*Cryptonymie, le verbier de l'Homme aux Loups*, 1976). It would appear that Török and Abraham used the English edition of Gardiner's book but translated its contents and all quotations from the Wolf-Man into French there. I have tried to be sensitive to these ambiguities and translational problems throughout the chapter.
3. Gardiner, ed., *The Wolf-Man*, 25–26.
4. Emil Kraepelin, *Compendium der Psychiatrie zum Gebrauche für Studirende und Ärzte* (Leipzig: Abel Verlag, 1883); Emil Kraepelin, *Psychiatrie. Ein Lehrbuch für Studierende und Ärzte*, I. Band, *Allgemeine Psychiatrie* (Leipzig: Verlag von Johann Ambrosius Barth, 1899); Emil Kraepelin, *Psychiatrie. Ein Lehrbuch für Studierende und Ärzte*, II. Band, *Klinische Psychiatrie* (Leipzig: Verlag von Johann Ambrosius Barth, 1899).
5. Gardiner, ed., *The Wolf-Man*, 59–60.
6. Gardiner, ed., *The Wolf-Man*, 69.
7. Sigmund Freud, *The Standard Edition of the Complete Psychological Works of Sigmund Freud*, ed. and trans. James Strachey (London: Hogarth, 1950), 17:2–123. Hereafter abbreviated *SE*.
8. The Wolf-Man also received a diagnosis of "neurasthenia" in 1907 from the Russian neurologist Vladimir Bekhterev, who attempted to cure him with hypnosis. James L. Rice, *Freud's Russia: National Identity in the Evolution of Psychoanalysis* (New Brunswick, NJ: Transaction, 1993), chap. 5. He was additionally seen by Theodor Ziehen in Berlin in 1908, who similarly found him suffering from a nervous disorder. Gardiner, ed., *The Wolf-Man*, 74.
9. Freud, *SE* 17:8.
10. Freud, *SE* 17:74.
11. Freud, *SE* 17:74–75.

12. Freud, *SE* 17:75.
13. Freud, *SE* 17:8.
14. Freud, *SE* 3:146. The French can be found in Sigmund Freud, *Gesammelte Werke* (London: Imago, 1952), 1:410. Here the German text in parentheses is Freud's and the French text in brackets my own, showing the French words Freud used for "mental degeneracy" and "neurasthenia."
15. In the foundational sixth edition of 1899, Kraepelin assigns a diagnosis he terms "obsessive insanity" (*Zwangsirresein*) to a category he labels "Psychopathic Conditions (Degeneration Insanity)" (*Die psychopatischen Zustände (Entartungsirresein)*)," which he separates entirely from the neuroses. In the seventh edition of the textbook from 1903–1904, *Zwangsirresein* becomes part of a new classificatory group called "Original Pathological Conditions" (*Originäre Krankheitszustände*), which similarly remains distinct from the neuroses, just as in the sixth edition. While a subcategory called "obsessional neurosis" (*Zwangsneurose*) does appear in the voluminous eighth edition of Kraepelin's textbook, he there gives obsessional neurosis simply as an identificatory symptom for manic-depressive insanity (*manisch-depressive Irresein*). Even had the Wolf-Man been characterized as a case of obsessional neurosis by Kraepelin, that description still would have returned him to the diagnosis of manic depression.
16. Wolfgang Burgmair, Eric J. Engstrom, and Matthias M. Weber, eds., *Emil Kraepelin. Persönliches* (Munich: Belleville Verlag Michael Farin, 2000).
17. H. Steinberg and M. C. Angermeyer, "Emil Kraepelin's Work at the Silesian Provincial Psychiatric State Hospital in Leubus," *Fortschritte der Neurologie, Psychiatrie* 70, no. 5 (2002): 252–58.
18. Holger Steinberg and Matthias C. Angermeyer, "Emil Kraepelin's Years at Dorpat as Professor of Psychiatry in Nineteenth-Century Russia," *History of Psychiatry* 12, no. 47 (2001): 397–27; Wolfgang Burgmair, Eric J. Engstrom, Albrecht Hirschmüller, and Matthias M. Weber, *Kraepelin in Dorpat 1886–1891* (Munich: Belleville Verlag Michael Farin, 2003).
19. Emil Kraepelin, *Memoirs*, trans. Cheryl Wooding-Deane (Berlin: Springer-Verlag, 1987).
20. H. Steinberg and H. Himmerlich, "Emil Kraepelin's Habilitation and His Thesis: A Pioneer Work for Modern Systemic Reviews, Psychoimmunological Research, and Categories of Psychiatric Diseases," *World Journal of Biological Psychiatry* 14, no. 4 (2013): 248–57.
21. Edward Shorter, *History of Psychiatry* (New York: Wiley, 1998), 79.
22. This approach was based on the findings of pathologico-anatomical research in neurosyphilis, which showed that the ailing brain developed lesions.
23. Flechsig believed that thought was the result of higher-order functioning in so-called psychic centers (*Associationscentren*). According to *Gehirn und Seele*, these centers, which he positioned in the cerebral cortex, combined the activity of different sensory organs to produce more sophisticated sensory impressions: sight, touch, hearing, and "cogitation" (thinking). Paul Flechsig, *Gehirn und Seele* (Leipzig: Verlag von Veit & Comp., 1896), 23–24. As one American critic observed at the time, this idea seemed to smack of Condillac's proposition that the faculties of mind could be reduced to the cumulative interaction of different sensations. Mary Putnam Jacobi, "Considerations on Flechsig's 'Gehirn und Seele,'" *Journal of Nervous and Mental Disease*, December 1897, 749. Whether Flechsig's stance was a Condillacian endeavor or not, his view of "normal" mental functioning formed the basis for his understanding of

psychopathologies. Mental illness, Flechsig claimed, was the simply the result of disturbances within the psychic centers. Triggered by memory, they would allegedly become overly excited, to psychopathological effect.

24. Flechsig, *Gehirn und Seele*, 10–11. Emphasis mine.
25. Eric Engstrom, *Clinical Psychiatry in Imperial Germany* (Ithaca, NY: Cornell University Press, 2003).
26. Engstrom, *Clinical Psychiatry.*
27. For example, when Griesinger became director of the psychiatric clinic at the Berlin Charité hospital in 1865, he instituted a massive reform program that stressed nonrestraint of patients and that differentiated between patients in need of short-term versus long-term care to reduce overcrowding. Engstrom, *Clinical Psychiatry.*
28. Engstrom, *Clinical Psychiatry*, 123–25.
29. Katja Guenther, *Localization and Its Discontents* (Chicago: University of Chicago Press, 2015), 71.
30. Shorter, *History of Psychiatry*, 80.
31. Guenther, *Localization*, 46; Andreas Killen, *Berlin Electropolis* (Berkeley: University of California Press, 2005), 37, 88.
32. Guenther, *Localization*, 45–46, 215n37.
33. Quoted in Steinberg and Himmerich, "Emil Kraepelin's Habilitation."
34. Gustav Theodor Fechner, *The Elements of Psychophysics*, trans. Helmut E. Adler (New York: Holt, Rinehart and Winston, 1966), 1:xvii; Gustav Theodor Fechner, *Elemente der Psychophysik* (Leipzig: Breitkopft und Härtel, 1860), 1:v.
35. Fechner, *Elements*, xxvii.
36. See J. F. Herbart, *Psychology as a Science, Newly Founded on Experience, Metaphysics and Mathematics* (*Psychologie als Wissenschaft, neu gegründet auf Erfahrung, Metaphysik, Mathematik*) (1824). See also chapter 1 of this volume.
37. Gustav Fechner, "Das psychische Mass," *Zeitschrift für Philosophie und philosophische Kritik* 23, no. 1 (1858): 6.
38. Fechner, "Das psychische Mass," 2.
39. "Instead of precise equal divisions made available by a material standard, what we need here [to determine a psychological standard] is the precise determination and statement of a law permitting us to relate the increments of stimulation and sensation to one another." Fechner, "Das psychische Mass," 7. Translation modified from Heidelberger, *Nature from Within: Gustav Theodor Fechner and His Psychophysical World View*, trans. Cynthia Khlor (Pittsburgh, PA: University of Pittsburgh Press, 2004), 201.
40. Gustav Theodor Fechner, *Elemente der Psychophysik* (Leipzig: Breitkopft und Härtel, 1860), 2:554.
41. Benjamin Rand, ed., *The Classical Psychologists* (Boston: Houghton Mifflin, 1912), 569. Gustav Theodor Fechner, *Elemente der Psychophysik*, 2:17.
42. Rand, *The Classical Psychologists*, 572. Fechner, *Elemente der Psychophysik*, 2:17.
43. Wilhelm Wundt, *Outlines of Psychology*, trans. Charles Hubbard Judd (Leipzig: Wilhelm Engelmann, 1897), 256.
44. See, for example, Helmholtz's chapter "Fechners psychophysiches Gesetz," in H. Helmholtz, *Handbuch der physiologischen Optik* (Leipzig: Leopold Voss, 1867). Kraepelin is occasionally characterized as a descendent of the Helmholzian biophysics approach, which, while technically accurate, neglects that he would have had much more direct access to psychophysics through Wundt. Ernst Mach, *The Analysis of Sensations and the Relation of the Physical to the Psychical*, trans. C. M. Williams

(La Salle, IL: Open Court, 1984); Charles Sanders Peirce, *Photometric Researches* (Leipzig: W. Engelmann, 1878).

45. In Freud's *Project for a Scientific Psychology* (1895), originally a series of letters Freud wrote to Wilhelm Fliess, Freud describes hoping to establish a psychology that represented "psychical processes as quantitatively determined states of specifiable material particles." Freud, *SE* 1:283–387. The idea is a direct reference to psychophysics as laid out in Fechner's *Elements*. Citations of Fechner also appear several times in the *Interpretation of Dreams*. There Freud credits Fechner with no less than the discovery of the dream scene's distinction from that of ordinary waking life.
46. Wilhelm Wundt, *Lectures on Human and Animal Psychology*, trans. J. E. Creighton and E. B. Titchener (London: Swan Sonnenschein & Co., 1907), 32. Italics mine.
47. Wundt, *Lectures on Human and Animal Psychology*, 59.
48. Wundt, *Lectures on Human and Animal Psychology*, 63.
49. Wundt, *Lectures on Human and Animal Psychology*, 63.
50. On Kraepelin's relationship to Wundt, see H. Steinberg, "Der Psychologe und Philosoph Wilhelm Wundt und eine Widmung seines Schülers Emil Kraepelin," *Nervenarzt* 72, no. 11 (2001): 884; On Kraepelin and psychology, see J. Allik, "Why Was Emil Kraepelin Not Recognized as a Psychologist?," *Trames* 20, no. 4 (2016): 317–35; K. Arens, *Structures of Knowing: Psychologies of the Nineteenth Century* (Dordrecht: Kluwer Academic Publishers, 1989); E. J. Engstrom, "La messenden individualpsychologie: sur le role de l'experimentation psychologique dans la psychiatrie d'Emil Kraepelin (second partie)" *PSN* 1, no. 2 (2003): 40–46.
51. A detailed picture of Kraepelin's time in Dorpat can be found in Burgmair et al., *Kraepelin in Dorpat 1886–1891*. Their work complements and expands summaries in other sources including M. S. Rogovin, "Emil Kraepelin. The Derpt Period," *Zhurnal nevropatologii i psikhiatrii imeni S.S. Korsakova* 74, no. 8 (1974): 1244; L. Mehilane, "Emil Kraepelin's Activities in Tartu (Dorpat)," *European Psychiatry* 11 (1996): 392; Steinberg and Angermeyer, "Emil Kraepelin's Years at Dorpat."
52. Emil Kraepelin, "Fechner, Ueber die psychophysischen Maassprincipien und das *Weber*'sche Gesetz.—Philosophische Studien IV, 2, p. 161–230," *AZfP* 44, no. 2 (1888): 150.
53. Kraepelin even reviewed one of his own psychophysics publications.
54. Emil Kraepelin, "Die Richtungen der Psychiatrischen Forschung," in Burgmair et al., *Kraepelin in Dorpat 1886–1891*, 55–80; Emil Kraepelin, "Psychologische Forschungsmethoden," *Humboldt*, January 1888, 12–14.
55. Eric Engstrom and Matthias M. Weber, "Classic Text No. 63: The Directions of Psychiatric Research by Emil Kraepelin, 1887," *History of Psychiatry* 16, no. 3 (September 2005): 350.
56. Engstrom and Weber, "Classic Text No. 63," 356.
57. Engstrom and Weber, "Classic Text No. 63," 356–57.
58. Kraepelin, "Psychologische Forschungsmethoden," 12.
59. Kraepelin, "Psychologische Forschungsmethoden," 13.
60. Kraepelin, "Psychologische Forschungsmethoden," 13–14.
61. Emil Kraepelin, "G. Th. Fechner, Elemente der Psychophysik. Zweite unveränderte Auflage, 2 Bände. Leipzig 1889," *AZfP* 47 (1891): 170–72.
62. Emil Kraepelin, "Vorwort," *Psychologische Arbeiten* 1 (1896).
63. Emil Kraepelin, "Der psychologische Versuch in der Psychiatrie," *Psychologische Arbeiten* 1 (1896): 1–90.
64. Kraepelin, "Der psychologische Versuch in der Psychiatrie," 28.

65. Kraepelin, "Der psychologische Versuch in der Psychiatrie," 43.
66. On the political environment in Dorpat at the time and its impact on Kraepelin's research, see Maike Rotzoll, "Dorpat University in the Late Nineteenth Century as a Transit Space for Psychiatric Knowledge," in *Explorations in Baltic Medical History, 1850–2015*, ed. Nils Hansson and Jonatan Wistrand (Rochester, NY: University of Rochester Press, 2019); B. Engmann and H. Steinberg, "Emil Kraepelin's Time in Dorpat—Did This Stay Make Marks in Russian and Soviet Psychiatry?," *Fortschritte der Neurologie-Psychiatrie* 85, no. 11 (2017): 675; Kuznecovs, "Psihiatrijas attīstība Krievijas attīstība Vidzemes, Kurzemes un Igaunijas gubernās 19. gadsimta beigas: Emāla Krēpelīna darbība (1886–1891)," *Acta Medico-Historica Rigensia* 12, no. 31 (2019): 22–66; Steinberg and Angermeyer, "Emil Kraepelin's Years at Dorpat"; E. Tammiksaar, "Political Atmosphere in Dorpat in Emil Kraepelin's Period," *Trames* 20, no. 4 (2016): 403–16.
67. Rotzoll, "Dorpat," 356.
68. Emil Kraepelin, "Ziele und Wege der klinischen Psychiatrie," *AZfP* 52 (1897): 841; M. M. Weber and E. J. Engstrom, "Kraepelin's 'Diagnostic Cards': The Confluence of Clinical Research and Preconcieved Categories," *History of Psychiatry* 8, no. 31, pt. 3 (September 1997): 375–85; Rotzoll, "Dorpat," 356; Steinberg and Angermeyer, "Emil Kraepelin's Years at Dorpat," 308. See also the discussion of the cards in relationship to Kraepelin's development of the dementia praecox classification in Yvonne Wübben, *Verrückte Sprache. Psychiater und Dichter in der Anstalt des 19. Jahrhunderts* (Konstanz: Konstanz University Press, 2012), 89–94.
69. Weber and Engstrom, "Kraepelin's 'Diagnostic Cards,'" 377.
70. Weber and Engstrom, "Kraepelin's 'Diagnostic Cards,'" 377.
71. A. Guttstadt, "Die Geisteskranken in den Irrenanstalten während der Zeit von 1852 bis 1871 und ihre Zählung im ganzen Staat am 1. December 1871 nebst Vorschlägen zur Gewinning einer deutschen Irrenstatistik," *Zeitschrift des königlich-preussischen statistichen Bureaus* 14 (1874): 248b; Weber and Engstrom, "Kraepelin's 'Diagnostic Cards,'" 378.
72. Many of the cards are held in the historical archives of the Max Planck Institute of Psychiatry in Munich. As Weber and Engstrom note in their overview of the cards, their categories and form changed over time. In general, they include headings for: "(1) personal data, e.g. name, age, profession, date and place of birth, relatives; (2) data concerning the psychiatric disorder, e.g. remarks on aetiology and heredity, medical history, age of first and actual onset, duration of treatment, psychopathological status, course of symptoms, correct diagnoses and diagnostic errors; (3) additional data, e.g. forensic remarks or anatomic diagnoses." Weber and Engstrom, "Kraepelin's 'Diagnostic Cards,'" 379.
73. Weber and Engstrom, "Kraepelin's 'Diagnostic Cards,'" 379.
74. Quoted in Weber and Engstrom, "Kraepelin's 'Diagnostic Cards,'" 379–81.
75. The first edition (1883) and editions two through four (1887–1893) have slightly different titles than all subsequent editions. In 1883, the work is entitled *Compendium der Psychiatrie. Zum Gebrauch für Studierende und Ärzte* (Compendium of psychiatry. For use by students and doctors). For the editions of 1887, 1889, and 1893 it is entitled *Psychiatrie. Ein kurzes Lehrbuch für Studierende und Ärzte* (Psychiatry. A short textbook for students and doctors). The title became *Psychiatrie: ein Lehrbuch für Studirende und Äertze* (Psychiatry: a textbook for students and doctors) in 1896, after which point the name remained unchanged. Kraepelin also switched publishers at this time. Editions one through four had been published through Ambr. Abel Press

in Leipzig, which specialized in popular scientific works. Beginning with the 1896 edition, however, Kraepelin began to publish with the older and more established publisher Johann Ambrosius Barth Press, which also specialized in scientific works but had a wider a range of scientific texts in its catalogue. The shift in publishers is a good indicator of Kraepelin's own sense of the scientific importance of his work.

76. Emil Kraepelin, *Psychiatrie. Ein Lehrbuch für Studierende und Ärzte.* (Leipzig: Verlag von Johann Ambrosius Barth, 1896), v.
77. Emil Kraepelin, *Psychiatrie. Ein Lehrbuch für Studierende und Ärzte*, I. Band, *Allgemeine Psychiatrie* (Leipzig: Verlag von Johann Ambrosius Barth, 1899), v.
78. Shorter, *History of Psychiatry*, 106–7.
79. These two differential diagnoses could also themselves be further subdivided, but such subdivisions merely represented subtypes of manic-depressive illness and dementia praecox, not new forms of psychosis. Kraepelin borrowed the term "dementia praecox" from the German psychiatrist Heinrich Schüle, who first used it in the 1880s in a different sense.
80. Emil Kraepelin, *Psychiatrie. Ein Lehrbuch für Studierende und Ärzte*, II. Band, *Klinische Psychiatrie* (Leipzig: Verlag von Johann Ambrosius Barth, 1899), 4.
81. Kraepelin, *Psychiatrie* II (1899), 6.
82. Gayatri Chakravorty Spivak, *An Aesthetic Education in the Era of Globalization* (Cambridge, MA: Harvard University Press, 2012), 220.
83. F. Plaut, "Worte der Erinnerung an Emil Kraepelin," *Zeitschrift für die gesamte Neurologie und Psychiatrie*, 108 (1927): 3.
84. Plaut, "Worte der Erinnerung an Emil Kraepelin," 5.
85. The clinical task force for the DSM-III did not so much as read Kraepelin's works as reinvigorate his methodology and classification system. They were largely insulted to be designated as "neo-Kraepelinians" at the time.
86. Over the past two decades, Wolfgang Burgmair, Eric J. Engstrom, and Mattias M. Weber have produced a nine-volume edited edition of Kraepelin's *Werke*, featuring archival material and his published articles (accompanied by detailed contextual commentary) in volumes that cover the different phases of his career. These volumes include: I. *Persönliches* [Personal materials], II. *Kriminologische Schriften* [Criminologial writing], III. *Briefe I* [Correspondence I], IV. *Kraepelin in Dorpat*, V. *Kraepelin in Heidelberg*, VI. *Kraepelin in München I*, VII. *Kraepelin in München II*, VIII. *Briefe und Dokumente I*, and IX. *Briefe und Dokumente II*. Wolfgang Burgmair, Eric J. Engstrom, and Mattias M. Weber, eds., *Emil Kraepelin. Werke.* (Munich: Belleville Verlag Michael Farin, 2000–2019).
87. Cited in Sander Gilman, *Seeing the Insane* (Brattleboro, VA: Echo Point Books and Media, 1982), 190.
88. "At the publisher's suggestion, I have decided to augment the book with a few photographic plates, handwriting samples, and graphs in order to increase clarity. The pictures for the plates were partly made by [Heinrich Erhard] Dehio, but mainly by [Ernst] Trömner, the microphotographs mostly produced by [Franz] Nissl. Unfortunately, and especially in the case of the latter, a great deal [of the images' appearance] is due to the reproduction process." Kraepelin, *Psychiatrie* (1896), vi. Kraepelin's attribution of the photographs to his research assistants (Heinrich Erhard Dehio and Ernst Trömner), and the microphotography to Franz Nissl indicates that the images of patients that appeared in 1896 were all most likely of Kraepelin's current German patients at the Heidelberg clinic, not those of Dorpat or Leipzig.

89. Emil Kraepelin, *Psychiatrie. Ein Lehrbuch für Studierende und Ärzte*, I. Band, *Allgemeine Psychiatrie* (Leipzig: Verlag von Johann Ambrosius Barth, 1909), 626, 598, 597.
90. Kraepelin, *Psychiatrie* I (1909), 581–82.
91. Kraepelin, *Psychiatrie* I (1909), 646.
92. Kraepelin, *Psychiatrie* I (1899), 275–80.
93. For an extensive discussion of Kraepelin's writing scale and how it worked, see Armin Schäfer, "Graphology in German Psychiatry," *History of Psychiatry* 27, no. 3 (2016): 307–19.
94. "Psychophysical graph showing pressure exerted on a piece of paper by individuals writing the numbers 'one' and 'ten.'" Kraepelin, *Psychiatrie* II (1899), 372–74. The diagram appears on 373.
95. See Gilman, *Seeing the Insane*, chap. 15.
96. Freud, *SE* 17:48.
97. Even research being done by prominent German and Austrian psychiatrists of his day, such as Richard von Krafft-Ebing, Theodor Ziehen, Karl Kahlbaum, and Ewald Hecker, place much more emphasis on psychodiagnostic assessment than Freud and were significantly more committed to psychiatry's institutional professionalization. Like him, however, they remained committed to understanding mental disorders on the basis of the external symptoms expressed by individual patients. Such symptoms, or clusters of symptoms, formed the proper ground for psychiatric diagnosis.
98. Friedrich A. Kittler, *Discourse Networks 1800/1900*, trans. Michael Metteer and Chris Cullens (Stanford, CA: Stanford University Press, 1990).
99. Kittler, *Discourse Networks 1800/1900*, 45.
100. Kittler, *Discourse Networks 1800/1900*, 42.
101. Kittler, *Discourse Networks 1800/1900*, 214–16.
102. Kittler, *Discourse Networks 1800/1900*, 307.
103. Kittler, *Discourse Networks 1800/1900*, 307.
104. Kittler, *Discourse Networks 1800/1900*, 309.
105. Kittler, *Discourse Networks 1800/1900*, 305.
106. Common in work on modernist studies, this position has also informed scholarship in media studies (to which Kittler's work foundationally contributed), in the history of science, and at the intersection of the two. The fascinating propositions made by this research could, in addition to exploring the way in which Freudian psychoanalysis and Kraepelinian psychiatry were both writing technologies, also benefit from considering the differences between the two systems in terms of the their respective uses of language and storytelling. See Cornelius Borck and Armin Schäfer, eds., *Psychographien* (Zürich: Diaphanes, 2005); Alexander Košenina, ed., "*Fallgeschichten. Von der Dokmentation zur Fiktion*," Special issue, *Zeitschrift für Germanistik* 19, no. 2 (2009); Yvonne Wübben, *Verrückte Sprache* (2012); Cornelius Borck and Armin Schäfer, eds., *Das Psychiatrische Aufschreibesystem* (Amsterdam: Brill/Rodopi, 2015).
107. Michel Foucault, "Cuvier's Situation in the History of Biology," trans. Lynne Huffer, *Foucault Studies* 22 (January 2017): 208–37. The diagrams can be found on 211–212.
108. Freud, *SE* 17:29.
109. Gardiner, ed., *The Wolf-Man*, 27.
110. Gardiner, ed., *The Wolf-Man*, 39.
111. Nicholas Abraham and Mária Török, *The Wolf-Man's Magic Word: A Cryptonomy*, trans. Nicholas Rand (Minneapolis: University of Minnesota Press, 1986), 19.
112. Abraham and Török, *The Wolf-Man's Magic Word*, 5.
113. Freud, *SE* 17:121.

## 3. Schreber's Law: Psychotic, Reading

1. Sigmund Freud, "Psychoanalytic Notes on an Autobiographical Account of Paranoia (Dementia Paranoides)," in *The Standard Edition of the Complete Psychological Works of Sigmund Freud*, ed. and trans. James Strachey (London: Hogarth, 1950), 12:3–88 (hereafter abbreviated *SE*); Jacques Lacan, *The Psychoses 1955–1956. The Seminar of Jacques Lacan. Book III*, ed. Jacques-Alain Miller, trans. Russell Grigg (New York: Norton, 1997). The Lacan epigraph to this chapter can be found on *The Psychoses*, 124.
2. Mortiz Schatzman, *Soul Murder: Persecution in the Family* (New York: Signet, 1974).
3. Holger Steinberg and Sebastian Schmideler, "Eine wiederentdeckte Quelle zu Büchners Vorlage zum *Woyzeck*: Das Gutachten der Medizinische Fakultät der Universität Leipzig," *Zeitschrift für Germanistik* 16, no. 2 (2006): 339–66.
4. Daniel Paul Schreber, *Memoirs of My Nervous Illness*, trans. Ida Macalpine and Richard A. Hunter (1955; New York: New York Review Books, 2000). The Schreber epigraph to this chapter can be found on 83n42 of the English *Memoirs*. The German edition of the text I refer to throughout this chapter is the reprint of Schreber's memoirs: Daniel Paul Schreber, *Denkwürdigkeiten eines Nervenkranken* (Berlin: Kulturverlag Kadmos, 2003). The book was originally published by Oswald Mutze Press in Leipzig. See 58 of the 2003 Kadmos edition for the epigraph in German.
5. This chapter shares some of the same title as Peter Goodrich's insightful book *Schreber's Law: Jurisprudence and Judgment in Transition* (Edinburgh: Edinburgh University Press, 2018). Goodrich examines the legal history of Schreber's case and looks at its connection to trans studies. I cannot recall if I settled on my chapter title before encountering Goodrich's book or did so having been inspired by it but without recollecting it was Goodrich's title. Having realized the overlap, however, I nevertheless decided to let my chapter title stand as a way of paying tribute to the research work on Schreber's relationship to the law that has already been written and to Goodrich's important reflections on sex and gender in the Schreber case. As this is a chapter concerned with repetitions, and historical repetitions in particular, a title that included a historical repetition (albeit with a difference) seemed fitting.
6. Zvi Lothane, *In Defense of Schreber: Soul Murder and Psychiatry* (Hillsdale, NJ: Analytic Press, 1992), 472.
7. On this topic see Eric Santner, *My Own Private Germany: Daniel Paul Schreber's Secret History of Modernity* (Princeton, NJ: Princeton University Press, 1996). The final chapter of Elias Canetti, *Crowds and Power*, trans. Carol Stewart (New York: Continuum, 1962), connects Schreber to the rise of German totalitarianism. Heinz Kohut, *The Analysis of the Self* (1971; Chicago: University of Chicago Press, 2009), analyzes Schreber's father as afflicted with a "healed over psychosis, similar perhaps to Hitler's" (255–56), building on research done by Niederland and Baumeyer. See William Niederland, "Schreber's Father," *Journal of American Psychoanalytic Association* 8 (1960): 492–99; William Niederland, "Schreber: Father and Son," *Psychoanalytic Quarterly* 28 (1959): 151–69; F. Baumeyer, "Der Fall Schreber," *Psyche* 9 (1955): 513–36. Reflecting on the growth of literature on Schreber and fascism, Erik Butler calls for a need to revisit discussions of Schreber's relationship to National Socialism and argues the work is best understood as a "case study in Bildungsbürgertum at the turn of the century." Erik Butler, "The Schreber Case Revisited. Realpolitik and Writing in the Asylum," *New German Critique* 104 (Summer 2008): 171–89.

8. Santner, *My Own Private Germany.*
9. Steinberg and Schmideler, "Eine wiederentdeckte," 341.
10. Steinberg and Schmideler, "Eine wiederentdeckte," 341.
11. Steinberg and Schmideler, "Eine wiederentdeckte," 349.
12. Walter Benjamin, "Books by the Mentally Ill. From My Collection," in *Selected Writings*, vol. 2, *1927–1934*, trans. by Rodney Livingstone et al., ed. Michael W. Jennings, Howard Eiland, and Gary Smith (Cambridge, MA: Belknap Press of Harvard University Press, 1999), 123–30.
13. Hans Blüher, *Die Aristie des Jesus von Nazareth* (Prien, 1921); Carl Friedrich Schmidt, *Leben und Wissenschaft in ihrene Elementen und Gesetzen* (Würzburg, 1842); Carl Gehrmann, *Körper, Gehirn, Seele, Gott* (Berlin, 1893).
14. Benjamin, "Books by the Mentally Ill," 123.
15. Benjamin, "Books by the Mentally Ill," 124. It is unclear whose diagnosis Benjamin is citing.
16. Benjamin, "Books by the Mentally Ill," 124.
17. Benjamin, "Books by the Mentally Ill," 124.
18. Benjamin, "Books by the Mentally Ill," 130.
19. Benjamin, "Books," 125.
20. Benjamin, "Books by the Mentally Ill," 128.
21. Benjamin, "Books by the Mentally Ill," 130.
22. Max Horkheimer and Theodor Adorno, *Dialectic of Enlightenment*, trans. Edmund Jephcott (Stanford, CA: Stanford University Press, 2002), 182. The German for "knowledge" in the quotation is *Erkenntnis.*
23. Horkheimer and Adorno, *Dialectic of Enlightenment*, 2.
24. Benjamin, "Books by the Mentally Ill," 123.
25. Steinberg and Schmideler, "Eine wiederentdeckte," 365.
26. *Entwurf eines bürgerlichen Gesetzbuches für das Deutsche Reich* (Berlin: Verlag von J. Guttentag, 1888), Erstes Buch, Dritter Titel, "Altersstufen. Entmündigung," §§25–29.
27. Goodrich provides an exegesis of the English and German title pages in chapter 1 of *Schreber's Law.* The translation I give here is a modification of his, for reasons indicated in the body of the text. Goodrich translates the subtitle as: "*with postscripts and an addendum concerning the question: 'Under What Premises Can a Person Considered Insane Be Detained in an Asylum Against His Own Declared Will?'*" (12). Santner and Lothane note the discrepancy between the English and German in their own work but do not expand on it.
28. "In the kingdom of ends everything has either a price or a dignity [*Würde*]. What has a price can be replaced by something that is its *equivalent*; what on the other hand is raised above all price and therefore admits no equivalent has a dignity." Immanuel Kant, *Groundwork of the Metaphysics of Morals*, trans. Mary Gregor (Cambridge: Cambridge University Press, 1997), 42.
29. Schreber, *Memoirs*, 350–51.
30. On the making of the BGB, see C. M. Barber, *The Making of a German Constitution: A Slow Revolution* (London: Bloomsbury, 2008).
31. Barber, *The Making of a German Constitution*, 196.
32. Barber, *The Making of a German Constitution*, 201.
33. Barber, *The Making of a German Constitution*, 201–2.
34. Barber, *The Making of a German Constitution*, 202.
35. Barber, *The Making of a German Constitution*, 202.
36. Barber, *The Making of a German Constitution*, 202.

37. Quoted in Barber, *The Making of a German Constitution*, 208.
38. See Schreber's medical chart in Lothane, *In Defense of Schreber*, 470–71; and Lothane's timeline of Schreber's illness in Lothane, *In Defense of Schreber*, 91–93.
39. Schreber, *Memoirs*, 101n53. Lindenhof, run by a Dr. Pierson, was a *Heilanstalt für Gemüths- und Nervenkranke* (treatment facility for patients with mood and nervous disorders) and was quite different from Flechsig's university clinic setting of Leipzig. Lothane, *In Defense of Schreber*, 260–61.
40. Schreber, *Memoirs*.
41. Daniel Devreese, Han Israëls, and Julien Quackelbeen, eds., *Schreber Inédit* (Paris: Éditions du Seuil, 1986), 220.
42. Devreese et al., *Schreber Inédit*, 222.
43. Lothane, *In Defense of Schreber*, 295.
44. *Bürgerliches Gesetzbuch* I no. 2, no. 6 (subsection 1), 1896.
45. Schreber, *Memoirs*, 10. Italics Schreber's.
46. Schreber, *Memoirs*, 411.
47. Schreber states in his appeal of 1901 that he received a promise from his father's publisher, Friedrich Fleischer in Leipzig, that his *Memoirs* could be released through them. Schreber, *Memoirs*, 379. In 1902, the court judgment that set Schreber free quotes a statement from the plaintiff that the *Memoirs* would be published with Nauhardt Leipzig, which had released his father's work "Medical Indoor Gymnastics." Schreber, *Memoirs*, 422. Neither press ultimately accepted the book.
48. Freud, *SE* 12:79.
49. Lothane, *In Defense of Schreber*, 521. Lothane is referring to R. H. Pierson, "Über Entmündigung wege Geistesschwäche," *Archiv für Psychiatrie und Nervenkrankheiten* 37 (1903): 1052; and Guido Weber, "Discussion of Pierson," *Archiv für Psychiatrie und Nervenkrankheiten* (1903): 1053.
50. Guido Weber, "Ein interessanter Entmündigungsfall," *Allgemeine Zeitschrif für Psychiatrie* (1905): 402–6. Reviews of Schreber's book at the time appeared in German psychiatric journals including *Centralblatt für Nervenheilkunde und Psychiatrie* (1903): 500; *Psychiatrische-Neurologische Wochenschrift* 5, no. 38 (1903/1904): 422–43; *Zeitschrift für Psychologie und Physiologie der Sinnesorgane* 37 (1904): 469; *Aerztliche Sachverständigen-Zeitung* 14 (1904): 298; *Deutsche Zeitschrift für Nervenheilkunde* 27 (1904): 352–53.
51. Otto Gross, "Zur Differentialdiagnostik netativistischer Phenomene," *Psychiatrische Wochenschrift* 6 (1904): 345–53, 357–63.
52. Emil Kraepelin, *Psychiatrie. Ein Lehrbuch für Studierende und Ärzte*, III. Band. *Klinische Psychiatrie*. II. Teil (Leipzig: Verlag von Johann Ambrosius Barth, 1913), 682n1, 854n1. There is also a long passage in this volume (872) that describes a patient with dementia praecox who insisted that he had a nervous illness. While there is no way to confirm that the reference is to Schreber, Kraepelin's earlier citations of the *Memoirs* make the connection a strong possibility.
53. Manfred Geier, "'Es wundert mich an.' Schrebers Denkwürdigkeiten: Ein paranoider Intertext," in *Die Schrift und die Tradition. Studien zur Intertextualität* (Munich: Wilhelm Fink, 1985), 34–55; Gerd Busse, "Schreber und Flechsig: Der Hirnanatom als Psychiater," *Medizinhistorisches Journal* 24, no. 3–4 (1989): 260–305; Gerd Busse, *Schreber, Freud und die Suche nach dem Vater*, Inaugural-Dissertation, Freie Universität, Berlin (Frankfurt am Main: Lang, 1990); Martin Stingelin, "Paul Emil Flechsig. Die Berechnung der menschlichen Seele," in *Wunderblock. Eine Geschichte der modernen Seele*, ed. J. Clair, C. Pichler, and W. Pichler (Vienna: Löcker, 1989); Martin

Stingelin, "Die Seele als Funktion des Körpers. Zur Seelenpolitik der Leipziger Universitätspsychiatrie unter Paul Emil Flechsig," in *Diskursanalysen 2*, ed. Friedrich Kittler, Manfred Schneider, and Samual Weber (Opladen: Westdeutscher Verlag, 1990); Martin Stingelin, "Psychiatrisches Wissen, juristische Macht und literarisches Selbstverhältnis in Daniel Paul Schreber's *Denkwürdicgeiten eines Nervenkranken* im Licht von Foucaults *Geschichte des Wahnsinns*," in *Scientia Poetica. Jahrbuch für Geschichte der Literatur und der Wissenschaften*, Band 4 (2000), 131–64; Holger Steinberg, "Arzt und Patient: Paul Flechsig und Daniel Paul Schreber," *Der Nervenarzt* 75, no. 9 (October 2004): 933–37; Holger Steinberg, "Paul Flechsig (1847–1929): ein Hirnforscher als Psychiater," in *200 Jahre an der Universität Leipzig*, ed. Matthias C. Angermeyer (Springer, 2005).

54. Stingelin, "Psychiatrisches Wissen"; Steinberg, "Arzt und Patient"; Steinberg, "Paul Flechsig (1847–1929)."
55. Thomas Dalzell, *Freud's Schreber Between Psychiatry and Psychoanalysis: On Subjective Disposition to Psychosis* (New York: Routledge, 2011).
56. Gilles Deleuze and Félix Guattari, *Anti-Oedipus*, trans. Robert Hurley, Mark Seem, and Helen R. Lang (Minnesota: University Of Minneapolis Press, 1983).
57. Jean-François Lyotard, "Vertiginous Sexuality: Schreber's Commerce with God," in *Psychosis and Sexual Identity: Toward a Post-Apocalyptic View of the Schreber Case*, ed. David B. Allison (Albany: SUNY Press, 1988).
58. Michel de Certaeu, "The Institution of Rot," in *Psychosis and Sexual Identity*, ed. Allison.
59. Friedrich Kittler discusses the Schreber case at length both in "Flechsig/Schreber/Freud: An Information Network of 1910," *Qui Parle* 2, no. 1 (Spring 1988): 1–17, and his book *Discourse Networks 1800/1900*, trans. Michael Metteer and Chris Cullens (Stanford, CA: Stanford University Press, 1990). Octave Mannoni described Schreber as a recording machine taking dictation from God in "Schreber als Schreiber," in *Psychosis and Sexual Identity*, ed. Allison. Wolfgang Hagen characterizes Schreber's *Memoirs* as a radio operating from within his delusional state to broadcast his delirium to the world as a scientifically exact discourse in *Radio Schreber: Der 'moderne Spiritismus' und die Sprache der Medien* (Weimar: Verlag und Datenbank für Geisteswissenschaft, 2001). Mark S. Roberts writes of Schreber's body as becoming progressively mechanized and machinelike because of the techniques used in his psychiatric treatment, a fact of which he was both aware and horrified. Mark S. Roberts, "Wired: Schreber as Machine, Technophobe, and Virtualist," *TDR* 40, no. 3 (Autumn 1996): 31–46. Avital Ronell mentions Schreber briefly in *The Telephone Book: Technology, Schizophrenia, Electric Speech* (Lincoln: University of Nebraska Press, 1989). Andrew Gaedtke argues that Schreber's *Memoirs* help readers interpret the "ontological and phenomenological" implications of the "technological features of the psychological theories" used to explain schizophrenia, pairing the work with modernist texts by Wyndham Lewis and Samuel Beckett, among others. Andrew Gaedtke, *Modernism and the Machinery of Madness* (Cambridge: Cambridge University Press, 2017).
60. Goodrich, *Schreber's Law*; Mark Sanders, "Psychoanalysis, Mourning, and the Law: Schreber's Paranoia as Crisis of Judging," in *Law and Mourning*, ed. Austin Serat, Lawrence Douglas, and Martha Merrill Umphrey (Amherst: University of Massachusetts Press, 2017), 117–47; Santner, *My Own Private Germany*.
61. On how Freud read Schreber, see C. Barry Chabot, *Freud on Schreber: Psychoanalytic Theory and the Critical Act* (Amherst: University of Massachusetts Press, 1982).

Fiction and art: see the Italian writer Roberto Calasso's *L'impuro folle* (Milan: Adelphi, 1974); Caryl Churchill's radio play *Schreber's Nervous Illness* (London: Bloomsbury, 2015); Brian Henderson's *Nerve Language, A Book of Poetry* (Pedlar, 2007); Fritz Kaiser and Peter Androsch's opera *Schreber. Ein Oper in acht Bildern, Musik von Peter Androsch* (Linz, 2000); and the Leipzig exhibition on Schreber in Thomas R. Müller, ed., *Angewundert: hundert Jahre "Denkwürdigkeiten eines Nervenkranken" von Daniel Paul Schreber: Katalog zur Ausstellung* (Leipzig: Sammlung Sächsisches Psychiatriemuseum, 2004).

62. Lothane, *In Defense of Schreber*, 67.
63. Lothane, *In Defense of Schreber*, 477.
64. Martin Stingelin has produced a concordance between Schreber's *Memoirs* and Flechsig's *Brain and Soul (Gehirn und Seele)*. Martin Stingelin, "Paul Emil Flechsig. Die Berechnung der menschlichen Seele," in *Wunderblock*, ed. Clair et al.
65. Schreber, *Memoirs*, 8.
66. Schreber, *Memoirs*, 82.
67. Schreber, *Memoirs*, 82–83n42.
68. Schreber, *Memoirs*, 82–83n42.
69. Schreber, *Memoirs*, 270–71.
70. Schreber, *Memoirs*, 271n113.
71. Karl Pörnbacher, Gerhard Schaub, Hans-Joachim Simm, and Edda Ziegler, eds., *Georg Büchner. Werke und Briefe. Münchner Ausgabe* (Munich: Deutscher Taschenbuch Verlag, 1988), 650.
72. Schreber, *Memoirs*, 60.
73. Schreber, *Memoirs*, 60–61.
74. Schreber, *Memoirs*, 96.
75. Immanuel Kant, *Anthropology from a Pragmatic Point of View*, trans. Robert B. Louden (Cambridge: Cambridge University Press, 2006), 103. Kant's italics.
76. Freud, *SE* 12:54.
77. Schreber, *Memoirs*, 55.
78. Sandra M. Gilbert and Susan Gubar, *The Madwoman in the Attic* (1979; New Haven, CT: Yale University Press, 2000).
79. Holger Steinberg, Adrian Schmidt-Recla, and Sebastian Schmideler, "Forensic Psychiatry in Nineteenth-Century Saxony: The Case of Woyzeck," *Harvard Review of Psychiatry* 15, no. 4 (July/August 2007): 173.
80. Steinberg and Schmideler, "Eine wiederentdeckte," 342.

## 4. Expressionist *Weltrevolution* and Psychopolitical Worlding

1. The term *Räterepublik* designates any republican system of government composed of councils of workers and is a form of council communism. As such, it does not necessarily imply affiliation with, control by, or other links to the Soviet Union—which, in any event, did not formally exist by that name until 1922. A number of such republics sprang up after World War I in Bremen, Hungary, and Slovakia. Allan Mitchel provides a detailed account of the Bavarian Soviet Republic in *Revolution in Bavaria, 1918–1919* (Princeton, NJ: Princeton University Press, 1965), 304–31. An extensive discussion of Toller's role therein can be found in R. Ellis, *Ernst Toller and German Society: Intellectuals as Leaders and Critics, 1914–1939* (Madison, NJ: Farleigh Dickinson University Press, 2013), 85–128.

2. A transcript of Toller's defense as delivered by his lawyer, Hugo Hasse, can be found in full in Stefan Großmann's eyewitness account of the proceedings, *Der Hochverräter Ernst Toller. Die Geschichte eines Prozesses* (Berlin: Ernst Rowohlt Verlag, 1919), 24–32. Toller reproduces this specific quotation in his autobiography as well.
3. Ernst Toller, *Masse-Mench: ein Stück aus der Sozialen Revolution des 20. Jahrhunderts* (Berlin: Gustav Kiepenheuer Verlag, 1930). The brevity of these lines belies their translational difficulty. Vera Mendel's 1923 English edition gives them as "Mother of new power and rhythm / Mother of new peoples and patterns" (Ernst Toller, *Masses and Man*, trans. Vera Mendel [London: Nonesuch, 1923]), and Louis Untermeyer's as "Bearer of new forms / Bearer of new folk-unity" (Ernst Toller, *Man and the Masses*, trans. Louis Untermeyer [Garden City, NY: Doubleday, Page and Co., 1924]). Neither of these variants, however, captures the sense of *Schwingen* as oscillations (as in the swinging of a pendulum) or *Volkerkreise* as, literally, circles of people. The latter is particularly problematic because it can be used in the anthropological sense of ethnic groups. Both English translations additionally struggle with how to convey Toller's use of *Gebärerin*, which is not "mother" but grammatically and biologically refers to a female progenitor.
4. The character is based on the Russian-Jewish intellectual and dissident Sarah Sonja Lerch, née Rabinowitz (1882–1918), an acquaintance of Toller's from 1918. Lerch was imprisoned for her participation in the Munich munitions strikes of that year and died in prison awaiting trial. Albert Earl Gurganus, "Sarah Sonja Lerch, née Rabinowitz: The Sonja Irene of Toller's *Masse-Mensch*," *German Studies Review* 28, no. 3 (October 2005): 607–20.
5. Once again, there are a number of translational obstacles in these lines. Mendel stretches Toller's German ("Flames the century in blood of expiation / The earth nails itself / To the cross"). Untermeyer inexplicably adds the term "pyre" ("The century is a red glare / Pyres are bloody with guilt / Earth crucifies itself").
6. Toller, *Masse-Mensch*, 17.
7. There is a vast array of secondary sources on this topic written from literary, historical, and sociological perspectives. While it would be impossible to list them all, a much-abbreviated overview of those focused on Central Europe and Russia might include Anson Rabinbach, *The Human Motor: Energy, Fatigue, and the Origins of Modernity* (Berkeley: University of California Press, 1992); Michael Cowan, *Cult of the Will: Nervousness and German Modernity* (University Park: Pennsylvania State University Press, 2008); Andreas Killen: *Berlin Electropolis: Shock, Nerves, Modernity* (Berkeley: University of California Press, 2006).
8. Unabhängige Sozialdemokratische Partei Deutschlands (Independent Social Democratic Party of Germany) and Kommunistische Partei Deutschlands (Communist Party of Germany). See Killen's description of neurasthenia and hysteria in *Berlin Electropolis*, esp. 85–86. Killen describes both as part of a sweeping "mass nervousness" that emerged in Germany in the 1890s.
9. *Weltgeschichte*, Erster Band, ed. Hans F. Helmolt (Leipzig und Wien: Bibliographisches Institut, 1899), v. Helmolt is explicitly using the term in the sense outlined by Ratzel. His *Weltgeschichte* notably concludes with a study of the relationship between human psychology and world history. See also Hartmuth Bergenthum, "Understanding the World Around 1900: Popular World Histories in Germany," in *Popular Historiographies in the Nineteenth and Twentieth Centuries*, ed. Sylvia Paletschek (Oxford: Berghahn, 2011), 54–72. Jessica Berman writes about Ratzel in the context of literary modernism's possible geographies.

10. I have chosen to retain the gendered sense of the German word *Mensch* (man, as in mankind) in English rather than opting to translate it as the more neutral "one," to keep the important gendering of the play. The title could, however, also be translated as: Many-One, Many and One, The Many's One.
11. Emil Kraepelin, "Psychiatrische Randbemerkungen zur Zeitgeschichte," *Süddeutsche Monatshefte* 16, no. 2 ("Kriegshefte") (June 1919): S. 171–83. Hereafter abbreviated as "PR" in the notes. Translated by Eric J. Engstrom as "Psychiatric Observations on Contemporary Issues," *History of Psychiatry* 3 (1992): 253–69. See also Fritz Gerlich, "Der Kommunismus in der Praxis," *Süddeutsche Monatshefte* 16, no. 12 ("Kriegshefte") (June 1919): S. 184–207; Paul Busching, "Die Revolution in Bayern," *Süddeutsche Monatshefte* 16, no. 12 ("Kriegshefte") (June 1919): S. 217–33; Hermann Losch, "Das denkende Pferd," *Süddeutsche Monatshefte* 16, no. 12 ("Kriegshefte") (June 1919): S. 244.
12. Kraepelin, "PR," 177; Engstrom, trans., 263.
13. Kraepelin, "PR," 177–78. Engstrom, trans., 263–64.
14. Kraepelin, "PR," 177–78. Engstrom, trans., 263–64.
15. The eighth edition appeared in four volumes. It is the last of these that was published in 1915.
16. Kraepelin, *Psychiatrie. Ein Lehrbuch für Studierende und Ärzte.* IV Band. *Klinische Psychiatrie.* III. Teil (Leipzig: Verlag von Johann Ambrosius Barth, 1915), 1974.
17. See Ernst Bloch, *Geist der Utopie* (Berlin: Paul Cassirer, 1923), 260; *The Spirit of Utopia*, trans. Anthony A. Nassar (Stanford, CA: Stanford University Press, 2000).
18. A complete list of financial contributors can be found in *Kraepelin Werke* IX, *Briefe und Dokumente* II, ed. Wolfgang Burgmair, Eric J. Engstrom, and Mattias M. Weber (Munich: Belleville Verlag Michael Farin, 2000–2019), 127–35.
19. Ernst Toller, *Autobiographisches und Justizkritik*, Band 3 in *Sämtliche Werke* (Göttingen: Wallstein Verlag, 2015), 178. Toller had gathered students at the University of Heidelberg to sign an appeal against the Vaterlandspartei. It subsequently inspired several articles criticizing the party in major newspapers during 1917 and 1918. Toller also wrote a skit entitled "Tragödie unserer Zeit" (The tragedy of our time), from which he read during the 1918 strike, that exposed the "inhumanity" of annexationist claims.
20. Emil Kraepelin, *Kraepelin in München* II, *Kraepelin Werke* VII, ed. Burgmair, Engstrom, and Weber, 175.
21. *Reichstrafgesetzbuch* (1871), Vierter Abschnitt: "Gründe, welche die Strafe ausschließen oder mildern."
22. Kraepelin, *Kraepelin in München* II, 176.
23. Kraepelin, *Psychiatrie. Ein Lehrbuch für Studierende und Ärzte*, IV Band, *Klinische Psychiatrie.* III. Teil (Leipzig: Verlag von Johann Ambrosius Barth, 1915), 2032, 2040, 1980.
24. Kraepelin, *Kraepelin in München* II, 176.
25. Kraepelin, *Kraepelin in München* II, 174.
26. Kraepelin, *Kraepelin in München* II, 174.
27. Wölfgang Frühwald and John M. Spalek, *Der Fall Toller* (Munich: Carl Hansler, 1979), 80.
28. Frühwald and Spalek, *Der Fall Toller*, 80, 93. Toller objected to Rüdin that many revered figures of history had suffered from hysteria ("Schiller, Napoleon, Schopenhauer") and that it clearly was not the kind of character flaw the psychiatrist made it out to be, whether he had "improved" or not.
29. Kraepelin, "PR," 177; Engstrom, trans., 264.

30. Kraepelin, "PR," 177; Engstrom, trans., 261.
31. Kraepelin, "PR," 177; Engstrom, trans., 262. Translation modified.
32. Kahn originally delivered the lecture to the Bavarian Psychiatrists' Association in August 1919.
33. Hugo Marx, "Ärztliche Gedanken zur Revolution," *Berliner Klinischer Wochenschrift* 2 (November 10, 1919), 1079.
34. H. Stelzner, "Pyschopathologisches in der Revolution," *Zeitschrift f. d. ges. Neur. u. Psych.* 49 (1919).
35. See Fidelis [Felix Boenheim], "Deutschlands Psychiater in ihrer Stellung zu den Revolutionären," *Das Forum* 4, no. 5 (February 1920): S.397–400; and Julius Moses, "Psychopathie und Revolution," *Die Freiheit* (Berlin) 514 (February 11, 1921).
36. The dramatic character's lightly fictionalized name damningly mixes a reference to the actual person with a phonic hint of the German term for "liar" (*Lügner*).
37. Ernst Toller, *Hoppla, wir Leben!*, in *Sämtliche Werke. Kritische Ausgabe*, ed. Bert Kasties, Karl Leydecker, et al. (Göttingen: Wallenstein Verlag, 2015), 2:13–162, 659, 667.
38. Frühwald and Spalek, *Der Fall Toller*, 110.
39. "This case does not concern theater censorship, but the police department's general obligation to maintain calm and order." See Frühwald and Spalek, *Der Fall Toller*, 113.
40. The references to *Gewalt* in the play help situate it within other contemporary dramatic and philosophical works treating the so-called *Gewaltfrage*. These include Ludwig Rubiner's *Die Gewaltlosen* (1917/1918), Erich Mühsam's *Judas* (1920), Georges Sorel's *Réflexions sur la violence* (1908), Erig Unger's *Politik und Metaphysik* (1921), and most famously Walter Benjamin's *Kritik der Gewalt* (1921). A number of works of critical scholarship have addressed the role of Toller's *Gewalt* in this broader context. See Birgit Schreiber, *Politische Retheologisierung: Ernst Tollers frühe Dramatik als Suche nach einer "Politik der reinen Mittel"* (Wurzburg: Königshausen & Neumann, 1997), 113–156; Ernst Toller and Wölfgang Frühwald, *Masse-Mensch: Ein Stück aus der sozialen Revolution des 20. Jahrhunderts* (Leipzig: Reclam Philipp, 2010), 99.
41. Renate Benson, *German Expressionist Drama: Ernst Toller and Georg Kaiser* (London: Macmillan, 1984), 6. Walter Rheiner, Iwan Goll, and Gottfried Benn, for example, all contested the existence of expressionism as such.
42. Walter H. Sokel, *The Writer in Extremis: Expressionism in Twentieth-Century German Literature* (Stanford, CA: Stanford University Press), 162–63.
43. Lisa Marie Anderson, *German Expressionism and the Messianism of a Generation* (Amsterdam: Rodopi, 2011), 16.
44. Toller is presumably citing the German sociologist Ferdinand Tönnies's opposition between *Gemeinschaft* (community) and *Gesellschaft* (society).
45. Bloch, *Geist der Utopie*, 5; *The Spirit of Utopia*, 3.
46. Bloch, *Geist der Utopie*, 3; *The Spirit of Utopia*, 1. "Ich bin. Wir sind. Das ist genug. Nun haben wir zu beginnen."
47. Bloch, *Geist der Utopie*, 5; *The Spirit of Utopia*, 3.
48. Ernst Toller, *Sämtliche Werke: kritische Ausgabe. Band 1. Stücke 1919–1923* (Göttingen: Wallstein Verlag, 2015), 364. Cordula Grunow-Erdmann, *Die Dramen Ernst Tollers im Kontext ihrer Zeit* (Heidelberg: Winter 1994).
49. Toller, *Sämtliche Werke* 1, 354.
50. Toller, *Masse-Mensch*, 76.
51. Toller, *Masse-Mensch*, 89.
52. Toller, *Masse-Mensch*, 94.
53. Toller, *Sämtliche Werke* 1, 354.

## 5. The Economic Hypothesis: Soul Markets of Soviet Fiction

1. A version of this chapter was previously published as Cate I. Reilly, "Russian Roulette: Speculation and the Medical Humanities in Vsevolod Ivanov's Novel Y," *Slavic and East European Journal* 66, no. 4 (Winter 2022), 518-537. Jean-Joseph Goux, *Symbolic Economies* (Ithaca, NY: Cornell University Press, 1990), 3.
2. Goux, *Symbolic Economies*, 5.
3. As Valentina G. Brougher and Alexander Etkind point out, the book's unusual title clearly refers both to the Cyrillic "У" and to the Latin "Y," particularly as used to designate a mathematical variable. For this reason, I have chosen to leave the title as "У" (rather than replacing it with the English transliteration "U"). Valentina G. Brougher, "Vsevolod Ivanov's Satirical Novel *Y* and the Rooster Metaphor," *Slavic Review* 53, no. 1 (1994): 160n1; Aleksander Etkind, "Zhit' u Kremlia i pisat' ne dlya pechati: romany Vsevoloda Ivanova 1930-kh godov," *Revue des études slaves* 71, no. 3 (1999): 639.
4. Tamara Ivanova, "Pisatel' obgonyayet vremya," in Vsevolod Vyacheslavovich Ivanov, *Kreml'; U: Romany* (Moscow: Sovetskiy pisatel', 1990), 516, 522.
5. Ivanov, *Kreml'; U: Romany*, 259. With the exception of a dream experienced by the protagonist Yegor Yegorych, *Y* has yet to be translated into English (Ivanov, "Yegor Yegorych's Dream"). Translations here are my own, unless marked otherwise. At the time Ivanov wrote the novel, the adjective "foreign" (*chuzhoy*) was associated with the belief that only foreign currency possessed guaranteed value, hence my choice of "thoughts belonging to someone else" for "*mysli v nikh chuzhiye.*"
6. Ivanov, *Kreml'; U: Romany*, 266, 373.
7. The novel is generically hybrid. Ivanova identifies the book as a "satirical philosophical novel," Shklovsky declared it reminded him of Petronius's *Satyricon*, and Etkind sees it as a part of the "novelistic tradition." Ivanova, "Pisatel'," 512, 519; Etkind, "Zhit'," 637.
8. Ivanov, *Kreml'; U: Romany*, 274.
9. Etkind, "Zhit'," 638.
10. Ivanov, *Kreml'; U: Romany*, 444.
11. Ivanov, *Kreml'; U: Romany*, 509.
12. V. I. Lenin, "VIII Vserossiyskiy s"ezd sovetov," *Polnoye sobraniye sochinenii* (Izdatel'stvo politicheskoy literatury, 1970), 42:158–59.
13. Ivanov, *Kreml'; U: Romany*, 263.
14. A paper shortage forced publishers to ration beginning in April 1928. On this topic, see Matthew Lenoe, "NEP Newspapers and the Origins of Soviet Information Rationing," *Russian Review* 62, no. 4 (2003): 614–36.
15. Ivanov, *Kreml'; U: Romany*, 324.
16. Ivanov, *Kreml'; U: Romany*, 525.
17. Ivanov, *Kreml'; U: Romany*, 266.
18. Ia. N. Shchapov, ed., *Russkaya pravoslavnaya tserkov' i kommunisticheskoye gosudarstvo 1917–1941* (Bibleysko-bogoslovskiy institut svyatogo Apostola Andreya, 1996), 281.
19. Vladimir Dal', *Tolkovyy slovar'* (Gosudarstevnnoye izdatel'stvo Khudozhestvennaya literatura, 1935), 2:381.
20. Ivanov, *Kreml'; U: Romany*, 264.
21. Georges Bataille, *Visions of Excess: Selected Writings, 1927–1939*, trans. Allan Stoekl (Minneapolis: University of Minnesota Press, 1985), 74.

22. Georges Bataille, *Inner Experience*, trans. Stuart Kendall (Albany: State University of New York Press, 2014), 112–13.
23. Alexander Etkind, *Eros of the Impossible: The History of Psychoanalysis in Russia*, trans. Noah and Maria Rubins (Boulder, CO: Westview, 1997); Martin Miller, *Freud and the Bolsheviks* (New Haven, CT: Yale University Press, 1998).
24. Ivanov, *Kreml'; U: Romany*, 271.
25. Birk Engmann and Holger Steinberg, "Emil Kraepelin's Time in Dorpat—Did This Stay Make Marks in Russian and Soviet Psychiatry?," *Fortschritte der Neurologie-Psychiatrie* 85, no. 11 (November 2017): 675, 677–78; Yu. V. Kannabikh, *Istoriya psikhiatrii* (Gostudarstvennoye meditsinskoye izdatel'stvo, 1928).
26. Kannabikh, *Istoriya psikhiatrii*.
27. Chizh published his own psychiatric textbook in 1911 that reflected the impact made by Kraepelin's work. Vladimir Fedorovich Chizh, *Uchebnik psikhiatrii* (Knigoizdatel'stvo Sotrudnik, 1911), 1–21.
28. Ivanov, *Kreml'; U: Romany*, 275–76.
29. Ivanov, *Kreml'; U: Romany*, 269.
30. Karl Marx, *Capital*, trans. Ben Fowkes (London: Penguin, 1990), 1:139–40.
31. Marx, *Capital*, 1:154–55.
32. Marx, *Capital*, 1:162.
33. Sigmund Freud, "Repression," in *The Standard Edition of the Complete Psychological Works of Sigmund Freud*, ed. and trans. James Strachey (London: Hogarth, 1950), 14:154.
34. Jacques Lacan, "The Function and Field of Speech and Language in Psychoanalysis," in *Écrits*, trans. Bruce Fink (New York: Norton, 2006), 223.

## 6. Monodrama as Mass Spectacle: The Soviet Self on Stage

1. Following his lecture at the Circle of Art and Literature in Moscow, Evreinov spoke again on the subject of monodrama in St. Petersburg, first at the Theatrical Club (February 21, 1909) and then again at the V. F. Komissarzhevskaya Theater (March 4, 1909), where he had recently been appointed chief artistic director. The lecture was published as an independent pamphlet in 1909. It has not been reprinted since. A substantially abridged version of the pamphlet appeared as the introduction to Evreinov's first monodrama *The Presentation of Love* (*Predstavleniye lyubvi*) published in the N. I. Kul'bina's edited volume *Studiya impressionistov* (St. Petersburg: N. I. Butovskoy, 1910), 51–57. Evreinov does not reference the "Introduction to Monodrama" there, but entire passages from it have obviously been transferred and rearranged.
2. N. I. Evreinov, *Vvedeniye v monodramu* (St. Petersburg: N. I. Butovskoy, 1909), 2. An English translation by Laurence Senelick, "Introduction to Monodrama," can be found in his *Russian Dramatic Theory from Pushkin to the Symbolists* (Austin: University of Texas Press, 1981), 183–99. I have modified Senelick's translation where noted. In general, Senelick translates *deystvuyushcheye litso* (the Russian for dramatis persona or character) as "active participant" to indicate Evreinov's emphasis on the dynamism he assigns to that role. I have restored the translation to "character" here and throughout.
3. See Evreinov's "Apologiya teatralnosti" (Apologia for theatricality, 1908).

4. Evreinov's reputation within Russian experimental theater of the early twentieth century has been eclipsed by that of his contemporaries such as Meyerhold and Mayakovsky. This is in large part because his emigration to Paris distanced him both geographically and ideologically from the famous productions of the revolutionary avant-garde.
5. See, for example, Erving Goffman, *The Presentation of Self in Everyday Life* (Garden City, NY: Doubleday, 1959); Erving Goffman, *Frame Analysis* (Cambridge, MA: Harvard University Press, 1974); Guy Debord, *La Société du spectacle* (Paris: Buchet/Chastel, 1967); and Clifford Geertz, *Negara: The Theater-State in Nineteenth-Century Bali* (Princeton, NJ: Princeton University Press, 1980).
6. Two dissertations on this topic include Spyros Papaioannou, "Performing Critique: Towards a Non-Representational Theatre in Britain," Goldsmiths College, University of London, 2012; and Hana Pavelková, "Monologue Plays in Contemporary British and Irish Theatre," Charles University, Prague, 2014. Variants on the genre in cinema can be found in recent popular American films, including *Being John Malkovich* (1999) and Pixar's *Inside Out* (2015), set inside a child's mind.
7. See, for example, his accusatory article directed at Meyerhold, "Originalnost' za chuzhoy schet" (Originality at someone else's expense), *Zhurnal zhurnalov* 1 (1915): 15–16. Tony Pearson has also written on the subject of Evreinov and Meyerhold's rivalry in *New Theater Quarterly* 8, no. 32 (November 1992): 325–29.
8. Kirsten Gram Holmström, *Monodrama, Attitudes, Tableaux Vivants. Studies on Some Trends of Theatrical Fashion, 1770–1815* (Stockholm: Almqvist and Wiksell, 1967), 40.
9. Spencer Golub, *Evreinov: The Theater of Paradox and Transformation* (Ann Arbor, MI: UMI Research Press, 1977; 1984). Golub's work is one of only two major monographs in English to have appeared on Evreinov, though several articles have been published on Evreinov's life, work, and especially his connections to Russian symbolism. The other major text in English is Sharon Marie Carnicke, *The Theatrical Instinct: Nikolai Evreinov and the Russian Theatre of the Early Twentieth Century* (New York: Lang, 1989). Carnicke's work is remarkably critical of Evreinov. In Russian, the recent bibliography by Aleksandrova, Lapidus, et al. contains a good overview of the secondary literature. See Nikolay Nikolayevich Evreinov, *Materialy k bibliografii* (St. Petersburg: Severnaya Zvezda, 2015).
10. Paul du Quenoy, *Stage Fright: Politics and the Performing Arts in Late Imperial Russia* (University Park: Pennsylvania State University Press, 2009). See also Mark Slonim, *Russian Theater from the Empire to the Soviets* (Cleveland: World, 1961).
11. Du Quenoy, *Stage Fright*, 253. Emphasis mine.
12. For an overview of Russian symbolist thought, see Evelyn Bristol's entry on "Symbolism" in *Handbook of Russian Literature*, ed. Victor Terras (New Haven, CT: Yale University Press, 1990), 460–64.
13. Golub, *Evreinov*, 39, has pointed out that many of the themes in *The Foundation of Happiness* and Evreinov's early plays reappear in *In the Stage Wings of the Soul*. These include the Demonic Woman, unorthodox subject matter presented through a mix of strange settings and odd circumstances, a preponderance of scenic effects, the threat of death, and the search for happiness.
14. *Starinnyy teatr* is difficult to render in English. It is most frequently translated by secondary literature as "Ancient Theater," but this translation fails to capture the sense of the adjective *starinnyy* as created or originating in the old days and having been preserved until the present. Whereas the English "ancient" merely gives a sense

of being old, the Russian *starinnyy* conveys the unchanging stability of the item described despite the passage of time. My use of the epithet "Ancient Theater" respects standard sources in English.

15. Golub, *Evreinov*, 37.
16. Evreinov, "Introduction to Monodrama," 183. Translation modified. Evreinov, *Vvedeniye*, 1.
17. Fasmer gives the etymology of the verb *zret'* as the Greek *ὁράω* (horéō), meaning "to look with the eyes (at someone or something)."
18. Evreinov, *Vvedeniye*, 23.
19. Evreinov, "Introduction," 187. Translation modified. Evreinov, *Vvedeniye*, 8.
20. There is some similarity here with Roman Jakobson's work on the empty shifter in "Shifters, Verbal Categories, and the Russian Verb," in *Word and Language*, vol. 2 (Berlin: De Gruyter, 1971). For Jakobson, shifters are "grammatical units in which the general meaning cannot be defined without reference to a specific message." Personal pronouns ("I" and "you") are a good example of shifters, insofar as these pronouns' meaning shifts based on context. Jakobson is translating "shifter" from the French *embrayeur*, and his discussion can be thought of in terms of how shifters are dependent on changing gears in correspondence with changes in reality. Evreinov's insistence on the use of the personal pronoun in the playbill intuits the central importance of such pronouns as linguistic markers that designate subjectivity as a form of pointing, rather than a fixed point.
21. Evreinov, "Introduction," 192. Translation modified. Evreinov, *Vvedeniye*, 17.
22. Evreinov, "Introduction," 187. Translation modified. Evreinov, *Vvedeniye*, 3.
23. See Holmström, *Monodrama*, 40; and Alain Cernuschi, "Pygmalion. Scène Lyrique," in Jean-Jacques Rousseau, *Oeuvres complètes. Édition thématique du tricentenaire*, ed. Raymond Trousson et al. (Geneva: Éditions Slatkine, 2012), 16:429–40.
24. The 1772 Vienna edition of Rousseau's text, by Joseph Kürzbock, preserves this synthesis visually by using three columns arranged adjacent to one another on the page. These detail the character of the instrumental music, give instructions on the length of musical interpolation at various segments, and offer specific directions for the acting. In addition to showcasing the nuts and bolts of the production, the Kürzbock edition revealed a great deal about how heavily monodrama relied on a strong directorial hand.
25. See Holmström, *Monodrama*, 47; and Don Michael Randel, ed., *The New Harvard Dictionary of Music* (Cambridge, MA: Harvard University Press, 1986), 481.
26. See Goethe's letter to Zelter in *Journal für Literatur, Luxus und Mode* 4 (1815). Quoted in Holmström, *Monodrama*, 105. The German tradition was the main channel by which monodrama reached England. It appeared there in the 1790s. William Taylor of Norwich, one of the first German scholars in England, had traveled extensively on the continent during the 1780s. Upon his return to England, he translated Goethe's *Proserpina* and then wrote two of his own monodramas, *Pandora* (1791) and *Oswald* (1792). Taylor's work is the first recorded instance of the use of the word "monodrama" in English. It influenced Tennyson's *Maud* (1855), often regarded as a monodrama (despite the fact that Tennyson did not title it as such).
27. See "Monodrama," in *Columbia Encyclopedia of Modern Drama*, ed. Gabrielle H. Cody (New York: Columbia University Press, 2007), 2:918–19.
28. Preceding monodramas that Evreinov conceivably would have been familiar with include Richard von Meerheimb's *Monodramen neuer Form* (1882), French symbolist iterations such as Mallarmé's interpretation of Hamlet as a monodrama in which all

the characters are emanations of the hero's consciousness, Gerhart Hauptmann's *Hanelles Himmelfahrt* (1893); August Strindberg's *Ett drömspel* (A dream play, 1902), Maurice Maeterlinck's *Der blaue Vogel* (1908), and Leonid Andreev's *Chernye maski* (Black masks, 1908).

29. A. Dwight Culler, "Monodrama and Dramatic Monologue," *PMLA* 90, no. 3 (1975): 375.
30. This is unsurprising given the traditional gender designations of Russian literature. Evreinov's use of an anxious male protagonist is a variant on the superfluous man (*lishniy chelovek*), a character who is "perceived—or regards [himself]—as being in a state of disharmony with the world around [him], rejecting it or being rejected by it," as Victor Terras writes in his *Handbook of Russian Literature* (454). Although Evreinov does not mention it in the "Introduction," his monodramas are also a testament to the continued importance of lamentation in the genre. They frequently feature men bemoaning their romantic plight.
31. A. Yu. Zubov, *Nikolay Evreinov, Demon teatralnosti'* (Moscow: Letniy sad, 2002), 306. Theater for oneself is also, as for subsequent playwrights such as Jerzy Grotowski and Peter Brook, an attempt at decommercializing the playing space.
32. *Samoye glavnoye* was formative for Luigi Pirandello and was the only non-Italian play chosen for production when Pirandello opened his theater in Rome in 1924. The play subsequently premiered at the Pasadena Community Playhouse and at Harvard before making its way to Charles Dullin in France in 1926. It has since been translated into over twenty-five languages and has also appeared on French radio and television.
33. The German translation of *V kulisakh dushi* was completed by the Austrian expressionist playwright Franz Theodor Csokor (1885–1969) and inspired a number of Csokor's own monodramas. See Franz Theodor Csokor, *Die Kulissen der Seele: Monodrama / Nikolaj Nikolajewitsch Evreinoff, Deutsch von Frantz Theodor Csokor* (Wien: Verlag der Wiener Graphischen Werkstätte, 1920); and Liudmila Antisferova, "Auf der Suche nach dem 'neuen Theater' um 1900: Franz Theodor Csokor in St. Petersburg," *Der literarische Zaunkönig* 3 (2007): 10–14. In Italian, the play appears as N. N. Jevrieinov, *La gaia morte ; Tra le quinte dell'anima ; Cio che piu importa*, trad. di Raissa Olkjenizkaja Naldi (Milano: Alpes, 1925). Additional information on Evreinov in Italy can be found in T. Baikova Poggi, "La fortuna di Nikolaj Evreinov in Italia negli anni venti," *Europa Orientalis* 1 (1982): 39–43. In France it was adapted by L. J. Proix as *Les coulisses de l'âme: un acte* in 1931. It played in Prague at the Rococo Theater in 1925.
34. The performances of Crooked Mirror initially took place at the Yusupov Palace Club (a former casino) and followed performances of Meyerhold's "The Strand." By 1910, however, Crooked Mirror had become an independently successful enough to move to the significantly larger Catherine Theater and play during normal hours.
35. Nikolay Nikolayevich Evreinov, "V kulisakh dushi," in *Dramaticheskiye sochineniya. P'yesy iz repertuara "Krivogo zerkala"* (Petrograd: Academiya, 1923), 3:32. The play has been discussed in English-language scholarship in Carnicke, *The Theatrical Instinct*; and Golub, *Evreinov*. More recently, it is the subject of Alexandra Smith's article "Nikolai Evreinov and Edith Craig as Mediums of Modernist Sensibility," *New Theater Quarterly* 26, no. 3 (August 2010): 203–16. English translations can be found in Marie Potapenko and Christopher St. John, *The Theater of the Soul. A Monodrama in One Act by N. Evreinov* (London: Bradbury, Agnew & Co., 1915); and Christopher Collins, ed. and trans., *Theater as Life. Five Modern Plays* (New York: Ardis, 2012). I have relied on my own translation here, which draws from both but also modifies each of these earlier

versions. For that reason, when I do not transliterate the Russian in the body of the text, I include the Russian original in the endnotes for short citations (alongside the pagination from the 1923 edition) and pagination alone in the case of longer citations.

36. Evreinov, "V kulisakh dushi," 33.
37. Nikolay Evreinov, *V shkole ostroumiya: vospominaniya o teatre 'Krivoye zerkalo'* (Moscow: Iskusstvo, 1998), 285.
38. Evreinov records that this was none other than the mother of the well-known actor and film celebrity Vladimir Vasil'evich Maksimov (1880–1937). Apparently the theater's directors and many of Evreinov's colleagues were also stunned by the monodrama. His memoirs claim that upon presenting a copy of the manuscript to the theater heads and his colleagues, no one would give him a straight answer as to whether it could be performed. Evreinov, *V shkole ostroumiyakh*, 283–84.
39. "О, заблуждение! . . . Оставьте ее! . . . оставьте...ведь это только ваше воображение! . . . " Evreinov, "V kulisakh dushi," 38.
40. "Она не такая! Вы целуете краски, вы ласкаете парик . . . Ей 40 лет . . ." Evreinov, "V kulisakh dushi," 38.
41. "С началом его речи 1-ый образ певички исчезает направо,—откуда 'Я' 1-ое выводит 2-ой образ певички, до комичного профанированный." Evreinov, "V kulisakh dushi," 38.
42. "Револьвер в правом кармане, сзади . . . Скорей! . . . скорей! . . . Мне слишком тяжело . . . Вернее целься! . . . Между третьим и четвертым ребром . . . Да, ну же, ну же! . . . Чего бояться? . . . Один момент. Скорее!" Evreinov, "V kulisakh dushi," 41.
43. There are major symbolist precedents for the streamers. Several similar devices appear in Aleksander Blok, *The Fairground Booth* (Balaganchik, 1906).
44. See S. Murata, "Mezhdu ritualom i iskusstvom," *Baltiyskiye sezony: deystvuyushchiye litsa peterb. stseny* [al'manakh] 8 (2003): 74–80. Murata examines Evreinov's *Stage Wings* as well as *A Merry Death* and *The Main Thing*. See also D. V. Fomin "N. N. Evreinov i khudozhniki: ot Starinnogo teatra k "Krivomu zerkalu" in *Russkoye iskusstvo, XX vek: issledovaniya i publikatskii*, ed. G. F. Kovalenko (Moscow: Nauka, 2008), 552–638; N. V. Rostova, "Khudozhestvennyye poiski novykh form na otechestvennoy stsene i v nemom kinematografe na rubezhe XIX–XX stoletiy," *Vestnik Chuvash. universiteta* 4 (2010): 282–90.
45. Paul de Man, *Allegories of Reading* (New Haven, CT: Yale University Press, 1979), 160.
46. De Man, *Allegories of Reading*, 151.
47. De Man, *Allegories of Reading*, 178.
48. De Man is quoting Heidegger here. See *Allegories of Reading*, 187.
49. De Man, *Allegories of Reading*, 180. The use of the French *défaut* for "lack" is Derridean in origin. In Derrida's lexicon, the French idiom "*il faut*" (it is necessary) is a technical term. It signals both the inseparability of essence and fact and the ways in which there is a "defect" or "default" (*dé*faut) in that inseparability. The relationship between *il faut* and *défaut* articulates the way in which necessity is always infected by contingency.
50. "В соответствии с этим, кулисы души рисуются в следующем виде. Рисует разноцветным мелом картину, которую он дальше описывает." Evreinov, "V kulisakh dushi," 34.
51. "Уходит; черная доска убирается; поднимается занавес, открывающий картинку души в том виде как она описана и зарисована профессором." Evreinov, "V kulisakh dushi," 34.

52. "Что? Алло? Плохо слышно? Но я говорю достаточно громко! . . . Гудит в ушах?"
53. James and the *Principles of Psychology* had first been introduced to Russia by an 1890 review in the *Questions of Philosophy and Psychology*, published by the Moscow Psychological Society. The review was written by Nikolay Grot, the journal's editor and founder. A Russian translation by L. E. Obolenskiy of the abridged, one-volume version (under the title *Nauchnye osnovy psikhologii* [The scientific basis of psychology]) came out in 1902. No full translation ever followed. See Joan Delaney Grossman, "Philosophers, Decadents, and Mystics," in *William James in Russian Culture*, ed. Joan Delaney Grossman and Ruth Rischin (Lanham, MD: Lexington, 2003), 110.
54. Sigmund Freud, "Ratschläge für den Arzt bei der psychoanalytischen Behandlung" (1912). Translation from Sigmund Freud, "Recommendations to Physicians Practicing Psychoanalysis," in *The Freud Reader*, trans. Peter Gay (New York: Norton, 1995), 360.
55. "Не дергайте нервы! . . . Ведь вам сказано . . . [Нервы гудят каждый раз, как до них дотрагиваются]."
56. Evreinov, "V kulisakh dushi," 34.
57. *Diderot's Selected Writings*, trans. Derek Coltman (New York: Macmillan, 1966), 186.
58. "Я сочту за драму только такое 'действие', которое я без насилия своей фантазии назову 'моею драмой.' Evreinov, "V kulisakh dushi," 34.
59. See *Tresor Dictionnaire de la langue Française XIXe et du XXe siècle.*
60. Evreinov, "Introduction," 194. Translation modified. Evreinov, *Vvedeniye*, 21.
61. P. Kerzhentsev, *Tvorcheskiy teatr. Puti sotsialisticheskogo teatra*, 3rd ed. (Moscow: Izdatel'stvo Vserossiyskogo Tsentralnogo Ispolnitel'nogo Komiteta Sovetov R. S. K. i K. Deputatov, 1919).
62. On Kerzhentsev's ideas about collective creation, see Stefan Acquilina, "Platon Kerzhentsev and His Theories on Collective Creation," *Journal of Dramatic Theory and Criticism* 28, no. 2 (Spring 2014), 29–48. Other work on Kerzhentsev in English is fairly limited, in part because *Creative Theater* has never been translated into English. See Robert Leach, *Revolutionary Theatre* (London: Routledge, 1994), 23–24; and Lynn Mally, *Revolutionary Acts: Amateur Theatre and the Soviet State* (Ithaca, NY: Cornell University Press, 2000). Kerzhentsev also receives mention in German scholarship in Malte Rolf, *Das sowjetische Massenfest* (Hamburg: Hamburger Edition, 2006), 74, 76.
63. Kerzhentsev, *Tvorcheskiy teatr*, 36–37.
64. See Golub, *Evreinov*; and František Deàk, "Russian Mass Spectacles," in *Drama Review* 19, no. 2 ("Political Theater Issue") (June 1975): 7–22.
65. Deàk, "Russian Mass Spectacles," 13.
66. Deàk, "Russian Mass Spectacles," 13.
67. "Задача предстоит режиссеру небывалая по сложности замысла." Evreinov, "Vzyatiye zimnego dvortsa," in *Zhizn' iskusstva* 596–597 (October 30–31, 1920): 1.
68. "Явилось желание вспомнить всенародно о событии, ставшем знаменательным для новой России, событии, положившем в ней фактически начало Советской Власти трудящихся." Evreinov, " Vzyatiye zimnego dvortsa," 1.
69. "Первые две сцены (каждая размером в длину по 20 саженей) решено было построить по бокам арки б. 'Генерального Штаба', бесценно декорировать их и соединить мостом."
70. Deàk, "Russian Mass Spectacles," 13. Responsibility for this platform was delegated jointly to Kugel' and Annenkov. Annenkov was also in charge of set design for both platforms.

71. Evreinov, "Vzyatiye zimnego dvortsa," 1.
72. There is no single authoritative document describing the event. The description here is compiled from numerous sources, including Huntley Carter's translation of an eyewitness recollection in *The New Theater and Cinema of Soviet Russia* (London: Chapman and Dodd, 1924) and René Fülöp-Miller's extensive description and photographs in *Geist und Gesicht des Bolschewismus* (Zürich: Almathea Verlag, 1926). I have additionally relied on Evreinov's published essays on the topic and those of his contemporaries, all of which appear in *Zhizn' iskusstva* (The life of art) magazine. A partial film of the spectacle can be found online: Константин Державин и Николай Евреинов. *Взятие Зимнего дворца*. Исторический фильм. Петроградский окружной фотокиноотдел [ПОФКО] (1920). From the performance of the mass spectacle of November 7, 1920, posted by "veragennadievna," December 13, 2012, http://www.youtube.com/watch?v=eyrAQiTbLhI.
73. Golub, *Evreinov*, 199.
74. "Высокая (с двухэтажный дом) будка, снабженная целым рядом телефонов и сигнальных звонков, построенная в качестве 'командного мостика' посреди площади (у самой колонны)."
75. "Речь идет об архитектонике драмы на принципе сценическаго тожества ея с представлением действующего." Evreinov, *Vvedeniye*, 8.
76. Golub, *Evreinov*, 197.
77. Katerina Clark, *The Soviet Novel: History as Ritual* (Chicago: University of Chicago Press, 1981), 18.

## 7. Something Wrong with Vero: Neural Landscapes of the Argentine Dirty War

1. A longer version of this chapter that did not include my discussion of psychopower was previously published in Cate I. Reilly, "Neuromimesis: Picturing the Humanities Picturing the Brain," *Frontiers in Integrative Neuroscience* 16 (October 14, 2022), https://www.frontiersin.org/articles/10.3389/fnint.2022.760785/full.
2. Santiago Ramón y Cajal, *Recollections of My Life*, trans. E. Horne Craigie (Cambridge, MA: MIT Press, 1996), 363.
3. Ramón y Cajal, *Recollections of My Life*, 363–64.
4. Maria Paz Soler Villalabos, "Su deseo primero: 'ser pintor,'" in *Santiago Ramón y Cajal. Trabajo, saberes y arte en la investigación científica*, ed. Fernando Bandrés and Santiago Delgado (Madrid: Gráficas 82, 2013), 193.
5. Laura Otis, *Membranes: Metaphors of Invasion in Nineteenth-Century Literature, Science, and Politics* (Baltimore: Johns Hopkins University Press, 1999).
6. Otis, *Membranes*, 64.
7. Otis, *Membranes*, 64.
8. Camillo Golgi, "The Neuron Doctrine—Theory and Facts," Nobel Lecture, December 11, 1906, https://www.nobelprize.org/uploads/2018/06/golgi-lecture.pdf.
9. Ramón y Cajal, "Neuronismo o reticularismo? Las pruebas objetivas de la unidad anatómica de las células nerviosas," *Archivos de neurobiología* 13, no. 2, 4–6 (1933): 1–144.
10. Lorraine Daston and Peter Galison, *Objectivity* (New York: Zone, 2007).
11. Ramón y Cajal, *Recollections of My Life*, 36.

12. Ramón y Cajal, *Recollections of My Life*, 36.
13. Ramón y Cajal, *Recollections of My Life*, 93.
14. Ramón y Cajal, *Vacation Stories*, trans. Laura Otis (Champaign: University of Illinois Press, 2001).
15. Ramón y Cajal, *Recollections of My Life*, 101.
16. Deborah Elise White, *Romantic Returns* (Stanford, CA: Stanford University Press 2000), 10.
17. Ramón y Cajal, *Recollections of My Life*, 62.
18. Ramón y Cajal, *Recollections of My Life*, 129–30.
19. Villalabos, "Su deseo primero," 192.
20. Ramón y Cajal, *Recollections of My Life*, 297.
21. Ramón y Cajal, *Recollections of My Life*, 363, 373.
22. Ramón y Cajal, *Recollections of My Life*, 293.
23. Ramón y Cajal, *Recollections of My Life*, 293.
24. Ramón y Cajal, *Recollections of My Life*, 297.
25. Ramón y Cajal, *Recollections of My Life*, 293.
26. In the 2015 Zaragoza exhibition "The Physiology of Dreams." See *Fisiologia de los Sueños. Cajal, Tanguy, Lorca, Dali . . .* (Zaragoza: Prensas de la Universidad de Zaragoza, 2015).
27. Gregorio Marañon, *Cajal: su tiempo y el nuestro* (Madrid: Espasa Calpe, 1950); Otis, *Membranes*; Miguel B. Márquez, "Santiago Ramón y Cajal: algo más que un fotógrafo," *Ámbitos* 11–12 (2004): 139–53; Pablo Garcia-Lopez, Virginia Garcia-Marin, and Miguel Friere, "The Histological Slides and Drawings of Cajal," *Frontiers in Neuroanatomy* 4 (2010); Javier DeFelipe, "Cajal and the Discovery of a New Artistic World: The Neuronal Forest," *Progress in Brain Research* 203 (2013): 201–20; Javier DeFelipe, *Cajal's Neuronal Forest* (New York: Oxford University Press, 2017); Miguel Ángel Rego Robles, "The Early Drawings and Prints of Santiago Ramón y Cajal: A Visual Epistemology of the Neurosciences," *European Journal of Anatomy* 23, suppl. 1 (2019): 57–66.
28. American Psychiatric Association, *Diagnostic and Statistical Manual of Mental Disorders*, 5th ed. (Washington, DC: American Psychiatric Publishing, 2013), 271.
29. Jacques Derrida, "Geopsychoanalysis: '. . . and the Rest of the World,'" *American Imago* 48, no. 2 (Summer 1991): 209; see also 205.
30. A. W. Stencell, *Seeing Is Believing: America's Sideshows* (Toronto: ECW Press, 2002), 185; Joe Nickell, *Secrets of the Sideshows* (Lexington: University Press of Kentucky, 2005), 283.
31. Nickell, *Secrets of the Sideshows*, 284.
32. Lucrecia Martel, dir., *La mujer sin cabeza* (Strand Releasing, 2008), 87 minutes, DVD.
33. On amnesia, see Quintín, "The Headless Woman," *Cinema Scope* 35 (Summer 2008): 42–43; Daniel Quirós, "'La época está en desorden': Reflexiones sobre la temporalidad en *Bolivia* de Adrián Caetano y *La mujer sin cabeza* de Lucrecia Martel," *A Contracorriente* 8, no. 1 (2010): 230–58; Deborah Martin, "Childhood, Youth, and the In-between: The Ethics and Aesthetics of Lucrecia Martel's *La mujer sin cabeza*," *Hispanic Research Journal* 14, no. 2 (April 2013): 144–58; Patricia White, *Women's Cinema, World Cinema: Projecting Contemporary Feminisms* (Durham, NC: Duke University Press, 2015); Karina Elizabeth Vásquez, "La poética del enrarecimiento en *La mujer sin cabeza* (2008), de Lucrecia Martel," *Hispanic Research Journal* 16, no. 1 (February 2015): 31–48. On trauma, see Cecilia Sosa, "A Counter-Narrative of Argentine Mourning: *The Headless Woman* (2008), directed by Lucrecia Martel," *Theory,*

*Culture, Society* 26, no. 7–8 (2009): 250–62; Matt Losada, "Lucrecia Martel's *La mujer sin cabeza*: Cinematic Free Indirect Discourse, Noise-Scape and the Distraction of the Middle Class," *Romance Notes* 50, no. 3 (2010): 307–13.

34. On concussion, see White, *Women's Cinema, World Cinema.* On confusion, see Martin, "Childhood, Youth, and the In-between." On lost bearings, see Paul A. Schroeder Rodríguez, "Little Red Riding Hood Meets Freud in Lucrecia Martel's Salta Trilogy," *Camera Obscura* 87.29, no. 3 (2014): 93–115. On guilty conscience, see Losada, "Lucrecia Martel's *La mujer.*" On the racist neocolonial order, see Vásquez, "La poética."
35. On altered state of mind, see Gerd Gemünden, *Lucrecia Martel* (Urbana: University of Illinois Press, 2019). On the erratic condition of consciousness, see Amy Taubin, "Identification of a Woman," *Film Comment*, July/August 2009, 20–23.
36. Ted Nannicelli and Paul Taberham, eds., *Cognitive Media Theory* (New York: Routledge, 2014), 4.
37. William Seeley and Noël Carroll, "Cognitive Theory and the Individual Film," in *Cognitive Media Theory*, ed. Ted Nannicelli and Paul Taberham (London: Routledge, 2014), 237.
38. Seeley and Carroll, "Cognitive Theory and the Individual Film," 237.
39. Seeley and Carroll, "Cognitive Theory and the Individual Film," 237.
40. Vittorio Gallese and Michele Guerra, *The Empathetic Screen*, trans. Frances Anderson (Oxford: Oxford University Press, 2020).
41. Gallese and Guerra, *The Empathetic Screen*, 111.
42. Gallese and Guerra, *The Empathetic Screen*, 116.
43. Mark Solms, *The Hidden Spring* (London: Profile, 2021), 195–96. I am indebted to one of the anonymous reviewers of my "Neuromimesis" article for this suggestion.
44. Daston and Galison, *Objectivity.*
45. Rodríguez, "Little Red Riding Hood," 98; Martin, "Childhood, Youth, and the In-between," 145.
46. Gemünden, *Lucrecia Martel.*
47. Sosa, "A Counter-Narrative of Argentine Mourning."
48. Sosa, "A Counter-Narrative of Argentine Mourning," 251.
49. Graça Castanheira, dir., *Thinking Existenz*, episode 3, "Lucrecia Martel" (Zurich: Pop Filmes, 2012), 30 min.
50. Castanheira, "Lucrecia Martel."
51. Seeley and Carroll, "Cognitive Theory and the Individual Film," 238.
52. Seeley and Carroll, "Cognitive Theory and the Individual Film," 240.
53. Francisco Ortega and Fernando Vidal, *Neurocultures: Glimpses Into an Expanding Universe* (New York: Peter Lang, 2011); Nicholas Rose and Joelle M. Abi-Rached, *Neuro: The New Brain Sciences and the Management of the Mind.* (Princeton, NJ: Princeton University Press, 2013).
54. Norbert Wiener, *Cybernetics* (Cambridge, MA: MIT Press, 1965), 5–6; Jean-Pierre Dupuy, *On the Origins of Cognitive Science: The Mechanization of the Mind*, trans. M. B. DeBevoise (Cambridge, MA: MIT Press, 2009).
55. Giacomo Rizzolati, Luciano Fadiga, Vittorio Gallese, and Leonardo Fogassi, "Premotor Cortex and the Recognition of Motor Actions," *Cognitive Brain Research* 3 (1996): 131–41.
56. Victoria Pitts-Taylor "Neurocultures Manifesto," *SocialText Online* (2012), https://socialtextjournal.org/periscope_article/neurocultures-manifesto; Victoria Pitts-Taylor, *The Brain's Body* (Durham, NC: Duke University Press, 2016); Cynthia Kraus, "What Is the Feminist Critique of Neuroscience?" in *Neuroscience and Critique*, ed.

Jan DeVos and Ed Pluth (New York: Routledge, 2016), 100–16; Victoria Pitts-Taylor, "Neurobiologically Poor? Brain Phenotypes, Inequality, and Biosocial Determinism," *Science, Technology, and Human Values* 44, no. 4 (2019): 660–85.

57. Rose and Abi-Rached point to the ways in which the neurosciences have left the "enclosed space of the laboratory and gained traction in the world outside" in *Neuro*, 8–9. Fernando Vidal describes the emergence of "brainhood" in the twenty-first century, which he characterizes in terms of the production of a "cerebral subject," in "Brainhood, Anthropological Figure of Modernity," *History of the Human Sciences* 22, no. 1 (2009): 5–36.
58. Elizabeth Grosz, *The Incorporeal* (New York: Columbia University Press, 2017).
59. Stathis Gourgouris, *Does Literature Think?* (Stanford, CA: Stanford University Press, 2003).
60. Sianne Ngai, *Our Aesthetic Categories: Zany, Cute, Interesting* (Cambridge, MA: Harvard University Press, 2012), 1.

## Afterword. An Aesthetic Education in the Wake of the Neurocognitive Turn

1. A portion of this chapter was previously published as Cate I. Reilly, "Neuromimesis: Picturing the Humanities Picturing the Brain," *Frontiers in Integrative Neuroscience* 16 (October 14, 2022). Nicolas Negroponte, "A 30-Year History of the Future," 2014, https://www.ted.com/talks/nicholas_negroponte_a_30_year_history_of_the_future.
2. Gayatri Chakravorty Spivak, *An Aesthetic Education in the Era of Globalization* (Cambridge, MA: Harvard University Press, 2012), 12.
3. Spivak, *An Aesthetic Education*, 3.
4. Antonio Damasio, *Descartes' Error: Emotion, Reason, and the Human Brain* (New York: Penguin), 248.
5. Mark Solms and M. Saling, "On Psychoanalysis and Neuroscience: Freud's Attitude to the Localizationist Tradition," *International Journal of Psychoanalysis* 64 (1986): 397–416.
6. Mark Solms, *The Hidden Spring* (London: Profile, 2021), 30.
7. Solms, *The Hidden Spring*, 44.
8. Solms, *The Hidden Spring*, 35, 44.
9. Solms, *The Hidden Spring*, 177.
10. Mark Solms, "New Project for a Scientific Psychology: A General Scheme," *Neuropsychoanalysis* 22 (2020): 5–35.
11. This is, admittedly, itself preferable to an older and more historically common practice in the Western European sciences: to see such objects as window dressing on scientific facts. The sporadic use of citations from literary works had the additional advantage of attesting to the researcher's cultured background.
12. Antonio Damasio, *The Stranger Order of Things* (New York: Vintage, 2018), 101.
13. Soares, in any event, writes of his soul as a "hidden orchestra," not one seeking disclosure.
14. Solms, *The Hidden Spring*. The chapter is supposed to illustrate predictive hierarchy in the nervous system. Eve, however, records "long-term leakage patterns" on the dam and is described as concluding her career in the local municipality with an

inquiry about a "reproductive department" that could produce more dams. This makes it difficult to think of the nervous system as the primary focus.

15. Solms, "New Project for a Scientific Psychology"; Solms, *The Hidden Spring.*
16. Nima Bassiri, "Freud and the Matter of the Brain: On the Rearrangements of Neuropsychoanalysis," *Critical Inquiry* 40, no. 1 (Autumn 2013): 83–108; Katja Guenther, *Localization and Its Discontents* (Chicago: University of Chicago Press, 2015); Elisa Galgut, "Against Neuropsychoanalysis: Why a Dialogue with Neuroscience Is Neither Necessary nor Sufficient for Psychoanalysis," *Psychoanalytic Review* 108, no. 3 (September 2021): 315–36.
17. Solms, *The Hidden Spring.*
18. Sigmund Freud, "Project for a Scientific Psychology," in *The Standard Edition of the Complete Psychological Works of Sigmund Freud*, ed. and trans. James Strachey (London: Hogarth, 1966), 1:360. Hereafter abbreviated *SE.*
19. Sigmund Freud, *Die Traumdeutung*, Bd. II/III, *Gesammelte Werke*, ed. Marie Bonaparte and Anna Freud (Frankfurt am Main: Fischer Taschenbuch Verlag, 1999), 541.
20. On Freud's metaphors, see Jacques Derrida, *Writing and Difference*, trans. Alan Bass (London: Routledge, 2001).
21. Solms, *The Hidden Spring*, 280, 282.
22. Solms, *The Hidden Spring*, 282–83, 285.
23. T. J. Clark, "Freud's Cezanne," in *Farewell to an Idea* (New Haven, CT: Yale University Press, 1999), 139–67.

# INDEX